VEDĀNTA EXPLAINED

VEDĀNTA EXPLAINED

Saṁkara's Commentary on The Brahma-sūtras

VOLUME I

By
V. H. DATE
With a Foreword by the late
PROF. R. D. RANADE, M.A., D.Litt.

Munshiram Manoharlal
Publishers Pvt. Ltd.

Munshiram Manoharlal
Publishers Pvt. Ltd.
54, RANI JHANSI ROAD, NEW DELHI-110055
Book Shop : 4416, NAI SARAK, DELHI-110006

Second edition 1973

Originally published in 1954
by Booksellers Publishing Co. Bombay

Printed in India by Raj Bandhu Industrial
Company, C 61 Maya Puri II, New Delhi 27

To

My Spiritual Teacher

–V. H. DATE

PREFACE

Srī Śaṁkarācārya has hitherto been shown as a great idealist and monist; but this expository treatment of his greatest work, viz. his commentary on the Brahma-Sūtras, which I am presenting in two volumes, aims at pointing out in addition the ethico-spiritual standpoint of his philosophy. It is not the mere intellectual understanding of the reality, but the moral and the spiritual awakening of man which is, according to Śaṁkara, responsible for the realization of the Ātman in this very life. If this be the truth, a new light will be flashed upon the philosophy of the great Ācārya. He will be seen to have built upon the foundations of renunciation and asceticism a new but an everlasting structure of moral and spiritual equality of all men before God and their identity in Him.

To achieve this purpose, a mere literal translation of his Bhāṣya, as a Sanskritist or a grammarian would like to have it, will not do. On the contrary, a free rendering in simple and philosophical language is desirable. I have remained absolutely faithful to Śaṁkara, though I have added a few lines here and there to bring out explicitly what is merely implicit in the commentary, my aim being to preserve the unity of ideas rather than that of mere words. I have tried to see that the ideas are connected logically, and that the arguments of Pūrvapakṣin and the Vedāntin develop in a natural manner. In other words, my aim has been to see that the entire book reads as a connected whole, as though it had been originally written in English. I believe that a readable account of the metaphysical position of Śaṁkara, as gathered from his commentary on the Brahma-Sūtras, will go a long way to understand his theistic and mystical position, which is mainly to be found in his minor religious works. People, in general, have still to understand that the monistic idealism of Śaṁkara is simply a prelude to his central teachings in philosophy which are mainly theistic and mystical in character. I shall therefore be more than rewarded if, while giving a readable but full account of his commentary on the Brahma-Sūtras, I show in his own words that the mystical knowledge of reality is the sole end both of philosophy and religion. I shall, however, have to wait, till the second volume is complete, to be able to write a critical survey of the philosophy of Śaṁkara, as developed in his commentary on the Brahma-Sūtras.

I shall then be able to point out how the doctrine of Māyā is not incompatible with its so-called rival doctrine of Cidvilāsa. Why Śaṁkara favours the one and not the other is because he finds that the doctrine of Māyā, unlike the other, serves the double purpose of bringing home to consciousness the reality of Brahman and the unreality of anything else, apart from Brahman. Had Śaṁkara been slow to understand the element of truth contained in the Cidvilāsa theory, it would have been impossible for him to explain the meaning of 'Sarvaṁ khalu idaṁ Brahma'. But the important point to note is that, to Śaṁkara, the 'sarvaṁ', like 'ahaṁ', is nothing else but Brahman, though he holds that the experience 'all this is Brahman' comes much later than the experience, 'I am the Brahman'. From the view-point of mere logic, as we shall see, the 'ahaṁ' and the 'sarvaṁ', that is, the 'I' and the 'world' have their existence apart from the other term viz. Brahman in the two propositions mentioned above. But from the view-point of spiritual experience or anubhava, there remains only the Brahman, as both the subject and the predicate of the proposition, and the consciousness of the 'I' or the 'world' as a separate entity drops down altogether. In order to preserve this truth, and in order not to allow the idlers and pretenders to say that they are having the Brahmanic anubhava, when, as a matter of fact, they are engrossed with the sensuous and sensual pleasures, Śaṁkara keeps himself away from the Cidvilāsa theory. The world may be a 'Vilāsa' of Brahman, but let it not be a 'vilāsa' for one who has not realized the Brahman. Better it would be if one were to think that the 'vilāsa' as divorced from Brahman is only transitory and insufficient to satisfy completely and finally, and that therefore it is as good as an illusion. I shall then be able to point out how the genesis of Māyā is due to the urge on the part of Brahman to become many which, instead of being conscious of the Brahman which is immanent in them, become conscious of themselves as finite and limited; how Brahman instead of being a blank is the repository of all the qualities, so much so, that Śaṁkara believes—to borrow a phrase from Rāmadāsa, a saint of Mahārāṣṭra—that Nirguṇa is just the same as Bahuguṇa; how Śaṁkara leads us on through the different stages of non-contradiction to the ultimate mystical criterion of Svānubhava; and how, finally, Śaṁkara shows us that the individual soul is a gainer and not a loser by being absorbed in the Brahman.

The transliteration and the literal meaning of the words in the Sūtras may create a taste for Sanskrit even in those to whom the language may be totally unfamiliar. The translation of the Sūtras is not simply aphoristic in nature; the additional words in the brackets are intended not only to explain the Sūtras, but also the topic and the context in which they arise. And, as indicated above, the rendering of the commentary is so presented that it gives a complete and unitary picture of the arguments for or against. Many of the Upaniṣadic and other references therefore which ought to have been explained or pointed out in the footnotes have been so incorporated in the body of the commentary that, sometimes, the argument begins with the form of a story or a dialogue in an Upaniṣad, and an attempt has been made to bring out the whole Vedāntic position with as much narrative interest as force of reasoning. If a particular argument consists of too many queries and replies, or doubts and counter-doubts, I have, instead of tiring out the reader by compelling him to go through these unending meanderings, simplified the issues and presented them as several points in the argument. I have taken utmost care, however, not to omit or neglect even the smallest point in the argument of the Pūrvapakṣin or the Vedāntin. As for the footnotes, they are given only when they are absolutely necessary.

Some more features of this undertaking deserve emphasis here. I have given at the end of each volume a broad outline or summary of the whole volume, so that one may have at a glance the relevant position of a particular philosophical thesis in the whole scheme, as well as be acquainted in a general way with the richness and extent of the field of inquiry covered by Śaṁkara. I have also thought it well to give separately almost all the important Upaniṣadic and other references in the commentary, so that such of my readers as may thereby be tempted to read Śaṁkara in the original may be encouraged to come in contact with that beautiful, simple and powerful work. The Sūtra-wise index of references too will be immensely useful for a comparative study of the different schools in Vedānta. I also intend to give at the end of the second volume some important philosophical passages in the original from the Commentary of Saṁkara which will explain my critical survey of his philosophy.

Professor R. D. Ranade, M.A., D. Litt., Ex-vice-Chancellor of the University of Allahabad, has been so intensely and unceassingly kind to me in all my affairs ever since he first taught me philosophy in 1923, that whenever my head touches his feet in gratitude, it is a wrench to take it away from them. He has not only made me what I am philosophically, but has also enabled me to a small degree at least, to value the way of the Spirit, and to understand sympathetically how Sanatkumāra must have been able to remove the grief of Nārada by imparting unto him the lore of the Ātman. I am therefore all gratitude to this great saint for having blessed my undertaking. Another great influence upon my life is of the 'philosopher-statesman' of India; for it is the writings of Professor S. Radhakrishnan which have inspired me to make philosophy understandable and to bring it within the reach of all. Truth is truth even if some are slow to understand it. But it is with respect to these 'some' that Dr. Rādhākrishnan has taught me that the truth must be given in the form in which it is acceptable. I can never be too grateful to him also for having blessed me.

My whilom colleague, Dr. K. R. Srinivasa Iyengar, Professor of English, Andhra University, Waltair, has exceedingly obliged me by reading the proofs and by making a number of valuable suggestions. It was he who persuaded me to publish my earlier book, 'The Yoga of the Saints' (Popular Book Depot, Bombay, 1944), and again it was he who voluntarily came forward to help me in this new venture. I am grateful to him for teaching me that friendship based on a sense of dedication to higher values does not easily fade away. Another friend of mine, and a Sanskrit scholar Dr. M. A. Karandikar, M. A., Ph. D., of the Elphinstone College, Bombay, has helped me in the selection of the Upaniṣadic and other sources in the original and in correcting their proofs. I am greatly indebted to him for this. Professor K. L. Varma, M. A., Principal of my College, is to be specially thanked in this connection for the very kind interest he has taken in the publication of this volume and the tangible encouragement he gave me by affording me facilities for the books which I required. One of my post-graduate students, Mr. Shyam Sundar Joshi, getting interested in my work, has helped me a lot in the correction of the galley-proofs, and my thanks are due to him in full measure. Nor must I omit to mention that my sons have been very helpful to me: Viśvanāth in preparing the Sūtra-wise index and in comparing the references with the manuscript, and Raghunāth, in addition to this, in doing the typist's job so willingly and so well.

It would have been impossible for me to bring out this volume had I not been fortunate in meeting the young, upright, and obliging gentleman, Mr. D. M. Tilak. With courage and generosity he has rendered me a great service, which I shall ever remember with gratitude. I cannot commend too highly the quick despatch, the sincerity of purpose, and the aesthetic sense he has displayed in the production of this volume.

My debt to Bhāmatī, as also to such eminent scholars as George Thibaut, Max Muller, Vāsudeva Śāstri Abhyankar and the Ācārya-bhakta Bapat, and others, is too obvious to require any special mention. It is in the company of the work of these pioneers in the field, that I have been able to evaluate to some degree the precious store of Ātmānubhava in the philosophy of Śaṁkara.

Finally, I am greatly indebted to the University of Rajputana for making a generous grant towards the cost of publication of this volume.

Maharaja's College,
Jaipur.
7th February 1954

V. H. Date

FOREWORD

I have great pleasure in writing this small foreword to a very important work of my former student and now Professor at Maharaja's College, Jaipur, Dr. V. H. Date, M. A., Ph. D. The translation of Śānkara Bhāṣya has been attempted by very few persons in the history of Sanskrit Scholarship, and I am glad that Prof. Date can be placed in that list. His translation has this particular characteristic about it, namely, that it is not merely literal but expository. Dr. Date makes his translation always readable by introducing some stories from the Upaniṣads and similar works. I think the book would be useful to University students and scholars alike. At the end of each volume Prof. Date intends to give a summary of the contents of the volume which will enable the reader to have a short glimpse of the Bhāṣya. The primary interest of the Śānkara Bhāṣya, as Dr. Date tells us, is ethico-spiritual, the metaphysical portion being in the background. सर्वं खलु इदं ब्रह्म as he points out, is an extension of the experience of अहं ब्रह्मास्मि. Śankarācārya has put this idea very beautifully in his śata śloki आदौ ब्रह्माहमस्मी त्यनुभव उदिते खल्विदं ब्रह्म पश्चात् । Dr. Date has kept before himself the model of Dr. Radhakrishnan's works on Indian philosophy, who, as everyone knows, has eminently succeeded in creating interest in the minds of his readers by his lucid and comprehensive exposition. The transliteration and the translation of the Sūtras, along with the clear exposition of the objections and answers in the shape of पूर्वपक्ष and उत्तरपक्ष will be found very useful by students of the Bhāṣya in India or outside. If Prof. Date sometimes undertakes to expound the texts of the Upaniṣads seriatim, his expositions will also be found eminently readable as they will introduce readers to the contents of the Upaniṣads at first hand in the same clear manner. Prof. Date is not merely well-versed in European Philosophy, but also in Indian Philosophy having learnt it, and particularly the Vedanta, from a Shastri of repute. Finally, I shall feel very glad, as Prof. Date will certainly feel, that his translation will enable some at least to rise on the ladder of Vedanta Philosophy to its real spirit, namely, a first-hand contact with Reality, which is the beginning, the end and the life of the world-Tajjalān.

5th February 1954. **R. D. RANADE**

CONTENTS

i	Preface	i
ii	Foreword	vii
I	Sanskrit Sūtras, Transliteration, Translation and Commentary	I
II	Sūtrawise Summary of Philosophical points	349
III	Extracts from Upaniṣads & other Sources as found in Śaṁkara's Commentary	371
IV	Sūtrawise index of Upaniṣadic references	393
V	Errata	401

VEDĀNTA EXPLAINED

(*Śaṁkara's Commentary on the Brahma-Sūtras*)

Adhyāya First

Pāda First

Śaṁkara's Introduction: Nature of Adhyāsa.

The words 'asmad' and 'yuṣmad'[1], that is, the words 'I' and 'thou', indicate the subject and the object in experience. The latter are so opposed in nature to each other like light and darkness that it is a plain truth that they can never be identical. Much less will the attributes of them be identical. It will be wrong therefore to superimpose the objects and their attributes on the self-illuminating subject, the cognition of which can be defined only by the word 'asmad'. Equally wrong will be the superimposition of the subject and its attributes on the object. And yet,

---

1 The word 'asmad' conveys undoubtedly the meaning of the subjective aspect in experience. The word 'yuṣmad' however presents a difficulty. On the one hand, being a personal pronoun like 'asmad' it also suggests the presence of an intelligent, experiencing subject, and therefore may not be supposed as necessarily contradicting the import of the word 'asmad.' On the other hand, it falls outside the scope of the meaning of the word 'asmad,' just as truly as any other non-intelligent thing of the world falls outside it. Any centre of experience denoted by 'yuṣmad' is not directly cognized as the 'I' is cognized. It is therefore on a par with other objects of the world. And yet the word 'yuṣmad' is more useful than the word 'this' or 'idaṁ' in bringing out the absolute contrast in nature between the subject and object. 'Idaṁ' may be combined with 'asmad' as in 'idaṁ ahaṁ' (it is I); but the word 'yuṣmad' cannot be so combined. Apart from this usage of language, 'yuṣmad' is a word which can be used not only while addressing our fellow beings who fall outside the scope of the 'I' in us, but also be used in an act of introspection for anything which, in a way, does not belong to the subjective side, except the pure self-illuminating subject itself. Thus, one may address (not metaphorically but literally) in an act of introspection, his own indriyas, mind, intellect and ahaṁkāra by the same endearing epithet 'thou.' One can mentally dissociate oneself from these and address them, as if they are one's own fellow beings. The mind, the buddhi, etc. are not merely separate from the Ātman; they are, according to Śaṁkara, of the nature of un-ātman. The word 'yuṣmad' therefore is as useful to convey this un-ātmic side of the mental or intellectual life as of the bodies of our fellow men in social life. The extension of the meaning of the word 'yuṣmad' to cover the ordinary, inanimate objects of the world is easy to understand. The world is un-ātmic, on the face of it; and if the word 'yuṣumad' can be used to

so natural and illusory[2] is the practice of the world to mingle the truth and falsehood and to superimpose one on the other, forgetting all the while that they can never be identical on account of their attributes being absolutely opposed to each other, that we readily have such expressions as 'I am this', 'This is mine'.

But what do we mean by 'adhyāsa' or 'superimposition' at all? It is the apprehension of something perceived previously but remembered[3] while perceiving something else. In the opinion of some, adhyāsa means the superimposition of the attributes of one thing on another thing.[4] Others define it as the illusion due to not being able to note the difference between the two things[5]. To some

---

denote one or two parts of the world, viz. our fellow beings, and our own senses, intellect etc. because they are un-ātmic, it can legitimately be used to denote the third part of it, viz. the inanimate objects on account of the same reason.

2 An illusion arises out of the ignorance of the real. The knowledge of the real therefore has got the power to cancel the illusion. Similarly, we may note in passing that bondage is simply illusory, not real; and therefore it is that knowledge of the real means the cancellation of bondage.

3 Adhyāsa is not the same as recognition. An object first perceived is recognised as the same when it is perceived a second time, due to remembrance. In adhyāsa, on the other hand, the remembered part of the object, e.g. silver, is not actually presented to the eye. In recognition, the two perceptions are with reference to one and the same object; in adhyāsa, they refer to different objects.

4. This definition covers both the views known as anyathākhyāti and ātmakhyāti. The first is the view of the Naiyāyikas and of the Bhāṭṭa school of Mīmāṁsā; while the second is of the Vijñānavādi Buddhist known also as the Sautrāntika. According to the first view, the object appears as 'anyathā,' as something other than what it is. The shell appears or manifests as something else, viz. as silver. It must however be noted that the criticism of the Vedāntin against this view is that the shell does not become the silver in spite of the manifestation of it on the shell. Otherwise the shell may be able to fetch the value of silver in the market. According to the second view it is the internal or mental idea of silver that comes out and manifests as external object after being superimposed on the shell. The Vedāntin would say against this that if all reality is mental in character, there would be no criterion to distinguish between truth and error. Cognition of silver as external is required to remove the error.

5 This is the view of the Prabhākara school of Mīmāṁsā. According to it, strictly speaking there is no error. Error consists in taking a composite view of two cognitions. The 'this' aspect of the shell in front of the eye is conjoined with the 'what' aspect of the silver which is only remembered and is not in contact with the eye. Due to some fault either in the medium or the sense-organ, etc., the glitter of the shell does not carry the mind beyond the mere 'that' of the shell to the 'what' of it; due to resemblance, however, the glitter of the shell leads the mind to the glitter of the silver. But the awareness of the glitter of the silver too does not lead the mind to the recognition of it as previously seen, but stops with the remembrance of silver in general.

others, still, it means the ascription of false attributes to a thing.[6] All these views however agree in representing adhyāsa as the false apprehension of the attributes of one thing on another, *e. g.* the appearance of silver on the mother-of-pearl[7], or the appearance of one moon as double.

How can, one may ask, the objects and their attributes be superimposed on the Ātman who, as has been said above, is never an object, and who is therefore said to be 'pratyak', *i. e.*, who manifests or shines as sat, cit and ānanda? The Ātman who is totally disconnected with the idea of 'yuṣmad', can hardly be said to be amenable to superimposition which one may experience with reference to objects in contact with sense-organs.

We reply that notwithstanding its being pratyagātman and its being unrelated to the objective world which is denoted by the word 'yuṣmad', the pure Ātman too is capable of being known as an object, whenever one becomes aware of oneself as 'I am',[8] as also of the intuitive certainty[9] of the existence of one's self. And it is not

---

Hence arises the non-apprehension of distinction between the shell and the silver. The criticism of the Vedāntin against this view is, that if there should really occur non-discrimination between what is presented and what is remembered, a person may very well experience in dream that he is blue. For the remembered 'blue' would then be combined with the presented self.

6 This is the view of the Mādhyamikas or the Śūnyavādins. Error consists in apprehending the non-existing silver as existing on the shell which also is a product of void. The Vedāntin objects to this that there can be no cognition of a non-existing thing.

7 The view of the Vedāntin is known as anirvacanīyakhyāti, since the cognition of silver on the shell is neither real nor unreal. For it is not so real as will not be cancelled by any later experience; and it is not so unreal as not to appear on the shell. Silver does appear on the shell; but while the appearance is unreal, that on which it appears, viz. the shell, is real. Hence it is that with the knowledge of the substratum, viz. the shell, the appearance of silver disappears.

8 Here the consciousness of the 'I' means the consciousness of the jīva, as bound by the upādhis of body, mind, senses etc. There is no possibility of the consciousness of being the 'doer' (kartā), the 'enjoyer' (bhoktā) with reference to pratyagātman, who is pure consciousness (caitanya). Jīva, on the other hand, is not conscious of being caitanya but is conscious of being kartā and bhoktā, because it is connected with the upādhi of buddhi.

9 The self-luminosity of the Ātman is capable of being intuitively felt by all without any doubt; and this constitutes the objective side of the Ātman. In other words, the Ātman is its own object.

a universal rule that objects in front of us or in contact with sense-organs should alone be superimposed on one another. The ākāśa though imperceptible is still called by ordinary people as having a coloured surface. Similarly it is no contradiction to superimpose the objects which are un-ātmanic in character, on the pratyagātman or the self-luminous imperceptible Ātman. Wise men call this kind of adhyāsa as avidyā[10]; and by contrast with this, they call it as Vidyā which enables them to discern the real nature of the Ātman (vastu). Such being the nature of vidyā and avidyā, neither the defects of the un-ātman nor the virtues of the Ātman will in any way affect[11] the substratum on which they are superimposed. It is due to this mutual superimposition of the Ātman and the un-ātman that there arise all the practical distinctions of ordinary and Vedic life, pertaining to knowledge and its objects, prohibitions and injunctions, as also pertaining to mokṣa.

How is it, it may be asked, that the means of right knowledge such as perception and others, and the various Srutis have their origin in avidyā ? The answer is not difficult to find. In the first place, the absolutely free and unattached Ātman cannot be said to be the knower unless the body, the mind and the senses are first superimposed upon it, and there arise the wrong notions such as, 'I am this', 'it is mine', etc. And, secondly, it is only after the knower is established that the body and the senses will be active[12], and the means of knowledge will be employed. In short, it is the avidyā in which is rooted the distinction between the knower and the known, and it is due to it that we employ the means of knowledge and

---

10 Avidyā is, strictly speaking, the cause of adhyāsa. Avidyā is not only the opposite of Vidyā, but is capable of being cancelled by Vidyā.

11 The Ātman is not affected by the qualities of buddhi and others such as hunger and thirst ; nor are buddhi and the senses affected by the qualities of the Ātman, such as consciousness and bliss.

12 Had the activities of the senses been dependent only on the body without reference to the Ātman which is superimposed on the body, they would have been active even during sleep, when there is no such superimposition.

follow the instructions of Śruti. In this respect there is no difference between a man and a lower animal[13]. A cow runs away through fear from a man who has a raised stick in his hand; but it moves towards him if he has fresh green grass with him. A man too approaches another, if the latter is of gentle behaviour; but he runs away from a fierce-looking strong person, who approaches shouting and flourishing a sword in hand. So, in spite of the difference of intelligence between men and animals, their cognitional and other activities of the practical worldly life are ultimately due to the mutual superimposition of the Ātman and the un-ātman.

Now what can we say about that kind of activity which is enjoined by the Vedas? No doubt a person who wishes to qualify himself for the performance of such actions, a sacrifice for instance, gets first the intellectual conviction that the soul ought to have a relation with the next world[14]. But this does not include the knowledge of the real nature of the Ātman who is, as the Upaniṣads tell us, beyond the bodily wants of hunger and thirst, beyond the distinctions of castes such as Brahmins and Kṣattriyas, and beyond the rounds of birth and death. As a matter of fact, this kind of knowledge has no purpose to serve for a person who has to perform a sacrifice; on the other hand, it goes against and disqualifies that person. But before the advent of such Aupaniṣadic knowledge of the Ātman, what can be said of the whole of the Karma-Kāṇḍa? The reply is, it has its basis in avidyā. Unless the distinctions of caste, āśrama, age, etc. are superimposed

---

13 The animal is aware of the distinction between itself and its environment; a man is not only aware of this distinction, but also knows that the body and the soul have got different characteristics. And yet so far as the mutual superimposition of the body and the soul is concerned, the man resembles the animal.

14 It is suggested by way of objection that a person, who wishes to attain the Svarga (heaven), and who therefore wishes to perform the jyotiṣṭoma sacrifice, must not be resorting to any kind of adhyāsa. For it is presumed that that person should know the simple fact that it cannot be the body which is burnt after death but that it must be the soul which ought to be connected with the fruit of the sacrifice. In other words, it is suggested that the person will have no illusion about the absolute difference between the body and the soul. On the contrary, he will have all the possible knowledge about the soul, and will not therefore superimpose the soul on the body.

upon the Ātman, there will be no possibility of the performance of a sacrifice by a Brahmin.

How this natural and endless superimposition operates in the world and creates the false knowledge that the soul is the doer and experiencer of actions and their effects, we shall explain by a few examples. A man considers himself happy or otherwise, as his wife and children are. He considers himself to be stout, lean, fair, mute, deaf or blind, when as a matter of fact his body or sense-organs are so. The desires, the doubts and the various modifications of his mind, as also the sense of empirical consciousness in the form of 'I am', are ascribed by him as belonging to the eternal Ātman in him, the witness of all[15]. And reciprocally, the Pratyagātman also is superimposed by him on body, senses, mind etc.[16]

With a view therefore to remove this adhyāsa which is the root-cause of all evil, and thereby to enable one to attain the knowledge of the unity of the Ātman, the study of the Vedānta is undertaken. And that all the Vedānta passages have this purpose alone, we shall prove in what follows, *viz.* the Śārīraka-mīmāṁsā[17].

The first Sūtra of this Vedānta-mīmāṁsā is as follows:

१ जिज्ञासाधिकरणम् । (१)

अथातो ब्रह्मजिज्ञासा । १

[*Atha—now ; ataḥ—therefore ; Brahma-jijñāsā—desire to know the Brahman.*]

NOW THEREFORE THE DESIRE TO KNOW THE BRAHMAN. 1

---

15 Qualities belonging to others and therefore constituting the 'social me' of a man or qualities belonging to his own body, or to his senses or mind or ahaṁkāra are all superimposed upon the Ātman. In other words, the superimposition takes place either through the social relations, or through the physico-psychological considerations.

16 It is on account of this type of adhyāsa viz. of the Ātman on the senses, intellect etc. that a man appears to be endowed with 'caitanya.' As opposed to this, the other kind of adhyāsa, viz. that of intellect, etc. on the Ātman, endows the man with the notions that he is the doer of actions and enjoyer of fruits.

17 The śarīra being dirty is known as śārrīaka ; and the jīva which dwells in hist body is known therefore as śārīraka. A discussion or Mimāṁsā whether this

The word 'now' indicates that the inquiry about the Brahman follows as a consequence of some prior event. It does not indicate the mere beginning of a new subject such as the nature of Brahman, after another subject has been finished. Nor does it make us aware of any prior event which is not connected as cause or condition of the inquiry of Brahman. To say that the word 'now' is used to indicate the auspicious beginning of a work, is also inadequate; for such a beginning is indicated by the mere sound of the word 'atha'. So far as its meaning is concerned, it is used then to denote a necessary connection.

What then is that necessary, antecedent, condition which, when fulfilled, makes one fit to enter upon the inquiry of the nature of Brahman? It cannot be the study of the Vedas exclusively, for it is the common antecedent of both the inquiries regarding the Brahman and Religious duty. Neither can the knowledge of Religious duty be said to be the antecedent, because one can have the knowledge of the Brahman even without the knowledge of such duty, by merely studying the Vedānta literature. Here there is no indication of the order of succession, as is indicated with reference to certain things to be done in a sacrifice. Knowledge of Religious duty and that of Brahman are not so related to each other that the study of the one will prepare a person to study the other. They differ in subject-matter and in results. Brahma-jñāna ends in salvation and eternal bliss, while Dharma-jñāna has transitory prosperity as its end. Dharma-jñāna enjoins performance of religious acts, while Brahma-jñāna does not. The fruit of one is dependent on human activity; in the other it is not so. Brahman being eternal and an ever-accomplished fact, the knowledge of it is not something which will accrue at some future time as the result of human effort. The fruit of Dharma, on the other hand, is to be accomplished at some future

---

Śārīraka is the same as Brahman or not is known as Śārīraka-Mīmāṁsā. The same discussion being the aim of all Vedānta passages, it is also known as Vedānta-Mīmāṁsā.

time by the performance of some religious acts. Besides, the intent of the Śruti statements differs entirely in the two inquiries. A statement in the Brāhmaṇa, such as "A person wishing to obtain svarga should perform the Agniṣṭoma sacrifice", informs us about Dharma, by urging us to act. But a statement from the Upaniṣads, such as "The Ātman is verily the Brahman", does not render a man inclined to do some activity, but instructs him straightway regarding the nature of the Brahman. In other words, whereas the knowledge about the Brahman is the immediate result of the Upaniṣadic statement, without requiring any intermediate human activity, the knowledge about Dharma is dependent not only on the statement from the Brāhmaṇa but on human activity too. Unlike Dharma-jñāna, then, the knowledge of the Brahman is like perceptual knowledge which arises as soon as there is contact of a sense with its objects. It does not wait to come into being till there is some human activity, for it does not require it. If Dharma-jñāna then is not the necessary antecedent of Brahma-jñāna, we must state what that antecedent is.

The real antecedent conditions are:—The discrimination between what is abiding and what is not abiding; non-attachment to the mundane and extra-mundane objects of pleasure and pain; possession of tranquillity, restraint and other virtues;[1] and the desire for final liberation. If these conditions are fulfilled, then alone, irrespective of the knowledge of Dharma, it is possible to enter upon an inquiry of the Brahman and to know it. The word 'now' therefore indicates that Brahma-jijñāsā is subsequent to the fulfilment of these four conditions.

The word 'therefore' supplies an additional reason as to why the four moral and spiritual means alone, and not Dharma-jñāna, are to be construed as the prerequisites of Brahma-jñāna. The statement from the Chāndogya Upa-

1 The other virtues besides 'Śama' (tranquility) and 'dama' (restraint) are known as uparati, (Dispassion), titikṣa (endurance), samādhāna (alertness), and Śraddhā (faith).

niṣad (8, 1, 6) regarding the 'perishable nature of the fruits of actions acquired in this or the next world', clears away the possible objection based on the belief that dispassion for fruits of the next world may not be had inasmuch as they are not perishable as the fruits of this world are. Thus while the fruits of Agnihotra and other sacrifices are declared by Veda itself as impermanent, the Taittirīya Upaniṣad, on the other hand, points out to us that "He who knows the Brahman becomes the Brahman" (2, 1) . From this it is clear that the above-mentioned qualifications, such as the discrimination that the Brahman alone is the Reality, are the only necessary antecedents of Brahma-jñāna.

The third and the last word in the Sūtra, *viz*., 'Brahma-jijñāsā' indicates that Brahman is the direct and principal object of inquiry. Of course this may imply other objects of inquiry, which are less important and therefore of a secondary nature, *e*. g. means of knowledge, reasoning, sādhana and its results. When someone says, " There goes the king ", what he means is that the king is going along with his retinue. Śruti also tells us that Brahman is the direct object of the desire for knowledge; *e*. g. we get in the Taittirīya Upaniṣad (3, 1) " That from whom these beings are born etc., desire to know that. That is Brahman." This desire for knowledge, again, has for its object not merely an intellectual understanding about the nature of the Brahman, but the realization of it; for it is this direct realization of Brahman which constitutes the Summum Bonum of human life, and which is necessary to root out all avidyā, the seed of all evil in this Saṁsāra.

Brahman is derived from the root 'bṛh' (to become great), and so means the Being having unlimited greatness. This quality of unlimited greatness, in its turn, implies that Brahman is eternal, pure, self-conscious and free.[1]

1 These are the primary attributes of Brahman, and constitute what is known a the 'svarūpalakṣaṇa' of Brahman. As distinct from this definition which deals with

The existence of Brahman is also known by its being the self of every thing. Every one has the consciousness of the existence of the self in the form of 'I am'. And yet, opinions differ regarding the specific nature of the self. The Lokāyatikas and the ordinary men believe that this body alone, when endowed with intelligence, is known as the self. Others say that the organs and the intelligence, or the mind alone is the self. To some others like the Buddhas, the momentary knowledge or the void itself is the self. It is, to some others, a being which is distinct from the body etc. and is responsible for actions. Some say the self is merely the subject of experience, while some others posit the existence of an omniscient, omnipotent Lord of all, and call him the real Self as distinct from the selves; while there are some others who call him the Self of selves. Thus it is that different people hold different opinions, and advance in support arguments and passages from Śruti which are only partly true. When such is the state, if a man accepts as true any one of the wrong views, he will not only not have the highest bliss, but will also be bound by the chain of births and deaths. So it is with a view to make possible the release of all that the author of the Sūtras has started the inquiry into the knowledge of Brahman, by resorting to arguments which are not inconsistent with Śruti.

२ जन्माद्यधिकरणम् । (२)

जन्माद्यस्य यतः । २

[*Janmādi—origin etc..; asya—of this; yataḥ—from which.*]

(BRAHMAN IS THAT) FROM WHICH (SUBSISTENCE AND DISSOLUTION) BEGINNING WITH THE ORIGIN OF THIS (WORLD PROCEED). 2

---

the primary nature of Brahman there is another definition of it known as 'Taṭastha-lakṣana.' It points out other derivative qualities of Brahman such as 'omniscience,' omnipotence,' 'omnipresence,' etc.

The word 'janmādi' is a compound which can be solved in two ways[1], and so may mean either the subsistence and dissolution merely without including the meaning of the word 'janma', *viz.* origin, along with them or the subsistence and dissolution which come after the origin. If we take the second meaning, then alone it is possible to relate the three states to this world, in the order of origin, subsistence and dissolution. For what comes into being alone endures and ceases to be in course of time. Śruti too points out the same order (Tai. 3, 1). The world that is qualified by these three states is this very world made up of names and forms, subjects and objects, causes and effects, and space and time. It baffles our imagination when we think about its wonderful construction. It is this world which is dependent for its origin, subsistence, and dissolution on the Brahman.

We need not however increase the number of states from three to six, as the sage Yāska has done it. For the motive of the sage was to speak about the nature of all created things after once the five elements have come into existence. In the first place, the three additional states of modification, growth and decay are involved in the three states already mentioned; the first two being a kind of origination, and the last a kind of dissolution. Secondly, if these six states are mentioned, they may refer to the five great elements as their cause and not to the Brahman. In order to ward away this possible suspicion, the author of the Sūtras has mentioned only the three states and not six. Even the origin of the five great Bhūtas must be referred back to the Brahman, which is both omniscient and omnipotent.

It is not possible therefore to attribute the origin etc. of the world to any other cause, such as the non-intelligent

---

1 The first variety gives 'janma' (origin) an adjectival function only; and so the word drops down the moment we are aware of the two substantions viz. subsistence tnd dissolution. The other variety treats the word 'janma' as substantive in character as the other two; and so all the three words are taken to constitute the meaning of ahe compound.

pradhāna of the Sāṁkhyas, or the atoms of the Vaiśeṣikas or the non-being of the Śunyavādins, or the transmigrating Hiraṇyagarbha. Nor can it be said that the world came into being spontaneously as the Lokāyatikas hold, because as inferred by those who believe in the existence of God, a particular place, time and cause are required for the production of an effect.

This does not however mean that the present Sūtra embodies one more similar argument without reference to Śruti. On the contrary, this and the other Sūtras merely afford an opportunity to collect the material from Śruti for thought and discussion, consequent on which, and not simply due to inference and other pramāṇas, there will spring up the knowledge of Brahman. But if inference too is brought forward to strengthen the conclusions of the Śruti, it is a welcome and serviceable instrument of knowledge. Śruti itself has admitted its utility. The Bṛhadāraṇyaka recommends the hearing and the thinking about the Ātman; and the Chāndogya declares that just as a man led astray by robbers would arrive back in his country of Gāndhāra after being guided by others and by his intelligence, even so one who has been guided by a spiritual teacher can employ his own reason also and achieve the knowledge of the Brahman.

Now, Brahma-jijñāsā is unlike Dharma-jijñāsā. For while in the latter the Śruti passages are alone capable of giving us knowledge, in the former, not only these but self-realization also is available as an authoritative source. Brahman as the object of knowledge is already an existing thing, and therefore can be apprehended only through intuitive knowledge. In the case of knowledge of a thing which is to be accomplished, there being no possibility of intuitive knowledge, Śruti would be the only possible means of proof. Besides, the thing to be accomplished, whether ordinary or vedic, depends on human activity which may be done or not done. A man may go to a place on horse-back or on foot, or not go at all, Similarly a man may or may not accept the Ṣodaśī cup of somarasa in the Atirātra sacrifice ; or a man may or may not make oblation before or after sunrise. In all such cases, injunctions and prohibitions, options and rules have a place, because they refer to the intellect of man. The knowledge of the Vastu (Brahman or Substance) has no reference to human intellect or activity, but is rooted in itself alone. To say with regard to a post that it is a man or something else is false knowledge; to say that it is a post is correct, because this knowledge is rooted in the thing itself. Even so the knowledge of Brahman depends entirely on Brahman alone, inasmuch as it is already an accomplished fact.

One may say that Brahman as an existing substance can also be known by other means of knowledge, and so the discussion of the Vedānta passages is not essential to know it. But this is not correct. For Brahman is not like the external things an object of the senses. We perceive the world but not the Brahman. Nor can we infer that the world is an effect of Brahman; for no invariable necessary connection can be established between an effect which is perceived and a cause which is incapable of being perceived. Therefore the present Sūtra does not refer to inference as the means of knowing Brahman; it refers to the Vedānta-passages which are capable of describing the Brahman. In the dialogue between Varuṇa and his son (Tat. 3, 1, 6), the Brahman is described as Bliss and as that from which beings are born, and that in which they live and merge after death. This and other passages referred to by the Sūtra point out therefore the single conclusion that Brahman is eternal, pure, intelligent, free and omniscient, and that it is the cause of this world.

To confirm this, we proceed:

३ शास्त्रयोनित्वाधिकरणम् । (३)

शास्त्रयोनित्वात् । ३

[*Śāstra—Śruti* ; *yonitvāt—from being the source.*]

FROM ITS BEING THE SOURCE OF ŚRUTI; OR ŚRUTI BEING THE MEANS OF ITS KNOWLEDGE. 3

If the compound Śāstrayoni be treated as Ṣaṣṭhitatpuruṣa and be dissolved as 'Śāstrasya yoniḥ', then the meaning of the Sūtra is that the Brahman is the source of the Śruti; but if the compound is treated as Bahuvrīhi and is dissolved as 'Śāstraṁ yoniḥ Kāraṇaṁ pramāṇaṁ yasy', then the meaning will be that the Śruti is the means of the knowledge of Brahman.

The Śruti, *i.e.* the Ṛgveda and other branches of study, is a mine of knowledge and light; nevertheless, it comes 'as a breath' (Bṛ. 2, 4, 10) from the omniscient and omnipotent Brahman, just as grammar comes from Pāṇini. Where else can we seek for the source of this omniscient quality of the Śruti ? Or the Sūtra may be interpreted to mean that the knowledge of the Brahman as the cause of the world is possible only through Śruti, as has been shown by quoting a passage in the preceding Sūtra. But as there was some room for doubt in the preceding Sūtra, whether or not there was in it a reference to inference, the present Sūtra is intended to remove that doubt and explicitly state that the Śruti is the means of knowing that Brahman is the cause of the Universe.[1]

४ समन्वयाधिकरणम् । (४)

Someone may raise an objection like the following : How can it be maintained that Śruti is the means of knowing Brahman ? For in the Pūrva Mīmāṁsā (Sūtra 1, 2, 1), Jaimini has stated that action is the sole end of Śruti, and so those Śruti passages which do not aim at action are useless. No doubt, there are many passages in the Veda which appear to have no connection with action,

---

1 The first interpretation would leave room for supposing that Brahman is inferred from Śruti, just as the first Sūtra has left room for supposing that Brahman is inferred from the world. But the mention of the fact that Śruti is the breath of the great Being as mentioned by the Śruti itself removes both these doubts.

that is, which neither enjoin nor prohibit any action. For example, 'Wind is a swift deity,' appears to have no relation to human activity when taken in isolation. But read in the proper context, it means that the action of sacrificing a white animal to the deity of Wind will bear the fruit as swiftly as the wind is swift. Similarly, 'the Fire wept on account of being confined by gods,' is endowed with meaning because it implies the censure of silver and the offering of it in a sacrifice, inasmuch as silver is produced out of the tears of Agni. Therefore, as Jaimini says (Pū. Mī. Sū. 1, 2, 7), such Vedic sentences, known as 'arthvāda' go to supplement by way of praise or censure other sentences which enjoin or prohibit actions. The mantras too, as Jaimini tells us (Pū. Mī. Sū. 1, 2, 40), are connected with either the actions or their means. For example, in the mantra, 'for strength, thee', (Yaj. Saṁ. 1, 1, 1), the action of cutting a branch is implied. No Vedic passage can therefore be said to have any meaning unless it refers to some action or to some means or fruit of action. The Vedic passages which are declared to refer to the Brahman as an accomplished fact are therefore either useless, because there are other means of proof such as perception; or if they are to be of any use, they must, in the first place, refer in a subsidiary manner to some action or agent; or secondly, to the means or fruit of action, as explained above by Jaimini; or thirdly, must point out the process of meditation for the sake of realizing the Brahman. In any case, they do not refer to Brahman directly or independently of any action.

In order to refute this the Sūtrakara says :—

तत्तु समन्वयात् । ४

[*Tat—that* ; *tu-but* ; *samanvayāt—being the result of harmony.*]

BUT THAT (BRAHMAN IS KNOWN FROM ŚRUTI); IS THE RESULT OF HARMONY (OF THE VEDĀNTA-PASSAGES). 4

1. The omniscient and omnipotent Brahman then is the cause of the origin, subsistence and dissolution of the world. This is the only harmonious and cumulative conclusion of the Vedānta passages, such as; 'Being alone was in the beginning, one, without a second' (Chā. 6, 2, 1); 'All this was in the beginning, the one Ātman alone' (Ait. Ār. 2, 4, 1, 1); 'This is the Brahman, without cause and without effect, having nothing else inside or outside; this Ātman is the Brahman, the spectator of all' (Bṛ 2, 5, 19); 'That which is seen in front of one's self is the immortal Brahman alone' (Mu. 2, 2, 11). When the words in these passages refer directly and undoubtedly to Brahman, it will be improper to imagine that they refer to an altogether different thing *viz.* action. To do so is to commit the error in two ways; it is to reject the Brahman which is categorically indicated and to accept the action which is not so stated.

2. Nor can it be said that these passages refer to the agent or the deity which is implied in every action. But passages like 'then by what means, he (the Ātman) should see whom?', (Bṛ. 2, 4, 13) remove the possibility of reference to agent, actions, means or the fruit thereof.

3. Notwithstanding that it is already of the nature of an existing thing, Brahman cannot be known through perception or other means of knowledge; for the fact that Brahman is the Self of all, cannot be understood except by means of Śruti passages, such as 'That thou art' (Chā. 6, 8, 7).

4. Nor can it be said that instruction regarding the nature of Brahman will serve no purpose, because Brahman is not something which is to be accepted or rejected. For it is exactly this knowledge of the Brahman as the self of all, which does not require the further doing or non-doing of anything, and which results in the Summum Bonum of man's life by making him free from all pain.

5. There may be certain passages in which the description of the deities is subordinate to the process of meditation. But Brahman is not described in this manner as an object of meditation. For meditation implies the duality of the meditator and the object of meditation. Once the knowledge of unity arises, and the sense of duality is uprooted, there will be no such distinctions as agents and actions, nor anything which will be desired or avoided. Hence Brahman can never be considered in a subordinate manner as an object necessary for the process of meditation.

6. There may be passages in Karma-Kāṇḍa in which it is easy to point out that certain sentences known as arthavāda, whose function is to praise or censure, are supplementary to other sentences which enjoin or prohibit action, and are therefore authoritative. But the Vedānta passages which impart the knowledge of the Ātman have their own direct fruit, *viz.* the final release. Valid by themselves they do not owe their validity to other passages which deal with activity such as meditation or inferential reasoning. It is clear, therefore, that Śruti is authoritative as a means of the knowledge of Brahman.

At this point, some others (Vṛttikāras) raise the following objections :

1. Brahman is still the object of the process of realization, even though we may accept that it is known through Śruti. Knowledge about the sacrificial post or about the 'Āhavanīya' fire cannot be had by ordinary means of proof ; it is given by Śruti. And yet the post and the fire are described in a subsidiary manner, because they are involved in other activities which are recommended or prohibited by the Veda. That the purpose of Śruti passages is to induce a man either to do or not to do a particular thing, is clear from the following extracts : 'The purpose of it (Veda) is to give the knowledge of some kind of activity' (Śāba. Bhā. 1, 1, 1); 'A statement inducing action is known as an injunction'

(Śāba. Bhā. 1, 1, 2); 'A statement which gives knowledge about religious duty is known as initiation or instruction' (Jai. Sū. 1, 1, 5); 'Let words be connected with the verb denoting action' (Jai. Sū. 1, 1, 25); 'Activity being the aim of Śruti, passages which have no such aim are useless' (Jai. Sū. 1, 2, 1). The Vedānta-passages too, inasmuch as they belong to Śruti, are purposive in the same way. Just as 'agnihotra' etc. are recommended as a means to attain to heaven, even so the knowledge of Brahman is recommended as a means for the attainment of immortality.

2. The Vedāntin may say that the objects of knowledge and the fruits thereof differ in the two Śāstras. According to Karma-Kāṇḍa, Dharma is to be accomplished in the future; according to the Vedānta, the Brahman is an already accomplished and eternal fact. The fruit in one, viz. heaven, is dependent on the performance of actions; the fruit in the other, viz. the release, is not the result of any actions. Therefore the analogy, that the knowledge of Brahman is recommended for the purpose of final release in the way in which a sacrifice is recommended for attaining heaven, is not correct. In refutation of this, we reply that the knowledge about Brahman given by the Vedānta-passages is only in connection with some actions. The desire to know the Brahman is produced in us on account of such directive statements: 'Verily, the Ātman must be seen' (Bṛ. 2, 4, 5); 'Search out and understand the sinless Ātman' (Chā. 8, 7, 1); 'One should worship the Brahman in the form of Ātman only, (Bṛ. 1, 4, 7); 'One should worship the Ātman only as his true nature' (Bṛ. 1, 4, 15); 'One who knows Brahman becomes Brahman' (Mu. 3, 2, 9). And to the questions, what is this Ātman? What is this Brahman?, which arise in the mind by reading the above-mentioned directive statements, we get the reply in other Vedāntic statements that 'The Ātman is eternal' (Ka. 2, 18), 'Omniscient' (Mu. 1, 9), 'all-pervading' (Śve. 3, 11), 'eternally content with itself' as well as

'eternally pure, self-conscious and free', and that 'the Brahman is of the nature of consciousness and bliss' (Bṛ. 3, 9, 28). The nature of the Brahman is thus described because the motive of the Vedānta-passages is primarily to enable a man to meditate on it in order to achieve the final release.

3. If the Vedānta-passages were mere statements of existing facts and did not refer to actions to be done or not to be done, as if they resemble statements like, 'there are seven continents on the earth,' 'the king is marching,' they would be useless in practical life. It is alleged that the fear of the serpent will be removed by the mere assertion of the statement that 'this is a rope, not a snake.' But it is a matter of common experience that the mere verbal knowledge of the nature of Brahman does not in any way remove the wrong notions about one's own self. On the contrary, a man having such verbal knowledge continues to be affected by pleasure and pain of saṁsāra.

4. Besides, as stated in the Śruti (Bṛ. 2, 4, 5), the śravaṇa (hearing) is to be followed by reflection and contemplation. This clearly shows that in so far as Brahman is known by Śruti, it becomes the object of the devotional process.

We say in reply that the objections are futile, because:

1. There is a great difference between the results of Karma-vidyā and Brahma-vidyā. (*i*) While the knowledge and practice of dharma and adharma result in sensuous pleasure and pain, the knowledge of Brahman results in final release which is free from pain and is beyond the ken of the senses. (*ii*) Unlike mokṣa, pleasure and pain arise on account of the contact of the senses and its objects, and are experienced by all the beings from Brahmadeva down to the blade of grass. Mokṣa, however, is impossible

for those who have not seen the Ātman. (*iii*) There is the difference of degree in the merits or demerits and in the consequent pleasures and pains, as also in the capacity of persons performing religious acts. There is no such difference either with reference to mokṣa, or with reference to persons who are capable of having it. (*iv*) Those who perform sacrifices and are given to learning and contemplation go after death by the northern path of light to Brahma-loka; while those who do the daily routine of agnihotra etc. or social service and exhibit moral[1] qualities go by the southern path of smoke to Candra-loka and live there till their merit is exhausted (Chā. 5, 10, 5). (*v*) Thus, in short, is described the transitory, fleeting nature of Saṁsāra of the embodied beings as opposed to the disembodied state of final release which is not certainly the result of actions as directed by Śruti. Saṁsāra is due to ignorance and is full of pleasure and pain, merit and demerit; mokṣa, on the other hand, cannot be the fruit of dharma. It means knowledge, the disembodied and original condition of purity and bliss, as is clear from the passages: 'The wise does not grieve, because he knows that the Ātman is bodiless though residing in the bodies, and is changeless though residing in the changing things. The Ātman is the greatest and the omnipresent being of all' (Ka. 2, 22.); 'He is pure, and without prāṇa and manas' (Mu. 2, 1, 2); 'This puruṣa is not attached to anything' (Bṛ. 4, 3, 15). In other words, these passages point out that the Ātman is without gross or subtle body, and is unattached to both of them. So it has been proved that mokṣa is the eternal disembodied state and is different from the fruits of actions enjoined by dharma.

2. Some may hold that the eternal nature of things is compatible with change(pariṇāminitya). The five elements of earth, water etc. or the three guṇas of the Sāṁkhyas, are eternal in the sense that they are recognised as identical even though under-going change for the sake of the evolu-

1 From the view-point of one who has achieved Brahman-jñāna, all talk about the two paths and lokas is irrelevant.

tion of the universe. But mokṣa is eternal in the true sense of the word; it dces not undergo any transformation, and is immovable (Kūṭasthanitya). All-pervading like ākāśa, existing by itself, content with itself, without body, parts or modifications, it is self-illuminating, timeless and unaffected by merit and demerit (Ka. 1, 2, 14). Therefore, mokṣa or the disembodied condition is the same as Brahman, and so the instruction of Brahman cannot be mere supplementary to action.

3. Consider the following: 'One who knows Brahman becomes Brahman' (Mu. 3, 2, 9); 'Ineffective become the actions of one who sees the Brahman as the support of the higher and the lower' (Mu. 2, 2, 8); 'He who has the Brahmanic joy fears on no account' (Tai. 2, 9); 'O Janaka, You have achieved fearlessness' (Bṛ. 4, 2, 4); 'Brahman knew itself as Brahman and so has become all this' (Bṛ. 1, 4, 10); 'How can infatuation and sorrow affect him who has seen oneness in all?' (Īś. 7); 'Seeing which, the sage, Vāmadeva, realized that he was Manu, he was the sun' (Bṛ. 1, 4, 10). All these Śruti passages indicate that mokṣa follows immediately after the realization of Brahman, or that there remains nothing to be done after Brahma-jñāna to attain mokṣa. If it be the result of any activity, one would get mokṣa, like heaven after a lapse of some time. But just as a man can sing while standing, even so there need not be any lapse of time between Brahma-jñāna and mokṣa.

4. Consider again the other passages which indicate that the only result of Ātma-jñāna is merely to remove the obstacles in the way of mokṣa. Bhāradvāja and other sages say to their Guru, Pippalāda, 'You are father unto us, because you have carried us to the other end of avidyā' (Pr. 6, 8); Nārada says to Sanatkumāra,' 'Since I have heard from men like thee that one who knows the Ātman overcomes grief, carry me then beyond my grief' (Chā. 7, 1, 3); 'Revered Sanatkumāra carried him beyond ignorance, because his sins were washed out' (Chā.

7, 26, 2). The author of Nyāya-śāstra, Gautama, too, holds the view that the successive destruction of false knowledge, faults, activity, birth and misery results in mokṣa (Nyā. Sū. 1, 1, 2). Unlike the Nyāya[1] view the Vedāntin holds that the destruction of false knowledge rẹsults from the knowledge of the identity of jīva and Brahman.

5. This knowledge of the identity of the jīva and Brahman is not due to make-believe (bhāvanā)[2] on account of the fact that consciousness is common to both, though a similar make-believe is referred to in the Śruti, 'infinite are the Viśvedevas and infinite is the mind in its modifications; so it is that the person who fancies the mental states as Viśvedevas gets the world that knows no finitude' (Bṛ. 3, 1, 9). The identity of the jīva and Brahman however is real and not imagined.

6. Nor is this knowledge of identity of the nature of superimposition (adhyāsa). Brahman is not superimposed on the jīva, in the manner in which it is recommended to be superimposed for the sake of meditation on mind or on the sun (Chā. 3, 18, 1; 3, 19, 1).

7. Nor again is the knowledge of the identity of jīva and Brahman on the pattern of the functional identity conceived between prāṇa and vāyu. The vāyu or wind is said to be the absorber of everything *e.g.*, of fire, sun etc. at the time of dissolution, and prāṇa is said to be the absorber of speech, sight, hearing etc. during sleep (Chā. 4, 3, 7; 4, 3, 3). It is on account of this common activity or function of the two, that the prāṇa is to be contemplated

1 The Naiyāyikas however believe in many ātmans; the Vedāntin believes in one Ātman only.

2 Bhāvanā is deliberate, though imaginary identification of two things on account of similarity. Adhyāsa is illusory identification, and cannot be deliberate. Bhāvāna is utilized in order to forget the lower in value by meditating upon the higher; e.g. the Viśvedevas are contemplated and imagined to have actually taken the place of the modifications of the mind, while the latter, though actual are forgotten in the process of meditation. In adhyāsa one is simply aware erroneously of the meaning or the 'what' of one thing on the 'that', of other.

as the wind. The jīva however is not identical with the Brahman in the sense that both of them have the common activity of growing.

8. Nor does this knowledge of identity mean the act of purification of the jīva in its activity of seeing the Brahman, as is implied in the seeing of ghee by the sacrificer's wife in the Upāṁśu Yāga. The seeing of the identity of the jīva and the Brahman is not referred to in any passage connected with sacrifice.

9 (*i*). To suppose that this knowledge of identity arises on account of make-believe etc. as mentioned above, is to set at naught the words in the following passages which clearly indicate that the identity is real and not imagined : 'Thou art that' (Ka. 6, 8, 7) ; 'I am Brahman' (Bṛ. 1, 4, 10) ; 'This Ātman is Brahman,' (Bṛ. 2, 5, 19). The cessation of avidyā as the result of this knowledge and the fact of the realization of the Brahman are clearly mentioned in the passages : 'The knot in the heart is broken, and all the doubts are cut'; 'He who knows Brahman becomes Brahman (Mu. 2, 2, 8 ; 3, 2, 9). (*ii*) Hence it is clear that Brahma-jñāna is not the result of some human activity, but exists in itself alone. It exists as certainly as an object that is perceived or inferred exists by itself. In other words, it is impossible to conceive Brahman or the knowledge of Brahman as in any way connected with human activity and treated as an effect. (*iii*) Brahman is not an object of knowing, because it is stated 'to be different from the known effect and the unknown cause.' (Ke. 1, 3) ; 'How can one know Him by whose power everything else is known' (Bṛ. 2, 4, 13). (*iv*). Nor again is Brahman the object of any religious worship ; for the tongue cannot say anything about it, though it is through its power that the tongue speaks. 'Know this to be Brahman and not that which is worshipped' (Ke. 1, 4, and 5).

10. If it is indescribable, how can Śruti be said to be the means of knowing the Brahman ? The reply is that

what Śruti aims at showing is that Brahman is the internal imperishable Ātman. It can never become the subject, because all the empirical differences of the knower, the known and the knowledge are caused by avidyā. The paradoxical statement that 'it is not known by those who think that they know it, but that it is known by those who say that they do not know it' (Ke. 2, 3), means that it transcends the triad of the known, the knower and the knowledge, and that it is only to be realized. The same idea is conveyed in the passage, 'You cannot see the seer of sight, hear the hearer of hearing, think the thinker of thought, and know the knower of knowledge etc.' (Bṛ. 3, 4, 2). In short, the Śruti denies the imaginary transmigratory nature of the Ātman, and thereby brings out the eternally free nature of the same; mokṣa, in other words, is not transitory.

11. To consider mokṣa as a thing to be produced like a jar, or brought into being by a modification in the original condition like curds from milk, or reached as if it is a place of journey, is to consider it as short-lived, and as dependent on some action of body, mind or speech. Mokṣa is nothing but Brahman or the Ātman, which is already present in all. Brahman is perfect and so nothing can be added to it; being eternally pure, there cannot be any flaw in it which requires to be removed. It is not amenable to any change, and hence mokṣa does not mean the manifestation of the real nature of the Ātman on account of the latter being purified by some action, as if it is a mirror which becomes clear when the dust over it is removed.

Again, it is the empirical soul and not the Ātman that gets itself associated with the body, and which, therefore, is said to be purified by actions such as bathing, sipping of water, and the wearing of the sacred thread. In the proposition, 'I am free from disease', the empirical soul signified by the word 'I' is nothing but the ahaṁkāra that arises on account of avidyā and gets itself associated with the body. 'Joined with the body, the senses and the mind, it becomes known as the enjoyer or bhoktā (Ka. 3, 1, 4), and as such, 'eats the sweet fruit'; while the other (the Ātman) merely looks on without eating' (Mu. 3, 1, 1,). Brahman is described to be 'the one God, the hidden Ātman in all beings, all-pervading, watching all activity, the support of all, and yet absolutely free from all qualities' (Śve. 6, 11), or again, as 'self-luminous, disembodied, without any scars or muscles, pure and without evil' (Īś. 8). Mokṣa, then, being the same as the Ātman or Brahman, cannot in any way be connected with action. It has its relation with knowledge alone.

12. Is not knowledge itself an activity of the mind? No, the two are entirely different. Action is dependent on the mind but independent of the nature of things, and so admits of being done or not done. This includes even mental actions like reflection and meditation on a deity, as are required to be done by the 'hotā' while he is saying 'vaṣaṭ', and the chief priest is engaged in making the offering (Ait. Brā. 3, 8, 1). Knowledge, on the other hand, is not dependent on the mind of man or the Vedic instructions. It depends on the thing itself and is made available by pramāṇas. The difference between action and knowledge will be clear from the following example. Meditation on man and woman as fire (Chā. 5, 7, 1 ; 5, 8, 1) is an action because it is dependent on the will of man and conveys a Vedic instruction. The idea of fire, on the other hand, constitutes knowledge because it refers to the actual perceived fire, and is not dependent on the mind of man or on some Vedic statement. The knowledge of Brahman too is in the same manner objectively real, that is, refers to Brahman alone and not to any human activity or Vedic instruction. The various imperative statements such as 'The Ātman should be seen, meditated upon etc.' become as inoperative as the edge of a razor when it is applied to a stone, because the Brahman, which is referred to by these statements, is not something which can be acquired or rejected. The only purpose

served by these imperative statements is that they enable us to turn our back against our common objects of like and dislike, as also against our activity which is directed in achieving them, and to enable us to direct our eye on the Ātman itself. That after the realization of the Ātman, there remains nothing to be achieved or rejected, is no defect, but on the contrary, constitutes the strength of the Vedāntic position. It is the fulfilment of all our duty and the end of our life. 'If one were to realize the Ātman and realize him as this very Puruṣa (Brahman) what and for whom will he wish anything and suffer in the body?' (Bṛ. 4, 4, 12); or as the Bhagavadgītā declares, such a person achieves the aim of his life. Brahman is not therefore expounded as the object of any activity.

13. The opinion of those who, following Jaimini, say that there is no portion of the Vedas which does not recommend or prohibit action, or which is not subservient to action, is not therefore only erroneous but is also the expression of boldness. For the Upaniṣadic description of the Puruṣa is only a statement of fact, and not a statement regarding any action. It is impossible to hold that this Upaniṣadic Puruṣa or Brahman, who is beyond birth and death, and who is unrelated to action which is involved in production, modification, acquisition and purification, does not exist or is not realized. His existence is implied by the very word 'Ātman' in the passage which tries to describe him negatively as 'not this', not this' (Bṛ. 3, 9, 26). To deny the Ātman is to posit him, for otherwise the very denial would become impossible.

It will be wrong to suggest that the Ātman need not be known from the Upaniṣads, and that any body will be aware of it as the object of consciousness. For what people are aware of is not the Ātman, but the empirical soul. The Ātman of the Upaniṣads is the witness of the soul, the in-dweller of all, the unchanging one and same to all. Knowledge about him cannot be had from

Karma-Kāṇḍa or Logic. He alone is imperishable among all perishable things, and so cannot be avoided; and being eternal, pure, intelligent and free, he is not like a thing which is to be got by effort. 'There is nothing beyond the Puruṣa; He is the highest Good' (Ka. 1, 3, 11). He is referred to 'as taught in the Upaniṣads' (Bṛ. 3, 9, 26). This clearly shows that the main concern of the Upaniṣads is to teach the doctrine of the Ātman.

14. Now even if we take Jaimini's dictum that action alone is the import of the Vedas, we shall find that within the domain of the Karma-Kāṇḍa portion itself, statements regarding 'soma' and 'curds', such as 'One should sacrifice with "soma" or "use curds" as offering', will become meaningless. The words 'soma' and 'curds' do not themselves indicate any action. If, on the other hand, it is contended that they have got all the meaning inasmuch as they form part of some action to be done, then why should we suppose that the Jñāna-Kāṇḍa portion of the Veda which gives instruction about the eternally existing, unchanging Ātman, has no connection with some future event which necessarily follows as a result? Though Ātman itself is not a part of action or is not subservient to action, one necessary result of the knowledge of the Ātman is the removal of false knowledge and of the consequent saṁsāra. The connection of a thing with action does not change that thing into action. Knowledge of things only as already existing facts is possible in both the spheres of Karma and Jñāna; and it is the common nature of both that they are necessarily connected with results peculiar to them.

Besides, if the dictum of Jaimini is pressed too far, some negative propositions from the Karma-Kāṇḍa itself which recommend abstinence from action will have to be considered as useless; for they are themselves neither actions nor subservient to actions, and so appear to be mere statements of existing facts. But such a conclusion is not desirable. If it is urged that a negative statement may imply a positive statement over and above the negation of some positive idea, then there would be no difference between actions which are enjoined and actions which are prohibited. The word 'not' in the sentence, 'a Brahmin should not be killed', has got the primary meaning of desisting from killing, and so should not be construed as merely having the secondary or the implied meaning, *viz.* of doing something else than killing, that is, abusing or tormenting him. The negative particle merely indicates the non-existence of that action with which it is connected and not any new action, unless from context in exceptional cases, it is certain that the negative sense constitutes an action. For example, in the Prajāpati-vrata, the Brahmacāri is asked not to see the rising sun. Here, 'not to see the rising sun' is not simply the absence of seeing the rising sun, but constitutes a positive action by itself. But excepting such cases, the negative particle indicates a neutral condition of the mind which arises on account of the negation of an action. It need not be maintained that this cognition of the negation and the consequent neutral condition of mind will last for a short time, and will again give rise to a desire to do the actions; for the fire is extinguished only after the fuel is burnt. Knowledge about the negation of an action will first destroy the desire for action and then destroy itself. In short, it is the neutral condition of indifference to actions that constitutes the meaning of a negative proposition, and not an action which is contrary to some prohibited action. So if there be any part of the Vedas which is meaningless, it is that which has no other aim but to narrate some stories.

15. We have proved so far that Vedic statements regarding existing facts are not purposeless, even though they do not point to any action. They are of the type, 'This is a rope, not a snake', and are therefore purposeful in the way in which this proposition is in removing the fear of the snake. No doubt, one who has merely an intellectual understanding of the Brahman may be found engrossed as before with the affairs of the world; but not

certainly one who has realized the Brahman. It is natural that a man who has falsely identified himself with his body should suffer from the effects of misery and fear; but he will never suffer in this way if he once realizes, as the Vedas tell, that he himself is the Brahman. A person who feels proud on account of his riches may mourn over the loss if he is robbed of them; but is it ever possible for a person to mourn over the loss, if he has renounced the world and has given up his attachment for wealth? Similarly, a person may derive pleasure from ear-rings because he has the sense of ownership, but is it possible for him to have the same pleasure in ownership, once he casts away the ear-rings and feels no attachment to them? As the Śruti tells, 'neither pleasure nor pain touches a man who has lost the egoism of his body' (Chā. 8, 12, 1).

16. As for the disembodied condition or mokṣa we have already said that it is eternal. One may perhaps say that the disembodied condition is possible after death, but that the Ātman may again assume the body on account of the merits and demerits incurred by it. But the Ātman is neither related with body nor with merit and demerit. To hold that the Ātman is related to the body because of merit and demerit, and that it incurs merit and demerit because it has got a body, is to argue in a circle. To hold again that the body, on the one hand, and merit and demerit, on the other, are endlessly related to each other as seed and tree, is to believe in a chain of blind men who will be unable to lead one another. No doubt, kings and great men are called authors of actions, although their servants do these for the sake of wealth. But there is no such link to establish the relation of master and servant between the Ātman and the body. Hence there is no other reason for the embodied condition except the wrong notion that the soul has got a body. Hence too arises the egoism in the form of 'I am the performer of sacrifice etc.' on account of the false knowledge that the 'I' is identified with the body.

17. Following the Prabhākara school, it need not also be said in this connection that the consciousness of the Ātman as the body arises on account of the transference of the idea and the name of one thing to another thing because of certain characteristics which are common to both. The meaning of the transferred name is only secondary and not primary. On seeing the bravery and similar qualities of a man, he may be called a 'lion' among men. But where there is no cognition of the two things as separate from each other, the transference occurs on account of error. In darkness, a post is taken for a man; there appears silver on the shell; for there is no clear and distinct apprehension of the post or the shell. So the meaning of the term 'man' or of 'silver' that is transferred to the post or the shell is not the secondary meaning, but the primary meaning due to error. Similarly, the application of the word 'I' and of the consciousness of that 'I' to the body-complex arises on account of the ignorance of the difference between the body and the 'I'. In the absence of the knowledge of the difference between the two, there will necessarily be the absence of the transference of the secondary meaning (if any) from one to the other. So it is on account of superimposition or error that the word and the meaning of 'I' are transferred to the body. This error is not peculiar only to shepherds and common people; even learned men who know the distinction between the Ātman and the body, commit it.

All this goes to prove two things; (*i*) that the embodiedness of the Ātman is due to false notion, and (*ii*) that the disembodied condition or mokṣa can be experienced even while living. From the view-point of one who has realized the Brahman, 'the body is like the cast off, dead slough of a snake; he himself, on the other hand, remains immortal, without the body, and becomes verily the Brahman and the Light' (Bṛ. 4, 4, 7). So perfect is the disembodied condition of such a person that he behaves 'as if he has neither eyes, nor ears, nor mind nor life.' The Bhagavadgītā too, while describing the characteristics of a Sthitaprajña, tells us that one who has realized the Atman is in no way connected with any kind of action. Thus, it has been proved beyond doubt that one who has realized the Brahman never returns to Saṁsāra; nor one who clings to Saṁsāra has realized the Brahman.

18. Finally, the objection that Brahman does not constitute an independent topic of inquiry but a subsidiary one to Dharma-jñāna is also not true. Reflection and contemplation as well as listening to narrations about the nature of Brahman are for the purpose of realizing the Brahman, and not for some other purpose. Had Brahman been subservient to the process of meditation, it would have been incorporated in Pūrva-Mīmāṁsā alone. At best, Jaimini would have made a separate chapter to deal with Brahman, as if it were an appendix to Dharma-Jijñāsā, as he has done with reference to sacrifice and Summum Bonum of life (Pū. Mī. Sū. 4, 1, 1). But nowhere in Pūrva-Mīmāṁsā is there any reference to the knowledge dealing with the identity of the Brahman and the jīva; and hence it is appropriate to have a separate branch of study for dealing with the subject of Brahman.

Therefore all the precepts regarding action and all the means of knowledge have their utility so long as the knowledge, 'I am the Brahman', has not dawned. Once there arises the knowledge of this non-dual Ātman, that can neither be accepted nor rejected at the will of a man, there remains neither the subject as the knower, nor the object as the known, nor again the means of knowledge. Hence it is said : 'The moment one knows that he is verily the Brahman, his secondary or false consciousness that he is related to his son or to his body drops down, and there remains nothing to be done by him.' The Ātman appears as the subject in relation to an object so long as it is not known in its true nature; but the moment the Ātman is known the person becomes one with the sinless Brahman.

५ ईक्षत्यधिकरणम् (५-११)

We have proved so far that the only aim and the motive of the Vedānta-passages is to make us aware of the fact that Brahman is the Self of everything, that it has no relation with action, and that, being omniscient and omnipotent, it is the cause of the origin, subsistence and dissolution of the world. The Sāṁkhya and other philosophers, however, rely on inference and not on Śruti. And so they think that the Vedānta-passages which deal with the problem of creation point out that the cause of the world is the connection of pradhāna with Puruṣa. The followers of Kaṇāda think that God and the atoms are the efficient and the material causes of the world. Others too take their stand on Vedānta-passages and use fallacious arguments and objections. Against all these opponents it will be shown that the only aim of the Vedānta-passages is to impart the knowledge of the Brahman. The views of the opponents will therefore be propounded and refuted.

To state first the view of the Sāṁkhyas. Pradhāna is the cause of the world, though it is non-intelligent and consists of the three guṇas. It can be said to be omnipotent, because it has the power to produce all its effects; and it is omniscient because 'knowledge comes out of sattva' (B. G. 17, 14). This is borne out by the fact that the yogins themselves become omniscient because they are endowed with body and senses (the effects of pradhāna), and possess the sattva quality of pradhāna in its highest degree. Even at the time of the dissolution of the world, when the three guṇas are in the condition of equipoise, the pradhāna has got the capacity for knowing all, in spite of its being non-intelligent. On the other hand, Brahman is incapable of having full or partial knowledge; for it is said to be solitary, devoid of body and other organs of sense and action; and though it is pure consciousness, it is conscious of nothing in particular. And what does omniscience of Brahman mean, except the capacity for all knowledge as in the case of pradhāna? For if we mean by it a perpetual actual cognition of objects, Brahman will be robbed of its freedom to know; and if we mean by it transitory cognition, then it will be robbed of its eternal consciousness which is said to be its essence. Besides, being without the means of action, like the body and the senses, it can neither have knowledge nor be able to create this world. It can never be the cause of the world because it is one and homogeneous. As opposed to this, the pradhāna is capable of modifications. It consists of more elements than one, and may therefore be the cause of the world.

To this the Sūtrakāra replies:

ईक्षतेर्नाशब्दम् ।५

[*Īkṣateḥ—on account of seeing; na—not; a-śabdaṁ—not found in veda.*]

BECAUSE 'SEEING' (IS REFERRED, THE PRADHĀNA) WHICH IS NOT FOUNDED ON THE VEDA, IS NOT (THE CAUSE). 5

The pradhāna cannot be the cause of the world; for being non-intelligent, it cannot perform the act of 'seeing' which is mentioned in the Śruti as performed by the cause. The word 'seeing' does not refer simply to the meaning of the root 'Īkṣ' (to see) but includes in it meanings of other words also which indicate possession of intelligence or knowledge, in the same manner in which the word 'Yaja' is used by Jaimini to indicate any sacrifice. The word 'this' in the following passages refers to this world of names and forms as caused by the intelligent Brahman alone. 'This was, in the beginning, the one, non-dual Being; it saw within it the desire, "to become many and produce much", and so created the fire' (Chā. 6, 2, and 3); 'This was in the beginning one Ātman alone, and nothing else had the capacity to move. He saw within him the desire to produce the worlds, and produced them' (Ait. Ār. 1, 1, 1). In one place, it is the Puruṣa consisting of sixteen parts[1] who is said to have 'seen and produced the prāṇa' (Pr. 6, 3). Similarly, in Muṇḍakopaniṣad (1, 1, 9) 'all this Brahman, that is the world of names, forms, and food', has been said to have come out of 'Him who is omniscient, and whose penance is the knowledge of all the lores'. All this clearly shows, that the cause of the world is the 'seeing' of the intelligent Brahman and not that of the non-intelligent pradhāna.

Pradhāna cannot be omniscient on account of its sattva-guṇa too; for the latter is in the condition of equipoise with the other two guṇas, and not predominant over others. Knowledge arises only when the sattva predominates. And if the presence of sattva in it is sufficient to consider the pradhāna as having the capacity to know all, the presence of rajas and tamas which prevent knowledge is sufficient to consider it as having the capacity to know little. Again there must be some conscious subject to whom the sattva will belong as a modified state; but the pradhāna is not a conscious subject. A yogin becomes omniscient because he is a conscious subject, and not simply because there is an excess of sattva in him.

Modifying his position, a Sāṁkhya may say that Brahman may be the witness, and yet it is on this very account that the pradhāna may possess in it the causal activity of the 'seeing' mentioned in the Śruti, just as a ball of iron which is not itself fire may possess the quality of burning on account of its conjunction with fire. But will it not then be more reasonable to say that Brahman alone is the cause of the world rather than saying that pradhāna, which is dependent on the Brahman, is the cause?

Besides, there is no incompatibility between the ever-lasting all-knowingness and the freedom of Brahman. Just as the ever-lasting heat and light of the sun are said

1 The sixteen 'kalās' are the four quarters, earth, heaven, the space between them, ocean, fire, sun, moon, lightning, breath, eye, ear and speech (Chā. 4, 5-8).

to have been given freely by the sun, even so the 'seeing' of the Brahman is a free act inspite of its eternal cognition. The all-knowing Brahman 'saw', is as clear a statement about the freedom of the Brahman, as the statement the sun 'shines' about the freedom of the sun, even when there is no object to be seen or no object to be illuminated. And if at all the 'seeing' should grammatically require some object to be seen, it will be no other than the very names and forms[1] of this world which were before creation present in the bosom of the Brahman as ideas to be seen or thought of. If the Yogins can have a perceptual knowledge of the past and the future on account of His grace, is it too much to suppose that He himself, the eternally pure, has an everlasting cognition of the creation, subsistence and dissolution of this world ? Like luminosity of the sun, eternal knowledge, being itself the essential nature of Brahman, does not require the means of knowledge. Being bound by avidyā, the individual soul may require body and other instruments for the sake of having knowledge. But as the following mantras tell us, God is free from every hindrance to knowledge. 'He has neither body nor senses; neither is there anyone who is equal or superior to him; manifold and extraordinary is his power; and his actions are the natural result of his knowledge. Handless and holding fast the things, without feet and moving swift, without eyes and yet having sight, without ears and yet hearing, He knows all that is knowable, but nobody knows him; they call him the first and the great Puruṣa'. (Śve. 6, 8, ; 3, 19).

No doubt, the individual jīva, though bound to saṁsāra is essentially not different from Īśvara, 'other than whom, there is no other seer or knower' (Bṛ. 3, 7, 23). And yet, just as a false notion arises regarding the existence of different portions of space on account of the existence of the limitations of things like jars and vessels in one

1 The names and forms cannot be distinct from Brahman, for they cannot manifest themselves ; neither can they be said to be non-distinct from it, for they are 'jaḍa', while Brahman is 'cetana.' In other words, having their origin in Māyā, they are 'anirvacanīya.'

space, even so there arises the false notion that the soul and God are different on account of the ignorance of the fact that the soul is attached to the limitations of body, and the senses. The Ātman is thus wrongly believed as the non Atman, and therefore requires the body and the senses for carrying on the affairs (lit. for 'seeing') of this saṁsāra.

One may ask if the non-intelligent pradhāna cannot be said to have 'seen' in the manner in which a bank of a river is figuratively said to be wishing to fall. The pradhāna too brings about the evolution of the universe as regularly, as a man should execute his plan of going to a village after taking his bath and dinner. Such a figurative use is made even in Śruti, 'The fire saw; the water saw' (Chā. 6, 2, 3 ; 4). Or else, if the 'seeing' refers to Brahman, there too it must be taken in a figurative sense, because, in the context where it is used, it refers more than once to non-intelligent objects, such as fire and water.

To this the Sūtrakāra replies :

गौणश्चेन्नात्मशब्दात् । ६

⟦*Gaunaḥ—secondary* ; *cet—if* ; *na—not* ; *Ātmaśabdāt—on account of the word* ' *Ātman* '.⟧

On account of the word 'Ātman' (being applied to the cause) the meaning (of the word 'seeing') is not figurative. 6

The Śruti passage which mentions the Sat (Being) as alone existing before the creation of this world, and as alone responsible for the creation of fire, water and earth on account of its 'seeing', mentions further that it was the divinity of Sat which thought of entering with its own jīvātman into the other divinities of fire, water and earth and so evolving the world of names and forms (Chā. 6, 2). If the 'seeing' or thought should refer in a figurative manner to the pradhāna, then the word 'divinity' too would refer to it; but in that case, how can 'jīvātman', which means both conventionally and etymologically the intelligent ruler of the body and the bearer of prāṇa, be the constituent nature of the non-intelligent pradhāna? But if by 'sat' we mean the Brahman which does the act of 'seeing', not in a figurative or secondary manner, but literally or primarily, the use of the word Ātman with reference to jīva will be intelligible. In a chapter of the Chāndogyopaniṣad (6, 8, 7), Śvetaketu is told that he is the Ātman, and that all this is the Ātman, the very subtle essence, the 'sat' or the Puruṣa.' As for fire and water, even though they are spoken of as possessing the 'seeing' in a figurative manner, and as being smaller divinities, they are in reality non-intelligent and created objects having names and forms.

It may still be urged that the word 'Ātman' may refer to pradhāna, in the same figurative manner in which a king may say about his servant, Bhadrasena, that he is his very soul. For the pradhāna is useful in making the jīva reap the fruit of his actions or have his salvation, just as the minister of a king is useful to him in peace and war. Or the word 'Ātman' may refer to both intelligent and non-intelligent beings, just as the word 'jyoti' indicates both a sacrifice and a flame, and hence the 'seeing' may still be taken in a figurative meaning.

To this the Sūtrakāra replies :

तन्निष्ठस्य मोक्षोपदेशात् ।७

[*Tanniṣṭhasya—of him who is devoted to Brahman ; mokṣopadeśāt—on account of release being promised.*]

BECAUSE THE INSTRUCTION IS THAT ONE WHO IS DEVOTED TO HIM, GETS FINAL RELEASE, (THE WORD ĀTMAN CANNOT BE USED WITH REFERENCE TO PRADHĀNA). 7

The passage from the Chāndogyopaniṣad which tells us that the subtle Being (Sat) is the Ātman and which further expounds the truth 'That thou art', is immediately followed by another statement which tells us that this knowledge of the identity of the jīva and the Ātman or the Sat is achieved by one who has got a spiritual teacher, and that he becomes one wit h the Ātman after the fall of the body. This means that mokṣa is possible for one by being devoted to the Sat or the Ātman. If, on the other hand, the Sat were to refer to the pradhāna, it would mean that a conscious human being, who is hankering after mokṣa is asked to believe that he is nothing but the non-intelligent pradhāna. This would only mean that he would not only not have mokṣa, but also be bound all the more by the ties of saṁsāra. His condition will be no better than that of a blind person who, wishing to reach his home, is ill-advised to take hold of the tail of an ox, and who therefore, instead of reaching his home, is merely hurt by the shrubs and stones on the way as he is carried away by the ox in any direction. Therefore it behoves us to say that the Śruti passages contain instructions regarding the means to realize the Ātman, just as it may behove one to say that Agnihotra and other sacrifices are recommended as means to attain to heaven (Chā. 6, 8, 7; 6, 14, 2; 6, 16, 3). The conviction 'I am the Brahman', will lead one to mokṣa as surely as the holding fast of a red-hot axe without being burnt was once considered to be the means of making a man free from the guilt of theft. That the word 'Sat' means the 'Ātman' is then literally true and not merely in a figurative sense. Otherwise, like devotion to the 'uktha' or the 'prāṇa', it will yield only transitory result (Ait. Ār. 2, 1, 2, 6).

Sometimes, words are used in a figurative sense no doubt; for instance, the word 'Ātman' in 'Bhadrasena is my Ātman. But to universalize the belief, and to say that the word 'Ātman' in 'I am the Ātman' is used in a figurative sense, is to create confusion. Which meaning is intended on a particular occasion, must be settled by reference to the context or to the qualifying word. So if we are not to be confused, we must take the word 'Ātman' in its literal sense with reference to sentient beings like Śvetaketu, or with reference to their actions, such as the 'seeing' performed by the Sat. But we should take it in the figurative sense with reference to non-sentient things, such as the senses and elements. Again, the interpretation of the word 'jyoti' is no key to the interpretation of the word 'Ātman'. The word 'jyoti' has got the derivative meaning of 'sacrifice', because the sacrifice indicates the primary meaning of the word, *viz.* light or flame in it. The word 'Ātman', on the other hand, cannot be transferred with its meaning which is available with reference to sentient beings, to the non-sentient pradhāna, because there is nothing common between the sentient Brahman and the non-sentient pradhāna.

हेयत्वावचनाच्च। ८

[*Heyatva—fact of being discarded* ; *avacanāt—there being no statement* ; *ca—and.*]

THERE BEING NO STATEMENT THAT IT IS TO BE DISCARDED (THE PRADHĀNA IS NOT MENTIONED BY THE WORD 'SAT'); AND. 8

The word 'Sat' has not been used to denote the pradhāna, even as a preliminary step, so that it should denote afterwards the Brahman or the Ātman. Had it been so, Śvetaketu's father who wished to instruct his son regarding the nature of the subtle Being or the Ātman, would have first asked him to descard the notion of the pradhāna being the Sat. But this has not been done. When the very small star of Arundhati is to be shown, the device adopted is to show first a bigger star near it as if it is the star of Arundhati, and then to direct the attention to the real star, thereby discarding the earlier false knowledge of the bigger star as Arundhati. But such a device has not been used in the case of the knowledge of the Ātman. The false notion of the pradhāna as the Sat has not been introduced first and discarded later, so that it should be an aid to the understanding of Śvetaketu that Ātman alone is the Sat or the real Being.

The sixth adhyāya of the Chāndogyopaniṣad deals with the direct statement of the Ātman as the real Being.

Even if the pradhāna is believed to be rejected, the word 'and' in the Sūtra indicates that there would arise the additional defect of contradicting the earlier statement, *viz.* the cause being known, everything else becomes known. For the sixth adhyāya begins with the statement of the question as to what it is which when known enables one to know what is ordinarily never known, hear what is never heard, and realize what is never realized. And the reply is given by saying that to know the clay as the cause is to know everything that is made out of clay; for all the modifications of clay are mere distinctions in name which have their origin in speech and not in clay as such. The truth is that all these modifications are clay only (Chā. 6, 1, 2–6). If the word Sat were to denote pradhāna, then the knowledge of pradhāna as the cause would have given us the knowledge of the individual souls. But this does not happen, because the souls which are sentient cannot be the effects of the non-sentient pradhāna. Therefore the word 'Sat' does not mean pradhāna.

A further reason why 'Sat' does not mean Pradhāna.

स्वाप्ययात् ।९

[*Sva—Ātman* ; *apyayāt—on account of absorption.*]

On account of (the individual soul) entering into the Ātman, (the word 'Sat' does not refer to Pradhāna). 9

It is with reference to the cause which is denoted by the word 'Sat' that it is said that the individual soul becomes one with the 'Sat' during sleep (Chā. 6, 8, 1). In the waking state, the soul apprehends the objects intellectually and becomes endowed with the consciousness of the body. The same soul goes by the name of the 'mind' when the person dreams on account of the desires which only are left behind. But when he becomes devoid of the two conditions, that is, when there are neither the external objects, nor the body, nor the senses, nor even the desires of which he should be conscious, he is said to sleep or enter, as if, in his true being viz. the Ātman. This interpretation of the word 'Svapiti' (he sleeps) as 'Svam apīto bhavati' (becomes absorbed in the Ātman) is analogous to the interpretation of the word 'hṛdaya' (heart) as 'hṛdi ayaṁ Ātmā' (the Ātman is in the heart. Chā. 8, 3, 3). Similarly, again, the words 'aśanāyā' and 'udanyā' are explained as 'water which carries the food eaten by him' (tadaśitaṁ), 'fire which carries away what has been drunk (talpitaṁ) by him (Chā. 6, 8, 3, 5). So it is impossible that the conscious Ātman will be resolved in the non-conscious pradhāna. Even if the word 'Sva' were to denote, not necessarily Ātman, but pradhāna as 'belonging to the Ātman,' there would be the same defect of the conscious being mixed up with the non-conscious. The soul then, 'embraced as he is by the conscious Ātman, knows nothing inside or outside' during sleep (Bṛ. 4, 3, 21); and so, it is not pradhāna, but the conscious Ātman alone which is the cause of the world, which is indicated by the word 'Sat' and in which all conscious beings go for rest.

Pradhāna is not the cause for a further reason :

गतिसामान्यात् । १०

[*Gati—knowledge ; sāmānyāt—on account of similarity.*]

ON ACCOUNT OF THE CONSENSUS OF OPINION (EXPRESSED IN DIFFERENT UPANIṢADS, BRAHMAN IS THE CAUSE, AND NOT PRADHĀNA). 10

Had the Vedānta-passages contradicted each other as the arguments of the logicians do, then it would have been plausible to hold that the cause of the world is either the intelligent Brahman or the non-intelligent pradhāna or something else. But there is the unanimous declaration that the intelligent Brahman alone is the cause.

Compare for instance : 'Just as sparks emanate from fire in all directions, even so, from the Ātman proceed the prāṇas, and from prāṇas the gods, and from gods the worlds' (Kau. 3, 3); 'From the Ātman has come forth the ākāśa' (Tai. 2, 1); 'All this has come out of the Ātman' (Chā. 7, 26, 1); 'From Ātman alone proceeds the prāṇa,' (Pra. 3, 3). So, just as the eyes of different men agree in having the same knowledge regarding colour, even so the views expressed in different Vedānta passages agree in holding the conscious Ātman or Brahman as the cause of the world. And the consensus of opinion is certainly a powerful argument.

A further reason in support of the omniscient Brahman as the cause of the world :

श्रुतत्वाच्च । ११

[*Śrutattvat—being mentioned in the Veda; ca—and.*]

AND BECAUSE IT IS MENTIONED IN ŚRUTI (THAT THE ALL-KNOWING BRAHMAN IS THE CAUSE). 11

The mantropaniṣad of the Śvetāśvataras tells us that 'He alone, the all-knowing God, indicated by the word 'Sva' is the cause and the Lord of lords, while there is none else who can be said to have produced him or be his lord' (6, 9). This means that the omniscient Brahman alone is the cause of the world.

६ आनंदमयाधिकरणम् । (१२-१९)

In the above and in the preceding nine Sūtras, what we have been showing by the help of suitable arguments is that the various Vedānta-passages aim at proving that the all-knowing and the all-powerful God is the cause of the origin, subsistence and dissolution of the world. The purpose of the remaining Sūtras is to show that Brahman assumes two forms, one without limitations as the object of knowledge, and the other with limitations as the object of devotion. Consider the following 'where there appears duality, one sees the other ; but when one becomes identified with the Ātman, who should see whom ?' (Bṛ. 4, 5, 15). When one sees nothing but the Ātman, hears or knows nothing but the Ātman, he is the greatest; but where one sees or hears or knows something else, it is a little thing ; he who is the greatest attains immortality, everything little is perishable' (Chā. 7, 24, 1). 'Having created all, the wise Being names them and calls them by their names' (Tai. Ār. 3, 12, 7). 'He is without limbs or actions, without any blemish or defect, unperturbed, unaffected, the bridge of salvation, and is like fire which has consumed the fuel of avidyā' (Śve. 6, 19). 'Not this, not this' (Br. 2, 3, 6). 'It is neither gross nor subtle' (Bṛ 3, 8, 8). 'Perfect is one abode, imperfect the other'. All these and several other passages show that Brahman as the object of knowledge differs from Brahman as the object of devotion. The latter however is the result of avidyā. So long as avidyā lasts, there arise different forms of devotion which either aim at prosperity, success in works or gradual liberation. 'As a man worships, so he becomes' (Chā. 3, 14, 1) ; 'Whatever one remembers at the time of death, he attains that' (B. G. 8, 6). Though the Ātman is eternal, unchanging, uniform and hidden in all the movable and immovable things, he becomes manifest in proportion to the degree of the excellence of the mind, and being endowed with power, dignity and glory' (Ait. Ār. 2, 3, 21; B. G. 10, 41) becomes an object of worship. Similarly, in the Brahmasūtras too (1, 1, 20 and 1, 1, 22), the sinless golden person who appears on the disc of the sun as well as the Ākāśa are declared to be the highest Being.

Thus, though Ātma-jñāna is the immediate cause of mokṣa, it must be settled whether it refers to Saguṇa or to Nirguṇa Brahman, and whether Brahman is the object of knowledge or of devotion. The sūtrakāra will solve this problem, as also incidentally explain in the remaining Sūtras the earlier point that Brahman, and not pradhāna, is the cause of the world.

आनंदमयोऽभ्यासात् ।१२

[*Ānadamayaḥ—a being full of bliss ; abhyāsāt—because of repetition.*]

ĀNANDAMAYA (MEANS THE BRAHMAN) BECAUSE (THE WORD ĀNANDA AS DENOTING BRAHMAN) IS REPEATED. 12

After having mentioned in succession several ātmans consisting of food, prāṇa, mind and intelligence, the Taittirīyopaniṣad tells us that the inner-most Ātman consists of bliss (2, 1, 5). The question to be solved in this connection is whether ānandamaya Ātman is the Brahman itself, the Being which is already pointed out as truth, knowledge and eternity, or like the selfs of food, prāṇa etc., it is different from the Brahman. The pūrvapakṣin contends that it is jīvātman only and not Brahman, because, in the first place, the ānandamaya comes last in the series of lower ātmans such as those that are made up of food etc.; secondly, even though innermost, it has joy etc. as its limbs, e.g. 'joy is its head'; and thirdly, it has, unlike the Brahman, the body viz. the preceding ātman made up of intelligence (Tai. 2, 6).

In reply to this, it is to be said that ānandamaya means the highest Ātman alone, for it is in this sense that the word 'ānanda' has been repeatedly used; e.g. after introducing the topic of ānandamaya as an embodied one, it is further said to constitute the essence of flavour (rasa). It is after getting this rasa that one finds the bliss ; if this bliss be not in the ākāśa of the heart, who would be able to breathe ? He alone makes one enjoy the bliss ; and the test of this bliss of the Brahman is that one who gets it does not fear anything, but reaches the Ātman and realizes that Bliss itself is the Brahman' (Tai. 2, 7-9 ; 3, 6). Again we have 'knowledge and bliss are Brahman' (Bṛ. 3, 9, 28). So the word bliss or 'ānanda' is repeatedly used for Brahman ; hence we say that 'ānandamaya' Ātman is Brahman only.

As for the objections, we say that they have no force. In the first place, the ānandamaya Ātman is the innermost reality of all, beyond which no other ātman is mentioned. The most ignorant of the people understand by the Ātman the body which is made up of food. So in order to suit the understanding of the common run of people, the Ātman is first shown to be that which is un-ātman ; then another un-ātman of the same shape but more real because inner than the first; then another still of the same shape, but much more real because inner than the second; and so on, till the innermost Ātman which consists of ānanda only is finally shown as the real one. Just as the very small star of Arundhati is shown last of all, after having first shown the bigger ones in the neighbourhood as aids to the eyesight, even so the un-ātmans made up of food, prāṇa etc. are shown in succession in order that people of ordinary intelligence may gradually eliminate the false ātmans, and posit the innermost Ātman consisting of ānanda as the only reality. Secondly, to speak of this Ātman as 'having the head of joy' or the 'body of intelligence' is but an imagination. The language of 'limbs' and 'body' is used with reference to this Ātman, because it is mentioned as the last link of the chain. Otherwise it has neither body nor limbs as the jīvātman has. Ānanadamaya Ātman is verily then the Brahman or the highest Ātman.

विकारशब्दान्नेति चेन्न प्राचुर्यात्। १३

[*Vikāraśabdāt—due to word denoting modification* ; *na* ; *iti* ; *cet—if* ; *na* ; *prācuryāt—due to abundance.*]

IF IT BE SAID (THAT ĀNANDAMAYA) DOES NOT (DENOTE THE HIGHEST ĀTMAN) BECAUSE IT IS A WORD DENOTING MODIFICATION, (THEN IT IS) NOT SO; (THE MEANING OF THE AFFIX 'MAYA') BEING ABUNDANCE. 13

If the affix 'maya' is said to change the meaning of the original word, then the word ānandamaya may mean 'made up of' or consisting of ānanda just as the word "annamaya" means 'made up of food.' The objection however is not valid, because 'maya', as Pāṇini tells us, (Pā. Sū. 5, 4, 21) may mean 'abundance' also. In 'annamaya yajña' e.g., the word 'annamaya means 'abounding in food', and so annamaya-yajña means a sacrifice in which there is plenty of food. Similarly, 'ānandamaya' means 'abounding in blisss', and so ānandmaya-ātman means Brahman itself as abounding in bliss. That the bliss of Brahman knows no measure is seen from the passage in the Taittirīyopaniṣad (2, 8), where the several blisses beginning with the bliss of man and ending with the bliss of Brahman are measured in ascending degree, each bliss being made up of hundred blisses of the preceding being.

तद्धेतुव्यपदेशाच्च। १४

[*Tat*; *hetu—cause*; *vyapadeśāt—because it is mentioned.*]

BECAUSE (BRAHMAN) IS MENTIONED AS THE CAUSE OF (THE BLISS, THE AFFIX 'MAYA' MEANS ABUNDANCE). 14

Just as a person who makes others rich must himself possess abundant wealth, even so the Ātman who 'causes bliss' (Tai. 7) himself must abound in bliss. As 'maya means 'abundance' 'ānandmaya' means therefore the highest Ātman only.

मान्त्रवर्णिकमेव च गीयते। १५

[*Māntravarṇikaṁ—as in mantra*; *eva*; *ca* ; *gīyate—sung.*]

(ĀNANDAMAYA IS BRAHMAN BECAUSE) THE SAME (BRAHMAN WHICH HAS BEEN MENTIONED IN THE MANTRA IS MENTIONED (IN THE BRĀHMAṆA). 15

The mantra and the Brāhmaṇa portions of the Taittirīyopaniṣad (2, 1, and 5) do not contradict by dealing with two different topics, but are consistent with each other in referring to the same Brahman. The mantra which first introduces the topic of Brahman by saying 'one who knows Brahman becomes Brahman,' describes it further as truth, intelligence and infinity, as giving birth to ākāśa and other elements, and to all movable and immovable things, and as residing inside the beings, and finally as being the innermost Ātman of the series of other ātmans. The same Brahman is spoken of by the Brāhmaṇa[1] as 'ānandamaya' and as being the innermost of all. Besides the vidyā known as Bhārgavī Vāruṇī centres round this 'ānandamaya'; and beyond this there is no mention of any other ātman. Therefore ānandamaya alone is the highest Ātman.

नेतरोऽनुपपत्तेः । १६

[*Na—not ; itara—the other ; anupapatteḥ—because not found.*]

(ĀNANDAMAYA IS) NOT THE OTHER (*viz.* THE JIVĀTMAN) BECAUSE (THINGS) DO NOT FOLLOW. 16

With reference to ānandamaya it is said, 'He wished to become many and to produce (the world) ; he made a penance and created this all' (Tai. 2, 6). Now it is impossible for the individual soul or for any other being except the highest Ātman to think, in the first place, about things to be created during this disembodied condition, and secondly, to create the things in such a way as will be non-different from himself.

भेदव्यपदेशाच्च । १७

[*Bheda—difference ; vyapadeśāt—being pointed out ; ca—and.*]

1 The Brahman which is described as 'ānandamaya' in the Brāhmaṇa portion of the Upaniṣad (Tai. 3-6) known as the Bhṛguvalli is also described in the same manner in the earlier portion (Tai. 2-5) known as Mantra.

AND BECAUSE THE DIFFERENCE IS POINTED OUT (THE ĀNANDAMAYA IS NOT THE JĪVĀTMAN). 17

The Taittirīyopaniṣad tells us (2, 7) that the individual soul gets the bliss of the Ātman after it first gets the taste of the Ātman ; for the Ātman is described as bliss itself and as flavour (rasa). It is clear that the attainer and the attained cannot be one and the same. No doubt, Śruti and Smṛti recommend the search of the Ātman, as there is nothing higher than the knowledge of the Ātman. In reality, the Ātman is in its own nature, Ātman alone. 'There is no other seer or hearer than the highest Lord' (Bṛ. 3, 7, 23) ; and hence no search of it is possible. Yet, in common experience owing to ignorance, the Ātman is identified with the non-ātman like body, senses etc., and so it is possible to say that the Ātman is to be searched or heard or attained.

The jīvātman who is really not different from God (Ātman) is unreal. He is the product of avidyā, and being embodied is responsible for his actions and the results thereof. The reverse cannot be said of God. We cannot say that God is unreal because he is identified with the jīvātman ; for he is the ground of avidyā. Just as a magician is the cause or support of an unreal prototype of him who climbs up a rope and holds a shield and a sword in his hands, or just as the unlimited ākāśa being limited by the adjunct of a jar appears distinct from the ākāśa in the jar, even so the Lord is different from the jīvātman, inasmuch as he is not only real but the support or the ground of the illusory nature of the jīva.

कामाच्च नानुमानापेक्षा । १८

[*Kāmāt*—*due to desire* ; *ca*—*and* ; *na*—*not* ; *anumānāpekṣā*—*necessity of inference.*]

AND ON ACCOUNT OF DESIRE (BEING EXPRESSED BY ĀNANDAMAYA) NO NECESSITY OF INFERRING (THE PRADHĀNA). 18

The desire on the part of ānandamaya to 'become many and to create' (Tai. 2, 6) precludes the possibility of the non-intelligent pradhāna being the cause of the world, or being the same as ānandamaya. The refutation of the Sāṁkhya doctrine was already done in the Sūtra 1, 1, 5, but is again incidentally done here to show that the Vedānta-passages are uniform in the view that Brahman is the cause of the world. Desire and 'ānanda' cannot belong to pradhāna even in a figurative manner.

अस्मिन्नस्य च तद्योगं शास्ति । १९

[*Asmin—in this* ; *asya—of this* ; *ca—and* ; *tadyogaṁ—union with that* ; *śāsti—teaches.*]

BESIDES, WITHIN THIS (ĀNANDAMAYA, THE UNION OF THIS (INDIVIDUAL SOUL) IS TAUGHT. 19

Besides, the ānandamaya does not denote the pradhāna or the jīva, because the jīva obtains salvation when it is joined or identified with the ānandamaya. The jīva, we are told, 'becomes fearless when he is lodged in that invisible, incorporeal, undefinable, unsupported and fearless Ātman; but the moment he feels himself even slightly away from the Ātman he encounters the fear of Saṁsāra' (Tai. 2, 7).

We must have our own say, however, in this connection (i.e. as against the view of the Vṛttikāras regarding the meaning of the word ānandamaya). How can the affix 'maya' mean 'modification' or 'product' when it is added on to words anna, prāṇa, manas and Vijñāna, and mean, all of a sudden, 'abundance,' when it is added on to the word ānanda in the same context? The words beginning with annamaya and ending with ānandamaya form one series, and accordingly how is it that only the last word of the series refers to Brahman? This is like supposing that a certain body consists partly of an old lady and partly of a young lady. We grant that Brahman is the chief topic of discussion (Tai. Chapter 2). But, in that case, if 'ānandamaya' were to denote the Brahman, 'annamaya' etc. too, would denote it. It may be said that ānandamaya points to Brahman because while other ātmans such as annamaya etc. have, each one of them, a further ātman beyond it, there is no such ātman beyond ānandamaya. But in The Taittirīyopaniṣad itself (2, 5) it is said with reference to ānandamaya that 'joy is its head, satisfaction is its right wing, delight is its left wing, ānanda (bliss) is its soul, and Brahman is its tail and support.' The same Brahman which is mentioned as truth, knowledge and infinity is mentioned here as the tail and support ; and it is to have the knowledge of this Brahman, that the imaginary description of the five sheaths, from annamaya to ānandamaya, is given. In saying therefore that ānandamaya does not mean Brahman, but that the tail of ānandamaya is the Brahman, we are not leaving (as the Vṛittikāra supposes us to do) the original and main context of the description of Brahman, and introducing the new topic of describing the jīva as ānandamaya.

Now, the description of Brahman as mere member or the tail of the ānandamaya may be said to reduce it to a subordinate position, and so if we are to stick to the context, once again, the ānandamaya may be recognized as the true Brahman. But this is to consider one and the same Brahman as at once the whole, viz. the ānandamaya, and as a mere part thereof viz. the tail. If we are to get away from this contradiction, we must locate the mention of Brahman either in the sentence referring to ānandamaya or in the sentence referring to the tail of it. The word 'Brahman' occurs in the latter sentence and not in the former; and so it is proper to say that the subject-matter of Brahman is chiefly, and not subordinately mentioned in the sentence referring to the tail, and that ānandamaya does not denote Brahman at all.

Our conclusion that Brahman is treated as the chief subject-matter in the sentence, 'Brahman is the tail and the support,' gains strength by what is told in the verse which immediately follows it, viz. 'If he knows the Brahman as non-existing, he himself becomes non-existent ; if he knows it as existing, he himself becomes so' (Tai. 2, 6). Without any reference to ānandamaya which is known to all, this verse tells us what one may gain or lose, if one only knows the being or the non-being of Brahman. The word 'tail' is not to be taken literally and construed as merely a member ; it is to be taken in the sense of support or resting-place of all the ānanda known to the world. As the Bṛihadāraṇyaka says, 'All the created beings live only on a very small portion of that Brahmanic ānanda' (4, 3, 32).

Notwithstanding the above, if we are to consider the ānandamaya as Brahman, then because it is endowed with qualities like joy etc. as its members, we shall have to consider it as saviśeṣa or saguṇa Brahman, as opposed to nirviśeṣa or nirguṇa Brahman, 'from which the speech and mind turn away being unable to comprehend it. One who gets the ānanda of this Brahman fears nothing' (Tai. 2, 9). Besides, 'ānandamaya abounds in bliss' means that it contains a little measure of pain too. But to hold this view about Brahman is to hold it in contradiction to another Śruti passage which tells us that 'that is Infinite or Brahman where nothing else is heard, seen or known' (Chā. 7, 24, 1). Moreover, as joy differs from man to man, the ānandamaya too will be different. Brahman, on the other hand, is 'imperishable, truth and knowledge and so cannot be divided' (Tai. 2, 1). 'It is the all-pervading God, the hidden inner Ātman of all beings' (Śve. 6, 11). It is to be noted again that it is not the word ānandamaya but the word ānanda which is repeated, (as we have already seen in Sūtra 12) ; and that the word 'ānanda' stands for Brahman is clear from Taittirīya as well as other Upaniṣads (Tai. 2, 7 ; 2, 8 ; 2, 9 ; 3, 6 ; Bṛ. 3, 9, 28). It does not stand for ānandamaya, which, as we have seen, is not Brahman. The passage in which the full word 'ānandamaya' is repeated only tells us that it too, like other preceding anātmans such as 'annamaya' etc., is to be discarded. No doubt the stage of ānandamaya is to be attained[1] in order to reach the Brahman. The passage, 'Let me be many, let me create,' (Tai. 2, 6) is nearer the sentence which refers to Brahman as the tail and support (Tai. 2, 5) than to the sentence which refers to ānandamaya, and so does not tell us that ānandamaya is the Brahman. Similarly, 'He is rasa,' (Tai. 2, 7) refers to Brahman and not to ānandamaya.

As for the objection that Brahman in the neuter gender is referred to by the masculine pronoun 'he' in the sentence 'He wishes to become many,' we reply that the masculine word Ātman too in 'from that Ātman has come forth ākāṣa' (Tai. 2 1) refers to Brahman, inasmuch as Brahman is the subject-matter of the chapter. As for the word 'ānanda' mentioned in the Bhārgavi Vāruṇī Vidyā, in the sentence 'He realized ānanda as Brahman (Tai. 3, 6), it denotes Brahman alone because there is neither the affix 'maya' nor any mention of the limbs such as joy as 'head' etc. Nowhere in the chapter is there any intention to refer to the saguṇa Brahman having qualities or members; on the contrary, as already said, it aims at having the knowledge of nirguṇa Brahman which transcends speech and mind. The conclusion therefore is that the affix 'maya' does not mean 'abundance' but means only modification or product, and so ānandamaya like 'annamaya' etc. does not refer to Brahman.

The Sūtras should therefore, be explained as follows: Sūtra 12—Brahman is the chief and not subordinate subject-matter, as is clear from its reference as the tail

1 In other words, it is to be attained only to be discarded, just as the previous stages are to be attained only to be discarded in favour of later ones. The ānandamaya is to be reached only to be discarded in favour of its 'tail and support', *i. e.* the Nirviśeṣa Brahman.

and support of the ānandamaya ātman (Tai. 2, 5) and from the repetition of the word 'Brahman in the immediately following verse, 'he becomes himself existent or non-existent who knows Brahman to be so' (Tai 2, 6). Sūtra 13—If Brahman is not to be considered as the chief topic on account of the word 'maya' meaning 'modification' or member (the tail e.g.), then the meaning 'abundance' too can be construed as standing for a group of members (such as head, wings, etc.). But the word 'tail' is not to be taken literally as a member, but as a sign for Brahman which is the real support of all. Sūtra 14—Brahman is said to have 'created all that exists' (Tai. 2, 6), all the modifications including the 'ānandamaya.' Being itself the cause of 'ānandamaya,' it cannot be said to be at the same time only a member of that ānandamaya. So also other sūtras[1] refer to Brahman alone and not to ānandamaya.

७ अंतरधिकरणम् । (२०–२१)

अंतस्तद्धर्मोपदेशात् । २०

⟦*Antaḥ—inside ; tad-dharma-upadeśād—his qualities being mentioned.*⟧

THE PERSON APPEARING IN (THE DISC OF THE SUN AND IN THE EYE IS THE HIGHEST GOD), BECAUSE HIS QUALITIES ARE MENTIONED. 20

In a passage of the Chāndogyopaniṣad (1, 6, 6), we are told that 'the person seen on the sun has bright golden beard and hair, and appears golden to the very

---

1 Sūtra 15— If the mantra and the Brāhmaṇa portions are not to contradict, then Brahman is the chief subject-matter in the Brāhmaṇa *i.e.* the passage referring to the tail (and not merely as a member) as it is in the mantra. Sūtra 16–Brahman, the tail, is not the ānandamaya jīvātman. Sūtra 17—Brahman is not ānandamaya, because the distinction is mentioned. Sūtra 18—It is not proper to infer that because Brahman is mentioned on the fifth occasion in the Bhṛguvalli, therefore it is the same as ānandamaya which is mentioned as the fifth and the last of the series of 'annamaya' etc. in the Brahma-Valli. For the affix 'maya' meaning modification in the word ānandamaya does not allow this interpretation. Sūtra 19—What is meant is that Brahman is mentioned as the tail. This is clear from what Śruti tells us *viz.* the ānandamaya jīvātman becomes one with Brahman, the moment it has the knowledge of it.

tips of his nails, that his name is 'Ut' inasmuch as he is free from every kind of evil, and that one who knows this becomes himself likewise free from evil.' And we are further told that the 'same person is seen in the eye' (1, 7, 5). The question which arises here is whether this person who is recommended as the object of devotion is merely an individual soul who has raised himself to eminence on account of knowledge and good actions, or whether he is the perfect and eternal God.

From the view-point of the pūrvapakṣa, the person in question is the individual soul for the following reasons. In the first place, the person is described as having some form and features, such as golden beard etc.; the highest God, on the other hand, is spoken of as 'imperishable and without form, sound, or touch' (Kau. 1, 3, 15). Secondly, the sun and the eye are mentioned as the abodes; about the abode of God, Sanatkumāra tells Nārada that 'He lives in his own glory, and that he is all-pervading and eternal like the ākāśa' (Chā. 7, 24, 1). And thirdly, the limit of the power of the person in the sun is indicated by saying that he is the lord of the people beyond the sun and of the desires of gods. Similarly, the power of the person in the eye is indicated by saying that he is the lord of the people below it and of the desires of men. On the other hand, 'unlimited is the power of God. He is the Lord and protector of all beings, and acts like a bridge or bund so that the worlds may not come to a chaos.' (Bṛ. 4, 4, 22).

In reply to this we say that the person on the sun must be God and not jīvātman, because the qualities of God alone are mentioned. In the first place, the person in the sun is named 'Ut' and declared to be free from all sins; the same name then is extended to the person in the eye. This freedom from all sins is the characteristic of the highest Ātman alone (Chā. 8, 7, 1). Secondly, the person in the eye who is declared to be 'Ṛk, Sāman, Uktha, Yajus, and Brahman,' is no other than the highest

God ; for it is God alone who is the inner Ātman and the cause of all. Besides, having first mentioned with reference to gods and men that the Ṛk and Sāman of each are the earth, fire, etc. and speech, breath etc. respectively, it is further said that with reference to both the gods and men, the Ṛk and Sāman are the joints of the feet of the two persons in the sun and the eye. (Chā. 1, 6, 8 and 1, 7, 5). This description too of the ādhidaivika and the ādhyātmika types of devotion[1] is applicable to the highest Ātman alone, on account of his being all-pervading. Similarly, the passage which tells us that 'people who sing unto Him to the Vīṇā become wealthy' (Chā. 1, 7, 6) refers again to the same God ; for as the Bhagavadgītā tells us, 'whatever wealth, power, or strength one may have, it is produced from a portion of his glory' (10, 41).

As to the features and golden form of the person, we have to remark that God may assume, on account of his Māyā, any form for the sake of showing his grace to his devotees. When the imperishable Brahman is described as without form, sound or touch, it is the nirguṇa aspect of it (Kau. 1, 3, 15); but for the sake of devotion the same may be described as saguṇa, as 'having all desires, actions, odours and tastes' (Chā. 3, 14, 2). Similarly, the Ātman who resides in his own glory, may be described as having an abode like the sun or the eye for the sake of devotion, or be described as having limits to his power and glory, in order to make him accessible to gods and men.

भेदव्यपदेशाच्चान्यः । २१

[*Bheda—distinction* ; *vyapadeśāt—being mentioned* ; *ca—and* ; *anyaḥ—another.*]

---

1 In the beginning of the Chāndogyopaniṣad, the Udgītha or the syllable Oṁ which is the essence of all the Vedas is mentioned as the object of two types of devotion, ādhidaivika and ādhyātmika. Ṛgveda and Sāmaveda, for example, which are the parts of Oṁ, are spoken of, on the one hand, as the earth and fire, and as speech and breath, on the other.

On account of the distinction being mentioned (the person who appears on the sun is another (from the individual soul residing in the body of the sun). 2

The Bṛhadāraṇyaka passage is clear on this point: 'He who dwells in the sun but whom the sun does not know, who lives inside the body of the sun and controls him, is the Ātman who lives in you too, rules and is immortal' (3, 7, 9). The Ātman who resides and rules from within is different from the individual soul as well as different from the body, whether in the case of the sun or of man.

आकाशशब्दवाच्यत्वाधिकरणम् । (२२)

आकाशस्ताल्लिंगात् । २२

[*Ākāśaḥ* ; *tat—that* ; *lingāt—on account of signs.*]

On account of the characteristic marks (of Brahman being mentioned) the ākāśa (is Brahman). 22

On being asked by Śālāvatya, a Brahmin, as to what the support of these worlds may be, the king Pravāhaṇa Jaivali replied (we are told in the Chāndogyopaniṣad 1, 9, 1), that it is ākāśa ; for it is out of this that all the beings have come forth and into this they shall return. Ākāśa alone is the greatest of all and is their support. There arises now a doubt as to the meaning of the word ākāśa. Is it to be taken in the sense of element or Brahman? The former meaning is well-known, but the latter too is possible; as, for instance, in the passages: 'If this ākāśa is not the same as ānanda etc.' (Tai. 2, 7); 'ākāśa is the cause of this world consisting of names and forms; it is the Brahman in which names and forms appear' (Chā. 8, 14, 1). In the first passage, the extraordinary quality 'ānanda' is mentioned, on account of which, ākāśa is taken to mean Brahman and not the element in which there is no possibility of ānanda ; in the second, the principal sentence involves the word Brahman as a substitute for ākāśa. Therefore it is that there arises the doubt as to whether the word ākāśa means the element or the Brahman.

The pūrvapakṣin states that inasmuch as the primary sense of the word ākāśa comes readily to the mind, we need not take it to have the secondary meaning of Brahman. 'That all these beings come from ākāśa can very well be explained without recourse to Brahman by reference to the element itself ; for after the 'coming forth of ākāśa from the Ātman', we are told that 'from ākāśa itself comes forth air, from air fire, etc.' (Tai. 2, 1). And with reference to other beings below it, viz. air, fire, water, etc. ākāśa, the element, can be considered as the greatest and as the abode of all.

To this we reply that the characteristic marks which are mentioned are applicable to Brahman alone. In the first place, all the Vedānta-passages agree with the above mentioned statement of the Chāndogyopaniṣad, viz. 'all these beings spring forth from ākāśa only' (1, 9, 1). If the element of 'ākāśa' be considered as the cause of wind, fire, etc., wind too can be considered as the cause of fire, water, etc., and fire too in its turn, be considered as the cause of water, earth, etc. ; and and the word 'only' would lose all its meaning. But if by ākāśa we mean Brahman, the word 'only' will exclude all other lesser causes like the elements of ākāśa, wind and others, and restrict the word 'ākāśa' to Brahman only as the cause of all beings, including the element of ākāśa. Similarly, the word 'all' in the above passage would unnecessarily narrow down the meaning to 'beings except the element of ākāśa,' if the element and not Brahman is to be taken as the proper meaning. Secondly, the clause, 'they return into the ākāśa,' likewise points to Brahman alone. Thirdly, not only Brahman alone is, relatively greater, just as the element of ākāśa is with reference to wind, fire, etc., but is also absolutely greater than all; for the Ātman alone is said to be 'greater than the earth, the sky, the heaven, and all these worlds' (Chā. 3, 14, 3). Fourthly, the

Ātman alone can be said to be the final support and resting place of all, because it is the ultimate cause of all; the Brahman is knowledge, and ānanda ; it is the abode of rest for him who gives alms and wealth' (Bṛ. 3. 9. 28). And fifthly, the ākāśa is mentioned as infinite which is an additional exclusive characteristic of Brahman. When Dālbha and Śālāvatya were engaged in discussion with the king Jaivali as to what may be the support of the Oṁ or the Udgītha which comes at the beginning of Sāmaveda, Dālbha declared that it was heaven. Śālāvatya pointed out thereupon that it must be the earth, because the heaven too is obtained on account of the actions performed on the earth. But being dissatisfied with the views of both of the brahmins, Jaivali said to Śālāvatya that his view too about the Sāman was wrong, because the earth and the objects on it had all sprung up from ākāśa. Now, if by ākāśa we are to mean the elemental substance, then Jaivali too stands self-criticised, inasmuch as he commits the same error of pointing out a perishable thing as the support, as was committed by Śālāvatya. Therefore in order to preclude the possibility of ākāśa being understood as the element, Jaivali brings it under the concept of Oṁ and declares that it is this Oṁ or the Udgītha with the eternal Ākāśa as its ātman, which 'is the greatest of all, and which is endless' (Chā. 1, 8, 8). In other words, the Udgītha owes its eternity, infinity and greatness on account of Ākāśa or Brahman which alone has got these characteristics.

So, in view of all the prominent marks of Brahma which are presented to the mind in the principal clauses of the Upaniṣadic passages cited above, we need not stick to the view that the original meaning of the word 'ākāśa' as 'an element' should alone be taken because it comes readily to the mind. It will be more appropriate to take the secondary meaning of the word as Brahman, as noted above. Besides, synonyms used for ākāśa, such as 'Vyoman' and 'Kha' are used for Brahman ; and so it is not a rule that ākāśa must always mean the elemental substance. For instance 'Ṛk and all other Vedas, as well as all the gods are secure in the highest and the imperishable vyoman or ākāśa,' (Ṛk. Saṁ. 1, 164 39). 'This knowledge, which was imparted by Varuṇa and achieved by Bhṛgu, culminated in ākāśa'[1] (Tai. 3, 6); similarly, 'Oṁ, Ka is Brahman; Kha (i.e. ākāśa) is Brahman' (Chā. 4, 10, 5); 'Kha is the oldest' (Bṛ. 5, 1). So the meaning of the word 'ākāśa' is to be taken as Brahman, just as the word 'Agni' in the sentence 'Agni studies a chapter' is to be taken in the sense of a 'boy' named Māṇavaka, who on account of his intelligence shines like fire, and not in its literal and primary meaning as 'fire.'

९ प्राणाधिकरणम् । (२३)

अत एव प्राणः । २३

⟦*Ataḥ—hence ; eva—also ; prāṇaḥ.*⟧

FOR SIMILAR REASONS PRĀṆA (IS BRAHMAN). 23

There is a passage in the Udgītha chapter of the Chāndogyopaniṣad (1, 10, 9) which makes us aware of the reply given by a certain Brahmin, named Cākrāyaṇa, to the priest Prastotā[2] who sings in the beginning of the sacrifice certain hymns of Sāmaveda known as the prastāva. The deity of this prastāva is 'Prāṇa.' For 'all these beings merge into prāṇa alone, and from it they arise' (1, 11, 4–5). Now here too there arises a doubt as to the meaning of the word 'Prāṇa.' Are we to understand thereby the air we breathe, or Brahman? Passages like, 'mind is fastened to prāṇa,' (Chā. 6, 8, 2), and the 'prāṇa of prāṇa' (Bṛ. 4, 4, 18), indicate that prāṇa means Brahman.

---

1 'Ka' means joy, and 'Kha' means ākāśa. Neither 'Ka' nor 'Kha' by itself is Brahman; for while mere worldly joy is transitory, mere elemental ākāśa is non-intelligent. It is the combination of 'Ka' and 'Kha', *i. e.* the intelligent ākāśa in the heart that can be said to be blissful Brahman.

2 Prastotā is the chief priest among the Sāmavedins. The other three priests known as Udgātā, Pratihartā and Subrahmaṇya are subordinate to Prastotā. The first three are to sing respectively the first three portions of the hymns of Sāma-Veda known as Prastāva, Udgītha and Pratihāra. The last portion of the hymns, known as Nidhana, is to be sung in chorus by all the four priests.

The pūrvapakṣin wishes to take the word prāṇa in the sense of the air we breathe; for when a man sleeps, the breathing alone continues, and so it can be said that all the organs of sense like the tongue and others, and the organs of action such as the eye, the ear as also the mind and intelligence merge into the breath, and that they all come out of breath alone when man awakes ' (Śat. Brā. 10, 3, 3, 6). The merging and coming out of the organs of sense and action is not in reality different from the merging and coming out of the beings, because the former are nothing but the essences of the latter. Besides, inasmuch as the 'sun' and the 'food' are told by Cākrāyaṇa as the deities of udgītha and pratihāra (the two later portions of hymns) immediately after he tells prāṇa as the deity of the prastāva, and inasmuch as the two deities of the sun and the food do not represent the Brahman, it is natural to suppose that prāṇa too cannot mean Brahman.

To this we reply that prāṇa means Brahman, because the characteristic marks mentioned in connection with prāṇa are applicable only to Brahman. In the first place, whereas the merging and coming out of the senses alone are spoken of with reference to breath during sleep, in the passage quoted at the beginning, the merging and coming out refer not only to the senses, but also to *all* beings including their bodies and senses ; and so the reference to prāṇa will not be adequately interpreted as reference to breath ; it is a reference to Brahman alone. Secondly, even if the word 'Bhūta' be interpreted as 'element' and not as 'being', the word prāṇa[1] would mean Brahman. Thirdly, the argument that a passage in Kaushītaki Upaniṣad (3, 3) speaks of the 'merging of the senses and its objects and of the union of the jīvātman with prāṇa during dreamless sleep,' is not, as is supposed, in favour of identifying prāṇa with breath, but on the

1 Breath is nothing but a modification of the element of 'wind', and so cannot be the cause of its cause.

contrary, is in favour of identifying it with Brahman.[1] Fourthly, mere contiguity of the word 'prāṇa' with the words 'sun' and 'food' need not be taken as a reason for a similar interpretation of the three words, as 'not standing for Brahman'; for in the principal sentence there are clear references to the characteristic marks of Brahman. And finally, as pointed out in the previous Sūtra, the words 'only' and 'all' in the Śruti passage, 'All these beings merge into prāṇa only, and from it they arise,' will serve no purpose, if Brahman is not to be taken as the meaning of prāṇa.

As to certain other passages such as, 'the prāṇa of prāṇa' (Bṛ. 4, 4, 18), 'Mind is fastened to prāṇa' (Chā. 6, 8, 2), quoted by certain Vṛttikāras, there is no point in discussing these, inasmuch as there is no doubt or ambiguity regarding the meaning of the word prāṇa. The grammatical position of words, and the context clearly indicate that the meaning of the word 'prāṇa' is Brahman and nothing else. The word 'prāṇa' used in the nominative is distinctly used for some thing different from that which is signified by the word prāṇa used in the genitive; the former is used for Brahman, and the latter for the air we breathe. Similarly, in the second passage the context shows that 'prāṇa' is used for Brahman. If the context shows that we are dealing with jyotiṣṭoma sacrifice, then the word 'jyoti' in that context clearly stands for 'jyotiṣṭoma sacrifice,' as in the passage, 'he is to sacrifice 'Jyotisā' in every spring.' So the word 'prāṇa' means Brahman.

१० ज्योतिश्चरणाधिकरणम् । (२४--२७)

ज्योतिश्चरणाभिधानात् । २४

[*Jyotiḥ*—*light* ; *ca*—*and* ; *caraṇa*—*feet* ; *abhidhānāt*—*being mentioned.*]

1, For here too, there are two characteristic marks of Brahman which are mentioned as being connected with prāṇa; one is the capacity of the jīva to become one with Brahman, and the other is the reference to the source in which everything else must merge at the time of dissolution.

ON ACCOUNT OF FEET BEING MENTIONED, (THE WORD) JYOTIH (I.E. LIGHT INDICATES BRAHMAN). 24

Here we are concerned with the doubt whether the word 'jyoti' in the following passage of the Chāndogyopaniṣad is used in the sense of the light of the sun etc. or of the highest Ātman : 'That jyoti or light which shines above the heaven, above the beings, in the worlds beyond which there are no better worlds, is the same light which is within man' (3, 13, 7).

According to pūrvapakṣa, the word 'jyoti' means the light of the sun and the like, and the arguments advanced are :—(i) It is well known that jyoti means light. Light and darkness are the opposites of each other; darkness of the night, for example, obstructs the activity of the eye, while that which helps it is the light of the sun, etc. (2) The word ' shines ' too refers in ordinary life to the sun light which has form and which is physical in nature. Brahman, on the other hand, neither possesses body nor form and so cannot shine. (3) Jyoti must mean the physical and the limited light, the effect of the sun ; for a physical boundary is mentioned with reference to it. It shines beyond heaven. There can be no boundary to Brahman which is the cause of all, and the Ātman of all. Now if some one would say that it is possible for the physical light of fire also to be seen on this side of the heaven, when there is no light of the sun, we may then assume that the light spoken of is the original, invisible first principle or deity of light in its own nature, and not the visible light, which is made up by mixing its own half portion with the one-fourth portions of the original, invisible principles or deities of water and earth. But this pre-tripartite original light is of no use, because being invisible it cannot either be made as the object of devotion or be used to dispel darkness. And as the tripartite nature of the three deities of light, water and earth was conceived by God in the very beginning (Chā. 6, 3, 3), it serves no purpose to assume a pre-tripartite light, existing before the ordinary light which is known to all. Besides, there is no evidence that the pre-tripartite light is spoken of as having a boundary. So, the light here is the ordinary light of the sun or the fire, seen either on this side or the other side of the heaven. (4) That it is described as shining beyond or below heaven is for the purpose of devotion. On the other hand, ' beyond heaven ' or ' on this side of heaven' cannot be an adequate description of Brahman, which is undivided and unsupported. (5) That this light beyond the heaven is not Brahman is also clear from the fact that it is said to be the same with the abdominal light, which in its turn is purely physical on account of its being known by the warm touch of the body and the sound we hear when we shut our ears (Chā. 3, 13, 7 and 8). The identity of one light with the other is possible because both are physical in nature. (6) One more reason why this light is not Brahman is that meditation on it makes a man celebrated and beautiful. This is incomparably low a fruit compared to the fruit of mokṣa which one may get by devotion to Brahman. (7) Besides no special characteristic mark of Brahman is mentioned in the passage dealing with the light. (8) Nor does the previous section deal with Brahman. It deals with Gāyatrī alone (Chā. 3, 12). And even supposing that the earlier section deals with Brahman, there is nothing in the present section which may enable us to say that the same topic is continued; for in the earlier passage the heaven is referred to as the support or place where ' His immortal three feet ' are said to exist, while in this passage the heaven is spoken of as the boundary. So in the absence of the characteristic marks of Brahman, the 'jyoti' means the physical light of the sun.

To this we reply; The word 'jyoti' means Brahman, for in the preceding passage Brahman has been spoken of as having four feet, ' three of which constitute the immortal Being in the heaven and the fourth is all these beings. Such is His greatness ; he is greater than what has been manifested etc.' (Chā. 3, 12, 6). And we have the recognition of Brahman in this passage because the heaven, above which jyoti is mentioned as shining, is mentioned in the previous passage too as the place in which the three feet of Brahman are said to be immortal. Notwithstanding this, if we interpret jyoti as light, we leave aside the subject under discussion and begin a new one without any reason. Not only Brahman is the topic under discussion of this and of the earlier passage, but it is also the topic of the next passage dealing with Śāndilya-Vidyā.

When the general topic of three continuous passages' dealing with Gāyatrī, jyoti and Śāndilya-vidyā respectively is Brahman, and further when Brahman alone is indicated on account of the relative pronoun 'which' (Yat) used for it, and on account of the characteristic marks such as 'heaven' and the 'four feet,' it will serve no purpose to argue that the words 'light' and 'shines' are commonly used to denote the physical light of the sun and the like. And supposing that this light is the physical effect, even then it can be construed that the light points not to itself but to its cause, viz. the Brahman, as is clear from the mantra 'That (Brahman) on account of which the sun becomes shining first and then shines everything else' (Tai. Brā. 3, 12, 9, 7). Nay, Brahman is not merely indirectly indicated as the cause by the word jyoti, but is also the direct meaning of it, as is clear from, 'a person sits' and behaves by the 'light of words only', which he may hear from another person in darkness and when he cannot use the light of his own eyes (Bṛ. 4, 3, 5). Similarly, 'the mind of man who eats ghee becomes light' (Tai. Saṁ. 1, 6, 3, 3), points out that the word 'jyoti' can be extended to anything which has the capacity of stimulating something else ; and as such, it can necessarily be applied to Brahman, because it is Intelligence and gives light to the whole universe. The same has been emphasised in the Śruti : 'Everything shines after He shines,' and to exclude the possibility of other things being self-luminous, it is further said, that 'by His light, everything else is lighted ' (Kau. 2, 5, 15) ; 'gods worship Him as the light of lights, as the Immortal Being ' (Bṛ. 4, 4, 16).

To speak of Brahman (jyoti) as if it occupies a particular region like heaven, is useful for meditation. Though truly speaking, there are no regions in Brahman, yet on account of upādhis and for the purpose of devotion, one is advised to meditate on it, as if it exists only in the sun, the eye, and the heart. Similarly, the visibility and audibility of the abdominal fire are merely symbolic of the devotion to Brahman. The objection that jyoti cannot mean Brahman, because such devotion is said to result in mundane gains, is pointless; because, whereas the knowledge of the Brahman as the Ātman would lead one to release, the devotion shown to saguṇa Brahman would give him various rewards, small or great. As the Chāndogyopaniṣad tells us, 'he who worships the eternal Ātman as the giver of wealth and devourer of food, becomes wealthy and of strong appetite ' (1, 9, 4). And finally, though the word 'heaven' is used in the locative in one passage, and in the ablative in another, and therefore means the ' support ' and ' boundary ' on different occasions, yet the relative pronoun ' which ' (yat) relates this 'heaven ' with the same word ' jyoti ' or Brahman of the earlier passage with the word ' jyoti ' of the passage under consideration. Hence the word ' jyoti ' means Brahman and nothing else.

छंदोऽभिधानान्नेति चेन्न तथा चेतोऽर्पणनिगदात्तथा हि दर्शनम् । २५

[*Chandaḥ—metre* ; *abhidhānāt—being mentioned* ; *na* ; *iti* ; *cet—if* ; *na* ; *tathā—so* ; *cetaḥ—mind* ; *arpaṇa—fixing*; *nigadāt—being recommended* ; *tathā* ; *hi—also* ; *darśanaṁ —Śruti.*]

IF IT BE SAID THAT (BRAHMAN IS) NOT (MENTIONED) BECAUSE THE METRE IS MENTIONED, (THE REPLY IS) NOT SO; BECAUSE THE FIXING OF THE MIND (ON BRAHMAN) IS RECOM-

MENDED (BY MEANS OF THE METRE); THIS IS SEEN ELSEWHERE ALSO). 25

In section twelfth of the third chapter of the Chāndogyopaniṣad, the pūrvapakṣin maintains that Gāyatrī is mentioned as constituting all the things which have been created, and that it is this Gāyatrī metre which has been further described as sixfold and four-footed ; sixfold because it is described as the beings, the earth, the body, the heart, the speech, and the breath, and four-footed because it consists of four parts of six letters each. Naturally, the 'greatness' mentioned in the mantra (Chā. 3, 12, 6) is with reference to Gāyatrī and not to Brahman. How can the mantra refer all of a sudden to Brahman, when in the Brāhmaṇa portion the Gāyatrī alone is described? The mantra and the Brāhmaṇa do not give us different versions. No doubt the word 'Brahman' occurs immediately after this mantra, but here too by Brahman we are not to understand the highest Ātman. In keeping with the context of Gāyatrī we should mean by it the 'Veda' and as pointing to Gāyatrī which is a part of Veda. Besides the meaning of the word Brahman as Veda is allowed by an earlier passage in the Chāndogyopaniṣad itself (3, 11, 3) ; 'for him who knows this Brahman there is no rising or setting of the sun ; it is one everlasting day.' In short, inasmuch as the Gāyatrī metre is mentioned, Brahman is not the topic under discussion.

In reply to this we say that if by Gāyatrī we are to understand a kind of metre, then it is nothing but a collection of letters, and so it cannot be said to be the Ātman of all. But if we take Brahman as the general topic of the section under consideration, then Gāyatrī would mean nothing but Brahman in the form of Gāyatrī, an effect, for 'All this is verily the Brahman' (Chā.3, 14, 1). To consider the metre of Gāyatrī as the Ātman of all is mere imagination; but to consider Gāyatrī as Brahman is to consider the Brahman as the cause of all, including even the Gāyatrī, and to give it the correct explanation of things by pointing out the identity of cause and effects (Bra. Sū. 2, 1, 14). Besides, the Gāyatrī metre is intended to direct the mind on the Brahman. Just as the Bahvṛchas, i.e. those who follow Ṛgveda, consider the highest Ātman to be present in the great Uktha, as the Adhvaryus, or the followers of Yajurveda, consider it to be present in the sacrificial fire, and as the Chāndogas, or the followers of Sāmaveda, consider it to be present in the Mahāvrata sacrifice (Ait. Ār. 3, 2, 3, 12), even so, in this passage concerning Gāyatrī as in the passage concerning jyoti, Brahman alone is meant to be the object of devotion.

Or, as the Vṛttikāras[1] think, Brahman is directly the meaning of the word Gāyatrī, and is not merely suggested or implied by it. The four feet of the metre are, as a matter of fact, the four feet of the Brahman, one constituting the movable and the immovable world, and the three being the immortal nature of it. Another word having the meaning of metre is used elsewhere also (Chā. 4 3, 8) in a different sense on account of similarity of number; and so the word Gāyatrī need not be said to be used in the sense of Brahman by way of exception, because both of them resemble in having four feet. The word 'Viraṭ,' for example, means a metre having ten letters in each of its parts (foot). 'Kṛta' also is assumed to mean the number ten, and so used for the collection of two groups of five, one indicating the ādhidaivika entities of wind, fire, the sun, the moon, and water, and the other indicating the ādhyātmika entities of breath, speech, eye, ear, and mind. So this collection of ten entities is also spoken of as 'Virāṭ' as in the Śruti, 'these ten are again the Virāṭ which eats the food' (Chā. 4, 3, 8). Just as Virāṭ, therefore, means (and not simply suggests) the collection of the ten entities and not the particular metre, even so, Gāyatrī means the Brahman and not the metre.

1 If the interpretation of the Vṛttikārs is accepted, the Sūtra will be translated thus : If it be said that (Brahman is) not (mentioned) because the metre is mentioned (the reply is) not so, because (owing to similarity between Gāyatrī and Brahman) that word (*viz.* Gāyatrī) on account of which the mind is directed (on Brahman) means (Brahman); this is seen elsewhere also.

भूतादिपादव्यपदेशोपपत्तेश्चैवम् । २६

[*Bhūtādi—beings and others*; *pāda—feet*; *vyapadesha—indication*; *upapatteḥ—due to existence*; *ca—and*; *evaṁ—thus.*]

AND (BRAHMAN IS THE TOPIC) IN THIS WAY (I.E. IN THE PASSAGE CONCERNING GAYATRI) BECAUSE THE BEINGS ETC. ARE MENTIONED AS FEET. 26

If Brahman is not the topic, then the mere metre of Gāyatrī will not be spoken of as possessing the feet of the beings, the earth, the body and the heart ; nor is it possible to speak of Gāyatrī as the Ātman of all things, as is said in the mantra, 'such is His greatness etc.; one foot etc.' The Puruṣasūkta too mentions the mantra with reference to Brahman (Ṛk. Saṁ. 10, 90). Similarly the Smṛti 'I support this world by a small portion of myself' (B. G. 10, 42) points to the same nature of Brahman. Besides, the section which immediately follows the section of Gāyatrī, deals with the five doorkeepers[1] of heaven situated in the five apertures of the heart, in which, as the section of Gāyatrī mentions (3, 12, 7-8, and 3, 13, 6-7), the Brahman with four feet resides. It is this same Brahman again which has been mentioned by the relative pronoun 'Yat' in the section concerning jyotiḥ.

उपदेशभेदान्नेति चेन्नोभयस्मिन्नप्यविरोधात् । २७

[*Upadeśabhedāt—on account of difference in description*; *na—not* ; *iti—so* ; *cet—if* ; *na*; *ubhayasmin-api—in either way* ; *avirodhāt—without contradiction.*]

IF IT BE SAID THAT (BRAHMAN CANNOT BE RECOGNIZED AS THE SAME) ON ACCOUNT OF DIFFERENCE IN DESCRIPTION, (WE REPLY THAT IT IS NOT SO, BECAUSE THERE IS NOTHING

1 The heart as the city of Brahman is imagined to have five gates, one in each direction and one at the top. These are protected by five door-keepers, i. e. five prāṇas; Udāna is the door-keeper at the gate which is at the top.

CONTRARY TO RECOGNITION IN EITHER OF THE TWO (WAYS OF DESCRIPTION). 27

Just as a falcon on the top of a tree is in contact with the tree by reason of its feet, but at the same time can be said to be above the tree so far as the rest of its body is concerned, similarly, Brahman which is in heaven so far as one foot is concerned (in its own glory as manifested in this world or in the heart of man) can be said to be beyond the heaven with its three immortal feet. Or, if the Brahman which is impossible to be touched by ākāśa and other upādhis is to be mentioned, then also it can be said to be above heaven or beyond heaven ; just as we may say that the hut is on the Gangā, even though it is impossible to have a hut on the waters of the Gangā. In this case, the words 'on', 'above' and 'beyond' mean only that the heaven or the ākāśa is next to or near the Brahman, just as 'the hut on the Gangā' means that it is on the bank of the river. In any case, the word heaven, whether used in the ablative or the locative, (divi or divaḥ) and therefore meaning in heaven or beyond heaven, points to Brahman alone. In short, from the feet being mentioned as these beings etc., from the greatness or glory mentioned in the mantra, from the sentence which refers to Brahman as residing in the apertures of the heart, and from the oneness of meaning of the words 'divi' and 'divaḥ', it is clear that the Brahman mentioned in one section is the same as mentioned in another.

११ प्रातर्दनाधिकरणम् । (२८–३१)

प्राणस्तथानुगमात् । २८

[*Prāṇaḥ* ; *tathā—like that* ; *anugamāt—as is implied.*]

PRĀṆA (MEANS BRAHMAN) AS IS IMPLIED ON ACCOUNT OF SEVERAL CHARACTERISTIC MARKS). 28

When Pratardana, the son of Divodāsa, went to the abode of Indra after winning a battle, Indra asked him to choose a boon. On being solicited by Pratardana to bestow upon him such a boon as would conduce to the highest good of man, Indra asked him to meditate on Indra himself as the 'Immortal Life' inasmuch as he was the 'Prāṇa, the intelligent Ātman,' which 'makes this body rise up,' which is the 'speaker,' and which is 'ānanda without age and death' (Kau. 3, 1, 2, 3 and 8). Though in an earlier Sūtra (1, 1, 21) Prāṇa means Brahman, we are presented here with marks which do not exclusively point to it. In the first place, the word 'prajñātmā' (intelligent Ātman) as an adjective negates the meaning of prāṇa as ordinary breath, and the reference to 'māṁ' meaning Indra himself as the object of devotion negates the highest Ātman too. In other words, prāṇa means the divinity of Indra himself. Secondly, the reference to prāṇa as the cause of the movement of the body indicates that prāṇa means the breath. Thirdly, the reference to the 'speaker' and not to speech as the object of meditation makes the word refer to the individual soul. As opposed to this, the description of prāṇa as intelligent Ātman, as ānanda, and as without decay and death, makes it a synonym of Brahman. A doubt arises therefore as to which of these meanings should be taken as the proper meaning of prāṇa.

If the pūrvapakṣin chooses to understand thereby the ordinary breath because it is the well-known meaning, then we reply that prāṇa must mean Brahman, if all things are to be duly considered. To begin with, Pratardana asks for a boon which will be of highest good not to him alone but for man as such. It seems highly improbable that the highest good should be of the changing nature of prāṇa. It cannot be achieved by any means except the knowledge of the Ātman. 'A man who knows him goes beyond death ; there is no other path to mokṣa' (Śve. 3, 8). 'If anyone knows me, then nothing can hinder him in his way of mokṣa, neither theft nor killing etc.' (Kau. 2, 1). 'No work will bind him, who has seen the Brahman which is both the higher and the lower '

(Mu. 2, 2, 8; Cf. B. G. 4, 37). How can air which is non-intelligent be intelligent, unless it is identified with Brahman? Besides, the characteristic marks of 'bliss,' 'immortality' etc. which come at the end of the passage cannot be fitted with the nature of any other thing or being, except the Brahman. Prāṇa again is spoken of as unaffected by good or bad actions, but as responsible for making men do such actions as will lead them (as he likes) to higher or lower worlds. He is described again as the guardian, the King and the Lord of the world (Kau. 3, 8). From all this, it is clear that Prāṇa means Brahman.

न वक्तुरात्मोपदेशादिति चेदध्यात्मसंबंधभूमा ह्यस्मिन् । २९

[*Na—not; vaktuḥ—of the speaker; ātmopadeśāt—because of reference to himself; iti cet—if so; adhyātma—saṁbandha-bhūmā—references to Ātman being numerous; hi asmin—because in this.*]

IF IT BE SAID THAT PRĀṆA DOES NOT (INDICATE BRAHMAN) BECAUSE THE SPEAKER REFERS TO HIMSELF (WE REPLY THAT IT IS NOT SO); FOR HERE (i. e. IN THIS CHAPTER) REFERENCES TO ĀTMAN ARE NUMEROUS. 29

It may still be contended by the pūrvapakṣa that inasmuch as Brahman is described as 'without speech or mind' (Bṛ. 3, 8, 8), and as such cannot be said to be the speaker in the legend of Indra and Pratardana, and inasmuch as, on the contrary, Indra, the speaker, mentions himself as prāṇa, as the intelligent ātman, and asks Pratardana to meditate on him, prāṇa cannot be Brahman. Besides, Indra has praised himself for having killed the three-headed Brahmin, Viśvarūpa, the son of Tvaṣṭā, and for having strewn before the wolves the bodies of persons who have renounced the world but are averse to Vedas. Prāṇa means 'power' and it is well-known that Indra is the deity of power; and if there be any deed of power, people call it the 'deed of Indra.' All these things are not possible in the case of Brahman which is without body. That Indra calls himself as prajñātmā is in keeping with the unobstructed knowledge of gods. The highest good of man may be inferred from the position of Indra himself as deity and as the object of devotion. As a deity, he is not affected by action ; as a resident in heaven, he has ānanda; and as lasting till the end of the universe he can be said to be without old age and death. So, Prāṇa must mean the soul of Indra and not Brahman.

We refute this by saying that if the Śruti-passage 'Life exists so long as prāṇa lasts in the body' (Kau. 3, 2), is not a tautologous proposition, we must mean by prāṇa the inner Ātman who has got the power of bestowing or taking away the life, and not a particular deity which comes into being in course of time. It is this prāṇa in the sense of Ātman that is described as the nave round which go forth the spokes of the senses, which in their turn are the support of the various objects (Kau. 3, 8). And, further, we have another Śruti which tells us that the 'Ātman is the omniscient Brahman' (Bṛ. 2, 5, 19) whereby we can say that Prāṇa is nothing but Brahman.

Why then has Indra made a reference about himself? To this the Sūtrakāra replies :

शास्त्रदृष्ट्या तूपदेशो वामदेववत् । ३०

[*Śāstradṛṣṭyā—as described in Śruti; tu—but; upadeśaḥ—instruction ; Vāmadevavat—like Vāmadeva.*]

As in the case of Vāmadeva, the statement (made by Indra about himself is due) to intuitive knowledge as described in Śruti. 30

Just as the saint Vāmadeva said about himself after having realized the Brahman that he was the Manu and the sun (Bṛ. 1, 4, 10), even so, Indra can be said to have instructed Pratardana to know him only, because he himself must have first realized that he was the Ātman. This intuitive knowledge, must have come to him on account of spiritual efforts like śravṇaa and manana done in previous lives. But this much is certain, that 'whoever among the gods realizes the Brahman, becomes the Brahman' (Bṛ. 1, 4, 10). The reference to the slaying of Tvaṣṭṛ's son is not so much to glorify himself as to extol the vijñāna, the intuitive knowledge of Brahman. In order to emphasise this very point, Indra tells immediately afterwards that 'not a hair' of his 'is harmed, in spite of the horrible deeds' done by him, simply for the reason that he had become 'one with Brahman.' Nay, Indra tells us further that no other person too, who realizes Indra (in the same way in which Indra had realized the Brahman) would in any way be robbed of his mokṣa for having committed horrible deeds (Kau. 1, 3). So, the object of knowledge which is praised by Indra is not his own self, but the Brahman alone, as mentioned in the sentence, 'I am prāṇa, the prajñātmā.'

जीवमुख्यप्राणलिंगान्नेति चेन्नोपासात्रैविध्यादाश्रितत्वादिह तद्योगात् । ३१

[*Jīva-mukhya-prāṇa-lingāt—on account of signs of soul and chief breath ; na ; iti ; cet ; na ; upāsanā traividhyāt—because of three-fold meditation; āśritatvāt—being accepted; iha—here ; tad-yogāt—being connected with that,*]

IF IT BE SAID THAT (BRAHMAN) IS NOT MEANT, BECAUSE THE CHARACTERISTIC MARKS OF JIVA AND THE PRINCIPAL PRĀṆA (ARE MENTIONED), (WE SAY) NO, BECAUSE (THERE WOULD RESULT) THREE TYPES OF DEVOTION; (BESIDES OUR VIEW) IS ACCEPTED (ELSEWHERE); AND BECAUSE (CHARACTERISTIC MARKS OF BRAHMAN ARE) CONNECTED. 31

The pūrvapakṣin may still insist on saying that though there may not be any reference to Indra as a deity, the reference to the 'speaker' as the object of knowledge is clearly a reference to the individual soul, and not to Brahman. Similarly, the reference to prāṇa or the intelligent ātman as the cause of the support of the body is the reference to the principal prāṇa itself. The parable of the principal and the lower prāṇas tells us the same truth. When the lower prāṇas, i.e. the speech, the eye, the ear and the mind, became dejected to see the impending fall of the body as the principal prāṇa was about to depart from it, the latter came forward and said to them, 'Do not be infatuated; for it is I who divide myself fivefold, and support this body' (Pra. 2, 3). Or the prāṇa may be said to support the body, because it first supports the intelligent jīva and the sense organs, which are the instruments of the intelligent being; and so prāṇa too may rightly be described as 'prajñātmā'. Whether prāṇa is the same as the individual soul, as in the Śruti 'What is prāṇa is prajñā, and what is prajñā is prāṇa' (Kau. 3, 3), or different from it, as in the Śruti 'together they live in the body and together they depart' (Kau. 3, 4), the words 'prāṇa and 'prajñātmā' may mean the individual soul and the principal breath separately or taken together. If by 'prāṇa', on the other hand, we mean Brahman, then who would depart from whom? So, prāṇa must mean either the individual soul or the principal breath, or may mean both; but, in no case, it means Brahman.

The above interpretation, we reply, is inadequate because it would mean that three kinds of devotion are recommended in one single context. That it is one single context is clear from how the passage begins and ends. 'Know me alone, meditate on me as Life and Immortality, for I am the prāṇa and the intelligent Ātman,' is the beginning of the passage; and that 'prāṇa is verily the intelligent Ātman, the ānanda, and is without old age and death,' is the end of the passage. As the beginning and the end of the passage are one and the same, it is natural to suppose that only one kind of devotion is mentioned, and not three. And whereas the ten bhūtamātras and the ten prajñāmātras, or whereas the senses and their objects have their support in Brahman alone, the characteristic marks of Brahman including the word 'prāṇa,' can hardly be ascribable to the jīva. Besides, the reference to the 'highest Good' of man in what Pratardana asks for points to Brahman alone. The function of prāṇa, again, in supporting the body, being itself due to the Ātman, can be ascribed only to the latter. As the Śruti tells, 'no one lives by the up-going prāṇa or the down-going apāna, but by Him, the Other, in whom they take their support' (Ka. 2, 5, 5). Again, the statements, 'I am Brahman,' 'Thou art that,' indicate that the jīva is not essentially different from Brahman. On the contrary, Brahman itself is known as the jīva, and as the doer and enjoyer of actions on account of the limiting adjuncts of buddhi etc. So, the intention of sentences like 'Know the speaker etc.' is to direct the mind on the Brahman by casting away the distinctions of upādhis, and thereby make the individual soul come face to face with the Ātman and to show that it is the same as the Ātman. That the jīvātman which is involved in speaking and other activities is Brahman itself is clear from another Śruti: 'That which is incapable of being spoken by speech, but which enables one to speak, know that alone as Brahman; not that which people worship' (Ke. 1, 5). Finally, inadequate is the argument that prāṇa does not mean Brahman, because prāṇa and prajñātmā are said to be separate, though together they live in the body and together they depart from it. For buddhi and prāṇa, being the sources of cognition and activity, and being the upādhis of the Ātman, can very well be spoken of as separate from each other. But the Ātman, being non-differentiated in its nature in spite of the two upādhis, the upādhis too, in the light of this oneness of the Ātman, may be identified as in 'prāṇa is prajñā.'

The Vṛttikāras explain the latter part of the Sūtra in a different way. According to them, there is no logical flaw in stating along with the characteristic marks of Brahman, also those which belong to the jīva and the principal prāṇa. For they hold that the devotion to Brahman is recommended under the three aspects of prāṇa, prajñā and Brahman itself. The meditation on 'life, immortality or the 'uktha' (strictly on 'uttha' i. e. which causes the movement of the body) refers to the prāṇa aspect of Brahman. The prajñā aspect stands symbolically for the jīva. The prajñā or buddhi has nāma and rūpa (words and meanings) as the objects of knowledge ; the nāma being created by speech, and the rūpa by the sense-organs. It is the jīva, in short, who by the means of his intellect makes use of his organs of sense and action, and thus experiences the various objects (Kau. 3, 4, 5). As for the devotion to Brahman itself it consists in the cognition that Prāṇa or the Brahman is the ultimate support of both the senses and its objects. As the portion of the wheel at the circumference takes its support on the spokes, and as the spokes take their support in the nave, similarly, the objects are dependent on the senses, and, the senses in their turn are dependent for their support on the Prāṇa (Kau. 3, 8). Thus, Brahman alone is the object of devotion, whether in its own nature or in the form of its two upādhis of jīva and prāṇa. In the Chāndogyopaniṣad too (3, 14, 2), Brahman is recommended as the object of devotion in the form of one of its upādhis: 'He is of the form of mind, prāṇa is his body.' Thus Brahman alone is the general topic of the section, because, in the first place, the beginning and the end of the section are the same, and secondly, the characteristic marks of prāṇa, prajñā and Brahman are present.

But (as against this view of the Vṛittikārs) we hold that Brahman alone is the topic (of knowledge, and not of devotion).

Adhāya First

Pāda Second

१ सर्वत्र प्रसिद्धाधिकरणम् । (१–८)

In the first pāda Brahman has been shown as the cause of the origin, subsistence and dissolution of the world including ākāśa and other elements. It may be presumed therefore that we have also pointed out by way of implication that Brahman possesses the qualities of all-pervadingness, eternity, omniscience, and of being the Ātman of all. It was further pointed out that all those Vedānta passages where the characteristic marks of Brahman were clearly manifest, but about which there was some doubt on account of some words which ordinarily do not mean Brahman, referred to nothing else but Brahman. Now in the second and the third pādas, we shall be concerned with certain other passages which too are doubtful on account of their not containing in them characteristic marks of Brahman. In the second pāda, we shall deal with Brahman as the object of devotion, and in the third, with Brahman as the object of knowledge.

सर्वत्र प्रसिद्धोपदेशात् । १

[*Sarvatra—everywhere; prasiddha-upadeśāt—what is well-known being told.*]

BECAUSE WHAT IS WELL-KNOWN EVERYWHERE IS INSTRUCTED (BRAHMAN IS THE OBJECT OF DEVOTION). 1

In a passage of the Chāndogyopaniṣad, we are told that after death man becomes that to which he is devoted in this life. He is therefore asked to meditate with a composed mind on the Brahman, which is verily all this world, and which is the cause of the origin, the movement and the end of this world, and is not affected by desire, anger, etc. He should perform the Kratu, i.e. he should meditate, because 'the Ātman, which consists of mind and of prāṇa as its body, is resplendent.' (3, 14). The doubt which arises here is whether what consists of mind etc. and is the object of meditation, is the individual soul or the Brahman.

According to the pūrvapakṣin it is the individual soul; for it is the ruler of the body and the senses, and its connection with the mind and prāṇa is well-known. Brahman, on the other hand, is said to be 'pure, without prāṇa or mind' (Mu. 2, 1, 2). The reference to Brahman in the above mentioned passage of the Chāndogya viz. 'All this is verily the Brahman,' is not with a view to indicate the devotion to Brahman, but to urge the man to keep his mind calm. For in the one, homogeneous Brahman from which all this world arises and in which it ends, there is no room for emotions like love and hate. One and the same sentence cannot at once enjoin the meditation on Brahman and the calmness of mind. The sentence 'He who consists of mind etc.' follows immediately after the sentence 'One should perform the Kratu'; so it is clear that the performer of this Kratu or devotion is the individual soul suggested by the characteristic marks of 'mind' and 'prāṇa'. Further the description that 'he is the doer of all actions,' and that 'all desires belong to him' (Chā. 3, 14, 4), is also applicable to the individual soul, though not actually at any particular moment, yet in successive periods of time and of lives. Besides, there are mentioned two more characteristic marks of the jīva in the Śruti 'This Ātman, which is smaller than a grain of rice or of barley resides in my heart' (Chā. 3, 14, 3). This lodgement in the heart and the minute nature can adequately be said to belong to the jīva whose size can be compared to the point of a goad; they are not the marks of the limitless Brahman. No doubt, the Ātman is immediately afterwards described as 'greater than the earth etc.'; but this greatness too can be said to belong to jīva in a secondary sense, inasmuch as the minute jīva becomes as great as Brahman when it attains mokṣa. The use of the word Brahman in the end of the passage, 'This is Brahman' (Chā. 3, 14, 4), can also be said to refer to jīva because the pronoun points to nothing else but jīva; and the word 'Brahman' may be said to indicate the future status of the emancipated jīva.

To this pūrvapakṣa, our reply is that the object of meditation is Brahman alone, because the meaning which is attributed to the word 'Brahman' in the passage 'all this is Brahman etc.' is the same meaning, which has been taught by all the Vedānta-passages viz. that Brahman is the cause of the world. If we are not to avoid the topic under discussion and turn to a new topic without any cause, it seems appropriate that the Brahman spoken of here is qualified by mind, prāṇa and lustre. It may be said the word 'Brahman' is used, not for its own sake, but for the sake of making us aware of the calmness of mind that is recommended afterwards. But it should be noted that the relative pronoun 'which' occurring in the dissolution of the compounds 'manomaya,' and 'prāṇaśarīra', e.g. that which is qualified by the upādhi of prāṇa as body, refers to the proximate word 'Brahman' alone in the previous sentence. The word denoting jīva, on the other hand, is neither proximate nor anywhere directly used.

विवक्षितगुणोपपत्तेश्च । २

[*Vivakṣita—worthy of being narrated*; *guṇa-upapatteḥ—qualities being avail-able*; *ca—and.*]

AND BECAUSE QUALITIES WORTHY OF BEING NARRATED ARE AVAILABLE (IN THE CASE OF BRAHMAN ALONE). 2

Now the qualities which will be useful for man in his meditation are such qualities which can belong to

Brahman alone. For example, the quality of satya-sankalpa belongs to Brahman or the highest Ātman on account of its unobstructed power in translating its desire of creating, maintaining and dissolving the universe, into an actuality. Similarly the Ātman is said to be 'free from sin' (Chā. 8, 7, 1); Brahman, again, is said to be 'like ākāśa' on account of its omnipresence; its being 'greater than earth' points to the same fact; that it is the 'cause of all activity' and 'of all desires' (3, 14, 4) mean again the Brahman itself. Brahman is the inner Ātman of all, and so the upādhis of mind and prāṇa too can be said to belong to Brahman. Hence it is that Śruti and Smṛti say about Brahman: 'Thou art woman, thou art man; youth, maiden and an old man walking by the aid of his stick, all art thou; with thy face turned in every direction, thou art born in all things' (Śve. 4, 3). 'With its hands and feet everywhere, with eyes, heads, mouths and ears everywhere, it stands supreme, having engulfed all this' (B. G. 13, 13). The only difference one can point out is between a Śruti which refers to nirguṇa or pure Brahman, and a Śruti which refers to saguṇa Brahman. Nirguṇa or pure Brahman is described as 'without prāṇa, without mind, and as being white (pure)' (Mu. 2, 1, 2); saguṇa Brahman, on the other hand, is described as 'manomaya,' 'prāṇaśarira' etc. (Chā. 3, 14, 2).

अनुपपत्तेस्तु न शारीरः । ३

[*An-upapatteḥ—being not available*; *tu—but*; *na—not*; *sārīraḥ—embodied one.*]

But as (the qualities intended to be expressed) do not belong (to jiva, the Ātman denoted by 'manomaya' etc.) is not the embodied one. 3

The present Sūtra is intended to show that inasmuch as descriptions such as, 'he whose purposes are bound to come out true, who is like ākāśa, who is without speech and other senses, who is ever content, who is greater than earth, ' are applicable only to Brahman, and cannot be made applicable to the jīva or the embodied soul, the qualities like ' manomayatva ' etc. too do not belong to the soul that resides inside the body. No doubt, God also resides inside the body, but he is not simply inside but outside as well and is all-pervading, as is clear from the Śruti : ' He is greater than the earth, greater than space, eternally present everywhere like ākāśa ' (Chā. 3, 14, 3). The jīva, on the other hand, resides within the body alone, because the body is the only place where he can experience the effects of his actions in the form of pleasure and pain.

कर्मकर्तृव्यपदेशाच्च । ४

[*Karma—activity*; *kartṛ—agent*; *vyapadeśāt—being mentioned* ; *ca—and.*]

AND BECAUSE THE AGENT AND ACTIVITY ARE (SEPARATELY) MENTIONED. 4

The word ' him ' in the passage, ' When I shall have left this body, I shall obtain him ' (Chā. 3, 14, 4) refers to the Ātman or Brahman as the object fit to be obtained by meditating upon him and as possessing the qualities of ' manomayatva' etc. The object of meditation is thus clearly stated to be different from the meditator or the jīva indicated by the words ' I shall obtain.' One and the same thing cannot be the subject and object ; and hence the jīva, which is embodied, cannot possess the qualities of ' manomayatva ' etc., nor Brahman which possesses these qualities be the embodied self.

शब्दविशेषात् । ५

[*Śabda—word* ; *viśeṣāt—being specially used.*]

ON ACCOUNT OF WORDS BEING SPECIFICALLY USED. 5

In another passage dealing with the same topic, we read that ' this golden person is inside the individual soul, and is like the grain of rice or barley or of canary' (Śāt. Brā. 10, 6, 3, 2). Here the Brahman indicated by the word 'person' in the nominative is distinct from the jīva indicated by the locative. Hence, the being possessing 'manomayatva' etc. cannot be the embodied soul.

स्मृतेश्च । ६

[[*Smṛteḥ—on account of smṛti : ca—and.*]]

AND ON ACCOUNT OF SMṚTI. 6

There is the evidence of Smṛti too for holding that the highest Ātman and the embodied soul are different. For instance the Bhagavadgītā tells us that 'God, seated as he is in the hearts of all beings, moves them all by his magical power, as if they were placed on a machine' (18, 61). It may be said, no doubt, on the strength of both Śruti and Smṛti, that there is 'no other seer' but the highest Ātman (Bṛi. 3, 7, 23), or that the 'Knower of all these bodies' is God alone (B. G 13, 2), and so it may be pointed out that the embodied soul is not different from the Ātman. This is true indeed. But just as the unlimited ākāśa appears limited on account of the upādhis of jars and vessels, similarly, the Ātman is spoken of by the ignorant people as embodied, on account of the upādhis of the body, the senses, the mind and intellect. So long as there has not dawned the consciousness of the Ātmanic unitive life, there exists the practical difference between the objects of activity and the agents. But the moment one realizes the Ātmanic life of unity which is contained in the advice 'Thou art that (i.e. Brahman),' there is an end to all the practical view of the world and its distinctions, like bondage and mokṣa.

अर्भकौकस्त्वात्तद्व्यपदेशाच्च नेति चेन्न निचाय्यत्वादेवं व्योमवच्च ।७

[[*Arbhakaukastvāt—abode being small ; tat—that ; vyapadeśāt—being mentioned ; ca—and ; na—not ; iti—so ; cet—if ; na ; nicāyyatvāt—being meditated ; evaṁ—thus; vyomavat—like ākāśa; ca.*]]

IF IT BE SAID THAT (BRAHMAN IS) NOT REFERRED BECAUSE THE ABODE IS SMALL AND IS SO MENTIONED, (WE REPLY THAT IT IS) NOT SO BECAUSE (BRAHMAN) IS TO BE MEDITATED THUS; AND LIKE ĀKĀŚA (THIS IS TO BE UNDERSTOOD). 7

The argument of the pūrvapakṣa, (as noted in Sūtra 1 also) that the reference to the small abode of the heart and to the very small size of a grain of rice or barley, would naturally point to the jīva and not to Brahman which is all-pervading, deserves to be examined a little further. It is true that a small thing like the embodied soul cannot be said to be omnipresent; but the omnipresent Ātman can be said to occupy a small space in order to satisfy some purpose. The ruler of the earth may also be called the ruler of Ayodhyā a part of it. Similarly, the intellect of man can conceive the existence of the all-pervading God within the lotus of the heart, and please Him by meditating upon Him. Just as the worship of the stone of śaligrāma stands for the worship of Hari, even so God is represented as occupying the heart for the purpose of devotion. Or, just as the all-pervading ākāśa is said to occupy the eye of a needle, even so with Brahman. It is to be remembered however that the abode and the small size of Brahman have meaning only with reference to devotion; otherwise, from the view-point of Brahman they are unreal. This consideration will dispose off the possible argument that like parrots in different cages and with different perishable bodies, Brahman also may be impermanent because it resides in different hearts and is likely to assume different bodies. But the abode and the size being both imaginary Brahman is free from this defect.

संभोगप्राप्तिरिति चेन्न वैशेष्यात् । ८

[*Saṁbhoga-prāptiḥ*—*to have experience*; *iti*—*so*; *cet*—*if*; *na*; *vaiśeṣyāt*—*because of difference.*]

IF IT BE SAID THAT (BECAUSE THE JIVA AND BRAHMAN ARE ONE) THERE MAY ARISE EXPERIENCE (OF PLEASURE AND

PAIN FOR BRAHMAN ALSO), WE SAY NO, AS THERE IS DIFFERENCE IN THE NATURE (OF THE TWO). 8

The pūrvapakṣin may say that inasmuch as the all-pervading and sentient Brahman is in the hearts of all beings and is identical with the jīva, it too must experience the pleasures and pains of life. If there is 'no other knower than the highest Ātman' (Bṛ. 3, 7, 23), the pleasures and pains of saṁsāra do belong to the Brahman itself.

In reply to this we say that there is no logical connection between Brahman's residing in the hearts of all and its being made the subject of pleasures and pains. For there is difference between the embodied soul and the highest God. While the former acts and reaps the fruits of his acts, acquires merits and demerits, and becomes subject to pleasures and pains, the latter has the opposite characteristics, such as being free from sins, and from pleasures and pains. If mere proximity of things were to produce similar effects, ākāśa also will begin to burn on account of its proximity with fire.

Those who believe that the individual souls are many and all-pervading, may contend that the soul of one man will also be inside the bodies of other men, and so the pleasures and pains of one will be experienced by the others Our reply is that a particular man becomes subject to pleasures and pains in his own body, because he has got that body as the fruit of his actions, and not because of the proximity of his soul or body with the souls or bodies of other men.

Let us further inquire of the pūrvapakṣin as to the source of his information that Brahman will become subject to pleasures and pains on account of its indentity with the individual souls. If it is the Śruti passages such as, 'Thou art that,' 'I am Brahman,' 'There is no other knower but the Ātman,' then you cannot accept or reject the authority as you please. The Śruti sentence 'Thou art that,' as a matter of fact, removes the possibility of the individual soul itself being subject to pleasures and pains, inasmuch as it teaches us that the soul is nothing but the sinless Brahman. Where then is the possibility of Brahman being subject to pleasures or pains? If, on the other hand, the knowledge of the pūrvpakṣin is not due to Śruti, we have to tell him that the individual soul becomes subject to pleasures and pains on account of ignorance in him, and not because the pleasures and pains are in any way connected with Brahman. Just as the sky, which has really no physical surface or colour, is said to have a blue surface, even so the Sūtrakāra says that it may be conceived through ignorance that the embodied soul becomes subject to pleasures and pains. From the view-point of true knowledge, however, the jīva and Brahman are identical, and so both are free from sins and from pleasures and pains. There is a fundamental difference between ignorance and knowledge. And so there will be no connection between the identity of jīva and Brahman apprehended through knowledge, and experience of pleasure and pain apprehended through ignorance. God can never be imagined to have any connection whatever with pleasures or pains.

२ अत्त्राधिकरणम् । (९-१०)

अत्ता चराचरग्रहणात् । ९

[*Attā—eater ; carācar a—movable and immovable ; grahaṇā t—being taken.*]

(THE ĀTMAN IS) THE EATER; FOR (HE IS MENTIONED AS) TAKING IN WHATEVER IS MOVABLE AND IMMOVABLE. 9

A passage in the Kaṭhavalli (1, 2, 25) raises the question as to who may be there, 'who knows the dwelling place of Him to whom the Brāhmaṇas and Kṣttriyas are but food, and death itself is like the sprinkling (of ghee) on the food.' This implies that there must be some eater. But there arises the doubt as to whether the eater is the fire, the individual soul or the highest Ātman; for a discussion involving questions and answers regarding all the three is available in the same Upaniṣad.

According to pūrvapakṣa, the eater must be the fire as is mentioned by Śruti (Bṛ. 1, 4, 6) and as is known by every one in ordinary life. Or if the mention of fire is out place in a metaphysical discussion and as the fire is only the destroyer, the eater may be the individual soul. It cannot be the highest Ātman, because as the Muṇḍakopaniṣad tells us, 'One of the two eats the sweet fruit, and the other merely looks on without eating' (3, 1, 1). The Ātman alone must be the eater, we reply. For there can be no other being except the Ātman who will consume or absorb in himself the whole movable and immovable world as his food. No doubt the two castes of Brāhmaṇas and Kṣattriyas alone are mentioned as the food ; but these two being the best things of all stand as representatives of the whole world as food ; and the ghee of death which is sprinkled over the food characterizes the world as perishable or consumable by the Ātman. It may be said that the Ātman is merely a 'looker on' and no eater, but the context of the passage in the Muṇḍakopaniṣad shows by way of contrast, that the Ātman, unlike the jīva, does not become subject to the effects of actions. The passage does not aim at denying the absorption of the world into the Brahman ; for like creation and subsistence, absorption too of the whole world into Brahman is declared by all the Vedānta-passages. Therefore, the eater is Brahman alone.

प्रकरणाच्च । १०

[*Prakaraṇāt—owing to context* ; *ca.*]

AND ON ACCOUNT OF THE TOPIC UNDER DISCUSSION. 10

The passage that the 'Ātman is not born, that it does not die' (Ka. 1, 2, 18), and the passage quoted in the last Sūtra indicating the knowledge of the Ātman as exceedingly difficult to achieve, show it clearly that the topic under discussion is the Ātman.

३ गुहाप्रविष्टाधिकरणम् । (११-१२)

गुहां प्रविष्टावात्मानौ हि तद्दर्शनात् । ११

[*Guhāṁ—into cave*; *praviṣṭau who have entered*; *ātmānaw —the two selves*; *hi—for*; *tat*; *darśanāt—being mentioned.*]

THE TWO WHO HAVE ENTERED INTO THE CAVE ARE ĀTMANS (THE JIVA AND THE ĀTMAN); FOR (THEIR BEING OF THE SAME NATURE) IS SEEN (BY NUMBER BEING MENTIONED). 11

In the Kaṭhavalli, we read that 'these two who taste the fruit of truth, and reside in the world i.e. the body which they have acquired by good deeds, and who have entered the cave of the heart, the excellent seat of the Brahman, are like shade and light. This is what those who know the Brahman say, as also those house-holders who keep the five fires or those who are tṛṇāciketa ' (1, 3, 1).

The question that arises in this connection is whether these two are buddhi and jīva or the jīva and the highest Ātman. As a matter of fact, both the alternatives are possible. We read in an earlier passage (Ka. 1, 1, 20) that Naciketas asks Death to tell him by way of granting his third boon whether there is not such a being as jīva who is different from body, senses, mind and buddhi and who takes a new birth after death. This means that in the present passage too, buddhi and jīva are intended to be different and hence referred to as having entered into the cave. Or it may be that the two are the jīva and the highest Ātman. For a question regarding the highest Ātman also has been previously asked viz. to tell him that which is different from merit and demerit, effect and cause, and the past and the future (Ka. 1, 2, 14).

Now someone may say that there is, as a matter of fact, no question or doubt to be solved, because there is no possibility of either of the two alternatives. In the first place, the attribute of 'drinking the truth' (ṛtapāna) or 'tasting the fruit' cannot be predicated of the non-intelligent buddhi, though it can be predicated of the jīva. The attribute however is stated to belong to both of them and not to one only. Therefore, the two beings who have entered into the cave cannot be buddhi and jīva. Secondly, they cannot be the individual soul and the Ātman, for the latter is spoken of as merely a looker on and not as an eater (Mu. 3, 1, 1).

The question or the doubt mentioned above cannot however be thus brushed aside. It does exist. For just as a group of people is spoken of as having taken an umbrella, even though only one of them has taken it, similarly the two are mentioned as 'drinking the truth' even though one of them is actually doing so. The dual form of the verb drink' (pibantau) meaning thereby that there are two beings who perform the act of drinking, can be explained as having reference to the jīva who actually tastes (drinks) the fruits of actions and to Īśvara who, in spite of his looking on merely without eating, is said to drink because he makes the jīva drink. The chief of the cooks, for instance, is said to cook even though he sits silent and makes his subordinate cook. Or the dual form of the verb may refer even to jīva and to the non-intelligent buddhi; for like a cook, the non-sentient fuel also is spoken of as cooking the food. Hence in the presence of both the alternatives, there is room for doubt.

The pūrvapakṣin is in favour of the first alternative; the two agents referred to are the individual soul and the buddhi. The reasons he gives are: In the first place, it is the cave (whether we mean by it 'body' or 'heart') wherein they have entered. The cave being a small and a special place, it will be more appropriate to think of finite agents as having made the entry than to think of the infinite and all-pervading Brahman. Secondly, the words 'in the world of good deeds' have definitely a reference to buddhi and jīva which are within the sphere of karma, but not to the highest Ātman who does not grow larger by merit, nor does he become smaller by demerit (Br. 4, 4). 23, And thirdly, like shade and light, they are opposed to each other in being intelligent and non-intelligent.

To this we reply that the mention of the number 'two' makes us aware, in the first place, that the two beings must be of the same nature. And when one of them (as even the pūrvapakṣin says) is the jīva, then the other also must be an intelligent being; and so, it is no other than the highest Ātman. A bull requires another bull as its companion, neither horse nor man. Buddhi and jīva being disparate in nature, the relation of the subordinate and the superior is merely external to them. Between the jīva and the Ātman, on the other hand, there is the internal relation of intelligence. It is present in both and is indicated by 'ṛtapāna.' That a special local position of the cave of the heart has been assigned to the omnipresent Brahman is also, in the second place, quite appropriate. It serves the purpose of meditation, so that we should have a clear vision of the Brahman. Śruti and Smṛiti, too, speak very often of the Ātman as residing in the cave. For instance, 'The wise man leaves off both dejection and joy, when he comes to know the ancient Puruṣa hidden in the cave, etc.' (Ka. 1, 2, 12); 'He who knows him hidden in the cave of the heart, in the highest ākāśa, experiences all bliss' (Tai. 2, 1); 'Search for the Ātman who has entered into the cave.' Similarly, in the third place, though the attribute of existing in the sphere of the results of good deeds, i.e. of being embodied, belongs to the individual soul only and not to Brahman, yet it can be said to belong to the Brahman too in a figurative way, just as a group of men is described as one having an umbrella though only one of them has it. And lastly, the jīva and the Brahman being also disparate in nature are appropriately described as shade and light. The jīva is subject to saṁsāra on account of avidyā, while the Ātman is not because it is real. Therefore, the two beings who have 'entered into the cave' are the individual soul and the highest Ātman.

विशेषणाच्च । १२

[*Viśeṣaṇāt—because of distinctive qualities* ; *ca—and.*]

And because the distinctive qualities (of both are mentioned, those who have entered into the cave are the jiva and the Brahman). 12

A subsequent passage of the Kāṭhakopaniṣad (1, 3, 3 and 9) speaks of the body as the chariot and the individual soul as the charioteer, who is making his journey through saṁsāra to the final release. Another passage (1, 3, 9) speaks of the highest Ātman as the place of Viṣṇu, and as the destination of the journey. Similarly, in the passage already quoted (in the commentary of the previous Sūtra) the jīva and the Ātman are distinguished as the meditator and the object of meditation. All this goes to show that the two beings who have got distinctive characteristics and who have 'entered into the cave' are the individual soul and the Ātman. Besides, the general topic is of the highest Ātman itself. And again, the reference in just the previous passage to the authority of those who have realized the Brahman, proves that the subject-matter of discussion between these persons must be Brahman alone. So, when one of the two beings who have entered into the cave is the individual soul, the other must be no other than the highest Ātman.

By parity of reasoning, the passage from the Muṇḍakopaniṣad also (3, 1, 1) speaks about the jīva and the Ātman and not about two ordinary birds. 'The eating of the sweet fruit' refers to the individual soul, and the abstinence from eating and the intelligence required in mere looking on, refer to the highest Ātman. In the subsequent mantra, again, the same difference is shown to exist between the two (Mu. 3, 1, 2). The individual soul is represented as mourning because he is infatuated by the wrong notion that he is impotent, while the Ātman is represented as the object of meditation, which is said to be the cause of the removal of the grief of the jiva who meditates on it.

A different interpretation of the passage from the Muṇḍakopaniaṣd is also possible. The Paingi-rahasya Brāhmaṇa, for instance, discredits both the interpretations of the pūrvapakṣin as well as of the siddhāntin. The ṭwo birds do not stand either for buddhi and jīva on the one hand, or for jīva and Ātman on the other. On the contrary, they stand for buddhi and the released soul. The being which eats the sweet fruit is the sattva or the internal organ by means of which a man dreams ; and the being which merely looks on without eating is the individual soul who, really speaking, is not the enjoyer, but is identical with Brahman. It is this meaning which is found to be correct even according to Śruti and Smṛti ; e.g. 'That thou art' (Chā. 6, 8, 7), 'Know me also to be the Kṣetrajña or the individual soul' (B. G. 13, 2). The attribute of being an enjoyer has been simply superimposed upon buddhi, on account of want of discrimination on the part of the soul of the difference in nature between the two. Neither of them can be called an actor or enjoyer ; neither the non-intelligent buddhi, nor the non-modifiable individual soul. Besides being the product of avidyā buddhi is all the more incapable of being an actor or enjoyer. And yet, it is in the sphere of avidyā that dualism exists, and 'one sees the other' as elephants in a dream. But 'when all this becomes the Ātman, how should one see the other ?' (Bṛ. 4, 5, 15) So this passage as well as the one from the Muṇḍakopaniṣad tell us that for one who has realized the Brahman, there is an end to all the distinctions of the practical worldly life.

४ अंतरधिकरणम् । (१३-१७)

अंतर उपपत्तेः । १३

[*Aṁtaraḥ—Person within ; upapatteḥ—being available.*]

THE PERSON WITHIN (THE EYE, IS BRAHMAN) ON ACCOUNT OF (THE CHARACTERISTICS OF BRAHMAN BEING AVAILABLE. 13

A passage in the Chāndogyopaniṣad states that 'the person seen in the eye is the Ātman; that being is the fearless, the immortal, Brahman. If ghee or water is sprinkled over the eye it is wiped away along with the eyelid' (4, 15, 1).

According to pūrvapakṣa, the person in the eye. is the image of some person standing before the eye. Or it may be the individual soul ; for it is he who sees the forms of objects through the instrument of the eye. Besides the word 'ātman' in the passage indicates that it must be jīva. Or, again, it may mean the sun, the deity of the sense of sight which causes the eye to see, as is clear from: 'he (the sun-deity) resides in the eye, by means of his rays' (Bṛ. 5, 5, 2). Qualities like 'immortality' etc. which are mentioned in the passage may be attributed to the deities in the sense that they live far longer than men. The passage however does not refer to the omnipresent God, because a special place like the eye is mentioned as if it is the seat of God.

To this we reply that the person in the eye must be the highest God ; for the word Ātman, as it occurs in the Śruti 'That is the Ātman,' 'That thou art' (Chā. 6, 8, 7), refers primarily to God. Immortality and fearlessness are repeatedly spoken of as his characteristics. The eye too is fittingly described as his residence ; for just as God is free from the stain of sin, even so the eye is not stained by water or ghee. Besides He alone is known as Saṁyadvāma, that is, 'one towards whom all (vāma) fruits of actions go. He is also called Vāmanī, and Bhāmanī, that is one who distributes the fruits to all, and shines in all worlds (Chā. 4, 15, 2). So it is that the person in the eye is God alone.

स्थानादिव्यपदेशाच्च । १४

[*Sthāna-ādi—place and other things ; vyapadeśāt—being mentioned; ca.*]

AND BECAUSE PLACE AND OTHER THINGS ARE MENTIONED (THE EYE CAN BE THE PLACE OF GOD). 14

It is no objection to say that the eye cannot be a fit place for the omnipresent Brahman to reside ; for just as the omnipresent ākāśa can fill in the eye of a needle, even so the Brahman can reside in the eye. The objection could have carried some weight, if the eye alone were mentioned as the place of residence. The 'earth' etc. are also mentioned as fit places. Besides not only place is mentioned, but forms and names also are mentioned as characteristics of Brahman which is, really speaking, devoid of names and forms. His name is said to be 'Ut' and he is spoken of as possessing 'golden beard' (Chā. 1, 6, 7, 6). The ascription of a special place, name or form to the Nirguṇa Brahman is, as we have already seen, for the purpose of meditation.

सुखविशिष्टाभिधानादेव च । १५

[*Sukhaviśiṣtha—blissful;—abhidhānāt being mentioned ; eva; ca.*]

AND BECAUSE THE BLISSFUL (BRAHMAN WHICH HAS BEEN THE TOPIC UNDER DISCUSSION) ALONE IS MENTIONED (HERE, THE PERSON IN THE EYE IS BRAHMAN ONLY). 15

As a matter of fact, there ought to be no dispute regarding the person in the eye being Brahman alone, inasmuch as the same section of the Chāndogyopaniṣad which deals in its latter part with the person in the eye, deals with the nature of Brahman and with the path of Brahman as told by the Guru, in its earlier or introductory part (4, 10, 5 ; 4, 14, 1 ; 4, 15, 1-2). On being told by the fires that 'breath is Brahman,' Upakosala, the disciple of Jābāla, said that prāṇa being great he could understand that it was Brahman, but could not understand how the sensuous pleasure and the elemental ākāśa denoted by 'Ka' and 'Kha' respectively, were Brahman. To this the fires replied, 'What is Ka is Kha, and what is Kha is Ka,' meaning thereby that neither mere sensuous pleasure which is transitory and dependent upon sense-object contact, nor mere elemental ākāśa which is non-sentient, is Brahman, but that a combination of Ka and Kha, one of them being substantive and the other adjective, is Brahman. In other words, that bliss which arises in the ākāśa of the heart, for instance, and which is not transitory and dependent on sensuous objects, is Brahman and is therefore the fit object of meditation. Thus it is that the blissful Brahman is introduced as the topic of discussion in the beginning of the section. After this Gārhapatya and other fires tell their own glory and say, "This is knowledge regarding us, and this again is the knowledge of the Ātman. As for the path, your teacher will guide you." This means that there is no room for introducing another topic. Add to this the words of the teacher, Jābāla, 'As water does not cling to the leaf of a lotus, so no sin will cling to him who knows it,' which show that the person within the eye is the Brahman itself, possessing the qualities of Saṁyadvāma and others. It is clear therefore from the context, as well as from the common characteristic of not being stained, that the person within the eye is Brahman.

श्रुतोपानिषत्कगत्याभिधानाच्च । १६

[*Śruta-upaniṣatka-gati—The path of one who has heard the Upaniṣads; abhidhānāt—being mentioned ; ca—and.*]

And because the (same) path by which one who has heard the Upaniṣads (goes after death) is mentioned (here also, the person within the eye is Brahman). 16

The Praśnopaniṣad (1, 10) describes the path of the gods : 'Those who seek the Ātman by penance, celibacy, faith and knowledge go (after death) by the northern path to the sun. This is the abode of the prāṇas, the immortal fearless and the highest support of all, reaching which none returns.' The Bhagavadgītā too says, 'Those who know the Brahman go to Brahman after their death by the path of fire, light, the bright fortnight and the six months, when the sun is on the north' (8, 24). The same is the path of those, we are told, (Chā. 4, 15, 5) who know the person in the eye: 'Let people perform obsequies for such a person or not; he first goes to the world of the fire, and thence to the sun, to the moon, and to the lightning. A celestial being leads him further by the path of gods to Brahman.' It therefore follows that the person in the eye is no other than the Brahman.

अनवास्थितेरसंभवाच्च नेतरः । १७

[*Anavasthiteḥ—being not permanent* ; *asaṁbhavāt—being impossible* ; *ca* ; *na* ; *etaraḥ—other.*]

(The person in the eye is) no other (than the highest Ātman), because (any other being) is not permanent and because (it cannot possess the characteristics of the person in the eye.) 17

If the person in the eye were only an image of some one else standing before the eye, then the devotion to it is merely impossible, because the image will last only so long as the object before the eye will last. The intention of the Śruti must be that the person in the eye is capable of being seen by the meditator, and as such must be located in his own eye, rather than in the eye of another. But on the supposition that the person is the reflected image, we have to remain satisfied with one of the two absurd alternatives. Either the devotee has to meditate on the image of his own person reflected in the eyes of another (who must be available at any time), or he has to meditate on the image of another object reflected in his own eyes. Besides, as the Śruti tells us this image perishes along with the body (Chā. 8, 9, 1). In other words, it does not possess immortality, fearlessness, etc. which are the characteristics of the person in the eye.

The jīva likewise cannot be the person in the eye. For it is vitally connected with the whole body and the sense-organs, and not merely with the eye. It may be suggested that this applies equally to the all-pervading Brahman, if it is taken as the person in the eye. But we have to remember that it is for the sake of meditation that Brahman is conceived as occupying a particular place like the eye or the heart. The jīva too, like the image, does not possess the qualities of immortality, fearlessness etc. No doubt, the jīva is not different from the highest Ātman, but so long as desires, works etc. are ascribed to it on account of avidyā, it will continue to be mortal and be full of fear. And because it lacks the glory of God, it cannot possess the qualities of saṁyadvāma and others.

The suggestion that the person in the eye may be the divinity in the sun appears plausible because the Śruti tells us that he resides in the eye by means of his rays (Bṛ. 5, 5, 2). And yet he cannot be called Ātman; rather he is un-ātman because he shines by the lustre of the Ātman. As Śruti speaks of his origin and dissolution, he cannot be called immortal etc. The deathlessness of the gods is only nominal ; only as compared with human life, they live longer. They derive their glory from the highest God, as is clear from : 'Through fear of the Brahman, the wind blows, the sun shines, fire and Indra do their work, and Death runs' to kill those whose life is to end (Tai. 2, 8).

Hence the person in the eye must be the highest God alone. And when it is said that he is 'seen,' it should be understood to mean that he is capable of being realized by those who rely on Śruti, and that it has the further motive of creating in the mind of the ignorant a desire to 'see' him.

५ अंतर्याम्याधिकरणम् (१८–२०)

अंतर्याम्यधिदैवादिषु तध्दर्मव्यपदेशात् । १८

[*Antaryāmi—controller within; adhidaiva-ādiṣu—in gods and others; tat-dharma-vyapadeṣāt—his marks being mentioned.*]

THE CONTROLLER OF GODS AND OTHERS FROM WITHIN (IS THE ĀTMAN), FOR THE CHARACTERISTICS OF THAT (ĀTMAN) ARE MENTIONED. 18

A passage from the Bṛhadāraṇyakopaniṣad tells us that the being who lives inside this and other worlds and in all beings, as well as inside the earth, the gods, the Veda, the sacrifice and the bodies of all, is immortal and the ātman; the earth does not know him, though it is his body; he lives inside and controls all. (3, 7, 1) Now who is this antaryāmin? Is he the Ātman or some divinity, or a yogin endowed with powers, or a new being altogether?

The pūrvapakṣin may hold that the antaryāmin is a new being altogether, inasmuch as the name used for it is not familiar. But it serves no purpose to suppose the existence of a thing whose nature is not known at all. The word, however, is not absolutely unfamiliar, because it means 'one who controls from within.' It may mean, then, some deity ruling over the earth, etc.; for such a deity may have 'earth as its dwelling, fire as its sight, and light as its mind, etc.' (Bṛ. 3, 9, 16); that is, it may be endowed with organs of action and so become capable of ruling. Or the being may be some yogin who is able to enter within all things on account of his supernatural powers. In no case, can the being be the highest Ātman, because the Ātman is not endowed with body and sense-organs which are necessary for ruling.

To this we reply that the antaryāmin must be the Ātman ; for the quality of controlling all can belong to the Ātman alone, who not only resides within all the created things including gods, earth, etc., but is the cause of them all. Immortality belongs to the Ātman alone. The fact that the deity of earth does not know him, even though he is inside, shows that the Ātman is different from the deity. The being is described in the passage as 'unseen' and 'unheard,' indicating thereby that it is the Ātman alone which is devoid of names and forms. Supposing that the body and senses are essential for the act of ruling, it is possible likewise to suppose that the Ātman is, on account of avidyā, related to the bodies and senses of those whom he wants to control and rule. As a matter of fact, by means of the unfathomable power of his māyā, the Ātman can control all things, even though he has no body. To suppose that the Ātman may necessitate the existence of another being superior to it, and so on *ad infinitum*, is not relevant. For really speaking, there is no difference between the individual soul and the Ātman. So the internal ruler is no other than the Ātman.

न च स्मार्तमतद्धर्माभिलापात् । १९

[*Na—not ; ca—and ; Ṣmārtaṁ—found in Smṛti ; atat—contrary to it; dharma—attributes; abhilāpāt—not being mentioned.*]

NOR IS (PRADHĀNA) AS THOUGHT BY (THE SĀṆKHYA) SMṚTI (THE INTERNAL CONTROLLER); FOR CHARACTERISTICS NOT BELONGING TO (PRADHĀNA) ARE MENTIONED HERE. 19

That pradhāna is not the cause of the world has already been shown while dealing with Sūtra 1, 1, 5. We deal with pradhāna here again, because a follower of the Sāṇkhya may say that as the qualities of 'not being seen or being devoid of form etc.' belong to pradhāna as well, the pradhāna may be considered as the antaryāmin. As the Manu Smṛti says the pradhāna 'is not discovered by inference, nor is perceivable by the senses, but being unconscious lies spread in all directions, as if in sleep.' (1, 5). The attribute of being the controller may belong to it because it is the cause of all.

To this we reply that this is not possible, because qualities not belonging to pradhāna are mentioned as belonging to the Ātman. The pradhāna cannot be seen ; nor is it able to see because it is an unconscious element. On the other hand, in the concluding sentence of the section dealing with the antaryāmin, the Ātman is characterized as 'unseen but seeing, unheard but hearing' unthought of but thinking, and unknown but knowing' (Bṛ. 3, 7, 23). Besides the word 'ātman' cannot be applied to the unconscious pradhāna.

The opponent may take a turn and say, if not pradhāna, then let us suppose that the individual soul is the antaryāmin ; it is conscious and is therefore the seer, the hearer and the thinker; it resides inside and therefore can be described as the Ātman; it has to reap the fruits of its actions, if not in this life, in lives yet to come, and therefore unlike body it must be considered as immortal; and. being the seer etc., it is natural to say that it is itself unseen The Śruti too tells us, 'you will not be able to see the seer of the sight' (Bṛ. 3, 4, 2). Lastly, being inside and having got to taste the fruits of actions, it possesses naturally the quality of controlling the body and the senses. For all these reasons, the opponent may hold that the individual soul is the antaryāmin.

The following Sūtra comes as a reply to this.

शारीरश्चोभयेऽपि हि भेदेनैनमधीयते । २०

[*Śārīraḥ—the embodied soul ; ca—and ; ubhaye—in both; api—even ; hi—for ; bhedena—as different ; enaṁ—this ; adhīyate—is studied.*]

THE EMBODIED SOUL TOO (CANNOT BE THE ANTARYĀMIN); FOR IN BOTH (THE VEDIC BRANCHES OF STUDY), IT IS LEARNT AS DIFFERENT (FROM THE ANTARYĀMIN). 20

The qualities of seeing, thinking etc. may belong to the individual soul; yet like the ākāśa confined in a jar, it is limited on account of the upādhis like the body and the senses. It cannot therefore dwell inside the earth and the several worlds, and control them from within. The Kāṇvas and the Mādhyandinas, moreover, make the distinction between the individual soul and the antaryāmin, and speak as much of the former as of the earth and other things as being worthy to be controlled by the latter. They are the dwelling places of the antaryāmin. The Kāṇvas say, 'he resides in the vijñāna;' and the Mādhyandinas say 'he resides in the ātman' (Bṛ. 3, 7, 22); and the words, 'vijñāna' and 'ātman' stand for śārīra and the embodied soul respectively.

The objection that may arise here is that there would be two seers in one body; one the embodied soul and the other, the God as the antaryāmin. Śruti itself is against this possibility, 'There is no other seer but he,' (Bṛ. 3, 7, 23). It denies the existence of any other seer, hearer etc., except the one antaryāmin under discussion.

In reply to this we say that what appears as a difference between the two seers, the śārīra, and the antaryāmin does not exist as a matter of fact. It arises on account of upādhis of body, senses etc., the effect of avidyā. There is only one Ātman, the experience of which can be had in the form, 'I am.' Anything else which is not the content of this experience is un-ātman. But owing to upādhis, the one Ātman is treated in practical life as if it were two, just as the one ākāśa is considered as two (mahākāśa and ghatākāśa) on account of the upādhi of a jar. So, it is on account of the upādhis of avidyā which create an interest in the practical world that Śruti makes the distinction between the knower and the known, the injunctions and the prohibitions, and the means of knowledge like perception and experience of saṁasāra. Or as Śruti puts it, it is in order to explain the practical world of avidyā, 'that there is the appearance of duality, and that one sees another ; but when the practical world vanishes before vidyā, when all this becomes the Ātman to him, then who should see whom ?' (Bṛ. 2, 4, 14, and 4, 5, 15). Hence too, on account of the distinctions of avidyā, there exists a controller as different from the controlled; otherwise there exists only one supreme Ātman.

६ अदृश्यत्वाधिकरणम् । (२१–२३)

अदृश्यत्वादिगुणको धर्मोक्तेः । २१

[*Adṛśyatvādi-guṇakaḥ—one who possesses invisibility and other qualities; dharmokteḥ—qualities being mentioned.*]

THAT WHICH POSSESSES THE QUALITIES OF INVISIBILITY AND OTHERS (IS BRAHMAN) ON ACCOUNT OF CHARACTERISTICS (PECULIAR TO IT) BEING MENTIONED (ALONG WITH INVISIBILITY). 21

A passage in the Muṇḍakopaniṣad tells us that 'the higher knowledge is that by which the Immutable is realized ; that which is invisible, which cannot be seized, which has neither origin nor qualities, which has neither eyes nor ears, nor hands nor feet, which is everlasting and yet manifold, which is all-pervading, subtle, imperishable and which is regarded by the wise as "Bhūtayoni," the source of all' (1, 1, 5 ; 6).

Now the qualities like invisibility being common, a doubt arises as to whether the Bhūtayoni means the Brahman or the pradhāna or the embodied soul. According to pūrvapakṣa, it must be the non-intelligent pradhāna, because in the passage subsequent to the one quoted above, it has been compared with non-intelligent things ; e.g. 'just as a spider creates and takes back the threads, or just as the herbs grow on the earth, or hairs arise from the body of a living man, even so the world arises from the Immutable' (Mu. 1, 1, 7). One need not say in this connection that the spider and the man are instances of intelligent beings, for it is impossible that the threads and the hairs will be produced without the non-intelligent bodies. The bodies may be governed by intelligence, but it is out of the bodies that the hairs and threads are produced. Similarly, the world must have been produced by the non-intelligent pradhāna, even though it may be guided by the intelligent Puruṣa. Besides, not only qualities like invisibility are found to belong to pradhāna, but there is also no mention of a quality which does not belong to it. Qualities like 'knowing all,' 'perceiving all,' which are mentioned in the concluding portion (Mu. 1, 1, 9), may however be pointed out as contrary to the nature of pradhāna; but it must be remembered that the earlier reference to the Immutable as invisible (1, 1, 5-6) is different from the reference to that which is higher than the Immutable (Mu. 2, 1, 2). Now that which is 'higher' may be 'all-knowing' and 'all-perceiving'; but that which is Immutable or the Bhūtayoni must be pradhāna. Or if the word 'yoni' were to mean the efficient cause, then Bhūtayoni may mean even the embodied soul ; for by resorting to merits and demerits the jīva too can be called the cause of the origin of things.

To this we reply that the Bhūtayoni is the highest God only. For omniscience can neither belong to the non-intelligent pradhāna nor to the embodied soul which is limited. Besides, the same Immutable Bhūtayoni, which is first said to be the original cause of all created things (1, 1, 7), is further spoken of as omniscient and as the cause of the created things. 'From him, who is omniscient and whose penance consists of knowledge, comes forth this Brahman in the form of subtle elements, the gross elements possessing names and forms, and food such as barley and wheat' (1, 1, 9). From the identity of reference, we believe that the same immutable Bhūtayoni is omniscient also, and is therefore Brahman; it is neither pradhānan nor jīva. Nor again in the passage (Mu. 2, 1, 2) which refers to 'that which is higher than the high Immutable,' is there anything meant except the immutable, intelligent Bhūtayoni under discussion. For prior to this passage, there is another passage from the same Upaniṣad (1, 2, 13) which recommends the Guru to impart the Brahma-vidyā to his disciple, so that the latter may realize that truthful, immutable being. As to why the word 'Immutable' has been used in the ablative, and as to what the 'higher than the high immutable' may mean, we shall make it clear when we deal with the next Sūtra.

We reach the same conclusion in another way. The Muṇḍakopaniṣad begins with the topic of Brahma-vidyā by telling us (1, 1, 1) that it was first imparted by the Creator to his eldest son Atharva. It is said to be both the foundation and the culmination of all other vidyās ; for it being known, everything else becomes known. (1, 1, 3). It differs in kind from all other types of knowledge, such as the knowledge of the Vedas, grammar etc. It is therefore known as parā vidyā, due to which the Immutable being or the Brahman is known (1, 1, 5), as distinguished from the aparā which is only a preliminary to the parā. The one leads to bliss, the other to mere worldly prosperity. Fools alone may consider the aparā or the lower vidyā as the Summum Bonum, and so become subject to old age and death over and over again. Unless one considers the 'boats of sacrifices, and the eighteen[1] Brahmins required for a sacrifice, as frail' means, unless one turns away with disgust from the lower knowledge which, by contrast only brings out the glory of the higher, and is convinced that the eternal Ātman cannot be achieved by means of transitory actions, one does not become fit to receive the higher knowledge. But once he knows the futility of the lower knowledge and of actions, he should with humility,

1 The eighteen Brahmins include the sixteen priests required for any sacrifice and the sacrificer and his wife.

and with fuel in hand, surrender himself unto the Guru or the Spiritual Teacher who is not only learned but also steadfast in the realization of Brahman (1, 2, 7; 1, 2, 12).

All this points out that the Immutable source of all, or the Bhūtayoni is Brahman alone. If this were not so, the knowledge of Brahman would not be considered as parā vidyā. And if Bhūtayoni is to be understood as pradhāna, there would result a third kind of pradhāna-vidyā besides the two mentioned in the Upaniṣad. At best, the knowledge of pradhāna will lead to the knowledge of its non-sentient effects viz. the things of enjoyment; but not of the conscious individual souls; and the knowledge of the souls will not likewise lead to the knowledge of things. In other words, the knowledge of pradhāna or jīva will not give rise to the knowledge of everything else, as it happens in the case of the knowledge of the Brahman. And above all, the knowledge of pradhāna has never been acknowledged by anyone as leading to mokṣa.

Lastly, the argument that Bhūtayoni must be non-intelligent because things compared to it, by way of illustration, are non-intelligent, is not sound. For there is no such rule like this. Even on the Sāṇkhya theory, the pradhāna is not considered as gross in nature , because in the example taken for comparison the earth is a gross element. For all these reasons, the source of all or the Bhūtayoni which possesses the qualities of invisibility etc. is the highest God.

विशेषणभेदव्यपदेशाभ्यां च नेतरौ । २२

[*Viśeṣaṇa—qualities*; *bheda—difference*; *vyapadeśābhyāṁ—the two being mentioned* ; *na—not* ; *itarau—the two others.*]

(BHŪTAYONI DOES) NOT (MEAN) THE TWO OTHERS (i.e. THE INDIVIDUAL SOUL AND THE PRADHĀNA); FOR SPECIFIC QUALITIES AND DIFFERENCE ARE MENTIONED. 22

The aupaniṣadic person who is the same as Bhūtayoni, is described as 'effulgent, bodiless, the same inside and outside, unproduced, without mind or prāṇa and pure' (Mu. 2, 1, 2). The individual soul, on the other hand, which wrongly considers itself as being limited by name and form, cannot possess the attributes of effulgence etc., and is therefore, different from the Bhūtayoni. Similarly, the same passage which mentions the highest Ātman as 'higher than the high Immutable' distinguishes the pradhāna from the Bhūtayoni. The word 'Immutable' (akṣara) means here the unmanifest potential source of names and forms, the support of the subtle five elements, that which is lodged in God and forms his upādhi, and which transcends all other effects but is not itself an effect. The intention of the Sūtra is not to admit the independent existence of pradhāna, so that we may first say that the akṣara and pradhāna are one and the same thing, and then distinguish the pradhāna from the Ātman. The intention is rather to distinguish the Ātman as transcending the akṣara or the immutable. If at all the pradhāna is to be assumed, then we have no objection to its being assumed in such a way as will not contradict the Śruti i.e. in the way in which the akṣara has been defined above. Then, too, as said above, the Bhūtayoni is different from the pradhāna, and is nothing else but God.

And for what reason, again, does Bhūtayoni mean God? This is told in the following Sūtra. :

रूपोपन्यासाच्च । २३

[*Rupa—form* ; *upanyāsāt—being mentioned*; *ca—and.*]

AND BECAUSE ITS FORM IS MENTIONED. 23

In the passages which follow the mention of the Being which is higher than the akṣara, there is first the description of the creation of all things from prāṇa. Then comes a statement of the form of this very Bhūtayoni as : ‘ Fire is his head ; the sun and the moon, his eyes ; quarters, his ears ; the Vedas, his speech ; the universe, his heart ; the wind, his breath ; the earth, his feet ; he is verily the inner Ātman of all ’ (Mu. 2, 1, 3, 4). In view of the entire context, it is proper to hold that this form belongs to God alone, and not to the jīva who is of a limited power, or to pradhāna which cannot be the ātman of all. This bodily form, however, instead of contradicting the quality of invisibility, is intended to show that the Bhūtayoni is the inner Ātman of all. For does not a person who has realized the Brahman sing the sāman ‘ I am the food, I am the eater of food’ (Tai. 3, 10, 6), only to indicate that the Brahman is the Ātman of all, even though he has no desire to eat the food himself?

Some others say in this connection that the passage quoted in the beginning (2, 1, 4) does not refer to the source of all beings but refers to creation, the inner self of which is not the Ātman but the Hiraṇygarbha or Prajāpati. For in the passage 2, 1, 3 and again from 2, 1, 5 to 2, 1, 9, are mentioned only the things that are created such as, prāṇa, mind, senses, the five elements, herbs, and juices. It seems improbable that, all of a sudden, in the midst of the two passages (2, 1, 3 and 2, 1, 5), there should be a reference to Bhūtayoni, as the Ātman of all. So in the intervening passage too (2, 1, 4), it seems reasonable to hold that a being born from the ultimate source of all, and not the source itself, i.e. the Bhūtayoni or Brahman is mentioned. That being must be the Prajāpati or the Sūtrātmā, about whose birth we get reference in Ṛgveda and other places : ‘ Hiraṇyagarbha was (born) in the beginning, as the first lord of the beings with the three worlds as his body; he made the earth and the sky ; him alone as God, we worship by offering oblations ’ (Ṛg. 10, 121, 1). Being the first-born Person with body, he too may be called the internal ātman of all other created beings, in the sense, that he lives in the form of the thread of prāṇa (Sūtrātmā) in all beings (Bṛ. 3, 9, 9 ; and Mu. 2, 1, 4). The reference to Bhūta-yoni or the Ātman, therefore, as the source of all comes in the end after the description of the whole of creation. In 2, 1, 10, for instance, he is described as the Puruṣa, who is all this universe, including karma, penance etc.

वैश्वानराधिकरणम् । (२४–३२)

वैश्वानरः साधारणशब्दविशेषात् । २४

[*Vaiśvānaraḥ*; *sādhāraṇa—ordinary* ; *śabda—word* ; *viśeṣāt —owing to qualification.*]

VAIŚVĀNARA IS (THE HIGHEST ĀTMAN) ON ACCOUNT OF A SPECIFIC QUALITY BELONGING TO (TWO) ORDINARY WORDS (VIZ. VAIŚVĀNARA AND SELF). 24

The Chāndogyopaniṣad tells us that six brahmins approached the king, Aśvapati Kekaya, in order to learn from him the nature of Vaiśvānara ātman ; and on being asked as to what beings they worshipped, they said turn by turn, that the heaven, the sun, the wind, the ākāśa, the water and the earth respectively were the objects which they worshipped. Hearing this the king replied that these constitute respectively the head, the eye, the prāṇa, the mid-portion of the body, the bladder, and the feet of the Vaiśvānara; for they indicate the lustre, the forms, the motion, the space, and the wealth, which are in the Vaiśvānara. Besides, his chest is the alter; hairs, the grass on the altar; and his heart, mind and mouth the three fires, Gārhapatya, Anvāhārya and Āhavanīya, respectively. The king then deprecated their mode of worshipping the Vaiśvānara Ātman in parts, and advocated the contemplation on it, as measured by a span, so that the devotee would be the eater of food in all the worlds and beings (5, 11, to 5, 18).

Now both the words in 'Vaiśvānara-ātman' are ambiguous. The word 'Vaiśvānara' may mean 'the abdominal fire,' 'the elemental fire' or 'the Fire-divinity', and the word 'ātman' may mean the individual soul or God. Which of these five meanings, then, are we to have by 'Vaiśvānara-ātman'? According to pūrpavakṣa we may mean by it, in the first place, the abdominal fire or 'the fire inside the human body, by means of which the food is digested' (Bṛ. 5, 9). Or secondly, it may mean the ordinary fire, 'as a sign of the day, i.e. the suu which the gods made for the world' (Ṛg. 10, 88, 12). Or thirdly, as the passage 'May the god Vaiśvānara, the king of worlds, favour us with pleasure and prosperity' (Ṛg. 1, 98, 1) shows, we may take it to mean a divinity. With reference to the word ātman which is used along with Vaiśvānara, it may mean the individual soul. The proximity of the abdominal fire, and measurement by a a span, indicate that it must be the embodied soul. But on no account, would Vaiśvānara mean the highest God.

To this we reply that because the heaven, the sun etc. are the head, the eye, etc., the Vaiśvānara must be the God or the ātman of the worlds, though he is described thus for the purpose of meditation. This is the distinctive meaning of the 'Vaiśvānara-ātman,' over and above the meanings put forth by the pūrvapakṣa. As the cause of all, God possesses within him all the stages of all the effects ; and so the description of the several worlds and beings as the limbs of God is adequate. The statement regarding the result of meditation on the Vaiśvānara, viz. 'He eats the food in all worlds, beings and selfs,' has meaning only with reference to God. Similarly, the statement, 'all his sins are burnt etc.' (Chā. 5, 24, 3), regarding one who meditates on the Vaiśvānara and knows him, shows that Vaiśvānara is nothing else but God. To add to this, the topic of the passage under discussion is the nature of the Ātman or Brahman. For all these reasons, Vaiśavānara means Brahman.

स्मर्यमाणमनुमानं स्यादिति । २५

[*Smaryamāṇaṁ—what is told in smṛti; anumānaṁ—inference ; syād—may be ; iti—because.*]

BECAUSE (FROM) WHAT IS TOLD IN SMṚTI, THE INFERENCE MAY BE (TO WHAT IS TOLD IN ŚRUTI, VIZ. THAT THE VAIŚVĀNARA IS THE HIGHEST GOD). 25

A verse from the Śantiparva describes the highest God as 'the ātman of the worlds, and as one whose mouth is fire, whose head is the heaven, whose naval is the ākāśa, and whose feet, eyes and ears are the earth, the sun and the quarters' respectively (M. Bhā. 47, 68). This Smṛti enables us to infer a Śruti corresponding and prior to it as its authority, because the Smṛti has in it the presence of the sign viz. ' the heaven as head, and fire as mouth' etc., which is also present in the Vaiśvānara Śruti of the Chāndogyopaniṣad. Even taking for granted that Smṛti passages are sometimes given to eulogise, we say that such a grand eulogy cannot be without the sanction of a prior Śruti. Vaiśvānara, therefore, is the highest God.

शब्दादिभ्योऽन्तः प्रतिष्ठानाच्च नेति चेन्न तथादृष्ट्युपदेशादसंभवात् पुरुषमपि चैनमधीयते । २६

[*Śabdādibhyaḥ—because of word and others; antaḥ—inside; pratiṣṭhānāt—on account of presence ; ca—and ; na—not ; iti—so ; cet—if ; na ; tathā—like that; dṛṣṭi-upadeśāt—being recommended to behold ; asaṁbhavāt—not being possible ; puruṣaṁ—person ; api—also ; ca; enaṁ—him ; adhīyate—is studied.*]

IF IT IS SAID (THAT VAIŚVĀNARA IS NOT THE ĀTMAN) ON ACCOUNT OF THE WORDS ETC. (HAVING A DIFFERENT MEANING) AND ON ACCOUNT OF THE RESIDING WITHIN (OF FIRE), (WE REPLY THAT IT IS) NOT SO; BECAUSE IT IS THUS RECOMMENDED TO BEHOLD (FIRE AS GOD), ALSO BECAUSE IT IS IMPOSSIBLE (TO THINK OF HEAVEN AS HEAD OF FIRE); AND BECAUSE HE (THE VAIŚVĀNARA) IS REFERRED TO AS PURUṢA (BY VĀJASANEYINS). 26

Vaiśvānara cannot be the highest God, because ordinarily the word Vaiśvānara means fire. In Śatapatha

Brāhmaṇa (10, 6, 1, 11) the word Agni is affixed to Vaiśvānara and there it means fire residing within man. In the Chāndogyopaniṣad (5, 18, 2), again, the three fires are mentioned as the heart, the mind and the mouth of Vaiśvānara; and in the same Upaniṣad (5,19,1) it is mentioned as the place where oblations of food to prāṇa are to be offered. For all these reasons Vaiśvānara is to be understood as abdominal fire. Or in view of the qualifications, 'heaven as the head etc.' (Chā. 5, 18, 2), Vaiśvānara may be taken to mean elemental fire. This is clear also from the mantra, 'The sun who has by his light covered both the earth and the heaven and the intervening space, is fit for being meditated' (Ṛg. Saṁ. 10, 88, 3). Or again, the heaven etc. may be the limbs of the powerful Fire-deity, if not of the elemental fire.

All these arguments are incorrect, we say in reply. For what is recommended here is that the abdominal fire itself should be meditated upon as a symbol of the highest God, just as the mind is recommended for being meditated upon as the symbol of Brahman (Chā. 3, 18, 1,). Or, what is recommended here is the meditation of the highest God as qualified by the abdominal fire, just as God is recommended to be meditated as qualified by the upādhis of mind, prāṇa and light (Chā. 3, 14, 2). Had there been no intention of the Śruti to refer to the highest God, and had the aim been merely to point to the abdominal fire, there would have been no specific references to 'lustrous heaven as the head' etc. in the passages quoted above. This applies equally, as we shall see while dealing with the next Sūtra, when the Vaiśvānara is interpreted as meaning the elemental fire or the deity of fire. The abdominal fire can be said to be within man, and not as the same as man or Puruṣa. The Vājasanyins however say that Vaiśvānara is Puruṣa, and that one who knows him as residing inside eats the food in all places. (Śata. Brā. 10, 6, 1, 11). So the highest God alone can be the Puruṣa as well as be inside the body of man.

There are some who read the last portion of the Sūtra, not as 'Vaiśvānara is the Puruṣa,' but is 'like Puruṣa.' Then the likeness of the Vaiśvānara or the highest God, with Puruṣa will be explained thus. With reference to the external world, it can be said that the heaven is his head, and the earth is his feet ; while with reference to man, he will be said to be located, as if between the chin and the head of the devotee.

अत एव न देवता भूतं च । २७

[*Ataḥ—hence* ; *eva—also* ; *na—not* ; *devatā—deity* ; *bhūtaṁ—element* ; *ca—and.*]

For the same reason (the Vaiśvānara) is neither the deity (of fire) nor (the elemental) fire. 27

The elemental fire which gives only heat and light cannot be supposed to have the heaven as its head, etc. The fire-deity too cannot have them as its limbs, because it has not produced the heaven etc. This power of production is derived from God. So it will be more appropriate to call the heaven and the like as the head etc. of God, rather than of the fire-deity. Besides, the word ātman in the 'Vaiśvānara-ātman' (as seen before) is thoroughly inapplicable to abdominal fire, the elemental fire and the fire-deity.

साक्षादप्यविरोधं जैमिनिः । २८

[*Sakṣād—directly* ; *api—even* ; *avirodhaṁ—without contradiction* ; *Jaimini.*]

No contradiction, says Jaimini, even if (the highest God is taken as the object of worship) directly. 28

According to Jaimini there will be no logical flaw if, instead of taking Vaiśvānara as the symbol or upādhi of God, we mean by it God himself, and so worship him directly rather than worship him as a symbol or as limited by upādhis. The possible objections against this view are (as already considered under Sūtra 26) : That the words Vaiśvānara and fire have different meanings, and that the Vaiśvānara resides inside the man, and that these suggest that Vaiśvānara means the abdominal fire. Apart from the refutation we have done while dealing with Sūtra 26, Jaimini says that the passage from the Śatapatha Brāhmaṇa (10, 6, 1, 11) does not at all refer to the inner residence of the abdominal fire because it is not the topic of discussion and contains no word which is a synonym for that particular fire. On the contrary, it refers to the supposed similarity of the highest God to man, and to his existence inside man, that is, on the portion of human body viz. the portion from forehead to chin. What is 'on' and ' of ' the body can be said to be ' inside,' because it is a part or a limb of the whole ; just as a branch of a tree can be said to be within the tree. Or, the passage may be said to refer to both the saguṇa and the nirguṇa aspects of the Ātman ; saguṇa, so far as he is said to be 'like man', on account of his ādhidaivika and ādhyātmika similarity from head to feet to the external world and to man, and nirguṇa so far as he is a mere onlooker, and so residing within all, without being affected by the upādhis. In keeping with this interpretation, the word ' Vaiśvānara, can be explained to denote the highest Ātman, thus : (1) Viśva—all, and Nara—jīva ; so Viśvānara means 'one who is the ātman of all things including the souls ; or, (2) Viśva–all modifications, and Nara–creator; so it means the cause of all; or again, (3) One ruler whose subjects are the souls. Thus the word Viśvānara, which is the same as Vaiśvānara means the highest Ātman, the cause, the ruler and the internal self of all. The word 'Agni' too means the highest Ātman ; Ag—'towards the agra' i.e. towards the end or fruits of actions, and Nī—to lead; so it indicaes 'one who makes the souls approach the fruits of their actions.' In other words, Agni or Agraṇi (one who is the leader) means Ātman. Similarly, the idea of the three fires in the heart, the mind and the mouth, and the offering of food as oblations appear to be adequate if Vaiśvānara is to mean Ātman alone.

If Vaiśvānara is to mean God how is it possible to measure him by a span? The Sūtrakāra answers :

अभिव्यक्तेरित्याश्मरथ्यः । २९

[*Abhivyakteḥ—because of manifestation; iti—that; āśmarathyaḥ.*]

ĀŚMARATHYA SAYS (THAT GOD IS SAID TO BE MEASURED BY A SPAN) BECAUSE OF (HIS) MANIFESTATION (TO DEVOTEES). 29

God transcends all measurements, no doubt; yet he shows his grace to his devotees and manifests before them in a form which may be a span in length.

अनुस्मृतेर्बादरिः । ३०

[*Anusmṛteḥ—on account of meditation; Bādariḥ.*]

AS BĀDARI SAYS (GOD IS SAID TO BE MEASURED BY A SPAN) ON ACCOUNT OF MEDITATION (ON HIM). 30

Just as the corn of barley which has its own size, is said to measure a 'prastha' (two pounds), because that particular measure is used, even so God, who is beyond measure, is said to be measured by a span. For he is meditated upon by devotees in their heart, which is measured by a span. Or, God is said to be a span in length, because the motive may be that he should be meditated upon, as if he has a form which is measurable by a span.

संपत्तेरिति जैमिनिस्तथाहि दर्शयति । ३१

[*Sampatteḥ—supposition; Jaiminiḥ; tathā-hi—the same; darśayati—tells.*]

ACCORDING TO JAIMINI, (GOD IS SAID TO BE A SPAN IN LENGTH) ON ACCOUNT OF MENTAL SUPPOSITION; (ŚRUTI TOO) TELLS THE SAME. 31

In the Vājasaneyi Brāhmaṇa where the same topic is being discussed, the various ādhidaivika members of the Vaiśvānara, such as the heaven and earth, are identified with the ādhyātmika members such as the forehead and eye of the human body, and the meditation of God is being recommended on the portion of the human body which measures a span, and which is between the forehead and the chin. 'The highest God was thus obtained by the several gods,' we are told, 'because they meditated upon him as if he was of the measure of a span.' And we are told how the King Ashvapati too said to his disciples that 'he would show unto them how the Vaiśvānara had that measure, and then, pointing by his finger successively to his forehead, eyes, nose, space, saliva within the mouth and to the chin, he said that they were respectively the heaven, the sun, the wind, the ākāśa, the wealth or water in the bladder and the feet of the Vaiśvānara.' All this account goes to show that the Vaiśvānara-vidyā of the Vājasneyi-brāhmaṇa (Śat. Brā. 10, 6, 1, 11) is the same as that of the Chāndogyopaniṣad (5, 11, to 5, 18), in spite of the minor differences between the two. The heaven and the sun are spoken of in the one as 'standing above,' and as 'possessing light,' while they are spoken in the other as 'possessing light' and as having 'infinite forms'. Both the texts make the identical use of the expression 'measured by a span'. So, as Jaimini says, it is appropriate to call the highest God as 'Prādeśamātra', because Śruti wishes Him to be so imagined for the purpose of devotion.

आमनन्ति चैनमस्मिन् । ३२

[*Āmananti—they think*; *ca—and*; *enaṁ—him*; *asmin—in him.*]

MOREOVER (THE JĀBĀLAS) THINK THAT HE (i. e. THE HIGHEST GOD LIVES) IN IT (i. e. THE SPACE BETWEEN THE FOREHEAD AND THE CHIN). 32

The infinite, unmanifest Ātman, says Yājñavalkya, resides in the souls which are not released ; and he says to Atri that the place of the soul is between the Nāsī (nose) and the Varaṇā (eyebrow) ; for it is the Varaṇā and the Nāsī which ward off and destroy the sins of the senses. It is this place which is the juncture of the heaven (head) and the earth (chin), and a contemplation on which, as if on God, destroys the sins. So what Śruti speaks of God, viz. as prādeśamātra is quite appropriate.

God is also known as abhivimāna, because, he is known as the subject of every individual soul; or because, being everywhere, he transcends all measurement; or because he is the creator of all. From all this, it follows that Vaiśvānara is the highest God.

ADHYĀYA FIRST

PĀDA THIRD

१ द्युभ्वाद्यधिकरणम् (१-७)

द्युभ्वाद्यायतनं स्वशब्दात् । १

[*Dyu—(heaven); bhū—(earth); ādi—beginning with; āyatanaṁ—abode; sva-śabdāt—on account of the word 'sva' (self).*].

THE SUPPORT OF THE HEAVEN, EARTH ETC. (IS BRAHMAN), BECAUSE THE WORD 'SVA' (i. e. ĀTMAN HAS BEEN MENTIONED). 1

The Muṇḍakopaniṣad (2, 2, 5) speaks of the being 'in whom the heaven, the earth and the ākāśa, as well as the mind and prāṇa are woven' and asks us 'to know that Ātman alone, and to leave off all other talking; for he is the bridge leading to Immortality.'

According to pūrvapakṣa, the being or the support referred to in the passage must be different from the Brahman. For the word 'bridge' reminds us that there is another bank towards which it leads; Brahman, on the other hand, being eternal and all-pervading 'is without end and has no other bank' (Bṛ. 2, 4 12). It can be said that pradhāna, as told by Smṛti, is the support, because it is the cause of all. Or, it may be the wind; for the wind is said 'to be the thread on which all these worlds and beings are strung together' (Bṛ. 3, 7, 2). Or, again, inasmuch as the word 'ātman' is used with reference to the support, it may be the individual soul. For though it is finite, it can be said to be the support of the objects of experience, on account of its being the author of actions.

To this we reply. The use of the word 'ātman' on account of its pervasive and sentient character, is adequate only with reference to Brahman, and not to the non-intelligent pradhāna or the finite soul. Corresponding to this word 'ātman' of the Muṇḍaka, Brahman is designated by the word 'Sat' in the Chāndogyopaniṣad; 'All these creatures have their root in the Sat, their residence in Sat, and their support in Sat' (6, 8, 4). Again, in the passages preceding (2, 1,10) and following (2, 2, 11) the passage from Muṇḍaka quoted in the beginning (2, 2, 5), Brahman alone is mentioned by various terms such as 'Puruṣa,' 'penance,' 'para', 'immortal,' and others. 'The Puruṣa is all this, sacrifice, penance, Brahman, the highest and the immortal;' 'That immortal Brahman is before and behind, to the right and to the left.'

It is likely that one may think at this point that the support will make us aware also of other things which have this support, and that the expression 'Brahman is all this' implies that Brahman is manifold in nature, just as a tree, in spite of its unity, consists of different parts such as branches, stem and roots. In other words, there may arise a dualistic conception of the world and the Brahman as separate from each other; Brahman considered as the substantive and the world as adjectival. It is therefore in order to ward off this suggestion that, in the passage under discussion, we are told to know 'him as the support or as the one Ātman only.' The Ātman is not to be considered as many and as qualified by this world of manifold effects; rather it is to be known as one homogeneous substance or support after removing from the mind the false knowledge of this worldly existence. If one is asked to bring the seat on which Devadatta is seated, he brings the seat and not the man. So the passages 'Know him alone as the Ātman,' 'Brahman alone is all this,' 'The Ātman is, like a piece of salt altogether, both inside and outside, full of knowledge' (Bṛ. 4, 5, 13), all aim at removing the wrong notion of the reality of this world. 'From death to death he goes, who sees any duality here' (Ka. 2, 1, 10) has been described the fate of the believer in the unreal world. That which is 'all' is said to be in reality nothing but Brahman; not that which is Brahman is intended to be 'all' or many. The 'all' is to be cancelled, and the Brahman retained. As for the word 'bridge' (setu) we must not be led away by what it suggests viz. that there is another bank, just as we must not suppose it as one made up of wood and clay. Rather, must we catch the meaning of it, the idea of holding together or lending support, which is in the etymology of the word, viz. 'si' to bind. Or, as suggested by some others, the bridge here indicates the means of attaining Immortality, which consists of the knowledge of the Ātman and the leaving off of idle talk, as recommended in the passage. It does not refer to the support of the heaven, the earth etc., and therefore the question of taking the word 'bridge' to mean pradhāna or something else than Brahman does not arise.

मुक्तोपसृप्यव्यपदेशात् । २

[*Mukta (liberated)-upasṛpya-(to be achieved); vyapadeśāt—because it is mentioned.*]

BECAUSE IT IS MENTIONED AS FIT TO BE ACHIEVED BY THOSE WHO ARE RELEASED, (BRAHMAN IS THE SUPPORT OF THE HEAVEN AND THE EARTH, ETC.). 2

It is a common experience of us all that we become subject to love and hatred because certain things which promote the well-being of the body please us, and certain other things which are harmful displease us. Disease and death to the body fill us with horror and infatuation, and yet being misled by avidyā, the feeling, that 'I am the body and other things of the not-self', binds us to perpetual misery. As against this condition of bondage, it is pointed out that the destination of the released is the Brahman. It is fit for them to resort to the support of heaven, earth etc., because 'When He who is both the cause and the effect is seen, the knots of the heart are broken, all doubts are solved, and the actions cease to effect (Mu. 2, 2, 8), and because, being free from the bondage of name and form, the wise man reaches the self-effulgent Person, who is greater than the great avyakta' (Mu. 3, 2, 8). Other Śruti passages too mention the Brahman as the fit abode of the released : 'When all the desires go away from his heart, he becomes immortal, and attains to Brahman in this very life' (Bṛ. 4, 4, 7). Pradhāna and other entities, on the other hand, are not admitted by any as fit objects to be achieved by the released. Besides, the condition of leaving off all speech, in order to know the support of the heaven and the earth etc. as told by the Muṇḍakopaniṣad, is exactly the same condition as told by the Bṛhadāraṇyaka to know the Brahman. The two upaniṣads prove thereby that the support of the heaven etc. is Brahman alone. 'The wise man should first know the Ātman and fix his mind upon that alone, and should cease to talk many words, for it is nothing but weariness' (Bṛ. 4, 4, 21).

नानुमानमतच्छब्दात् । ३

[*Na-not; anumānaṁ-inference; atat-śabdāt-owing to want of any word indicating it.*]

ON ACCOUNT OF THERE BEING NO WORD TO DENOTE, (THE SUPPORT OF THE HEAVEN ETC. IS) NOT WHAT IS INFERRED (i. e. PRADHĀNA). 3

There is not a single word which will exclusively denote pradhāna, or vāyu; we cannot therefore take them as support of the heaven etc. On the other hand, terms like 'Omniscient' etc. indicate that the support is an intelligent being (Mu. 1, 1, 9).

प्राणभृच्च । ४

[*Prāṇa-bhṛt-beaerr of life; ca-and*].

(NOT) THE BEARER OF PRĀṆA (i. e. THE INDIVIDUAL SOUL) TOO. 4

The individual soul to cannot be the support of heaven etc., because though it can be called as intelligent and ātman, it is not omniscient. Besides being limited by upādhis, it is not all-pervading. The jīva may be considered as an instrumental cause of this world, because the unseen store of merit and demerit of the jīva requires the world for enjoying the fruits ; but on no account the jīva can be called the material cause of the world.

भेदव्यपदेशात् । ५

[*Bheda-vyapadeśāt–distinction being shown.*]

ON ACCOUNT OF DISTINCTION BEING SHOWN (THE JĪVA IS NOT THE SUPPORT OF THE HEAVEN ETC.). 5

The passage 'Know him as the Ātman' indicates the knower as the jīva, and the known 'Ātman' as separate from it. The jīva is that which has the desire of mokṣa; hence Brahman indicated by the word 'Ātman' is the support of the heaven etc.

प्रकरणात् । ६

[*Prakaraṇāt–because of context*].

ON ACCOUNT OF THE CONTEXT (THE JĪVA IS NOT THE SUPPORT OF THE HEAVEN ETC.). 6

The whole chapter deals with the nature of the highest Ātman. It begins with the inquiry as to what it may be, which when known, everything else becomes known (Mu. 1, 1, 3). So it is the knowledge of the Brahman which is referred to here.

स्थित्यदनाभ्यांम् च । ७

Sthiti-danābhyāṁ–on account of presence and eating; ca–and.]

AND BECAUSE THE TWO CONDITIONS OF (MERE) PRESENCE AND EATING (INDICATE BRAHMAN AND JĪVA RESPECTIVELY).

That Brahman is the support of the heaven and the earth etc. (as mentioned in the passage under discussion: Mu. 2, 2, 5) is again strengthened by a further passage in the Muṇḍakopaniṣad (3, 1, 1) where 'the two birds, the inseparable companions of each other' are mentioned as the Īśvara and the jīva. One of them is referred to as being merely present, and the other as eating the fruits of actions. Had there been no reference to Īśvara first in the passage 2, 2, 5, as the support of the heaven etc., a reference to him, all of a sudden, in 3, 1, 1, and in distinction from the jīva, is entirely without meaning. The same is not however, true of the jīva, who unlike Īśvara is an object of common experience. Therefore, even a casual reference to jīva afterwards without a prior reference need not strike us as unreasonable. The motive of the Śruti is to make us acquainted from the very beginning with the fact that Īśvara, who is not the object of common experience, is the support of the heaven etc. and that he is distinct from the jīva who is limited by upādhis. To take the jīva to be the supporter of the heaven etc. in the first passage is to render the reference to Īśvara in the second passage out of place to suppose the Īśvara to be so, however, is not to render the reference to jīva un called for, but to explain the fact that jīva though identical with Brahman is considered as separate because it eats the fruits of its actions.

Our conclusion remains unaffected even though the two birds are taken to mean the buddhi and the upādhi-less jīva, as stated in the Paingi Upaniṣad. For, just as the ākāśa contained in a jar is nothing but the infinite ākāśa without the jar, even so the jīva is nothing else but the highest Ātman, when viewed without the adjuncts of internal organ, body etc. Our contention is (1) that the jīva as limited by the upādhis is not the support of the heaven etc ; but (2) that the highest Ātman is the support. According to Paingi Upaniṣad too the jīva that appears different in different bodies is not the support ; but the upadhi-less jīva who is identical with the highest Ātman is the support. The conclusion of the two passages therefore is the same as that of an earlier passage still (Mu. 1, 1, 5-6), viz. the Bhūtayoni is the highest Ātman ; for 'in it the heaven, the earth and the sky are woven.'

२ भूमाधिकरणम् । (८-९)

भूमा संप्रसादादध्युपदेशात् । ८

[[*Bhūmā ; Saṁprasādāt-adhi–after state of deep sleep; upadeśāt–being mentioned.*]]

THE BHŪMAN (IS BRAHMAN); FOR (IT IS MENTIONED AFTER SAṀPRASĀDA (i. e. THE STATE OF SLEEP IN WHICH PRĀṆA KEEPS AWAKE). 8

The seventh chapter of the Chāndogyopaniṣad begins with a dialogue between Nārada and Sanatkumāra. Approaching with humility as a disciple, Nārada requests Sanatkumāra to initiate him in the knowledge of the Ātman, so that he may be relieved of his worldly sorrows. In the course of the conversation, Nārada asks if there was anything greater than name; and Sanatkumāra says in reply that it was speech. Then there is a series of questions and answers as to which is greater and greater still, so that, every succeeding member of the series becomes greater or higher in importance than the one preceding. Following the name, we get the series consisting of speech, mind, sankalpa, citta, dhyāna, vijñāna, power, food, water, fire, ākāśa, memory, hope and prāṇa (7, 1 to 15). And a little later (7, 23 and 24) Sanatkumāra says: 'One must know the Bhūman (*i. e.* the great) which when known, one sees nothing else; hears nothing else, and when one sees something else, hears something else, that is ' little '.

Now what is meant by ' Bhūman ' ? Whether, on account of the proximity of passages, we should mean by it the prāṇa, or whether, in connection with Nārada's grief, we should mean by it the highest Ātman, knowledge of which alone would remove that grief?

According to pūrvapakṣa the 'Bhūman' means the prāṇa; for, (1) though there is series of questions and answers as to what is greater and greater still, from the name to the prāṇa, there is no such question or answer after the positing of prāṇa as the greatest of all. (2) But soon after, the Bhūman is so described as to mean prāṇa. (3) Sanatkumāra calls the person who knows the prāṇa as the 'ativādin' *i. e.* one who can make a statement regarding the greatest of all things, and recommends that such a person need not disown that he is an 'ativādin' (7, 15, 4). (4) Therefore, the sentence which follows this, but precedes the description of Bhūman, *viz.* 'But this person who speaks the truth is the real ativādin' (7, 16, 1) does not refer to something else but refers to the greatness of prāṇa alone. The pronoun 'this' in 'this person' refers to the person who knows the greatness of prāṇa; so without breaking away from the topic of prāṇa, the description goes on from the ativādin of prāṇa, through another series, so to say, from truth to Bhūman. Bhūman therefore means prāṇa. (5) That Bhūman indicates a condition in which one does not see or hear anything else need not offer any difficulty, because the same may be seen to be applicable to prāṇa. In deep sleep when all other senses become merged in prāṇa (Pra, 4, 2, 3), it is the prāṇa that keeps awake. (6) The 'Bliss' of the Bhūman (Chā. 7, 23), again, can be explained as belonging to prāṇa because in deep sleep, when the jīva sees no dream, there is happiness (Pra. 4, 6). (7) Similarly, the 'immortality' of Bhūman (Chā. 7, 24, 1) may refer to prāṇa also (Kau. 3, 2). (8) That the Upaniṣad begins with the statement, that the knowledge of the Ātman enables one to overcome grief, need not again deter us from holding that prāṇa alone is considered here as the Ātman of all; for in the seventh chapter itself (15, 1) we are told that prāṇa alone is the 'father, mother, brother, sister, teacher and Brāhmaṇa.' (9) Besides, prāṇa is conceived as the 'nave' of the wheel in which all the 'spokes' of the things in the world are fixed; prāṇa, therefore, is conceived as Bhūman.

To this we reply. (1) The sūtra clearly states that the reference to Bhūman comes after the reference to 'Saṁprasāda' or the joy. That saṁprasāda points to deep sleep and not to jīva is clear again from its separate mention along with the waking and dreaming conditions (Bṛ. 4, 3, 15). As prāṇa alone is awake in deep sleep 'Saṁprasāda' then indicates the prāṇa to which it belongs. So the Bhūman which is described later than prāṇa must indicate an entity different from prāṇa. (2) On the other hand, if Bhūman were the same as prāṇa, there would be no sense in saying that prāṇa is mentioned after prāṇa. The series of members beginning with 'name' and ending with 'prāṇa' has in it every term as different and new from its preceding term. It is natural therefore to hold that what is told about Bhūman is different and new from what is first told about the prāṇa. (3) The statement regarding the 'ativādin' is not made exclusively with regard to the man who has the knowledge of prāṇa, as our opponent supposes, but it is made a second time and by way of contrast regarding an altogether different man with special reference to his knowledge of truth. (4) This too may be challenged, and it may be pointed out that a truth-speaking Agnihotrin is not an Agnihotrin because he speaks the truth, but because he performs the agnihotra, and yet truth-speaking is his special quality. Similarly, truth-speaking may be pointed out as a special quality of the person who is called ativādin on account of his knowledge of prāṇa; not that the person is ativādin simply because he speaks the truth. But to offer this explanation is not only to give up the direct meaning of the Śruti passage according to which the ativādin becomes so 'on account of truth', but also to ignore the meaning of the particle 'but' which intends to break away, by way of contrast, from the context of prāṇa, and to begin with the new topic of the person who is known as ativādin through truth. In short, the quality of being an ativādin does not refer to the knowledge of prāṇa, but to that of Brahman through the series of truth and other things. (5) Nor does it stand to reason to suppose that a new topic has not been introduced simply because the question-and-the-answer form is not there. When the conversation goes on regarding a brahmin who has studied one Veda, if someone says about another, 'but he is great who has studied four Vedas', we do understand without the question and the answer that a new topic has been introduced. Similarly, even though there is no new question asked by Nārada, after the hierarchy of entities was closed by the mention of prāṇa, Sanatkumāra, being filled with compassion, tells as if, of his own accord, that the quality of being an ativādin is a false thing, if it arises merely on account of the knowledge of a false thing like prāṇa, but that he alone is an ativādin who becomes so on account of truth. Now this truth is nothing but Brahman; for as Śruti tells 'Brahman is truth, knowledge and infinite' (Tai 2, 1). It is in this way that Nārada is led on beyond prāṇa by a series of steps of Vijñāna etc. to Bhūman, which is the same as the highest Ātman or the truth, the knowledge of which would really make a person an ativādin. (6) This interpretation of ours is quite consistent with the genesis of the whole discussion *viz.* the grief of Nārada and his desire to put a stop to it by means of the knowledge of the Ātman, as also with the result of the inquiry, *viz.* 'his faults being removed, he was shown the other side of darkness' by the revered Sanatkumāra (Chā. 7, 1, 3 and 7, 26, 2). The word 'ātman' cannot be applied in the real sense to prāṇa; and the cessation of grief cannot take place without the knowledge of the Ātman. 'There is no other path to mokṣa' (Śve. 6, 15). (7) That prāṇa, again, is not the last word of Sanatkumāra's teaching is seen from the fact that it is further told that the 'prāṇa springs forth from the Ātman alone' (Chā. 7, 26, 1). Neither can it be said that the topic of Ātman comes last of all, and that therefore one is free to say that 'Bhūman is prāṇa'. For being asked by Nārada as to the abode of the Bhūman, Sanatkumāra answers that he resides in his own glory (7, 24, 1), and further continues the same topic of the Bhūman to the end of the chapter, with the only change of the word Ātman for Bhūman. The greatness of the Bhūman as well as its self-existence are far more fittingly applicable to the Ātman than to prāṇa.

धर्मोपपत्तेश्च । ९

[*Dharma-attributes; upapatteḥ-being fit; ca-and.*]

And because the attributes (of Bhūman and Ātman) agree, (Bhūman is Ātman). 9

(1) The inapplicability of ordinary perception and, other sense-activities to Bhūman is found to be the same in the case of the Ātman too. 'Where one sees nothing else, hears nothing else etc. That is the Bhūman' (Chā. 7, 24, 1). Identically the same we read in another Śruti passage regarding the Ātman, 'When all this becomes the Ātman, who should see whom?' (Bṛ. 4, 5, 15). Regarding prāṇa, too, it can be said that during deep sleep there is the absence of activities; but if we remember that the topic under discussion is Ātman, we shall see that the alleged absence of activities, instead of referring to prāṇa, merely means the inapplicability of them to the Ātman. inasmuch as the Ātman is not attached to anything, (2) The bliss of deep sleep, again, does not refer to prāṇa but to Brahman or Bhūman, because it is 'great' and not 'little' (Chā. 7, 23, 1). And because it removes ths ordinary pleasure which is mixed with misery, the bliss of the Ātman is also spoken of as the 'highest' and a, constituting its very nature, 'on a small portion of which all the creatures live' (Bṛ. 4, 3, 32). (3) The immortality of Bhūman again (Chā. 7, 24, 1), as distinguished from the relative immortality of long life of prāṇa or other things, is intended to remind us that Bhūman is Brahman

or the ultimate cause of all, excepting which, as the Bṛhadāraṇyaka says, everything else is perishable (3, 4, 2). (4) Similarly, the qualities of truth, omnipresence, Self-existence and being the Self of all, mentioned as belonging to Bhūman, can belong to the highest Ātman also.

२ अक्षराधिकरणम् । (१०-१२)

अक्षरमम्बरान्तधृते: । १०

[*Akṣaraṁ–the syllable Oṁ; aṁbara–heaven; anta–end; dhṛteḥ–because it supports.*]

(AKṢARA IS BRAHMAN); BECAUSE IT SUPPORTS (ALL THINGS) INCLUDING ĀKĀŚA. 10

'What is that' asked Gārgī, 'in which the ākāśa, in its turn, is filled in all directions?' 'It is Akṣara, as the Brāhmaṇas say', replied Yājñavalkya; 'it is neither large nor small etc.' (Bṛ. 3, 8, 7; 8). Now the doubt that arises here is whether the word 'akṣara' means a syllable or the highest Ātman.

The pūrvapakṣa view is that akṣara means by convention a syllable. The 'akṣara-samāṁnāya' (or the collection of fourteen Sūtras which Paṇinī, the grammarian is said to have received from god Śaṅkara) contains in it such syllables. Śruti mentions this 'all as Oṁ' (Chā. 2, 23, 4); and as a symbol of Brahman, it is said to be the Ātman of all, and as such, fit to be meditated upon.

To this we reply that akṣara means the highest Ātman. Having first mentioned that all the things in the world, either of the past, the present or the future have their support in the ākāśa Yājñavalkya, further tells Gārgī that the ākāśa too finds its support in the akṣara; but to be the support of all things cannot be the quality of any being except Brahman. Akṣara therefore means, in the first place, that which is not kṣara or perishable;

and secondly, that which pervades (from the root 'aśa' to 'pervade'). Akṣara then means Brahman. That Oṁ is said to be all this is simply a sort of praise, because Oṁ is considered as a symbol of Brahman for meditation.

A follower of the Sāṇkhya school may say that if cause can be said to be the support of all its effect, then the akṣara too may be construed to mean pradhāna, and not necessarily Brahman. To this the Sūtrakara replies:

सा च प्रशासनात् । ११

[*Sā–this; ca–and; praśāsanāt–because of command.*]

THIS (LENDING OF SUPPORT) IS DUE TO THE COMMAND (OF GOD). 11

'It is due to the command of this akṣara, O Gārgī that the sun and the moon stand supported (Bṛ. 3, 8, 9); and the command must be the work of God alone, and not of the non-intelligent pradhāna, for otherwise clay also may be called to produce a jar on account of a command.

अन्यभावव्यावृत्तेश्च । १२

[*Anya (different)-bhāva (nature)-vyāvṛtteḥ–being excluded.*]

AND BECAUSE EVERY THING POSSESSING A DIFFERENT NATURE (FROM BRAHMAN) HAS BEEN EXCLUDED, (THE AKṢARA IS BRAHMAN). 12

The akṣara has been described as 'unseen but seeing, unheard but hearing, unperceived but perceiving etc.' (Bṛ. 8, 3, 11). No doubt, the qualities of being 'unseen,' 'unheard' etc. may be said to belong to the pradhāna; but the other opposing qualities which, at the same time, belong to the Akṣara are found lacking in the non-intelligent pradhāna. Akṣara, therefore, is not pradhāna. Similarly the same passage which tells us that 'there is no other seer but the akṣara, no other hearer or knower but the akṣara, excludes the possibility of the plurality of individual souls. Nay, the upādhis too are excluded from the nature of the akṣara ; for it is said to be 'without eyes, without ears, and without speech or mind etc.' (3, 8, 8). So the akṣara does not mean the embodied soul at all. Undoubtedly, then, it is nothing else but Brahman.

४ ईक्षतिकर्मव्यपदेशाधिकरणम् । (१३)

ईक्षतिकर्मव्यपदेशात्सः । १३

[*Ikṣati–seeing; karma–action; vyapadeśāt–being mentioned: saḥ—he.*]

BEING MENTIONED AS THE OBJECT OF SEEING, HE (IS THE HIGHEST BRAHMAN, WHICH IS MEDITATED BY MEANS OF Oṁ). 13

During the course of the discussion of meditation on Oṁ, in the fifth section of the Praśnopaniṣad, the sage Pippalāda tells Satyakāma that it is by means of this 'Oṁ which is both the saguṇa and the nirguṇa Brahman, that a person attains to one of them,' and that he who meditates on Oṁ with its three parts, a, u, ṁ, goes to the highest Puruṣa (5, 2 ; 5, 5). The doubt that may arise in this connection is whether the object of meditation is the lower or the higher Brahman.

According to the pūrvapakṣa, it is the lower Brahman ; for one who meditates on Oṁ consisting of three parts, enters first into the sun, and from there he is carried by the Sāman to Brahmaloka, a locality which is restricted by limits, and which therefore cannot be the fit reward for one who has known the higher Brahman. No doubt, such a man is said to reach the 'highest' or 'para-Puruṣa'; but the word ' para ' has got only relative significance with reference to the physical body which is gross. So the 'para-Puruṣa' is nothing but the Hiraṇyagarbha or the

Sūtrātmā-prāṇa or the lower Brahman, or the lord of Brahmaloka.

To this we reply. The nirguṇa or the highest Brahman alone is the object of meditation. For, this same object of meditation is spoken of afterwards as the object of sight. The man who meditates 'beholds the Person of his meditation too,' the person who dwells in the town of body, and who is greater than the jīva-ghana or the Hiraṇyagarbha. If it is a question of meditation alone, it matters little if the object of meditation is even imaginary ; a rope can be meditated upon as a serpent. But if the meditation of a thing is to turn into a vision, the object must be real and existing. And so the transcendent Being which is spoken of as the object of sight of the devotee who meditates upon it, must be an existing entity. It is the highest Ātman, the object of both meditation and the perfected sight or intuition ; it is not the lord of Brahmaloka for he may be the object of meditation, but not of intuition because the reality that belongs to him is imaginary and due to upādhis.

An objection may be raised in this connection. It may be pointed out that so far as meditation is concerned the person is said to be 'transcendent' simply ; but when the person is said to be intuited, he is described as 'transcending the transcendent Jīvaghana.' How should one know then that the person as the object of meditation and the person as the object of vision are not two but one and the same person ?

The persons appear as two, we say in reply, if the 'jīvaghana' is supposed to be the object of meditation, so that the Person 'transcending the jīvaghana' will be a different person as the object of sight. What we hold is that the jīvaghana is not at all the object of meditation, as is clear from the two words 'para' and 'puruṣa' which are both present in both the passages dealing with meditation and vision. It is the 'transcendent Puruṣa ' or the highest Ātman which is the object of meditation and continues to be the object of vision too. As for the meaning of the word ' jīvaghana ' which again is said to be 'transcendent,' we solve the compound not as that which is ' composed of (ghana) the jivas,' but as ' one having the characteristics of the jīva.' Now this jīvaghana or jīva, though, in reality, it is the same as the Ātman, is to be understood as limited on account of its upādhis, just as a piece of salt, though it is in essence nothing but salt in general, is a specific different portion from it on account of its being limited. And the jīvaghana is said to be 'transcendent,' because it transcends the senses and their objects. And yet we have to remember that in spite of the transcendent character of the jīvaghana, it is not the object either of meditation or of vision. As said above, it is the Puruṣa or Brahman which' transcends the transcendent jīvaghana ', and is the object both of meditation and of vision.

Or, jīvaghana may be interpreted, as some others do it, as the Brahmaloka, the residence of Brahmadeva or as Brahmadeva himself. The Brahmaloka is said to be higher than all other lokas or worlds, and the Brahmadeva or the Hiraṇyagarbha is said to be the cosmic Person including in him all the jīvas. So when it is said that the man who meditates upon the Oṁ with its three parts is lifted by the power of the Sāman-hymns to the Brahmaloka, it means that he does not stop here, but goes further along with the jīvaghana or Brahmadeva in having the vision of the highest Ātman which transcends the jīvaghana and yet is the in-dweller of all the bodies. Thus also, we come to the same conclusion that the highest Ātman, who transcends the transcendent Brahmaloka along with the Lord of that loka, is the only object both of meditation and vision.

Besides, Śruti also tells us that para-Puruṣa means Brahman; 'higher than the Puruṣa there is nothing; and that is the limit, the end of all ' (Ka. 1, 3, 11). So it is this highest or the nirguṇa Brahman which was first distinguished from the lower or the saguṇa Brahman, but which was said to be along with the latter identical with Oṁ, is told afterwards as the object of both meditation and vision. ' That a man becomes free from sin, as a snake becomes free from slough ' (Pr. 5,5) shows us further that this freedom from sin must proceed as a result of meditation on the highest Ātman, and not from meditation on anything different from the highest Ātman. Then, again, the man who meditates on Oṁ as the saguṇa aspect of the Ātman need not be said to receive a small reward by way of his being lifted to Brahmaloka ; rather it is his first reward. For in course of time he may get the highest reward, viz. the clear vision of the Ātman and become free. In other words, he attains to mokṣa by degrees along with the lord of the Brahmaloka.

५ दहराधिकरणम् । (१४-२१)

दहर उत्तरेभ्यः । १४

[*Dahara–small; uttarebhyaḥ–due to what follows.*]

THE SMALL (PORTION OF ĀKĀŚA IN THE HEART IS THE HIGHEST ĀTMAN) ON ACCOUNT OF THE FOLLOWING (REASONS). 14

In a passage of the Chāndogyopaniṣad (8, 1) one is recommended to 'search and understand that small portion of ākāśa, which is inside the small lotus-like palace of the City of body (Brahmapura).' Now, inasmuch as the word ākāśa means both the elemental ākāśa and Brahman, we must settle in which of the two senses the word ' dahara ' is used. Similarly, the word ' Brahmapura ' which means the city of Brahma may mean either the city of the jīva or of the Brahman, and so may give rise to a further doubt as to whether the jīva or the Brahman is the lord of the city.

According to pūrvapakṣa, (1) the dahara or the small ākāśa means the elemental ākāśa (the bhūtākāśa); for that is the conventional meaning of the word ākāśa. No doubt, the bhūtākāśa is all-pervading, yet it is spoken of as small, because it is located in the heart. And though there is one ākāśa, it is conceived for the purpose of meditation as two, one inside and the other outside; and hence a comparison is possible between them and they are said to be equally large allowing 'heaven and earth to contain' in them (Chā 8, 1, 3). (2) Or the word 'dahara' may mean the individual soul, inasmuch as the word 'Brahma' means jīva in a subsidiary manner; and hence the word 'Brahmapura' would mean the city in the form of body of that jīva; and the jīva in its turn, would be known as the lord of the city of body, inasmuch as it has acquired it as a result of actions. It dwells in the heart, because it is the seat of mind; and it is spoken of as small because it is compared to the point of a goad (Śve. 5, 8). That it is compared with the all-pervading ākāśa only shows that it is not different from Brahman. (3) Or again, the 'dahara' may be an attribute of something else residing inside the small ākāśa which itself is inside the heart. But on no account can it be said that 'dahara' means Brahman, because Brahman is not connected with the body.

In reply to this we say that daharākāśa means nothing but the highest Ātman; for in what follows after the statement of dahara, a possible question regarding the nature of that which is to be searched and understood is anticipated on the part of the disciples, and the reply which the teacher ought to give is stated thus; 'the ākāśa within the heart is as large as the elemental ākāśa, and hence contains within it heaven and earth, fire and wind etc.' (Chā. 8, 1, 2-3). This means that the teacher's reply is intended to silence the possible doubt of his disciples who must have thought that the heart is small, that the ākāśa within it must be smaller still, and that, therefore, it may contain nothing which is to be searched and understood. In other words, the teacher first wishes to cancel the erroneous idea that the 'dahara' is small because the heart inside which it is located is small, by declaring that it is as large as the elemental ākāśa; and secondly, because he compares the inner with the outer ākāśa, it can be said that he wishes to cancel the equally erroneous idea that the dahara means the elemental ākāśa, and thereby suggest that the two are different entities. Comparison requires two things which have a real difference between them and which at the same time are similar. Ākāśa being one cannot be compared with itself; and even supposing that there is a difference between the inner and outer ākāśa, the two cannot be compared in point of extent. We may suppose an imaginary difference, only when there is no possibility of an actual difference which, however, is possible if by dahara we mean the highest Ātman. If some one would say on this account that the highest Ātman (supposing dahara to be the Ātman) too cannot be compared with the ākāśa, inasmuch as 'the Ātman is greater than ākāśa' (Śat. Brā. 10, 6, 3, 2), we have to reply that the intention of the comparison of the dahara with the elemental ākāśa is only to negative the smallness of the dahara, which is erroneously ascribed to it on account of its being enclosed by the lotus of the heart, and not to indicate its extent. Nor can it be said that the purpose of the comparison is twofold, viz. to negate the erroneous idea and to indicate the extent; for the science of Mīmāṁsa forbids us to have two meanings of one and the same sentence. Besides, if dahara means only a small portion of ākāśa enclosed by the lotus of the heart and is so conceived as to be different from the elemental ākāśa on account of the upādhi, it is impossible that it will contain within itself the heaven and the earth etc. And finally, the dahara cannot be the bhūtākāśa, because the qualities, which belong to the Ātman and are ascribed to the dahara, cannot belong to the non-intelligent bhūtākāśa. The dahara, which is, in the immediately following passage, referred to as the Ātman by the pronoun 'this,' is mentioned as free from sin, old age, death, grief, hunger, and thirst; it is mentioned again as one whose purposes and desires are the embodiment of truth (Chā. 8, 1, 5). The dahara then is the highest Ātman.

Dahara does not mean the individual soul also, though the word ātman may mean it. For, in the first place, being enclosed in the small lotus of the heart, and being exceedingly small like the point of a goad, how can it be compared with the elemental ākāśa which is all-pervading and is the support of heaven and earth etc.? If, to escape this difficulty, it be said that the individual soul is in reality not different from Brahman, and therefore it is that one may ascribe these attributes to it, the reply would be that they may be more appropriately attributed directly to the Brahman itself rather than to the individual soul. The daharākāśa then would connote the Brahman and not the jīva. Secondly, the word 'Brahmapura' need not mean the city in which the individual soul resides, but with reference to the word 'Brahma', it means the city of Brahman. In the Praśnopaniṣad we are told that the devotee 'beholds the transcendent Puruṣa as dwelling in the city of body' (5, 5); 'This Puruṣa dwells in the bodies of all' (Bṛ. 2, 5, 18). We learn from Śruti, then, that this body is not only the abode of Brahman but is useful for its realization. And even supposing that Brahmapura means the city of jīva, the Śruti passage intends to inform us primarily that Brahman resides in the body in close proximity with the devotee, just as the image of Viṣṇu is said to be available in the Śāligrāma stone. Add to this, in the third place, what is told in a further passage of the Chāndogyopaniṣad regarding the imperishable nature of the results which accrue from the knowledge of the daharākāśa, in contrast with the perishable nature of the results of works, and it becomes absolutely clear that the dahara means the highest Ātman and not the individual soul. 'Those who, after having realized the Ātman, which is the only imperishable object of desire, depart from this world, become free to move anywhere they like' (Chā. 8, 1, 6).

As regards the further point of the pūrvapakṣa that the object to be sought for and understood is not the daharākāśa but something else contained in it, we have to point out that the comparison of the outer with the inner ākāśa then will not serve any purpose. Instead of comparing the two ākāśas, the teacher might have, in that case, given some information regarding the contents of the daharākāśa. If the daharākāśa is told to be as large as the bhūtākāśa for the simple reason we should become aware that heaven and earth, etc. are held within it, which is inconceivable on the face of it, the remaining portion of the section which deals with the dahara would be entirely out of place. The words ' This ' and ' and ' which refer to the sinless Ātman and to persons who attain freedom by knowing the Ātman and the desires located in the Ātman, refer necessarily to the previously mentioned daharākāśa and the heaven and earth etc., contained in it. In other words, both the beginning and the end of the Śruti section intimate to us that the daharākāśa means the highest Ātman only.

गतिशब्दाभ्यां तथा हि दृष्टं लिंगं च। १५

[*Gati-sabdābhyāṁ–because of movement and word; tathā-hi–the same; dṛsṭaṁ–seen; lingaṁ–mark; ca–and.*]

(DAHARA IS BRAHMAN) BECAUSE MOVEMENT (TOWARDS IT) AND THE WORD (BRAHMALOKA USED AS SYNONYM FOR IT ARE AVAILABLE); THIS IS SEEN (ELSEWHERE) TOO; REASON FOR INFERENCE (TOO IS AVAILABLE). 15

In continuation of the context of dahara, we are told further that 'all the beings go unto Brahmaloka, everyday, but are not able to find him,' because they are attracted outside by untruth. (Chā. 8, 3, 2). It is clear that here the word ' beings ' is used for individual souls, and the word ' Brahmaloka ' for dahara. So, dahara means Brahman. In another place of the Chāndogyopaniṣad (6, 8, 1) we read that 'during sleep the jīva becomes one with the Truth.' In the light of the Śruti meaning, probably, we say of a man who has gone to sleep, that he is taking rest in Brahman. Some may like to dissolve the compound Brahmaloka as 'the loka of Brahma' and so mean thereby the world of the Brahmadeva. But instead of treating the compound as Ṣaṣṭhi-tatpuruṣa, if we take it as Karmadhāraya, we shall dissolve it as 'Brahman, the same as Brahmaloka.' And the reason for not accepting the first meaning is that it is absurd to believe that people go everyday to the world of Brahmadeva. Brahmaloka, therefore, which is put for dahara is nothing but Brahman. Dahara then is Brahman.

धृतेश्च महिम्नोऽस्यास्मिन्नुपलब्धेः । १६

[*Dhṛteḥ–because of support; ca–and; mahimnaḥ–because of greatness; asya–of this; asmin–in him; upalabhdeḥ–because it is found.*]

AND BECAUSE THE GREATNESS OF LENDING SUPPORT (ATTRIBUTED TO DAHARA) IS FOUND IN HIM (i. e. THE HIGHEST GOD, DAHARA MUST BE THE HIGHEST GOD). 16

The same daharākāśa which was first characterised as being inside the lotus of the heart, which was compared then with bhūtākāśa, and shown as the support of heaven and earth etc., and which was then declared as the Ātman and so being free from sins, is further said to be the support and the bank which prevents the worlds from coming to a chaos (Chā. 8, 4, 1). Just as a dam prevents the flood of water from carrying away the crops in the fields, even so, this Ātman prevents the various people who differ in castes, āśramas and mental equipment, from being mixed together and confused. It is this greatness of dahara which has been shown by Śruti as belonging to the highest God ; 'It is by the command of this Akṣara, O Gārgī, that the Sun and the moon are held up (Bṛ. 3, 8, 9) ; 'He is the highest God, the Lord and the protector of all beings, the support and the dam to prevent the people from falling into confusion' (Br. 4, 4, 22). Dahara, therefore, is the highest God.

प्रसिद्धेश्च । १७

[*Prasiddheḥ–being well-known; ca–and*].

AND BECAUSE (ĀKĀŚA) IS KNOWN TO MEAN (BRAHMAN, DAHARA IS BRAHMAN). 17

Śruti passages like 'Ākāśa alone manifests the names and forms' (Chā. 8, 14), 'all these beings spring forth from ākāśa' (Chā. 1, 9, 1), show that the word ākāśa means Brahman. It will lead to no meaning if we take ākāśa in the sense of bhūtākāśa; for we have already seen that ākāśa cannot be compared with itself.

इतरपरामर्शात्स इति चेन्नासंभवात् । १८

[*Itara–other; parāmarśāt–owing to reference; saḥ–he; iti–thus cet–if; na–not; asaṁbhavāt–being impossible.*]

IF IT BE SAID THAT IT (i. e. THE INDIVIDUAL SOUL IS MEANT) ON ACCOUNT OF THE REFERENCE TO THE OTHER ONE, (WE SAY) NO; FOR IT IS IMPOSSIBLE (THAT DAHARA MAY BE THE JĪVA). 18

If dahara means the highest God on account of a reference to the latter in a passage subsequent to the one in which dahara is discussed, then the word dahara may mean the individual soul also, on account of a similar reason. The pūrvapakṣin may say so, and bring forth the evidence thus: 'It is this 'Saṁprasāda' which after having risen from this body meets the highest Light and appears in one's own form, that is known as the Ātman (Chā. 8, 3, 4). Now the word 'Saṁprasāda', which usually conveys the meaning of deep sleep according to other Śruti passages, must convey the same meaning in this passage also, and so refer to the individual soul who alone is said to be qualified by deep sleep. And just as wind and other elements are said to arise from ākāśa which is their support, even so the individual soul rises up from this body; and just as the word ākāśa means the highest God (as shown by the Vedāntin in the previous Sūtra) even though it is not ordinarily done so, because the word is used along with the qualities of God, even so, the word dahara may denote the individual soul, because the qualities of 'Saṁprasāda' etc. (as shown above) refer to it only.

We say in reply that this is not possible. For, in the first place, the individual soul which falsely thinks itself to be limited by the adjuncts of buddhi etc. cannot be compared with the unlimited ākāśa. And secondly, qualities such as freedom of sin etc. cannot belong to a being which erroneously thinks itself bound by upādhis. This has already been explained, in the first Sūtra of this adhikaraṇa (1, 3, 14), but we mention it again only to remove the additional doubt of the soul being thought of as different from the Ātman. That the so-called reference to the individual soul is, as a matter of fact, a reference to the Brahman will be shown in Sūtra 1, 3, 20.

उत्तराच्चेदाविर्भूतस्वरूपस्तु । १९

⟦*Uttarāt–due to what is subsequent; cet–if; āvirbhūta–become manifest; svarūpaḥ–one's own nature; tu–however*⟧.

IF IT BE SAID (THAT DAHARA IS JĪVA) ON ACCOUNT OF SUBSEQUENT (STATEMENTS, WE SAY THAT IT IS) HOWEVER, (ONLY THAT JĪVA) WHOSE REAL NATURE HAS BECOME MANIFEST. 19

The aim of the preceding Sūtra was to show that dahara cannot be the jīva inasmuch as qualities such as freedom from sin etc. which are spoken of as belonging to dahara, and which are found only in the highest Ātman, are not found to belong to the jīva. And yet the argument of the pūrvapakṣa may be revived, and presented in a new form, in view of the dialogue which comes after dahara-vidyā, between Indra and Virocana on the one hand, and Prajāpati on the other. The utterance of Prajāpati at the outset (Chā. 8, 7, 1) is dealt with reference to the Ātman who is free from sin, old age, death, hunger, thirst, mourning etc.; and it is this Ātman, says Prajāpati, who must be sought for and realized. And yet, again and over again, promising that he would explain the nature of the Ātman, he points to the existence of the individual soul only. For instance, he first tells Indra and Virocana that the person seen in the eye is the Ātman, thereby indicating that it is nothing but the individual soul in the wakeful condition (8, 7, 4). He again refers to the same individual soul in its dreaming and sleeping conditions by pointing out to Indra its joyful wanderings and perfect repose (8, 10,1, and 8,11, 1). And yet he says that the individual soul is the immortal, fearless Brahman. Further when Indra complains that the sleeping soul recognises neither itself nor anything else, Prajāpati once again promises to instruct him in the true nature of the Ātman and nothing else. But once again, censuring the body he exhibits the jīva alone as the 'excellent Puruṣa,' inasmuch as it is the jīva, as he says, which rises in the form of 'Saṁprasāda' from the body, meets the highest Light and appears in its own form (8, 11, 3 and 8, 12, 3). From this it appears that the qualities of the highest God are possible in the individual soul; and so one may say that the daharākāśa within the heart means the individual soul.

We say in reply that what Prajāpati means to convey is not that individual soul which, as the pūrvapakṣin has understood, is qualified by the three states of wakeful, dreaming and sleeping consciousness, but that individual soul which has manifested in its real nature, or its own form, after rising beyond the consciousness of body and after coming in contact with the highest Light, viz. the Brahman, which is free from sin etc. The individual soul referred to in this Sūtra (and in the preceding Sūtra as against the pūrvapakṣin) is nothing but the highest Brahman, the nature of which is eternal, unchanging consciousness or pure intelligence and is expressed by such propositions as 'I am Brahman,' and 'That art thou.' It is not the false individual, the aggregate of body, sense and mind, the notion of which arises on account of avidyā, and which therefore can be compared to the wrong notion arising out of illusion. The person who has 'known the Brahman and has therefore 'become the Brahman' as the Muṇḍakopaniṣad says (3, 2, 9), is the only type of the individual soul as meant by Prajāpati.

One may raise an objection here. If the individual soul in its original real status is Brahman itself, what then is meant by saying that it gets its own real nature? It cannot be said that its real nature is concealed, so that it should be revealed afterwards ; for what can there be which will outshine the eternal light of the consciousness of the Ātman ? Then, again, like ākāśa the Ātman remains ever unaffected by anything. It cannot be compared with gold which shines in its true lustre after it has been separated from dross by means of acid; nor with the stars, which though self-effulgent become invisible on account of the outshining light of the sun, but again re-appear in their own glory by night. The individual soul is, in its nature, endowed with the activities of seeing, hearing, thinking etc., and it is not necessary that it should rise beyond the body in order to exhibit this nature. The whole practical life will be impossible without these activities of the soul, and without its connection with the body. What then is meant by the so-called rising of the soul beyond the body ? And what is meant by the appearing of the soul in its own form?

We meet the questions by saying that just as a piece of crystal which is white and transparent is not discerned to be separate from the upādhi of the red or blue colour, even so the individual soul which is in reality pure consciousness or light appears to be of the nature of the upādhis of body, sense and mind, and so to be endowed with the activities of hearing, seeing etc., on account of absence of discrimination. But the moment the discriminative knowledge arises, the crystal which was already white and transparent appears so, as if for the first time; even so, the rising of the individual soul beyond the body is nothing but the dawning of the discriminative knowledge on the part of the soul, whereby it does not understand itself any more as made up of body, sense, mind etc., but understands itself as the pure Ātmaṇ. As a result of this knowledge, the individual soul appears, so to say, in its original form of the Ātman.

From this it follows that the embodied or the disembodied condition of the soul is the result of the absence or presence of discriminative knowledge. To have or not to have the body is irrelevant from the view-point of the Ātman. For as the Bhagawadgītā declares (13, 31), ' The Ātman is not affected by anything, even though it resides in the body '. ' It has no body, though it dwells within the bodies ' (Ka. 1, 2, 22). Notwithstanding the possession of body, the soul is without the body, only if it has the knowledge that it is one with the Brahman and has nothing to do with the upādhis. It manifests in its real, original nature of the Ātman if it possesses this knowledge; it remains as an individual soul, different from Ātman and bound up with the upādhis, if it has no such knowledge. And though due to ignorance, the individual soul and the highest God appear as separate and two, from the view-point of the highest God, they are identically the same. Whether manifest or unmanifest, there is only one Ātman; the distinction between the jīva and the Ātman as two is false.

All this becomes clear from what Prajāpati has told Indra and Virocana. Having first referred to the jīva as the person in the eye, Prajāpati characterises it as the fearless, immortal Brahman, meaning thereby that the two are not different. That Prajāpati has refrained from saying that the reflection in the eye is the symbol of Brahman only speaks about his honesty of purpose. And so, when he goes on to describe as to what happens in the dreaming condition, he refers to the same person in the eye, as is clear from the assurance he gives to Indra that he would explain the nature of the self-same jīva further. And this need not be doubted because, it is a common experience that a man who does not claim to see in waking life the elephant he saw in the dream, claims, however, that he is the same person who continues to exist in the two states. Therefore what Prajāpati means is that the person in the dream, being the same person in the eye, cannot be different from Brahman. Again, when he passes on to the description of the sleeping condition, the 'destruction' he speaks of is the destruction of specific knowledge of a thing during sleep and not of the knower or the Self. As Śruti says, 'There is no destruction of the Knower's capacity to know' (Bṛ. 4, 3, 30). And finally, when Prajāpati repeats the assurance that he would explain the nature of the same being, and censuring the body as mortal, describes the 'Saṁprasāda' as rising beyond the body and appearing in its own form when it approaches the highest Light, he refers to the self-same jīva of the earlier stages as being always in essence identical with the highest Brahman.

Some people are of opinion that instead of taking the individual soul as the topic of what Prajāpati had said on the first three occasions, and the highest Ātman as the topic of what he said on the fourth occasion, it would be appropriate to consider that the highest Ātman alone which is spoken of as free from sin etc. is the topic of the whole of his speech from the first to the end of fourth occasion. But this is incorrect. For, in the first place, the pronoun 'this' in the sentence which Prajāpati spoke, *viz.*, 'This I shall explain to you again', refers to the proximate substantive *viz.* the jīva. Secondly, the word 'again' refers back to the topic once discussed, and does not indicate a new topic each time. Had Prajāpati done so he would have been accused of practising deceit. Hence what we hold stands correct, *viz.* that the topic of the speech of Prajāpati is the individual soul. The only thing to note is that the individual soul is gradually being shown as nothing but the highest Ātman. Just as the knowledge of the rope destroys the serpent which appears on it through ignorance, even so, the illusory nature of the individual soul, so far as it is erroneously understood to be separate and distinct from the highest God, and on account of which various evils and distinctions of desires, doers etc. arise, vanishes the moment there arises the true knowledge. The so-called individual soul then is nothing but the highest God, who possesses the qualities of sinlessness and others.

In the opinion of some others still, (Mīmāṁsakas as well as Vedāntins of a different school), the individual soul is a real entity by itself. In order to silence such people by expounding unto them the unity of the Ātman, the Sūtrakāra has begun this Śārīraka-śāstra. It aims at teaching that there is one eternal unchanging highest God; there is none else except him who is knowledge incarnate (Bṛ. 3, 7, 23); and yet, like a magician, he appears in diverse forms on account avidyā or māyā. Śruti may hold this view; but what about the Sūtrakāra, one may ask, who has suggested the existence of difference between the individual soul and the Brahman, when, e. g. he says that daharākāśa is not jīva, but the highest Ātman (Sūtras: 1, 3, 18; 1, 1, 16) ? The Sūtrākāṛa, we reply, makes this difference only because he has to disprove the erroneous doctrine of duality. He believes that the highest Ātman is one, eternal, pure, intelligent, free, unchanging, formless and unaffected by anything; and yet he finds that opposite characteristics of the individual soul are erroneously ascribed to it, just as blue colour is ascribed to the colourless ākāśa. It is to refute the current dualism of the practical world that the Sūtrakāra makes use of such arguments and of Śruti sentences such as 'That thou art', 'there is nothing else but the Ātman'. And though he makes the difference of the highest Ātman from the individual soul, he does not make the difference of the individual soul from the

Ātman. The Ātman as the support is certainly different from the things imagined to be existing; but the imagined things cannot exist apart from the support, on account of which, they are imagined. The rope exists by itself and is different from the serpent. The serpent, however, which is imaginary cannot exist apart from the rope. The difference, then, which the Sūtrakāra allows between the highest Ātman and the jīva (and not vice versa) is only with the view of making people aware that the whole of Karma-kāṇḍa with its prohibitions and injunctions implies a dualism which is purely imagined and non-existent, and therefore does not affect the Vedānta position that there is one Ātman alone. The Sūtrakāra has already referred to this unity of the Ātman in Sūtra 1, 1, 30, and to the difference in spheres of Karma-kāṇḍa and jñāna-kāṇḍa in Sūtra 1, 1, 4. Performance of sacrifice may be said to affect the soul, so long as the consciousness of body etc. exists; but the same learned man, if he comes to know that the Ātman is not at all affected by action, may, without performing a sacrifice, remain content with the knowledge of the Ātman.

अन्यार्थश्च परामर्शः। २०

[*Anya (other)-arthaḥ-(meaning); ca-and; parāmarśaḥ-reference.*]

AND THE REFERENCE (TO THE INDIVIDUAL SOUL) IS INTENDED TO MEAN OTHER (VIZ. THE ĀTMAN 4). 20

Having pointed out that the purpose of the Prajāpati passages is not to describe the nature of the individual soul, but to prove that the individual soul is nothing but the Brahman, the Sūtrakāra points out now that in the subsequent sentence to the 'daharākāśa' too, the reference to the individual soul is intended to mean the Brahman. The individual soul, which is described by the word 'Saṁprasāda' becomes tired with the activities during the waking and the dreaming conditions of life, and so being desirous of taking rest goes beyond the consciousness of the gross and subtle bodies, during deep sleep; it then reaches the highest Light or Brahman, and so appears in its own real nature. Here too, the reference to the individual soul is for the purpose of making us aware of its real nature, which is manifested by reaching the highest Light and reappearing through it in its own form as the very sinless Brahman.

अल्पश्रुतेरिति चेत्तदुक्तम् । २१

[*Alpa (small)-Śruteḥ–being mentioned by Śruti; iti–thus; cet–if; tat–that; uktaṁ–said.*]

IF IT BE SAID THAT (ĀKĀŚA CANNOT MEAN THE HIGHEST ĀTMAN) ON ACCOUNT OF ITS BEING MENTIONED BY ŚRUTI AS SMALL, (WE REPLY THAT) IT HAS BEEN ALREADY CONSIDERED. 21

The argument of the pūrvapakṣin that the highest God cannot be meant by dahara, because of his all-pervasive character, but that it may mean the individual soul because of its comparison with the point of the goad, has already been met with while dealing with the Sūtra, 1, 2, 7. It was shown there that God, though all-pervading, is capable of being meditated even in the small heart. Besides, Śruti itself has contradicted the smallness, by saying that the internal ākāśa is as large as the external one. So the dahara means the Brahman.

६ अनुकृत्यधिकरणम् । (२२-२३)

अनुकृतेस्तस्य च । २२

[*Anukṛteḥ–Because of action after; tasya–his; ca–and.*]

ON ACCOUNT OF (EVERYTHING) ACTING (I. E. SHINING) AFTER (HIM), AND OF (THE WORD) 'HIS', (BRAHMAN IS THE SOURCE OF THE LIGHT OF ALL). 22

The Muṇḍaka and the Kāthaka Upaniṣads give us the verse: 'The sun does not shine there, not do the moon and the stars and the lightnings, much less the fire. After he shines, everything else shines; all this is lighted by his light' (Mu. 2, 2, 10; Ka. 2, 3, 15). The doubt that arises here is whether that being, which when shining everything else shines, is some luminous entity or the Prājña Ātman.

According to pūrvapakṣa it must be some luminous substance other than the sun, moon etc. For, firstly, it cannot be anyone of the latter, since it is said in the above mentioned verse itself that these do not shine 'there'. Secondly, just as the moon and the stars do not shine when the sun is shining, even so there must be something else which when shining, the sun too does not shine. And thirdly, the words 'shining after' indicate that imitation is possible only when there is some-body else whom to imitate. One can imitate walking when another walks. Therefore, there must be some luminous body other than the sun, moon etc. referred to in the passage.

To this we reply that it must be the Prājña Ātman; for as the Śruti says, 'Light is his nature; and his thoughts are true' (Chā. 3, 14, 2). On the other hand, experience does not show that the sun, the moon, etc. shine after some other luminous body. Besides, luminosity being the common nature of all, there is no need that one should shine first and the rest should shine afterwards. One lamp need not shine after another lamp. It is not a rule, again, that imitation should depend upon similarity of things. Iron is different from fire, dust is different from wind and yet a red-hot iron ball burns things like the fire; the dust on the ground blows after the blowing wind. The word 'his' (tasya) in the fourth part of the verse, makes us aware that the Prājña Ātman is the cause of the light of the sun and the moon etc. As the Śruti says, 'the gods worship Him as the light of lights, as the immortal Being' (Bṛ. 4, 4, 16). This obviously does not refer to the physical light of the sun, the moon, etc.; nor, as said above, does experience show that these physical lights are there on account of some other physical light. As a matter of fact, on the other hand, one physical light is surpassed by another physical light.

Or we may not restrict the meaning of the verse as referring to the cause of the light and the shining of the heavenly bodies, but understand it as referring to the cause of 'all this' (Sarvaṁ idaṁ) world which consists of names and forms, and of persons and their actions and fruits thereof. Just as the sun's light is the cause of the manifestation of colour, even so the light of Brahman is the cause of this all, including the light of the sun etc. Besides, the word 'there' in the verse shows us the context on account of which also we take the Brahman as the source of all. The word 'there' is used by way of a reply to the question, 'How is Brahman the light of lights'? which arises in view of an earlier verse in the Upaniṣad (Mu. 2, 2, 9) : 'In that transcendent golden sheath, there is that passionless and partless Brahman ; it is the stainless light of lights, and is known by those who have realized the Ātman.' That Brahman is the topic under discussion is shown by an earlier verse still (Mu. 2, 2, 5) where it is mentioned as that, 'in whom the heaven the earth and the intervening space are woven.'

So Brahman being the only self-luminous entity beyond the sun, and the moon etc., every thing that exists and shines does so on account of the light of Brahman. It manifests everything, but is not manifested or perceived by any other light. For, 'The Ātman is incomprehensible'; 'It is by the light of the Ātman, that a man sits, and goes etc.' (Bṛ. 4, 2, 4 ; 4, 3, 6).

अपि च स्मर्यते । २३

⟦*Api–also; ca–and; smaryate–is told in smṛti.*⟧

AND SMṚTI TOO SPEAKS (OF HIM IN THE SAME WAY). 23

We read in the Bhagavadgītā, 'That is my highest abode, reaching which none returns; neither the sun, nor the moon nor the fire illumines that.' And yet, 'that light of the sun which shines all over the world, and that light which is in the moon, and in the fire, know that all to be mine' (15, 6 and 12).

७ प्रमिताधिकरणम् । (२४-२५)

शब्दादेव प्रमितः । २४

[*Śabdāt–due to Śruti; eva–only; pramitaḥ–is measured.*]

THE (PERSON) MEASURED (BY A THUMB, IS THE HIGHEST ĀTMAN) ON ACCOUNT OF ŚRUTI-WORD ITSELF (VIZ. THE ĀTMAN IS THE CONTROLLER). 24

The Kaṭhopaniṣad tells us that 'the person of the size of a thumb stands in the middle of the body, and is like smokeless light. He is the controller of the present and the future; he is eternal the same, today and tomorrow. This is that (Brahman)' (2, 4, 12, 13).

According to pūrvapakṣa, the person referred to is the individual soul; for no measure can be predicated of the Ātman who has infinite length and breadth. But the Vijñānātman or the jīva being limited by Upādhis can be spoken of as somehow being measured by a thumb. In the Smṛti too, Yama is told to have dragged out forcibly by his noose the thumb-sized, helpless person out of the body of Satyavān (M. B. 3, 297, 17). It is impossible for Yama to have taken out the Ātman, as Yama himself admits that Viṣṇu is his controller. So, the Smṛti, too, is in favour of taking the thumb-sized person in the sense of 'saṁsāri-jīva.'

The person must be the Ātman alone, we say in reply. For there is none else who can ceaselessly control the present and the future. Besides, the words 'this is that' in the end of the passage, come as a reply to

Naciketa's question as to what it may be 'which is neither this nor that which is seen, which is neither the effect nor the cause, and which is neither the past, nor future' (1, 2, 14). This means that Brahman was the topic under discussion ; and so the word 'controller' as used in the Śruti itself is a far greater evidence than the words 'thumb-sized person' to indicate that the person is the highest God and not the individual soul.

How then can the all-pervading Ātman be spoken to have the small dimensions? To this the Sūtrakāra replies :

हृद्यपेक्षया तु मनुष्याधिकारत्वात् । २५

[*Ṛhdi–in the heart; apekṣayā–with reference to; tu–however manuṣya–man; adhikāratvāt–having a right.*]

WITH REFERENCE TO THE HEART, HOWEVER, (THE ĀTMAN IS SAID TO BE OF THE SIZE OF A THUMB) ; FOR MEN HAVE A RIGHT (TO STUDY THE VEDAS). 25

We have seen above that though the size of a thumb can more appropriately belong to the finite jīva and not to the infinite Brahman, yet the word 'controller' as used by Śruti is indicative of Brahman and not of jīva. Therefore, the small dimensions of a thumb can be said to belong to Brahman in a secondary way, with reference to its lodgment in the heart, just as the ākāśa is spoken of as having the measure of a cubit with reference to a portion of a bamboo stick. The hearts of different animals may be varying in dimensions, but by 'heart,' here, we mean the heart of man; for men alone have a right to the study of the Vedas. They alone have got the capacity to learn, have certain desires, and are not prohibited to learn. The upanayana ceremony can be performed only amongst men. As Jaimini has examined the question as to who has got a right, (Pūrva Mī. Sū. 6, 1), we need not say anything further. The heart then of a man has the size of his thumb.

In view of such statements, then, as 'That is the Brahman' 'That thou art' etc., we have to understand that the jīva or the saṁsāri soul which is of the size of a thumb is in reality the Brahman. The aim of the passage under discussion is not to describe the dimension of any thing in particular, but to bring home the identity of the jīva with the Brahman, by reference to the abode of the latter in the heart. A Vedānta-passage of this type has therefore a different aim from another whose aim is to make us aware of the Nirguṇa Brahman directly; this makes us aware of it by reference to individual soul which is nothing but Brahman in reality. That is why Śruti recommends one 'to draw out with courage that Person from inside his body as one would take out the delicate fibre from inside the blade of grass, and to know it as the pure immortal thumb-sized Ātman residing in the heart of people' (Ka. 2, 6, 17).

८ देवताधिकरम्। (२६–३३)

तदुपर्यपि बादरायणः संभवात्। २६

(GODS) ABOVE THEM (I. E. MEN) ALSO (HAVE A RIGHT TO STUDY THE VEDAS) AS BĀDARĀYAṆA HOLDS, ON ACCOUNT OF POSSIBILITY OF (SIMILAR REASONS). 26

Gods too, as Bādarāyaṇa holds, have a right to the knowledge of Brahman, for they too may become disgusted with indulgence in sensual pleasures, and may hanker after mokṣa. They are known to be endowed with bodies, from the descriptions we read about them in Itihāsa, Purāṇas, mantras, and arthavāda, and from paintings and images in ordinary experience.[1] They are not prohibited like Śūdras from having the knowledge. Vedas being manifest to them, no upanayana-ceremony is needed in their case. They accept discipleship; e.g., Indra lived as a disciple of Prajāpati for one hundred and one years (Chā. 8, 11, 3); Bhṛgu approached his father Varuṇa with the request

1 Indra is described to have the Vajra (thunderbolt) in his hand.

to teach him the knowledge of Brahman (Tai 3, 1). Gods and sages may be incapable of action such as a sacrifice, as Jaimini holds (Pūrva Mī. Sū. 6, 1, 5), because either there are no further gods whom they should please, or there are no other sages to whose family they may belong. But so far as knowledge of Brahman is concerned, no action is to be performed either with reference to any god or by the help of any sage. So far as the size of the Person is concerned, it may be measured by the thumb of a god, just as in the case of men, it is to be measured by the thumb of a man.

विरोधः कर्मणीति चेन्नानेकप्रतिपत्तेर्दर्शनात् । २७

[*Virodhaḥ—obstruction* ; *Karmaṇi—in action* ; *iti—so* ; *cet—if* ; *na—not* ; *aneka—various* ; *pratipatteḥ—due to assumption* ; *darśanāt—being observed.*]

IF IT BE SAID THAT (POSSESSION OF BODIES BY GODS WOULD CREATE) OBSTRUCTION TO (SACRIFICIAL) ACTIVITY, WE SAY THAT IT IS NOT SO; FOR IT IS OBSERVED THAT (GODS) ASSUME VARIOUS (FORMS). 27

If gods have bodies, it is conceivable that they should be present like priests on the occasion of a sacrifice. But how will it be possible for the god Indra, for example, to remain present at many sacrifices, if they are performed at the same time ?

The reply to this is contained in a passage from the Bṛhadāraṇyakopaniṣad (3, 9, 1, 2), which beginning with the number of gods as 303, and again as 3003 declares a little afterwards that these are nothing but the powers of gods, who, however, number thirty-three[2] only. These thirty-three gods are again reduced to six, then to five and finally to one God viz. the Prāṇa. This means that

2 The 33 gods are : 8 Vasus, 11 rudras, 12 ādityas, Indra and Brahmadeva. The six gods are : Fire, earth, wind, ākāśa, sun and svarga. If the first and the second, the third and the fourth, etc., are combined, they make three only. These three again are reduced to two *viz.*, food and prāna; and finally prāna alone is the one god.

it is the one God of Prāṇa who assumes various forms. In the Smṛti also, it is mentioned that the yogin, who acquires supernatural powers like possession of subtle body etc., can divide himself in thousand forms, and can have various experiences in life, such as enjoyment, penance etc. at one and the same time, and can collect back all these forms into himself, just as the sun takes back all his rays within himself (Ma. Bhā. 12, 110, 62). If this is possible for a man, how much more it should be in the case of a god who has naturally got all these powers? So, a god may divide himself in many forms and remain present at various sacrifices at one and the same time, himself remaining unseen.

Or we may offer another explanation. Just as a Brāhmaṇa who cannot be fed by different people at the same time, can nevertheless be bowed by them all simultaneously, even so, one God can, without leaving his place, be the common object of reverence of several persons who may, at the same time, give their offerings to him. The embodiedness of gods then is in no way a hinderance to the sacrificial activity.

शब्द इति चेन्नातः प्रभवात्प्रत्यक्षानुमानाभ्याम् । २८

[*Śabda—word; iti—that; cet—if; na—not; ataḥ—from this; prabhavāt—because it originates; pratyakṣa—anumānābhyāṁ—from perception and inference.*]

IF IT BE SAID THAT THE (VEDIC) WORD (WILL BE CONTRADICTED OWING TO THE SUPPOSITION THAT GODS HAVE BODIES) WE REPLY THAT IT IS NOT SO, BECAUSE PERCEPTION AND INFERENCE SHOW THAT EVERYTHING ORIGINATES FROM THE WORD. 28

Even though there may be no hindrance to sacrificial activity, the supposition that gods have bodies may be pointed out as being inconsistent with the position of 'word' in the Vedas. According to the 'Autpattika

Sūtra' of Pūrva Mīmāṁsā (1, 1, 5) the Vedas are considered to have self-validity ; for the words which constitute the Vedas are said to be eternally related with their meanings. Names of gods such as, Vasus, Rudras, Ādityas etc. being words in the Vedas, they too must therefore be supposed to be eternal. But if gods possess bodies, they become subject to birth and death just as men are. That is, the names of gods being connected with transitory meanings will themselves be untrustworthy. In other words, the Vedas will lose their self-validity, and shall have to depend on something else for being authoritative. Even if we reply that the whole world, along with the gods springs forth from 'word' it may be pointed out that, in the first place, as against our present position, Brahman was once said to be the origin of the world (B. S. 1, 1, 2) ; and that secondly, as is seen in common experience, the word or name comes into existence after the thing which is given that name. A child is born first, and then the name Yajñadatta is given to him. And just as the things are transitory even so the words or names denoting them will not only be not self-valid but non-eternal too.

The objection cannot stand. For there would arise from Substance, Quality and Action, individuals only and not species. The jāti or the species is eternal, and the words are connected with the species and not with individual objects, which may be infinite in number and transitory in nature. Words like 'Vasu,' 'Āditya' etc. are names of eternal species, and not of transitory objects. Besides, the words connote some permanent meanings on account of the presence of which they may be extended to new individual objects. Whoever leads the army is the 'army-leader.' The name will be applied to the individual object, if it presents the jāti or holds the permanent meaning ; and it is in this sense that the individuals are said to originate from the words, and not in the sense that the word is, like Brahman, the material cause of the universe.

The evidence, however, for believing that the universe arises on account of the efficient cause of the word lies in perception and inference. By 'perception' we mean Śruti, for the validity of perception is not dependent on anything else ; and by 'inference' we mean Smṛti ; for though inference is based on an invasiable sign, yet so far as the origin of the universe is concerned, inference or Smṛti must be backed by perception or Śruti. The Ṛgveda describes (9,62) how the god Brahmadeva produced the different deities, because the word 'ete.' (these) reminded him of the deities who preside over and do good to the various senses, how he produced men on account of the word 'asṛg' (blood), and how he produced the manes, the planets, the hymns, the weapons and the beings from the words 'Indu' (moon), 'tiraḥpavitra' (Concealer of holy things) 'āśu' (which includes), 'Viśva' (which enters) and 'abhisaubhaga' (beneficial) respectively. The Bṛhadāraṇyaka mentions him as having thought over the union of mind and speech (1, 2, 4) ; meaning thereby that thinking is impossible without word. The Śāntiparva (M. B. S. P. 233, 24) too mentions the 'Self-born Being as having first produced the eternal, celestial Vedic word which again, in its turn, produced all activities.' What is meant by production of this beginningless and endless Vedic speech is that it is being imparted orally from the teacher to the disciple So it is 'the Vedic words through which Maheśvara has produced the names and forms of all beings, and has set forth activity' (M. B ; Śantiparva 233, 25 ; and Manu Sm. 1, 21). As in common experience we find that a jar is made after conceiving the meaning of the word jar ; even so, there occurred in the mind of the Creator first the Vedic words and then corresponding to them, he created the universe. He created the earth, for instance, after uttering and knowing the meaning of the word 'bhūr', the heaven after the 'bhuvaḥ' (Tai Brā. 2, 2, 4 2).

1 Blood is essential to men; the manes remain in the moon; the planets drank the holy soma and hid it in their bosom; the hymns include ṛcās (sentences); weapons are ṛcās which enter into a sacrifice; creatures are benefited

What then must be the nature of the word, and how may it be said to cause the universe? According to grammarians, it is the 'sphota' which first arises in the mind after a word is uttered, and it is on account of this that the sense of the word becomes known. To them, the sphota which is different from the letters is the eternal entity; the word made up of letters is not eternal, for as soon as the letters are uttered, they perish. Gods etc. cannot arise from the perishable words, but from the imperishable sphota. That the letters are perishable can be seen from the fact that on different occasions they are perceived in different ways. The voice of Devadatta sounds differently from the voice of Yajñadatta; the letters uttered by one person vanish, though similar letters are uttered by another afterwards. As for the meaning of the word, we get it from the sphota and not from the letters of the word. For, (1) if every letter is to give us a meaning, the letters 'go' in गो and gotra ought to give us the same meaning; and if we have it, then the letters which follow would be useless. (2) Nor can all the letters taken together be said to produce one meaning, for the letters come one after another. (3) Nor again can it be said that the perception of the last letter combines with the mental impressions of the previous letters and produces the sense; for in order to understand the meaning of a word, it is necessary to become aware of the connection between them, just as we understand first the smoke that exists, and then from the knowledge of the connection which the smoke has with fire, know the meaning of fire too. But the impressions on the mind are incapable of being perceived, and as such, except the last letter of the word, there will be no perceptual knowledge of the word. (4) Though not perceivable, the impressions can still be inferred, one may say, from the fact of their being remembered; and so it may be maintained that the meaning of the word becomes manifest on account of inference when the impressions become combined with the last letter. But this too is impossible. For the remembering of the successive letters is not itself a single event which happens in one moment of time; but, on the contrary it is made up of different events of remembering the successive different impressions of letters. As such, the inferred impressions too cannot simultaneously be combined with the last letter and produce the meaning of the word.

The word then is of the nature of sphoṭa; and the manner in which it presents itself to buddhi is this. The several letters sow, as it were, the seed of impressions in the mind, and when with the combination of perception of the last letter, it becomes mature, there appears all of a sudden the sphota in the form of one single mental apprehension, which however, is not the remembering of the several succeeding letters. The difference that appears between two or more voices of men is due to the letters of the word, and not to sphoṭa which is recognised as eternally the same. It is sphoṭa therefore, and not letters, which manifest the meanings of the word and it is sphoṭa, therefore, which can be considered as the cause of this world, consisting of actions and the doers and results of actions.

As against this view of the grammarians, Upavarṣa holds that the word is made up of letters only, inasmuch as there is no separate perception of the sphoṭa over and above the perception of the letters. The letters too are not short-lived, because they are recognised to be the same, and because this fact of recognition is neither based on similarity, as in the case of hairs, nor contradicted by any other means of knowledge. Again it is not the recognition of the species or jāti of a letter, so that we may say that we hear a letter similar to the one heard before, both of which belong to a class. On the contrary, we hear the same letter as being uttered more than once. The word 'cow', when uttered twice, can never mean that two different words belonging to the same class are uttered. The letters are not different individuals that go to form a class, just as there are different individual cows which belong to one class. The letters c, o, and w, are each one of them the same on different occasions. That they appear to be different on account of pronounciation of different men is not thus due to their own inherent nature, but to the fact that they are dependent for the sake of pronounciation on the contact or otherwise of the wind with the palate, teeth etc. The grammarians too who maintain that letters are different individually have to admit, for the sake of explaining the fact of their being recognized as similar, the existence of a species or jāti to which they belong ; they have to admit again that the differences, such as 'udātta' and 'anudātta' in the manner of uttering them, are due to external conditions such as contact etc. Instead of making these two admissions, is it not a simpler way of explanation that the individual letters have their own intrinsic nature on account of which they are recognized as the same, and that they appear to be different in point of being 'udātta' 'anudātta' etc. by external conditions ?

Recognition of a letter as the same is thus the refutation of its being conceived as being different on different occasions. And yet, the same 'ga' when pronounced by different persons at the same time, appears to be different as udātta, anūdatta, svarita, nasal and non-nasal, because the expression of it is connected with the contact of the abdominal wind with the various parts of the mouth, such as palate, teeth etc. Or else, the difference may be attributed to the difference in dhvani or tone. A sound, which is indistinct because it is far off, becomes clear and distinct as it comes nearer. Though recognized as the same, it is differentiated as 'soft' or 'harsh.' So the better way of explaining would be that the distinctions of udātta, anudātta etc. are due to dhvani rather than to the process of conjunction and disjunction, which is not a matter of perception. In any case, the letters are recognized as the same in spite of their appearing different on account of difference in dhvani.

Besides being recognized as the same, it is the letters which have got the meaning of the word, and so there is no necessity to imagine the existence of sphoṭa. The object of cognition is not sphoṭa, an additional something which is suddenly perceived after the accumulation of the successive impressions of the letters as the grammarian supposes ; it is the letters themselves which constitute the word. For if sphoṭa, which is something different from the letters of a word were to be the object of cognition, then the meaning of these letters or word like the meaning of any other word or group of letters would not be apprehended at all. But this is against experience. So what appears to the grammarian as the sphoṭa is in reality nothing but an act of remembrance of the letters of the word. Besides, experience tells us that we may have one single cognition of a number of objects grouped together ; e.g. we speak of numbers as ten, hundred, thousand etc. Similarly, the many letters in a word go to express one meaning only. This does not however mean that the letters in a word if written in the reverse order would mean identically the same. For then the word 'rājā' (king) would mean the same thing as the word 'jārā' (a profligate); or the word 'pika' (cuckoo) would mean the same thing as 'kapi' (monkey). The letters though many, will have one meaning only when they succeed some fixed order.

The theory then that the letters of a word which succeed each other in a certain order give all the meaning they have directly to the buddhi in one single act of cognition is simpler than the sphoṭa theory which disregards that which is given in perception directly, viz. the letters, and something new which is never perceived, viz. the sphoṭa. It is unnecessary to imagine the additional factor of sphoṭa to explain the manifestation of meaning from the letters of the word. Anyway, whether the word is of the nature of letters, jāti or sphoṭa the theory that the gods originate from the eternal words remains unaffected.

अत एव च नित्यत्वम् । २९

[*Ataḥ—Hence ; eva—same ; ca—and ; nityatvaṁ—eternity.*]

AND BECAUSE OF THE SAME REASON, THE ETERNITY (OF THE VEDAS). 29

The preceding Sūtra was devoted to meet an objection against the theory of the Pūrva-Mīmāṁsā, viz. the eternity of the Vedas. The objection that the word (Veda) too must have been produced in the same manner in which the world of gods etc. has been produced from the word, was refuted by pointing out that the eternal species of gods etc. came out of the eternal words. The present Sūtra too confirms the same conclusion, viz. that the Veda is not merely the source but the eternal source of the universe. The Ṛg-Veda (10, 71, 3) tells us how the eternal speech which was dwelling in the sages was found out by those who performed the sacrifice. Vedavyāsa too says that 'being permitted by Svayaṁbhū, the sages obtained by means of penance the Vedas and the Itihāsa which were hidden at the close of yuga' (M. B. Śānti-Parva)

समाननामरूपत्वाच्चावृत्तावप्यविरोधो दर्शनात्स्मृतेश्च । ३०

[*Samāna (similar)-nāma—rūpatvat—because of names and forms; ca—and; āvṛttau—repeated cycles of births and deaths; api—even; avirodhaḥ—freedom from contradiction darśanāt—from Śruti ; Smṛteḥ—from Smṛti ; ca—and.*]

NOTWITHSTANDING THE REPEATED ORIGINATION AND DISSOLUTION (OF THE UNIVERSE), THE ETERNITY OF THE WORD IS NOT CONTRADICTED ON ACCOUNT OF SIMILARITY OF NAMES AND FORMS; AS (IS CLEAR) FROM ŚRUTI AND SMṚTI. 30

The eternity of the Vedas will not indeed be affected if words like Indra etc. would connote not the individuals but the eternal species, and consequently there would be an unceasing succession of several Indras and other gods one after another. But if, as Śruti and Smṛti tell us, all the three worlds of names and forms including Indra and other gods are some time to undergo complete dissolution and are to be born again, how indeed can there remain the same meaning attached to words like 'Indra,' and how can Vedas be believed to be eternal? The reply to this is also found in Śruti and Smṛti. The eternity of the Vedas is not affected, because the names and forms of each new creation are the same as those of the preceding world that was dissolved. The wheel of Saṁsāra as a whole is eternal, in spite of dissolutions and creations,—a point to be explained later on in Sūtra 2, 1, 36. Just as a man who has awakened from sleep goes on with the affairs of the world as he was going on before he slept, even so one creation of the world is connected with the previous one without being hindered by the intervening dissolution of the same. That dissolution and creation are like the sleeping and wakeful conditions of man is seen from what the Kauṣitaki Upaniṣad tells us (3, 3), viz. that when a man is in dreamless sleep, he becomes one with prāṇa and that all his senses and the objects of the senses become merged in prāṇa, but when the same man awakes, the prāṇas and everything else spring forth from the Ātman, like sparks from fire, and occupy their respective places.

It may be said that the mahāpralaya or the utter annihilation of the universe resembles death rather than the sleeping condition of man ; and so the idea that a new creation should be continuous with the old seems as improbable as the idea that the present life of a man is continuing with his life in the previous birth. Besides all men do not sleep at the same time ; so that when a few of them become awake, they are reminded of their rpeceding wakeful life by looking to the person who are already awake and are busy in doing something. The pralaya, on the other hand, destroys everything at the same time.

The objection is invalid. For we must remember that the higher beings and gods cannot be said to have the same deficiency as men have. Though all the beings including men are animated, knowledge and power are seen to decrease as we pass downwards from men to animals, and from animals to trees ; or what is the same thing from another point of view, they increase as we rise up from man to Hiraṇyagarbha. It is possible therefore that the Hiraṇyagarbha and other gods may remember all that was going on in the preceding Kalpa, and so, having received the grace of the highest God, may continue their existence, as if they are coming in the wakeful condition after sleep. We are told in the following Śruti that this is possible : 'Being anxious to be released, I surrender unto God, who delivered the Vedas to the Brahmadeva after having first created him, and who illumines the buddhi in order to impart the knowledge of the Ātman' (Śve. 6, 18). 'The hymns of the ten mandalas of Ṛg-veda were seen by Madhuchandas and other sages,' as Śaunaka and other ṛṣis tell us. This vision of the Vedas by the gods and ṛṣis appears to be so indisputable a fact, that a person, who performs a sacrifice by means of a mantra, without knowing the ṛṣis, the metre and the deity of that mantra, is said to fall into a pit, or be born as a pillar or a stone.

Having discussed so far that lapse of time involved in the period of dissolution or death of the universe does not stop the continuation of the same, inasmuch as there is the certainty of the perpetual vision of the Vedas by Hiraṇyagarbha and by other gods and ṛṣis on account of the grace of the highest God, we give the additional reason of Adṛṣṭa. Dharma enjoins and prohibits actions in order that man should get pleasure and ward off pain. The desire for having pleasures and avoiding pains is therefore the motive whioh leads men to act. The present world thus is nothing but the result of actions of beings done in the preceding creation ; secondly, it allows them to reap the fruits of their actions in the form of pleasures and pains ; and thirdly, it induces the beings again to do certain actions and prepares thereby the way for a fresh creation of the same nature. So, the whole of saṁsāra including the worlds, gods, animals, men, castes, āśrams, duties and their fruits, appears in the same form again and again, because it moves perpetually from desires to actions, from actions to pleasures and pains, and from pleasures and pains to desires again. Like actions produce like results ; and according as they are right or wrong, harmless or cruel, there arise like desires or impressions to do similar acts again. So there remains always a potentiality of the world to rise again into actuality by the same names and forms, and by the same desires and actions, in spite of its apparent dissolution. The new creation is not an effect without a cause. Just as there is a necessity that governs the relation of the five senses with their objects, even so, the actuality of the present creation is bound up with the potentiality of the earlier creation which is hidden in the period of dissolution. That is why the whole world including the sun, the moon etc., is arranged by the highest God, on the pattern of the arrangement of the previous world (Ṛk. Saṁ .10, 190, 3). That the names and forms of this created world are exactly those of the previous one is seen from what the Taittirīyopaniṣad tells us regarding the genesis of the god of Fire (3, 1, 4, 1). The person who desired to become Agni in a succeeding world offers oblations of cooked rice by placing them on eight earthen pots to the god Agni presiding over the Kṛttikā stars. This means that the names and forms of the two Agnis are the same. Similar is the case with ṛṣis and other gods. In short, like the seasons coming after one another with the same characteristics, things of the world too appear and reappear with identical names and forms.

मध्वादिष्वसंभवादनधिकारं जैमिनिः । ३१

[*Madhvādiṣu—in Madhu-vidyā and others; asaṁbhavāt—being impossible ;anadhikāraṁ—without fitness; Jaiminiḥ.*]

JAIMINI HOLDS (THAT GODS ARE) INCAPABLE OF (LEARNING BRAHMA-VIDYĀ) BECAUSE IT IS IMPOSSIBLE (FOR THEM TO LEARN) MADHU-VIDYĀ ETC. 31

In the third chapter of the Chāndogyopaniṣad, we read that the sun is conceived as the honey of gods, the ākāśa as the beehive, the Vedic hymns as the bees, the sacrifices as the flowers, and the offerings of Soma, milk, etc. as the honey itself. The sacrifices are conceived as producing five kinds of honey or nectar which get themselves deposited in the different portions of the sun as red, white, blackish, dark and pearl-like in colours., Led by Agni, Indra and others, the gods like Vasus, Rudras, Ādityas, Maruts and Sādhyas live upon this nectar. We are further told that whoever thus meditates on the sun becomes satisfied even by the sight of the nectar, and is endowed with all the glory of gods like Vasu. Now this is possible only for men and not for those who are already gods; for this will involve the conception of another sun or another Vasu as the objects of meditation for the existing sun and the existing Vasu. How can gods themselves become at once the meditators and the objects of meditation? And again, when certain divinities, such as Fire, Wind, Sun, Directions, are each declared to be a pāda (one foot) of Brahman, and as such, are recommended to be the objects of meditation for the sake of men (Chā. 3, 18, 2 ; 3, 19, 1 ; 4, 3, 1), it is not possible for them to meditate on themselves. Similarly, the right and the left ears are to be meditated upon as Gautama and Bhāradvāja respectively (Bṛ. Up. 2, 4, 2); but it is not possible that these ṛṣis should meditate on themselves. Therefore it is that Jaimini holds that gods and ṛṣis are incapable of learning the Brahma-vidyā.

ज्योतिषि भावाच्च । ३२

[*Jyotiṣi—luminous bodies ; bhāvāt—on account of being used ; ca—and.*]

AND BECAUSE (THE WORDS ĀDITYA AND OTHERS) MEAN (THE SPHERE OF) LUMINOUS BODIES, (THE GODS HAVE NO CAPACITY TO LEARN BRAHMA-VIDYĀ). 32

It is known from ordinary experience as well as from Vedic usage that the words āditya and others refer to the sphere of luminous bodies, which are revolving day and night and illuminating the world. 'The āditya rises in the east and sets in the west'; so says the Śruti in the later portion of Madhu-vidyā (Chā. 3, 6, 4). This clearly shows that āditya means the sphere of light or of the sun, which being non-intelligent like clay, has no connection whatsoever either with the body or heart of a god, or with intelligence or wish of any being. Similarly, the word Agni means fire only.

It is said, no doubt, that mantra, arthavāda, itihāsa, purāṇa and ordinary experience are all in favour of the belief that gods have a body. Indra, e.g. has the thunderbolt in his hand, says the mantra ; 'the fire wept' is the arthavāda ; the itihāsa and purāṇas describe gods as being pleased by sacrifices ; and men draw the paintings of Yama or Varuṇa as having a staff or a noose in hand. But it is to be noted that what goes by the name of ordinary experience is not an independent means of knowledge; rather its value depends on perception, inference etc., which, however, are not available with reference to the descriptions of gods. Itihāsa and purāṇas are human works, and so must be tested by independent means of knowledge again. The arthavāda is nothing but the praise of certain Vedic passages which recommend the doing or non-doing of actions, and, as such, have nothing to do with the embodiedness or otherwise of gods. And lastly, the mantras are meant to make us aware of the manner of performance and the various things involved directly in the performance of sacrifice. The mantras therefore have no authority to say whether the gods are embodied or not. In short, the gods and other beings have no capacity to have the knowledge of Brahman.

भावं तु बादरायणोऽस्ति हि । ३३

[*Bhāvaṁ—Existence* ; *tu—on the other hand* ; *Bādarāyaṇa* ; *asti—is* ; *hi—certainly.*]

BĀDARĀYAṆA, ON THE OTHER HAND, HOLDS (THAT GODS AND OTHERS) ARE CAPABLE OF (HAVING THE KNOWLEDGE OF BRAHMAN); FOR THERE IS (EVIDENCE TO SHOW THIS). 33

It may be that gods and others are incapable of participating in the Madhu-vidyā etc., because they themselves happen to be the objects of meditation or worship in those vidyās ; but so far as knowledge of pure Brahman is concerned, there is no reason why they should not be capable of having it. For as Bādarāyaṇa holds, their capacity for the knowledge of Brahman is revealed by several facts such as their wish to know it, the vow of celibacy and non-attachment which some of them could keep, the necessary strength which they possess, and the absence of any mention that they are not fit for Brahma-vidyā. Because they are excluded in one sphere, it does not follow that they are excluded in all spheres. A Brahmin, for instance, is not allowed to perform the Rajasūya sacrifice, but is not prohibited on this account to perform all the sacrifices. Besides, the Bṛhadāraṇyaka makes an explicit statement with reference to gods and ṛṣis along with men that whoever amongst them, whether, god, ṛṣi or man, knows himself as the Brahman, becomes one with it (1, 4, 10). The Chāndogya goes a step further and describes the gods and the demons too as hankering after the knowledge of the Ātman which would fulfil all their desires, and mentions how Indra and Virocana, the representatives of gods and demons respectively, went to Prajāpati for this purpose (8, 7, 2). Smṛti too describes, for the same purpose, the Gandharva-Yājñavalkya-saṁvāda.

As for the objection that the words āditya etc. mean only the non-intelligent spheres of light, we say in reply that over and above this meaning, they also stand for the intelligent and powerful divinities who reside in the form of light. This is possible because gods can assume any form they like. Indra, for example, assumed the form of a ram and carried away Medhātithi, the descendant of Kaṇva (Ṣaḍviṁśa Brā. 1, 1). Āditya approached Kunti after having assumed the form of a man. Even such substances as earth are regarded as being ruled over by intelligent beings, as is clear from 'the earth spoke,' etc.

To deal now with another objection regarding mantra and arthavāda: It was pointed out by the pūrva pakṣin that they cannot be looked upon as trustworthy evidence for believing in the embodiedness of gods, because what they refer to is not their own meaning but some thing other than that, *viz.* the things mentioned in the sacrifice, or the eulogy of some action. We say in reply that the question, whether a sentence has its own primary meaning or not, is not necessarily determined by the reference or otherwise of that sentence to something else. Rather, it is determined by the fact whether or not its alleged primary meaning is contradicted by some other experience. In other words, it is not the absence of reference to something else, but the uncontradicted presence of meaning, which gives the reality to a sentence. As opposed to this, it is not the presence of reference to something else but the absence of any meaning (or which is the same thing as contradicted meaning) which gives unreality to the sentence. The grass and the leaves seen by a traveller by the side of a road and given expression to in a proposition, have all the reality and meaning, even though the purpose of the traveller is something else, *viz* the journey.

The objector may intervene, and say that the grass and the leaves become the objects of direct perception; but this is not possible in the case of an arthavāda type of sentence, because its purpose being merely to say something by way of eulogy, is so intimately connected with the vidhi-vākya or the main sentence which recommends an action, that the meaning of one is included in the meaning of the other. Just as the words 'one should drink wine' cannot be detached from the word 'not' in the given sentence 'one should not drink wine', and then interpreted as if they have a separate affirmative meaning over and above the given negative meaning, even so the arthavāda has no separate meaning of its own over and above the meaning of the vidhi-vākya.

To this we reply. The prohibitive sentence quoted above cannot be split into two parts, because all the words in that sentence together make up one meaning. The words of the arthavāda sentence, on the other hand, can have a distinct and complete meaning of their own inasmuch as they describe a thing which already exists. It is only afterwards, when we think about the purpose which they subserve, that the same words are seen to be used in order to glorify some vidhi-vākya. To illustrate what we mean; Every word in the vidhi-vākya, 'He who desires to have prosperity, should offer a white animal to Vāyu' (Tai. 2, 1), is connected with the intended action. But the words in the arthavāda sentences, such as, 'Vāyu is a very swift deity, towards which he approaches fast; Vāyu leads him on to prosperity' (Tai. 2, 1), are not in like manner directly connected with the action. The words of the two types of sentences are not so connected with each other as will enable us to have such absurd sentences out of them as 'Vāyu should offer', or 'the swift deity should offer'. Rather they form two independent unities of their own, which in their turn get related in order to serve some additional purpose. The arthavāda sentence, in other words, which has an independent and complete meaning of its own and which refers to an already existing fact, is found to be related in a subordinate manner to the vidhi-vākya, because it fulfils the additional purpose of glorifying the intended ection. The arthavāda sentence referred to above, for axample, has got a complete meaning of its own, inasmuch sa it refers to the swift nature of Vāyu; it is only afterwards that it comes in relation to the vidhi-vākya when it serves the purpose of praising the Vāyu and making an offering to that divinity.

Further, the arthavāda sentence may be of two types. Either it is a statement of fact which already exists and is known through other means of knowledge; or it is a statement of some quality only, because the factual knowledge which is conveyed by it is contradicted by experience. 'Fire is the medicine of cold' is an example of the first variety known as 'anuvāda'; experience confirms that fire is a remedy against cold. 'The sacrificial post is the sun' is an example of the second variety known as 'guṇavāda'; for this makes us aware only of the guṇa or quality of luminosity of the sun which is seen on the post. The sentence is not to be interpreted literally for it runs contrary to experience; the sun is not the post. Where however experience is not contradicted, or what is told is not proved by any means of knowledge, it is better to interpret the arthavāda sentence as belonging to the first variety rather than to the second. It is not guṇavāda, because it is not contrary to experience; but the freedom from contradicting other means of knowledge leaves room for supposing that such means though not known must be available, inasmuch as the sentence is from Śruti. For example, 'Indra has a thunder-bolt in his hand' is a statement which can neither be proved nor disproved by the ordinary means of knowledge. And yet, as it is a Śruti statement, it leaves room for supposing that there must be some other means of knowledge for taking it as a fact; and so construed, it is an 'anuvāda'. 'The thunder-bolt in the hand,' therefore, suggests that Indra is a god having body. The mantra sentences too, in short, have meanings of their own corresponding to facts (*e.* g. the embodiedness of gods), though they fall beyond the ordinary means of knowledge.

There is another reason still for believing that gods are embodied. The very injunctions which recommend certain offerings to Indra and other gods imply that gods have some features. The sacrificer is asked to 'take in his hand the offering and remember the god to whom it is to be given at the time of uttering vaṣat' (Ai. Brā. 3, 8, 1). Without this mental representation, there would be no offerings to gods. The mantras by themselves cannot be considered as constituting the features or the forms of gods; for the mantras are merely words. It is the meaning of the words which convey to us the forms which the gods possess. Therefore all those who believe in the authoritativeness of the word cannot but admit the embodiedness etc. of gods like Indra, which is spoken of in mantra and arthavāda. And inasmuch as mantra and arthavāda are the foundation of itihāsa and purāṇa, the latter too are trustworthy evidence. Besides, they owe their origin to the perceptual knowledge of Vyāsa and other sages who, it is told in Smṛtis, were holding conversation with gods. To deny this is to deny the variety of the world. There is at present no single ruler of the whole earth; from this it does not follow that there was no such ruler in the past too. For in that case, the rājasūya sacrifice which is to be performed by one who desires to be the ruler of the whole earth, will be without any purpose. The whole of the Dharmaśāstra too will be useless, if one were to argue from the disorderly condition of varṇa and āśrama at the present time that they must have been so even in ancient times. It is therefore appropriate to hold that on account of their dhārmic excellence, people of the ancient times were capable of conversing with gods, which fact is also vouchsafed by the yoga-sūtras (2, 44). That yoga enables one to acquire extraordinary powers cannot simply be denied. The Śvetaśvataropaniṣad speaks of the greatness of yoga: 'When the five qualities of earth, water, fire, wind and ākāśa arise in the body by the power and fire of yoga, then no more will illness, old age or pain overtake that body (2, 12).' It is wrong to infer from our ability the ability of ṛṣis who had the power to visualize the mantras. Naturally, the itihāsa and purāṇas which have been composed by them must be trustworthy. Our ordinary experience too, if based on itihāsa and purāṇas, can also be possibly taken as true.

The result is that mantra, arthavāda etc. go to prove that gods and others have got bodily forms; and being endowed with desires etc. they can be considered as having the capacity to know the Brahman. Besides the conception of gradual release,—*viz.* that after death man first becomes Gandharva, then Pitara, and then god,—is possible only on the view that gods too get the release or are capable of having Brahma-jñāna; otherwise even after attaining godhood, man would be deprived of mokṣa.

९ अपशूद्राधिकरणम् । (३४–३८)

शुगस्य तदनादरश्रवणात्तदाद्रवणात्सूच्यते हि । ३४

[*Suk–grief; asya-his; tad-anādara–śravaṇāt–hearing his disrespectful words; tad–that; ādravaṇāt–due to approach; śūcyate–is indicated; hi–only.*]

THE SORROW WHICH HE (JĀNASRUTI) FELT ON HEARING THE DISRESPECTFUL WORDS OF THAT (SWAN BIRD) IS ALONE INDICATED (BY THE WORD ŚŪDRA); FOR THAT (SORROW) MADE HIM RUN (TOWARDS RAIKVA). 34

If gods can learn Brahma-vidyā, what can we say about the Śudras? Or are the twice-born alone capable of doing so? According to pūrvapakṣa, the Śūdra has a claim to it; because he has got a desire and capacity to learn. Besides, nowhere has he been debarred from learning it, just as he has been debarred from performing sacrifice because he does not preserve sacred fire (Tai. Saṁ. 7, 1, 1, 6). So far as Brahma-jñāna is concerned, the preservation of āhavanīya and other fires is not necessary. Besides, the circumstance that Raikva calls Jānśruti by the epithet 'Śūdra' (Chā. 4, 2, 3) in connection with Saṁvarge-vidyā or Vāyu-vidyā (a part of Brahma-vidyā), and asks him to take away the chariot, wealth and cows which he had brought as presents shows that the Śūdra is fit to have the knowledge of the Brahman. Śūdras like Vidura too are spoken of by Smṛti as possessing Brahma-jñāna.

We reply that the Śūdra cannot be considered capable of studying and understanding the Vedas even though he may be physically sound and has a desire to learn. For he is not allowed to undergo the upanayana ceremony which is considered as the necessary condition of the studying of the Vedas, which again in its turn, if not properly done under the guidance of a Guru, makes him unfit both for sacrifice and knowledge. Besides, the mere presence of the word 'Śūdra', without any backing of argument will not enable us to say that the Śūdra as such will be considered fit for saṁvarg and other Vidyās. At best, he may be fit for Saṁvarg-Vidyā alone ; but this too is not possible, because the word 'Śūdra' occurs in the arthavāda sentence alone *viz.* 'This vidyā cannot be obtained by money.' Or the word 'Śūdra' may be nterpreted in altogether a different manner, so that it may refer to a twice-born and not a Śūdra by caste. The word may refer to the grief of Jānaśruti and not to Jānaśruti himself. Raikva alludes to it only to show that he had the knowledge of the grief, though Jānaśruti was far away when he felt it at the disrespectful words of the hamsa bird. 'Śūdra' means the ādravana, the rushing forth of 'śuc' or grief. Whether Jānaśruti came to grief or grief fell on him, or whether he rushed unto Raikva on account of grief, the word 'Śūdra' points to one of the three things and not to the caste.

क्षत्रियत्वगतेश्चोत्तरत्र चैत्ररथेन लिंगात् । ३५

[*Kṣatriyatvagateḥ–caste of a Kṣatriya being known; ca–and; uttartra–later on; Caitrarathena–with Caitraratha; lingāt –due to sign.*]

AND BECAUSE OF THE SIGN (HE IS MENTIONED) LATER ON ALONG WITH CAITRARATHA, IT IS KNOWN THAT (JĀNAŚRUTI) IS KṢATRIYA (AND NOT ŚŪDRA). 35

In the arthavāda sentence of Saṁvarga-Vidyā, Jānaśruti is mentioned along with one Kṣatriya Abhipratārin known as Caitraratha. As equals are mentioned together, we gather that Jānaśruti also is a Kṣatriya. We have the same inference, from the power and glory which Jānaśruti exhibited by sending men in search of Raikva, as also by the numerous presents he sent to him.

संस्कारपरामर्शात्तदभावाभिलापाच्च । ३६

[*Saṁskāra—ceremonies ; parāmarśāt—being mentioned; tadabhāva—its absence; abhilapāt—being mentioned: ca—and.*]

THE SAṀSKĀRAS BEING MENTIONED (IN THE CASE OF THE TWICE-BORN) AND THEIR ABSENCE BEING MENTIONED (IN THE CASE OF THE ŚŪDRAS, THE LATTER ARE NOT FIT TO STUDY THE VEDAS). 36

In various places, where the vidyās are being discussed, mention has been made of saṁskāras like upanayana etc. in the case of the twice born. For example, Śat. Brā. 11, 5, 3, 13 ; Chā. 7, 1, 1 ; Pra. 1, 1. In the Chāndogyopaniṣad (5, 11, 7), the King Aśvapati, we are told, did not insist on the upanayana ceremony being performed in the case of certain Brahmins. An exception like this proves only the existence of a rule which applies to the twice-born. The Śūdra, on the other hand, is said to be born once only, and not a second time because there is no upanayana in his case (Manu. 10, 4). He is said not to incur sin, just as the twice-born incurs by eating what ought not to be eaten (Manu. 10, 126).

तदभावनिर्धारणे च प्रवृत्तेः । ३७

[*Tadabhāva; nirdhāraṇe—being convinced; ca; pravṛtteḥ—due to being active.*]

AND BECAUSE (GAUTAMA) PROCEEDED (TO INITIATE JĀBĀLA) AFTER BEING CONVINCED THAT (HE) WAS NOT THAT (VIZ., A ŚŪDRA). 37

The Chāndogyopaniṣad tells us that Gautama was pleased to know that Jābāla spoke the truth when he said that he did not know his gotra or the family name, and that Gautama concluded from this that inasmuch as jābāla possessed the quality of speaking the truth, he must have come from Brahmin parents. So after being convinced that he was not a Śūdra, Gautama showed his willingness to initiate Jābāla (4, 4, 5).

श्रवणाध्ययनार्थप्रतिषेधात्स्मृतेश्च । ३८

[*Śravaṇa—hearing ; adhyayana—study ; artha—meaning; pratiṣedhāt—being prohibited ; smṛteḥ ; ca.*]

AND BECAUSE (THE ŚŪDRA) IS PROHIBITED BY SMṚTI TO HEAR AND STUDY (THE VEDAS) AND (TO KNOW) THEIR MEANING. 38

From the prohibition to hear the Vedas follows the prohibition to study and to know their meaning. For how will one know the meaning without study and how again one will study without hearing what he studies? We find however explicit statements regarding these things in Gautama-Dharmaśāstra. 'The ears of the Śūdra who hears the Vedas are to be filled with molten lead and lac' (12, 4). 'If he utters a Vedic word, his tongue should be cut, etc.' (12, 5, 6). 'The twice-born alone are entitled to study, sacrifice and to the receiving or giving of gifts' (10, 1). 'Knowledge should not be imparted to the Śūdra' (Manu. 4, 80). Vidura and Dharmavyādha had knowledge, but it was the result of deeds in their previous births; and the fruit of knowledge too is inevitable. Though the Śūdras are prohibited to study the Vedas, they may however get the knowledge through itihāsa and purāṇas.

१० कंपनाधिकरणम् । (३९)

कंपनात् । ३९

[*Kampanāt—On account of trembling.*]

On account of trembling (of the world, the prāṇa is Brahman). 39

After having incidentally considered as to who is fit for receiving Brahma-jñāna, let us return to our main topic of the inquiry into the purpose of the vedānta-passages. We read in Kāṭhakopaniṣad (2, 6, 6) that 'The whole world trembles in the prāṇa ; that this prāṇa is a great terror, a raised thunderbolt as it were, and that those who know it become immortal.' Now the pūrvapakṣin maintains that prāṇa means the air we breathe with its five modifications; and that the thunderbolt too is a manifestation of wind when it assumes the form of rain and lightning. And he cites Śruti to explain immortality: 'One who knows that air is everything, conquers death '(Bṛ. 3, 3, 2).

We reply that prāṇa means Brahman, because both before and after the passage under discussion, Brahman is the topic of enquiry. How can, all of a sudden, air intervene as a relevant topic? The preceding passage describes the Brahman as the immortal, resplendent support of all beings, transgressing which none can go (Ka. 2, 5, 8). So on account of proximity, as also on account of its being the support of all, Brahman alone can be the topic in the passage under discussion. 'The whole world trembles in prāṇa,' means that prāṇa or the Brahman is the support of the world. That prāṇa means Brahman or the highest Ātman is stated in the expression 'prāṇa of prāṇa' (Bṛ. 4, 4, 18). To cause the whole world tremble is possible for the highest Ātman, and not for the mere wind; for it is not by means of the wind, 'prāṇa and apāna, that anyone lives ; we live on account of another being in whom these two prāṇa and apāna find rest' (Ka. 2, 5, 5). In the passage subsequent to the one under discussion, the wind, the fire and the sun, as also Indra and Death, are spoken of as doing their duties through the fear of Brahman. The Taittirīyopaniṣad says exactly the same thing (2,8,1). So, once again, on account of proximity and on account of the cause of fear, the raised thunderbolt and the terror referred to in the passage under discussion denote the general fear of Brahman which may fall on the heads of the disobedient beings. That prāṇa means Brahman is due to one more reason mentioned in the passage, viz., the knowledge of it leads one to mokṣa. This is borne out by another Śruti passage, 'A man who knows him alone goes beyond death; there is no other way' (Śve. 6, 15). The immortality of the wind spoken of by the pūrvapakṣin is not absolute but relative only with reference to the life-span of man; for immediately in the next chapter of the Bṛhadāraṇyaka, the wind and other elements are said to be perishable. And, finally, the subject-matter of the passage under discussion, started by Naciketas in his request to tell him that 'which is neither this nor that, neither effect nor cause, neither past nor future,' makes us aware that the word prāṇa means the highest Ātman, and not wind.

११ ज्योतिरधिकरणम् । (४०)

ज्योतिर्दर्शनात् । ४०

[*Jyotiḥ—light; darśanāt—being seen.*]

BECAUSE (BRAHMAN) IS SEEN, THE LIGHT (MEANS BRAHMAN). 40

A passage in the Chāndogyopaniṣad tells us 'that the serene being or the saṁprasāda rises from the body, and appears in its own form as soon as it meets the highest light' (8, 12, 3). Now the word 'light' in this passage is understood by the pūrvapakṣin as meaning the ordinary physical light of the sun which dispels darkness. No doubt, the word 'light' from the third chapter of the same Upaniṣad was decided (Sūtra 1, 1, 24) to mean Brahman, because the topic of the Gāyatrī-passage is Brahman; but there is no such reason to take that word here too in the same sense. Besides, in the chapter known as the Nāḍikhaṇḍa of the Chāndogyopaniṣad, it is stated that when a man aspiring for release,' departs from his body he is drawn upwards by the rays to the Sun' (8, 6, 5).

We reply that the word 'light' means Brahman only. For in the whole chapter Brahman is the topic of discussion. It is introduced in 8, 7, 1, as the 'Ātman which is free from sin,' and is said to be the object of inquiry. It is again referred to (8, 9, 3 ff) as the object requiring explanation, and so is told to be the disembodied being to which pleasure and pain do not touch (8, 12, 1). Now this disembodied condition is not possible except in the case of Brahman. The sun, on the other hand, is an embodied divinity. Finally, the light is spoken of as the 'highest light', and as 'the highest person' (8, 12, 3). True release, as we shall see later on, does not involve departing upwards to the Sun.

१२ अर्थान्तरव्यपदेशाधिकरणम् । (४१)

आकाशोऽर्थान्तरत्वादिव्यपदेशात् । ४१

[*Ākāśaḥ* ; *arthāntartva-ādi—being different in meaning from* ; *vyapadeśāt—because it is mentioned.*]

ĀKĀŚA IS (BRAHMAN), AS IT IS MENTIONED TO BE DIFFERENT ETC. 41

'What is known as ākāśa is the cause of the manifestation of names and forms. That in which these are contained is the immortal Brahman, the Ātman' (Chā. 8, 14, 1).

According to pūrvapakṣin, the word ākāśa stands for the bhūtākāśa because this is the accepted conventional meaning. The bhūtākāśa can be said to be the cause of the manifestation of names and forms, because it affords them room to exist. Besides, there is no clear and distinct indication on account of which the ākāśa can be said to be the cause of the creation etc. of the world, so that we may interpret it to mean Brahman.

We reply that the container must be different from the contained. The Brahman contains within it the names and forms ; therefore the ākāśa must be nothing else but Brahman. Nothing except Brahman can be different from names and forms. The bhūtākāśa too is included in the world of created things having names and forms ; and so it cannot be different from them. Besides for the manifestation too of names and forms, the creative power of Brahman is ultimately responsible, as is clear from the Śruti, 'Let me enter into them in the form of jīvātman and manifest the names and forms' (Chā. 6, 3, 2). Though the bhūtākāśa is said to afford room for all the objects of names and forms and so to manifest them, yet this is possible only in the case of objects which have been already created by the highest Ātman, and not in the case of those which have not been created. The mention of jīvātman in the Śruti passage is only to show that the jīvātman is not different from the Brahman. Besides the words 'Brahman, Immortal, and Ātman' are indicative of Brahman alone. The present Sūtra is only an additional explanation of what was told in Sūtra 1, 1, 22.

१३ सुषुप्त्युत्क्रान्त्यधिकरणम् । (४२–४३)

सुषुप्त्युत्क्रान्त्योर्भेदेन । ४२

[*Suṣupti-utkrāntyoḥ—during sleep and departure*; *bhedena—because of difference.*]

AND BECAUSE OF DIFFERENCE (BEING MENTIONED OF THE HIGHEST ĀTMAN FROM THE JĪVA) IN THE STATES OF SLEEP AND DEPARTURE (FROM THE BODY). 42

A passage in the Bṛhadāraṇyaka describes the Ātman as 'he who is within the heart and the prāṇas, and the person consisting of light and knowledge' (4, 3, 7). Now the prāṇas being the upādhis of the jīvātman, the reference to the person having knowledge in this as well as in the concluding passage, 'this great unborn Ātman, consisting of knowledge and residing in the prāṇas' (4, 4, 22) is, according to pūrvapakṣa, the reference to the jīvatman only. The intermediate passages too which deal with the waking and other states must be taken as referring to the embodied soul.

We say in reply that the passage does not give any additional information regarding the jīvātman, but tells us only about the nature of the highest God. In the first place, the God is pointed out as being different from the individual soul by reference to what happens to the latter in deep sleep. 'Being embraced by the prājña Ātman, this person knows nothing either inside or outside.' In other words, it is during the condition of sleep, that the jīvātman forgets everything of the nature of un-ātman. It forgets itself and becomes one with God, who is always intelligence or knowledge. Similarly, the jīvātman is spoken of as groaning while he is passing away from the body, because he is being presided over by the highest God. Here too God is mentioned as distinguished from the embodied soul.

The so-called characteristics which, according to pūrvapakṣa, indicate the nature of jīva are, as a matter of fact, merely used to indicate, the jīva as identical with the highest God. Śruti gains nothing by describing the nature of jīva which is already so well known ; Its aim is to make us aware of the unknown nature of the Brahman from the known nature of the jīva, and of the fact that the jīva is nothing else but Brahman. That is why immediately in the subsequent passage, the Ātman is described to be 'thinking as if' or 'moving as if', when as a matter of fact the Ātman neither thinks nor moves. That which thinks is the buddhi, and that which moves are the indriyas. Similarly, in the concluding passage, the words which appear to indicate the jīvātman, viz. 'the person consisting of knowledge and residing in the prāṇās,' indicate, as a matter of fact, the highest God, because the same person is referred to as being the 'great, unborn Ātman.' And if both in the beginning and in the end of the chapter, the aim of Śruti is to describe the nature of the highest Ātman, then to say that in the intermediate portion of the same, the jīvatman is described is to allow the possibility of a man who has gone in the east being found in the west. The description of the wakeful and other conditions is not intended to refer to jīva, but to the highest God who is free from such conditions. The reference to these only serves the purpose of denying these in the case of the highest Ātman. So here too Śruti makes the progress from the known nature of the jīva to the unknown nature of the Ātman. This is further evident not only from the repeated request of Janaka to tell him only what concerns mokṣa ; but also from the repeated answer of Yājñavalkya that 'the puruṣa being unattached to anything is not, affected by any of these enjoyments' (Bṛ. 4, 3, 14-16). The Ātman is further described 'as having nothing to do with merit or demerit, because it then overcomes all the sorrows.' We therefore conclude that the aim of the passage is to describe the nature of the Ātman alone.

पत्यादिशब्देभ्यः । ४३

[*Patyādi—like Lord and others*; *Śabdebhyaḥ—on account of words.*]

AND ON ACCOUNT OF WORDS LIKE 'LORD' ETC. 43

The words 'pati,' 'vaśī,' and 'īśāna' used in the Bṛhadāraṇyaka (4, 4, 22) further make us aware that it is the highest God who is spoken of as the Lord, the controller and protector of all. Obviously they cannot refer to jīva, because it is not possible for him to control and protect all beings. Similarly, the quality of being neither greater by good deeds nor smaller by evil deeds is not ascribable to any being except God.

ADHYĀYA FIRST

PĀDA FOURTH

१ आनुमानिकाधिकरणम्। (१-७)

आनुमानिकमप्येकेषामिति चेन्न शरीररुपकविन्यस्तगृहीतेर्दर्शयति। १

[*Ānumānikam—that which is inferred; api—even; ekeśām of some ; iti cet—if it be said ; na—not ; Śarīra—body rūpaka—simile ; vinyasta—referred ; gṛhiteḥ—because it is mentioned ; darśayati—Śruti says; ca—and.*]

IF IT BE SAID THAT (PRADHĀNA) TOO WHICH IS INFERRED (IS MENTIONED BY THE WORD 'AVYAKTA') ACCORDING TO SOME, (WE REPLY THAT) IT IS NOT SO ; FOR (THE BODY) WHICH IS MENTIONED IN THE METAPHOR OF THE BODY IS REFERRED (THEREBY); AND (ŚRUTI) TELLS (THE SAME). 1

Starting with the inquiry into the nature of Brahman we defined it as the cause of the origin, subsistence and dissolution of the world (Sū. 1, 1, 2). We then noticed that pradhāna can not be defined in this manner, because Śruti does not mention the 'seeing' in its case, as it mentions it in the case of Brahman. (Sū. 1, 1, 5). And further we proved that the common purpose of all the Vedānta passages is to show that Brahman, and not pradhāna, is the cause of the world (Sū. 1, 1, 10) And yet so long as the view that there are still some Śruti words which appear to favour the doctrine that pradhāna is the cause, has not been shown to be erroneous, our own theory that the omniscient Brahman is the cause of the universe cannot be said to be firmly established. So, we now proceed to show in this chapter that the passages containing such words really have a different meaning than that which is sought by the Sāṅkhyas.

The doctrine of pradhāna is said to have got the authority of Śruti because the three entities admitted by the Sāṅkhya Smṛti, viz. the mahat, the avyakta and the puruṣa are exactly the entities which are named and mentioned in the same order in Śruti. The Kāṭhaka, for example, reads: 'Beyond mahat, there is the avyakta and beyond avyakta, there is the Puruṣa' (1, 3, 11). Now, the word 'avyakta' is accepted to mean pradhāna according to the Sāṅkhya Smṛti; and pradhāna being without the qualities of sound, touch etc. is said to be the meaning of avyakta.

We say in reply that the passage from the Kāṭhaka does not refer to pradhāna though the word 'avyakta' may refer to anything subtle and difficult to discern. Besides the meaning of a thing does not depend upon the mere position it occupies or the order in which it comes. It is foolish to argue that a cow is a horse, because it is tied in the place of a horse. On the contrary, if we judge from the general subject matter, we shall find that avyakta does not refer to the imagined entity of pradhāna but to the body mentioned in the metaphor of the chariot.

The passage under discussion comes after another passage in which there occurs the metaphor of the chariot; and the various entities, viz. the soul, the body, the buddhi, the mind, the senses and their objects are respectively conceived as the lord of the chariot, the chariot, charioteer, the reins, the horses and their way of going (1, 3, 3, 4). It is told that a man who has no control over his mind and senses returns to saṁsāra, but that a man who has got it goes to the excellent abode of Viṣṇu. Then, while describing this abode of Viṣṇu as the end of all, it has been further mentioned that 'beyond the senses are their objects, beyond objects the mind, beyond mind the buddhi beyond buddhi the great ātman, beyond the great the avyakta, and beyond avyakta the Puruṣa; but that beyond Puruṣa there is nothing, and that Puruṣa is the highest goal, the end of the journey' (Ka. 1, 3, 10, 11). Now if we are to avoid the mistake of leaving the topic in hand and pursuing a new one, we must suppose that we are dealing with the same entities in this passage as were previously mentioned in the metaphor of the chariot. The senses, the mind and the buddhi are commonly referred to in both the passages, under the same names. The objects of the senses refer to the ways of the horses. That the objects go beyond the senses is confirmed by what Śruti has told, viz. 'The senses are grahas,' i.e. those which catch hold of ; but the objects of the senses are greater still in this respect, because the senses are dependent for their attractive power on the presence of the objects (Bṛ. 3, 2). In the same way, mind is superior to both the senses and their objects, for both these depend on the presence of the mind. The mind too, in its turn, being dependent on the discriminative power of buddhi the buddhi is superior to or goes beyond mind. Higher than buddhi is the great ātman or the soul, which is referred to in the earlier passage as the lord of the chariot. It is natural that the bhoktā or the soul that enjoys should go beyond the means of enjoyment ; he is like the master to his servants. Or the words 'mahān ātman' may mean the buddhi of Brahmadeva or Hiraṇyagarbha who was the first to be created, and was given the vedas (Śve. 6,18) ; for it is his buddhi which can truly be considered the support of all the intellects of beings. So though in the former passage, the word 'buddhi' comes once here it is referred to twice ; and so by 'buddhi' we may mean the human intellect, and by 'mahān ātman' the intellect of 'Hiraṇyagarbha. Then the word soul or jīvātmā in the former passage has its corresponding word 'Puruṣa' in the second passage, because jivātmā and paramātmā are in reality one and the same. Eliminating the five words from the first passage with the corresponding five words,—as a matter of fact six words as shown above—from the second passage, we get only one word as the remainder from the first passage, viz. the 'body' which must be equated with the one word which remains from the second passage viz. the 'avyakta.' It will be impossible therefore to bring out any meaning of the Śruti passages, if according to the Sāṅkhya view, the avyakta is to mean pradhāna.

The aim of the entire section of the Upaniṣad is to show how owing to avidyā the jīvātman is bound to the body, senses, mind etc., but how in reality it is nothing but Brahman. The metaphor of the chariot shows us the saṁsāra of the soul, but we know its final destiny too, viz. the highest and the excellent abode of Viṣṇu which 'though hidden in all beings is seen by those who have a subtle and one-pointed intellect (Ka. 1, 3, 12). The way to know him is through the practice of yoga ; It consists first in controlling the activities of speech and other senses and resting in mind only ; then to control and stop the doubtful mental activities too and rest in the decision of the intellect; then again restrain the personal buddhi into the fundamental, great intellect of the Hiraṇyagarbha, and finally to compose this too in the calm of the highest Ātman, the end of all. If we thus consider the full context, we find that there is no place for the hypothesis of pradhāna.

सूक्ष्मं तु तदर्हत्वात् । २

[*Sūkṣmaṁ—subtle ; tad—that ; arhatvāt—because it is proper.*]

(THE WORD AVYAKTA MEANS) HOWEVER THE SUBTLE (BODY); BECAUSE THIS IS THE PROPER (MEANING) OF THAT (WORD). 2

So, with the help of the context and the process of elimination employed while comparing the two passages regarding the chariot and the abode of Viṣṇu, it has been shown in the preceding Sūtra that avyakta means the body and not pradhāna. Yet it may be suggested that the actual physical body being perceptible, it ought to have been denoted by the word ' vyakta ' and not avyakta.

To this the reply of the Sūtrakāra is that the word avyakta means the subtle causal body, which consists of the subtle parts of the elements, and as such is further applied to the effect thereof *viz.* the gross, physica! body. This usage of naming the effect by the same term by which the cause is denoted is not uncommon. 'Mix the soma with cows' (Ṛg. 9, 46, 4) means 'mix the soma with milk of the cows'. Here cows means 'the milk of the cows'. Similarly, 'all this was then not manifest' (Bṛ. 1, 4, 7) means 'all this world of names and forms was in a former condition merely potential or seminal, *i. e.*, devoid of names and forms'. In other words, the present manifest world is referred to by the former non-manifest condition of the world.

तदधीनत्वादर्थवत् । ३

[*Tad-adhīnatvāt–being dependent on him;arthavat–serves the purpose.*]

BEING DEPENDENT ON HIM (*i. e.* GOD, THE FORMER NON-MANIFEST CONDITION OF THE WORLD IS NOT PRADHĀNA; AND) IT SERVES THE PURPOSE (OF MAKING GOD RESPONSIBLE FOR CREATION). 3

May not this antecedent condition of the world in which nothing is manifest be called as pradhāna ?

It is not pradhāna, we reply. For the previous condition of the world is not an independent cause. It is, on the other hand, dependent on the highest God. It is the power of God, with which he creates the world. It is this potential, premordial power of the highest God which is known by several names, such as, 'avidyā', 'māyā', 'avyakta', ākāśa, and akṣara. It is the great sleep on account of which the individual souls being ignorant of their real nature become engrossed in saṁsāra It is known as ākāśa, because of its unlimited extent, or because of its being the cause of ākāśa. It is akṣara because it does not cease to exist until there is knowledge.

It is known as māyā on account of its wonderful creation; and finally it is known as avyakta because being the power of Brahman it cannot be different from Brahman; nor can it be non-different from Brahman, because Brahman is knowledge, while its power is of the nature of ignorance (Bṛ. 3, 8, 11; mu 2, 12; Śve 4, 10).

The avyakta is said to be beyond mahat according to the Kāṭhakopaniṣad, because mahat, in the sense of the intellect of the Hiraṇyagarbha, originates from the avyakta. Or even if we understand by mahat the individual soul, the avyakta is beyond it, because the soul is dependent on avyakta or avidyā. The very being and continuation of the soul is on account of its relation to avidyā. Now as the cause and the effect are identical, the quality of transcending the mahat has been transferred from avyakta (the cause), to the body (the effect of it), and so the word avyakta too is mentioned in the sense of body. Such a transference of quality and name from cause to the effect it not made in the case of other products of avyakta because the senses etc. are mentioned by their own names in the two passages of the chariot and the abode of Viṣṇu. It is body alone which has not been so shown by its own name, and so has to be denoted by the word avyakta.

Some people give a different interpretation of the last two Sūtras. According to them, both the gross and the subtle bodies are previously compared to a chariot. But the word 'avyakta' means here the subtle body only. The bondage and release of the soul again are possible on account of this subtle body. For it is due to the subtle body that desires bind the soul after death, and it is due to the destruction of the subtle body by means of knowledge , that the soul gets its release.

To this we reply that just as the word chariot would stand for both the gross and the subtle bodies, even so, the word avyakta may stand for both of them. There seems no sufficient reason, excepting the word avyakta meaning subtle as to why both the bodies, gross and subtle, should have been mentioned first, and only one of them, *viz.* the subtle, be mentioned afterwards. The context is the same; and if we are to avoid the fault of leaving the subject in hand and taking to a new one at will, we must so interpret the two Śruti passages as to make a complete whole of meaning. And this can be achieved only when the passages concerned give a common topic. Therefore it is that both the bodies must have been referred to by 'avyakta', just as they were referred to by 'chariot'. Besides, the question is not regarding the distinction between the gross body and the subtle body; it is rather to point out a series of things in order of excellence, and thus to show that beyond the highest abode of Viṣṇu, though hidden, there is nothing superior. And yet, even taking for granted that the word 'avyakta' denotes the subtle body, the one conclusion, about which there is no uncertainty, is that the Kāṭhaka passage has no reference to pradhāna.

ज्ञेयत्वावचनाच्च । ४

[*Jñeyatva–a thing to be cognized; avacanāt–There being no mention.*]

AND BECAUSE THERE IS NO MENTION OF (AVYAKTA) AS A THING TO BE COGNIZED (IT CANNOT MEAN PRADHĀNA). 4

According to the Sāṅkhyas, the knowledge of pradhāna or the constituent guṇas as distinct from Puruṣa is considered to be essential for achieving the liberation of the soul. Or else, as held by them sometimes, the pradhāna is to be meditated upon for the sake of obtaining extraordinary powers. But, so far as the passage under discussion is concerned, the avyakta is not mentioned either as an object of knowledge or meditation. In other words, the knowledge of it serves no human end. Avyakta therefore cannot be said to mean pradhāna. On our view, on the other hand, the word avyakta has been merely incidentally used for body after the passage of the chariot is over to show the nature of the highest abode of Viṣṇu.

वदतीति चेन्न प्राज्ञो हि प्रकरणात् । ५

[*Vadati–says; iti cet–if it be said; na–not; prajñaḥ-intelligent Ātman; hi–for; prakarṇāt–from context.*]

AND IF IT IS SAID THAT (PRADHĀNA AS THE OBJECT OF KNOWLEDGE) IS MENTIONED (BY ŚRUTI), WE SAY THAT IT IS NOT SO; FOR, ON ACCOUNT OF THE GENERAL SUBJECT-MATTER, THE INTELLIGENT ĀTMAN IS MEANT. 5

The Sāṅkhya may again quote a passage from the same Upaniṣad and say that the entity described therein as that which goes beyond mahat is nothing but pradhāna. *E.* g., 'He who perceives that which is without sound, touch, form, decay, taste, or smell, which has neither beginning nor end, and which is beyond the mahat and is constant, is freed from the jaws of death' (Ka. 2, 3, 15).

We reply that the object of perception described in the passage is not pradhāna but the intelligent highest Ātman, which alone goes to form the general subject-matter. The Puruṣa alone is said to be the goal; for there is nothing beyond him. Though he is hidden and therefore difficult to be known, the wise people can have a vision of him by resorting to the control of senses and other means, and thus achieve the liberation from the jaws of death. On the Sāṅkhya theory, too, liberation is not possible by merely perceiving the pradhāna; they too believe that the release from death is possible after the knowledge of the intelligent Puruṣa, as distinct from pradhāna. Besides qualities such as being without taste smell etc. are said to belong to the highest Ātman alone in all the Vedānta—passages. Pradhāna, therefore, is neither spoken of as the object of knowledge, nor referred to by the word 'avyakta'.

त्रयाणामेव चैवमुपन्यासः प्रश्नश्च । ६

[*Trayāṇāṁ*—*of three* ; *eva*—*only* ; *ca*—*and* ; *evaṁ*—*thus*; *upanyāsaḥ*—*reply* ; *praśnaḥ*—*question*; *ca.*]

AND THUS THE QUESTIONS AND REPLIES REFER TO THREE THINGS ALONE (AND NOT TO PRADHĀNA). 6

In Kaṭhavalli there occurs the story of Naciketas and Death. Being sent by his father, Naciketas approached Death and got three boons. In this connection, Naciketas asks him three questions regarding the sacrificial fire (1, 1, 13), the individual soul and the highest Ātman. The second question seeks to know as to what happens regarding the individual soul after death (1, 1, 20), and the third is a query regarding that 'which is neither this nor that, neither cause nor effect, neither again past nor future' (1, 2, 14). The god of Death, we are told, has given three corresponding answers to these questions. Firstly, he tells Naciketas that fire is the beginning of the world, and so tells him the number of bricks etc. required for the sacrificial alter. Secondly, promising him to reveal the hidden knowledge of Brahman, he tells Naciketas that according to merits or demerits, some souls enter the womb in order to have a new body after death, and that others appear in the form of trees or stones (2,5,6,7). And thirdly, he answers the third question by saying that the Ātman has no birth or death etc. (1, 2, 18) There being therefore no separate question or answer regarding pradhāna, it cannot be said that it is either the object of knowledge or is indicated by the word avyakta.

An objection may be raised at this point. If the second question is resumed as the third, then there are only two questions and not three ; and if the third is a distinct and new question from the second, then taking into consideration Naciketas' first boon regarding his father, there will be four questions and not three. And if it is no mistake to ask a question in addition to the three boons conferred, then it is likewise no mistake to have an additional explanatory answer regarding pradhāna.

To this we reply that the number of questions indeed is in no way greater than the number of boons. The first boon does refer to the wished-for kindness to him from his father; the second refers to the fire, and the third to the nature of the soul and Ātman. Now so far as the three questions are concerned, the first refers to the fire, and the second and the third refer to the soul and the Ātman taken together as the subject-matter of the third boon. Naciketas himself says after making inquiry about the destiny of the soul after death, that it constitutes his third boon. So, the first boon takes the form of a demand ; and the second and the third boons the forms of three questions, as explained above. This means that the second and the third questions relate to the single topic, only with this difference that the second deals with it under the aspect of individual soul, and the third under the aspect of the Ātman. And this is possible because the individual soul and the Ātman are really one and not two.

We see the proof of this unity of the jīva and Ātman in a number of ways. (1) Passages like 'That thou art' affirm it. (2) In the present Upaniṣad again, the denial of birth and death in the case of the individual soul is itself an assertion of the non-difference of the soul and Ātman. For there is no point in denying them of the highest God where there is no possibility of their existence. Denial of something has got meaning only when that something has the possibility of existence somewhere. The embodied soul, for example, has got the possibility of birth and death on account of its connection with the body. Therefore the denial of these in the case of the individual soul means that the real nature of the individual soul is to be disembodied. The denial, in other words, points out the unity of the soul and the highest God. (3) Similarly, another passage, which declares the cessation of all sorrow by knowing that the real 'perceiver of all the objects in the waking and the dreaming conditions is the great and omnipresent Ātman itself,' clearly suggests that the jīva is not different from the Prājña (2, 4,). It is a doctrine of the Vedānta that the knowledge of Prājña puts an end to all sorrow ; and this is achieved by the knowledge of the real nature of the jīva. (4) Again, the passage (2,4,10), 'what is here is there and what is there is here ; he who finds any difference goes from death to death, contains a censure of a person who holds that the jīva and Prājña are different. (5) The fact that Naciketas remains firm regarding the choice of his third boon, viz. the question relating the condition of the soul after death, in spite of the various temptations offered by the god of Death, and the fact of subsequent praise of Naciketas and his question, and the form of answer given by the latter, show that the jīva and Prājña are not different from each other. Knowing that Naciketas was not moved by desires for pleasures, the god of Death imparts him the knowledge of the distinction of Vidyā and avidyā, and of the pleasant and the Good, and tells him how by the process of meditation the wise people find out with great difficulty that ancient and hidden God and go beyond both joy and sorrow (1, 2, 4 ; 1, 1, 12). (6) If Naciketas had left the question which had earned him so much praise, and asked a fresh question, it would have simply meant that the praise was wasted on him. His sticking on to the same question only means that the third question about the highest Ātman is really the carrying forward of the second question regarding the individual soul. (7) And, finally, a slight difference in language need not be construed as a difference in the subject-matter of the two questions. For we hold that whereas the second question is with reference to the existence of the soul as apart from the body, the third is merely with reference to its being or not being subject to saṁsāra. So long as avidyā is there, the jīva appears to be endowed with attributes etc. ; but the moment avidyā vanishes the soul too is seen to be one with the Prājña, as is told by the Śruti, 'That thou art'.

As a matter of fact the thing itself does not undergo any change by the presence or absence of avidyā. The rope itself remains as rope whether it appears as a snake or not. Even so, the jīva is, in its real nature, one with the highest Ātman, though it appears to be different in connection with the attributes, the body and the Saṁsāra.

In short, in the Sūtra as well as in the Śruti, the questions and the answers are said to refer to three things only, viz. the fire, the individual soul and the highest Ātman. As against this, there is neither the mention of a question, nor of an answer, which may favour the theory of pradhāna.

महद्वच्च । ७

[*Mahat-vat—like mahat ; ca—and.*]

AND (THE WORD AVYAKTA IS) LIKE (THE WORD) MAHAT (IN NOT BEING ABLE TO REFER TO PRADHĀNA). 7

The Sāṅkhyas have used the word mahat in the sense of sattā or buddhi because it is the first product of pradhāna and because it is buddhi which enables a man to achieve both prosperity and mokṣa. The vedic meaning of mahat, however, is Puruṣa or Ātman knowing whom there is an end to all sorrow. This is clear from the passages, 'The great Ātman is beyond the intellect' (Ka. 1, 2, 22); 'I know that great Person' (Śve. 3, 8). The Vedic word avyakta too like wise cannot mean pradhāna.

२ चमसाधिकरणम् । (८-१०)

Just as the word avyakta is shown to have been put for its effect, viz. the body, and not pradhāna, even so, the attributes, red, white and black indicate fire, water and food respectively, and not pradhāna.

चमसवदविशेषात् ।८

[*Camasavat—like the cup ; aviśeṣāt—there being no special characteristic.*]

As in the case of camasa, (ajā cannot mean pradhāna) because no special characteristic is mentioned. 8

The followers of Kapila may yet find the support of Śruti for their theory of pradhāna in the mantra (Śve. 4 5), which speaks of 'one ajā (She-goat) of red, white and black colours and of her innumerable similar offspring.' We are further told that 'she is loved by one goat but abandoned by another.' Now, obviously, the word 'ajā' does not mean a 'she-goat.' It means the un-born source of all, the pradhāna or prakṛti, which on account of attachment to it deludes some souls into believing that they are subject to pleasure and pain of saṁsāra, but which cannot affect the other souls because they achieve their release through discrimination and non-attachment to it. The sattva is said to be white, because it is pure or shining; the rajas is red because it colours the mind, and tamas is black because it envelopes the mind like darkness.

We reply that taken by itself the mantra is unable to justify any particular doctrine. For the words, 'aja' etc. have different meanings, and there is no special reason, like context for instance, why any particular meaning can be selected and shown to be favourable to any particular doctorine. A parallal example of this occurs in the Bṛhadāraṇyakopaniṣad (2, 2, 3); 'Camasa is a cup with its mouth below and bottom upwards.' Taken by itself, the mantra cannot determine any particular cup. But the sentence that follows determines this, and we get the sense that the so-called cup is the 'head.' Even so, may we not be able to determine the meaning of the word 'ajā' with reference to some other passage? The next Sutra comes as a reply.

ज्योतिरुपक्रमा तु तथा ह्यधीयत एके । ९

[*Jyotiḥ-upakramā—beginning with light; tu—but; tathā—in that manner ; hi—because ; adhīyate—study ; eke—some.*]

(AJĀ) HOWEVER (MEANS THE THREE ELEMENTS) BEGINNING WITH LIGHT; FOR SOME STUDY THEIR TEXT IN THIS MANNER. 9

As said above, we can determine the meaning of the word 'ajā' in the Śvetāśvataropaniṣad by reference to what has been said in the Chāndogyopaniṣad (6, 4, 1) viz. that the colours, red, white and black are the colours of the three elements of fire, water and earth and that these elements have sprung forth from the highest God. The words red, white and black are used to denote their primary meanings, viz. the colours or the elements and not the secondary meanings, viz. guṇas that go to form the pradhāna. The same conclusion is therefore possible to be inferred in the Śvetāśvataropaniṣad. For generally a doubtful passage is interpreted in the light of another passage whose meaning is accepted as beyond doubt. Starting with the question of the Brahman as the cause of the world, the Upaniṣad tells us, just previous to the passage under consideration, how those who had taken resort to meditation could see the power of the highest God, though it is hidden by his qualities. It is this power which is described in this passage (Śve. 1, 1) as creating the entire universe, and subsequently described as māyā or prakṛti, and as belonging to the Mayāvin or the Maheśvara. He is the one lord and support of not only the original yoni or Māyā but of several māyās which are the effects of the original one (4, 10-11). Naturally, in the passage which intervenes (4, 5) the word 'ajā' cannot mean the Sāṁkhya prakṛti or pradhāna as the independent cause of the world. Rather, the context or the subject-matter shows that, as in the ajā passage also, the same divine power in which the names and forms have not become manifest is the cause or the antecedent condition of the world of names and forms. Now this divine power or māyā is said to possess three colours because the three elements of fire, water and earth, which are the effects of māyā, possess the three colours of red, white and black respectively. Just as is the effect so also is the cause.

If 'ajā' is taken to mean the three elements according to the Chāndogyopaniṣad, and not original māyā which is really (ajā) unproduced, a doubt may arise as to how the three elements can either be conceived as having the form of the she-goat or be thought of as unproduced, inasmuch as the three elements are the products of māyā. To this the Sūtrakāra replies :—

कल्पनोपदेशाच्च मध्वादिवदविरोधः । १०

[*Kalpanā-upadeṣāt—being mentioned under the image of; ca—and; madhu-ādi-vat—like honey and others; a-virodhaḥ —not contradictory.*]

LIKE THE (METAPHOR OF) HONEY ETC. THERE IS NOTHING CONTRADICTORY IN MENTIONING (THE DIVINE POWER) UNDER THE IMAGE (OF AJĀ). 10

Just as the sun is imagined as honey, or the speech as cow, or the heavenly world as fire (chā. 3. 1; Bṛ. 5, 8; 6, 2, 9), even so, the prakṛti which consists of fire, water and earth, is imagined as she-goat. The prakṛti can neither be conceived as having the form of a she-goat, nor as unproduced. This original ajā is simply imagined like an ordinary she-goat to produce all the inanimate and animate beings possessing the three colours of the elements like herself, and as being loved by some ignorant souls who are held in bondage by avidyā, but abandoned by those who have attained true knowledge. This distinction between souls and souls does not however mean the doctrine of the multiplicity of souls as the Sāṁkhyas believe, but is merely meant to distinguish bondage from release. The distinction itself is not real but is due to upādhis, which are there on account of false knowledge. As the Śruti says, 'He is the one all-pervading God who is hidden in all beings as the inner Ātman of all' (Śve. 6, 11). It stands to reason then that ajā means fire, water and earth taken together.

३ संख्योपसंग्रहाधिकरणम् । (११–१३)

न संख्योपसंग्रहादपि नानाभावादतिरेकाच्च । ११

[*Na*—*not* ; *saṅkhyā*—*number*; *upasaṅgrahāt*—*being mentioned*; *api*—*even* ; *nānābhāvāt*—*on account of many differences* ; *atirekāt*—*due to excess* ; *ca*—*and.*]

NOT EVEN ON ACCOUNT OF THE NUMBER BEING MENTIONED (CAN IT BE SAID THAT PRADHĀNA HAS THE AUTHORITY OF ŚRUTI); FOR THE PRINCIPLES ARE DIFFERENT (EVERY ONE OF THEM), AND ON ACCOUNT OF EXCESS (OVER THE NUMBER). 11

To show that his doctrine of pradhāna has got the authority of Śruti, the Sāṁkhya again, cites the mantra, 'I believe him alone to be the Ātman, in whom the ākāśa and the panca pancajanas live; knowing him as the immortal Brahman, I become immortal' (Bṛ. 4, 4,17). Here the word 'panca' comes twice, and so, the two words together mean five groups of five, i.e. twenty-five. This, says the Sāṁkhya, is exactly the number of the principles as mentioned in the Sāṁkhya-Kārikā, 3—'The original prakṛti or pradhāna is not an effect; mahat, ahaṅkāra and the five tanmātras are the seven effects of prakṛti, but are causes too of the sixteen which are effects only, viz. the five gross elements and eleven indriyas; and the puruṣa who is neither the effect nor the cause. 'Thus the common element of the number twenty-five in both the Śruti-passage and the Sāṁkhya-Kārikās is taken to mean as the ground for believing that pradhāna has got the support of Śruti.

To this we reply:

Śruti cannot be shown to be the authoritative ource of the pradhāna-theory in this way. For (1) each one of the twenty-five principles of the Sāṁkhyas is different from the others. (2) They cannot be classified into five groups of five principles, there being no common quality in the members of any group; for, a classification into groups presupposes that the members of a group, whether two or three or more, must have some common quality. (3) The words 'panca, panca' are not to be said as forming the number twenty-five by multiplication, just as the words 'five' and 'seven' in the statement, 'Indra did not rain for five and seven years,' can be said to indicate the number of twelve years by the addition of five and seven. For where it is possible to mention the number directly as twenty-five, it is not correct to say that it has been indicated indirectly as five groups of five. (4) Besides, the second word 'panca' is not independent like the first word 'panca,' so that we can mean by both of them the number 'five.' The second word 'panca,' on the other hand, enters as a member in the compound word 'pancajana' as in the passage पंचानां त्वा पंचजनानाम् (Tai. Saṁ 1, 6, 2, 2), and therefore has not got a separate genetive case-termination as the first word 'panca' has got it. The word 'panca' then is not alone repeated twice so as to indicate five times five. Nor can the first word 'panca' be an adjective of the second word 'panca,' which also is an adjective. (5) Nor can it be said that inasmuch as the word 'panca' qualifies the compound word 'pancajana,' the expression 'panca pancajana' would suggest the number twenty-five on the analogy of the expression 'panca pancapuli,' which means twenty-five wooden or other similar vessels. For the word 'pancapūli' is a 'samāhāra-dvigu' compound and means a collection of five vessels; and so, if some one were to ask as to how many 'panchpūlis' are mentioned, the answer that there are five (panca) such groups or twenty-five vessels in all would naturally take the form of the expression 'panca pancapūlis.' But the word 'pancajana,' on the other hand, instead of indicating a 'dvigu' compound indicates directly the idea of five distinct persons. In other words, there being no idea of groups, there arises no occasion to know the number of groups, and so the word 'panca' cannot be said to be an adjective of another compound word 'pancajana' meaning a group of five persons. The expression 'panca pancajana' does not indicate then even indirectly the number twenty-five which may be useful for the Sāṁkhyas to denote the number of their principles. (6) Besides, in the passage where the expression 'panca pancajana' occurs, the words Ātman and ākāśa, which are already included in the twenty-five principles of the Sāṁkhyas, are again mentioned separately. So if the intelligent principle of the Ātman as also the ākāśa are to be counted again along with the supposed number of twenty-five indicated by the expression 'panca pancajana,' the total number would be twenty-seven. The Ātman which is mentioned as the immortal abode in which the 'panca pancajana' live cannot itself be taken again as one which lives in the abode. Similarly, the separate mention of 'ākāśa' would increase the number of the Sāṁkhya categories. (7) Again, the bare reference to a certain possible number as mentioned in the expression 'panca pancajana' can in no way lead us to the number twenty-five of the Sāṁkhyas, for the simple reason that it has been mentioned nowhere else in the Śruti. Besides the word 'jana' does not mean a principle or a category. (8) And if arbitrarily we are to interpret the expression 'panca pancajana,' then it may mean any other group of twenty-five things, and not necessarily the Sāṁkhya principles.

How, then, it may be asked, are we to interpret the word 'pancajana'? It is a name, we reply. For, according to Pāṇini (2, 1, 50) words indicating direction or number are compounded with other words and then mean only a name of something or person. So the word 'pancajanāḥ' does not indicate the number five, but indicates only a particular class of beings; and so again, the expression 'panca pancajanāh' does not indicate the number twenty-five of the Sāṁkhya principles, but indicates that beings known by the name 'pancajana' are five in number, just as the beings known as 'Saptarṣi' are seven in number.

Now to the question what these 'pancajana' things are, the next Sūtra comes as a reply.

प्राणादयो वाक्यशेषात् । १२

[*Prāṇādayaḥ-prāṇa and others; vākyaśeṣat-from complimentary sentence.*]

PRĀṆA AND OTHERS (ARE THE PANCAJANĀḤ, AS IS CLEAR) FROM WHAT FOLLOWS. 12

With a view to describe the nature of Brahman, the mantra which comes immediately after (Bṛ. 4, 4, 18) the mantra in which the pancajanāḥ are mentioned (4, 4, 17) tells us that 'those who know the breath of breath, the eye of the eye, the ear of ear, the food of food, and the mind of mind, are alone able to ascertain the nature of that eternal Brahman. So it is clear that the pancajanāḥ are no other but the beings which are mentioned so closely upon them, *viz.*, the breath, the eye, the ear, the food and the mind. The argument that the word 'jana' does not mean breath etc. tells equally against the word 'jana being taken in the sense of the Sāṁkhya categories. But our interpretation has this much in its favour, *viz.*, (1) the two mantras as shown above are in close proximity; (2)The breath, the eye, etc. have got an actual connection with 'jana' *i. e.*, a being or a person; (3) The word 'puruṣa' which is a synonym for 'jana' is used in the Upaniṣads to denote prāṇa etc.; e. g. 'These are the five Brahmapuruṣas', 'Breath is father, mother etc.'. (Chā. 3, 13, 6; 7, 15, 1); and finally (4) The word jana can, without any contradiction, be taken in its conventional meaning, just as we do in the case of the words 'Udbhid', 'Yūpa', and 'Vedi'. A word of unknown meaning becomes known as possessing some meaning because we see it used in connection with another word of known meaning. For instance, the word 'udbhid' in the sentence, 'he is to sacrifice with udbhid', enables us to know that 'udbhid' is the name of a sacrifice; the word 'yūpa' in 'he cuts the yūpa', means a wooden post; and the word 'vedi' in 'he makes the vedi', means the alter of sacrifice. So once we decide that the word 'pancajana' is a compound which is formed according to the above mentioned rule of Pāṇini and therefore means the name of a thing or person, it is very easy to show, as is shown in the above instances, that the name refers to prāṇa and other beings.

The word 'pancajanāḥ' has been taken by some commentators to mean the five beings of gods, fathers' gandharva, asuras and rākṣasas. Others say that it means the four castes of Brahmins etc. with Niṣādas added to them. We find it used in Ṛgveda to denote the created beings in general (8, 53, 7). We may take any meaning we like, but what the Sūtrakāra intends by choosing the meaning as prāṇa etc., is only to show that (whatever else may be the meaning) the word 'pancajana' does not mean the Sāṁkhya category.

Now it is a fact that the Kāṇva recension of the Upaniṣad does not mention the being of food, while the Mādhyandina mentions it along with the other four. To this the next Sūtra comes as a reply.

ज्योतिषैकेषामसत्यन्ने । १३

[*Jyotiṣā–by light; ekeṣām–of some; asati—when not mentioned; anne–food.*]

NOTWITHSTANDING FOOD BEING NOT (MENTIONED) BY SOME, JYOTI BEING (MENTIONED, THE NUMBER OF BEINGS IS STILL FIVE). 13

The Kāṇva recension no doubt, makes no mention of the being of food; but we must remember that just in the preceding mantra, the jyoti or the light of the sun has been mentioned only to remind us of the nature of Brahman and the way of devotion to it. But it may be pointed out that if 'jyoti' refers to Brahman, it cannot at the same time refer to the light of the sun; and that there is no reason why the Mādhyandina recension should not include it to make the number five, but that the Kāṇva one should include it, even if both the recensions refer to jyoti. The reply is that the choice to include the jyoti or not to include it is dependent on the requirement of the followers of the two branches. The Mādhyandina get all the five beings of prāṇa and others in one and the same mantra, while the Kāṇvas do not; and so it is that though the former do not, the latter do require to include the jyoti in order to make the number five. This is consistent with a similar Mimāṁsā usage of either accepting or not the Ṣoḍaśin-cup at the atirātra sacrifice.

It has been proved so far that pradhāna is not mentioned in Śruti. That the doctrine of pradhāna has neither been backed up by Smṛti nor by reasoning will be shown later on.

४ कारणत्वाधिकरणम् । (१४–१५)

कारणत्वेन चाकाशादिषु यथाव्यपदिष्टोक्तेः । १४

[*Kāraṇatvena–as cause; ca–and; ākāśa–ādiṣu–of ākāśa and others; yathā—as; vyapadiṣṭokteḥ–as is said to be mentioned.*]

AS (IN ONE, SO IN ALL OTHER VEDĀNTA-PASSAGES, BRAHMAN) BEING MENTIONED AS THE CAUSE OF ĀKĀŚA AND OTHERS, (THERE IS NO CONFLICT IN THE PASSAGES). 14

What we have seen so far from the very beginning is: (*i*) The nature of Brahman, as stated in the Sūtra 'Janmādyasya yataḥ' (1, 1, 1); (*ii*) That Brahman is the uniform topic of all the Vedānta-passages which we have so far considered while discussing Sūtras from 1, 1, 2 to 1, 3, 43; and that (*iii*) the doctrine of pradhāna is not at all mentioned in Śruti, as has been clear from the last thirteen Sūtras of this pāda.

Now, however, there comes forth a new objection. It may be said that it is neither proved that Brahman is the cause nor that it is the uniform topic of all the Vedānta-passages, inasmuch as they are seen to contradict each other. For instance the order in which the creation has been mentioned to have taken place varies from place to place. In one place, we are told that ākāśa has come forth from the Ātman (Tai. 2, 1); in another the Sat is said to have produced the fire (Chā. 6, 2, 3); in another place still, the Puruṣa is said to have produced the prāṇas, and the prāṇas the belief etc. (Pra. 6,4). As against all these statements in which some order of creation is mentioned, we get also an account of creation in which there is no mention of order; for instance, in the Aitareyopaniṣad, we are told that the Ātman has produced the three worlds of heaven, earth and pātāla. The creation is also said to have begun from non-existence (Tai. 2, 7: Chā. 3 19, 1). As opposed to this, non-existence is discredited, and existence mentioned as the beginning of the world (Chā. 6, 2, 1—2). Spontaneously, again, the world is said to have come into existence. That which was merely undeveloped originally has itself become developed by the means of names and forms (Br. 1, 4, 7). Thus, there being various contradictions regarding creation, and inasmuch as Brahman is already an accomplished fact, the Vedānta-passages cannot be trusted so far as they claim that Brahman is the cause of the world. Rather, taking our stand on Smṛti and reasoning, we should accept pradhāna or some other entity as the cause of the world.

To this we reply. Though there may exist contradictions in the Vedānta-passages regarding the order or otherwise of the created things, such as ākāśa and others, there is no such contradiction regarding the creator. For, as in one passage, so in all other Vedānta-passages, the creator is described as one who is omniscient, the lord of all, the inner Ātman of everything, and as the one and the only cause, without a second. Consider, for instance, the description of Brahman as the cause in the Taittirīyopaniṣad. The words 'knowledge' and 'desired' which are used with reference to Brahman, indicate that it is endowed with intelligence. The description that it is 'independent' of anything else applies only to God. The fact that it is this God who has further been referred to as the Ātman and as residing in the innermost sheaths known as made up of body, prāṇa etc. clearly indicates that he is the internal soul of all. The statements 'Let me be many', 'Let me produce the beings', show us how the Ātman himself has become many and is therefore not different from what he has become. And finally, the passage, 'He created all this', tells us that before the creation of the world, he alone existed as the cause (Tai. 2, 1, & 6). Now as in this passage, so in other passages too Brahman is described as possessing the same characteristics. For instance, in the Chāndogya, 'Being alone, and nothing else' is said to have been 'in the beginning; it thought to become many and to grow; it produced fire' (Chā. 6,2, 1,—3). We have the same idea in another passage of the Aitareyopaniṣad : 'All this was the Ātman in the beginning; there was nothing else neither movable nor immovable he thought to produce worlds' (1, 1;). So, even if there are conflicting statements regarding the order of creation, all the Vedānta-passages are thus seen to agree in saying that Brahman is the cause of the world. No doubt, these contradictions regarding creation will be reconciled by the Sūtrakāra later on, in the first Sūtra of the third pāda of the second adhyaya. For the present, we are, in no way, concerned with these contradictions. For to describe the order or nature of creation is not at all the aim of Śruti. The welfare of man does not depend on these matters. Taking into consideration both the introduction and conclusion of several such passages, we find that they are only subservient to the main topic of Brahman.. The passage, for instance, which asks 'to seek after the root of food, *viz.*, water, and then to seek after the root of water , *viz.* fire, and then again to seek after the root of fire, *viz.* the truth' (Chā. 6, 8, 4), ends in the search of Brahman alone. All accounts of creation, which involve the illustrations of clay, iron, sparks etc., are in the opinion of the experts who have the knowledge of Śruti, only the means for the acquisition of the knowledge of Brahman, in which there is no difference whatever (Mā. Gauda. Kā. 3, 5). Knowledge of Brahman, on the other hand, is mentioned to carry its own fruit : 'He who realizes it reaches the highest' (Tai. 2, 1); 'He who realizes the Ātman overcomes grief' (Chā. 7, 1, 3); 'One who realizes him goes beyond death' (Śve. 3, 8). Direct is the fruit of the experience of this knowledge; for, the moment the truth of the statement, 'That thou art,' is realized and the Ātman is seen to be not affected by the rounds of birth and death, that very moment, vanishes the illusion of the Saṁsāra.

As for the assertion that there exist contradictory statements even with the nature of the cause, *e.g* whether it was existent or non-existent in the beginning, we shall refute it in our discussion of the next Sūtra.

समाकर्षात् । १५

[*Samākarṣāt–being lnihed up.*]

As (THE WORD 'ASAT' IN THE PREVIOUS PASSAGE) IS LINKED WITH THE WORD 'SAT' IN THE NEXT PASSAGE, 'ASAT' INDICATES BRAHMAN AND NOT NON-BEING. 15.

A passage in the Taittirīyopaniṣad (2, 1) tells us that 'all this, verily, was in the beginning, non-being (asat)'. But the 'asat' need not mean absolute non-existence; for, in the preceding passage of the same Upaniṣad, we are told on the authority of those who have realized the Brahman that 'one who knows the Brahman as non-existing becomes himself non-existing; while one who knows it to be existing exists himself' (2, 6, 1). This is at once a clear denial of the absolute non-being like that of the horn of a hare and the affirmation of the being of Brahman alone. It is this same Being or Brahman which is further referred to as the innermost Ātman of the various sheaths of food, prāṇa etc., as the creator because he 'desired to become many', and as the ultimate Truth. It is only after this narration of the nature of Brahman, and therefore as connected with it, that we get the mantra: 'non-being indeed was this in the beginning'. If, instead of the generally accepted necessary connection between the Brāhmaṇa portion and the mantra of the Upaniṣad, the word 'asat' were to mean absolute non-existence, there will be no continuity of context at all. The conclusion therefore, would be that if the word 'sat' indicates the being of Brahman with all the manifest forms and names, the word 'asat' indicates the same being of Brahman without the names and forms. It indicates, in other words, the condition of the world prior to its origination, the condition in which Brahman appears to be 'asat', as if.

The passage in the Chāndogyopaniṣad too must be construed in the same manner. The statement, 'This was originally asat', is immediately followed by 'it then became sat'. It means therefore that the non-being referred to by the pronoun 'it' cannot be the absolute non-being, but on the contrary, means the sat or the Brahman (3, 19, 1). Similarly, the reference to the opinion of others in another passage of the same Upaniṣad viz. that 'non-being was this in the beginning' (6, 2, 1), does not mean the optional assertion of absolute non-existence, but means, on the contrary, the refutation of such a vulgar doctrine with a view to strengthen the position that Brahman alone was in the beginning. For there cannot be any optional view with regard to reality, as there can be with regard to action.

This enables us to interpret another passage still from the Bṛhadāraṇyakopaniṣad (1, 4, 7) which may appear to favour the view that the world came into existence without a creator. The reference to the world which was originally without names and forms, but which developed in course of time into one with names and forms, is not a reference to the world which came into being of its own accord and without a ruler. It is rather a reference to the world in which the author of it is said to have entered to the 'very tips of the nails of the fingers.' If the world is to be supposed as having come into existence by way of natural evolution, and if the authorship of the Ātman is to be denied, the pronoun 'he' in the sentence 'he entered into the effects' would serve no purpose. On the contrary, we are immediately told that the being which has so entered is known by various names, such as, the eye, the ear and the mind, because it does the function of seeing, hearing and thinking. We are told, in other words, that the being which has entered is no other than the intelligent Ātman; and it is clear that the authorship of the Ātman is as much necessary for the manifestation of names and forms at the beginning of the world as it is today, if at all we are not to assume something against experience. The Chāndogyopaniṣad also tells us that the evolution of the world has taken place under the supervision of the omniscient seer. 'Let me evolve the names and forms by entering into the beings by means of the jīvātman' (6, 3, 2). No doubt we have the intransitive expression, 'The world evolved itself', but it only shows the ease with which the Lord must have created the universe. We know it is the farmer who reaps the field, and yet we sometimes say that the 'field reaps.' Or else, the expression 'the world evolves' may be said to imply an author who evolves it, just as, the expression, 'the village is being approached' implies some person who approaches the village.

५ बालाक्यधिकरणम् । (१६–१८)

जगद्वाचित्वात् । १६

[*Jagat—world ; vācitvāt—being denoted.*]

BECAUSE (THE WORD 'KARMA') MEANS THE WORLD, (BRAHMAN IS THE AUTHOR OF ALL THIS AS ITS KARMA). 16

There is a dialogue in the Kauṣītaki-Brāhmaṇa between the king Ajātaśatru and a brahmin, by name Bālāki; and in the course of it the king tells the brahmin that 'verily he is fit to be known, who is the maker of the persons and of this work' (4, 18). Now the question to solve is whether the object to be known is the individual soul, or the chief prāṇa or the highest Ātman.

The pūrvapakṣin holds that what is meant is the chief prāṇa; for, in the first place, 'prāṇa' is the support of the activity or movement which it said to be its work. Secondly, the word 'prāṇa' which is used in the immediately following complementary sentence, viz. 'The jīva becomes one with prāṇa, during sleep' (4, 20), is well-known as denoting the chief breath. Thirdly, as Bālāki had already declared, prāṇa is the creator of the persons in the sun, the moon etc.; or as the Bṛhadāraṇyaka says, (3, 9, 9) the sun and the other deities are nothing but the modifications of the one God, viz. prāna or Brahman.

Or else, according to the pūrvapakṣin, the being fit to be known may be the individual soul. The 'work' of the soul then would mean the deeds of merit or demerit and the soul itself will be considered as the cause of the persons in the sun etc., inasmuch as the sun, the moon etc. can be said to be the sources of pleasure and pain to be experienced by the soul. Besides, a little further we get a characteristic mark of the individual soul. In order to instruct Bālāki that the being which really experiences the pleasures and pains is not prāṇa but the soul, Ajātaśatru went near a sleeping man and shouted at him by different names of prāṇa to wake him up. But the man was not awakened at all. Ajātaśatru then pushed the sleeping man with a stick and woke him up, and thus proved that the jīva is different from the prāṇa. Again, a little further, in section 20, we get another characteristic mark of the individual soul. The individual self as well as the other selves in the sun and the moon etc. are doing mutual obligations on each other. The individual soul is known as prāṇa only in a secondary manner, inasmuch as it is the support of prāṇa. And as there are no characteristic marks of the highest God, we must conclude that it is either the individual soul or the prāṇa that should be considered as the fit object of knowledge.

To this we reply. The beginning itself of the section is sufficient to show that God is the author of the persons mentioned in the sun, the moon etc.and is therefore the object of knowledge. It is Bālāki who begins the conversation with the statement that he would tell what Brahman is, but remains silent only after mentioning the persons residing in the sun, the moon etc. (4, 1). Ajātaśatru thereupon ridiculed Bālāki for having vainly said that he would describe the Brahman, and told him in return that the creator of these persons must be somebody else, viz. the Brahman. If Ajātaśatru too, who censured Bālāki for his boast, were also simply to mention some non-Brahmanic persons and remain silent, then there would be no point in the censure and the introductory statement of Bālāki regarding Brahman. Therefore it is that the creator of these persons is none else but God. Besides, God alone, unlike prāṇa and jīva, can be said to be truly independent in creating the persons in the sun etc. The word 'Karma' too does neither indicate the movement nor the merit and demerit accruing from it, so that we may refer to it as prāṇa or jīva. For neither of the two meanings, movement or merit etc. is the topic under discussion. Nor can the word' 'Karma' denote the persons in the sun etc. for the word puruṣa' is masculine and is used in genetive plural, while the word 'karma' is of neuter gender and is used in the singular number. Neither, again, the activity of producing the persons nor the result of that activity can be the meaning of the word 'karma' for both these are included in the agent or the author without whom they would not exist.

Examinating, then, all the possible alternatives, we conclude that the pronoun 'this' and the word 'karman' in the sentence, 'He of whom this is the karman,' point out the world that we see before us, even though there is no explicit reference to it. For the reference to the entire world can be inferred, not only from the explicit reference to a part of it, as constituted by the persons in the sun etc, but also by the additional words in the Śruti, viz. 'Or, this karman.' The reference to the 'persons' in the sun etc. as being created is meant to exclude the possibility of their being construed as Brahman, as Bālāki suggested, and to make them only a part of the entire world which is nothing but the work of God. When one says that both the Parivrājakas (i.e. the Brahmins who have renounced the world) and the Brahmins should be fed, what he means is that all the Brahmins should be fed. Similarly, the reference to a specific part of the world, and again to the entire world, is to affirm only emphatically that the highest God alone, as indicated by all the Vedānta-passages, is the creator of the whole world.

जीवमुख्यप्राणलिंगान्नेति चेत्तव्द्याख्यातम्। १७

[*Jīva—soul; mukhya—principal; prāṇa—breath; lingāt—due to marks ; na—not ; iti cet—if it is said ; tat—that; vyākhyātaṁ—already refuted.*]

IF IT BE SAID THAT IT IS NOT SO, ON ACCOUNT OF THE CHARACTERISTIC MARKS OF THE JĪVA AND PRĀṆA (BEING MENTIONED IN A COMPLIMENTARY PASSAGE) WE REPLY THAT THAT HAS BEEN ALREADY REFUTED. 17

As already explained while discussing Sūtra 31 of the first pāda, there may arise three objects for meditation, viz. the jīva, the prāṇa and the Brahman, if along with our view the view of the pūrvapakṣin is also to be adopted. But this is not acceptable to us. For, as seen in the preceding Sūtra, the beginning of the Śruti passage shows that the topic under discussion is Brahman and nothing else. The conclusion of that section too shows that Brahman is the topic; for he who knows Brahman is said to have been receiving the highest reward, viz. eminence among all beings, supremacy over all, and independence (Kau. 4, 20).

If the refutation has already been made in 1, 1, 31, while dealing with the statement of Pratardana, where then, it may be asked, is the necessity of this Sūtra? The reply is that the 'work', viz. the creation of this world, was not referred there to Brahman. But as the doubt may arise whether the 'work' is referred to prāṇa, on account of its one meaning viz. movement, or to jīva on account of its other meaning viz. the unseen fruit of it, it was felt necessary to have this Sūtra, and settle that the word 'work' refers to Brahman. As for the word 'prāṇa' in a subsequent passage, we have to remember that it is used in the sense of Brahman, as in the passage, 'the mind becomes tied with the prāṇa' (Chā. 6, 8, 2). And similarly, if the beginning and conclusion of the passage justify us to say that the topic deals with Brahman, then, whatever characteristics we may have about jīva, we shall be justified in considering them as indicative of Brahman, inasmuch as the jīva is identical with Brahman.

अन्यार्थं तु जैमिनिः प्रश्नव्याख्यानाभ्यामपि चैवमेके । १८

[*Anyārthaṁ—for another purpose ; tu—but; Jaiminiḥ; praśna-vyākhyānābhyāṁ—on account of question and answer ; api—also ; ca—and ; evaṁ—so ; eke—some.*]

JAIMINI, ON THE OTHER HAND, (THINKS) THAT ON ACCOUNT OF THE QUESTION AND ANSWER (THE REFERENCE TO THE INDIVIDUAL SOUL) HAS ANOTHER PURPOSE; SOME OTHERS TOO (READ THEIR TEXT TO INDICATE THIS PURPOSE). 18

There is no reason, according to Jaimini, to dispute whether the topic under discussion is the individual soul or Brahman. For he holds that even accepting that there is a reference to the individual soul, it is to indicate the knowledge of Brahman. And the reason for his opinion is the nature of the question and the answer in this connection. After having proved to Bālāki that the soul is different from prāṇa, Ajātaśatru asked as to where the person was asleep and whence he came back to the waking life. And the reply we get is that 'during dreamless sleep a person becomes one with this prāṇa (Brahman) alone'; and that it is 'from this Ātman alone that all the prāṇas depart to their abode; and that from prāṇa depart the gods, and from gods the beings' (Kau. 4, 19 and 20). And it is the Vedānta doctrine that during sleep the soul becomes one with Brahman, and that from Brahman it is that the world and the prāṇa proceed. Therefore that, in which the sleeping soul becomes devoid of cognitions of the waking life and enjoys a tranquil life, is Brahman itself ; and so it is the only object fit to be known. The Vājasaniyas, especially, in their text of the dialogue between Bālāki and Ajātaśatru, ask a similar question regarding the vijñānamaya or the soul as distinct from the highest Ātman, and have the reply that it lies in the ākāśa within the heart (Bṛ. 2, 1, 16 and 17). Now this small ākāśa is nothing but the highest Ātman (Chā. 8, 1, 1) ; and because the empirical selves are said to have come forth from the Ātman (Bṛ. 2, 1, 20), the Vājasaniyas suggest that the Ātman alone is the source of all. Thus, the question and the answer are not only able to intimate to us the existence of the soul beyond the prāṇa, but also the existence of the Ātman beyond both prāṇa and jīva.

६ वाक्यान्वयाधिकरणम् । (१९-२२)

वाक्यान्वयात् । १९

[*Vākya—sentence; anvayāt—on account of connection.*]

On account of the connection of the sentences, (the meaning of the word 'Ātman' in 'The Ātman is to be seen' etc. is the highest Ātman alone). 19

In the Maitreyi-brāhmaṇa of the Bṛhadāraṇyakopaniṣad, we are told that nothing becomes dear for its own sake, but that everything becomes dear for the sake of the Ātman, and that therefore all this becomes known when the Ātman is seen, heard, thought about and meditated (Bṛ. 3, 5, 6). Now there arises the doubt whether the object to be seen etc. is the individual soul, on account of the dear things such as, husband, etc., with which it is connected as the subject of experience, or the Ātman on account of the fact that everything else becomes known when the Ātman is known.

The pūrvapakṣin maintains, as indicated above, that all the objects of enjoyment in this world, such as, husband, wife, riches and son, are dear on account of the individual soul, and therefore it is the object of sight, etc. Besides, the section begins with the discussion of the individual soul; and if, in spite of this, the object is to be considered as something else, there would be no sense in making the beginning with the topic of the individual soul. Towards the middle of the dialogue, again, the great being or the Ātman which is endless, unlimited and full of knowledge is shown as springing forth from the five elements in the form of the individual soul, and meeting with destruction after them, so that there remains not a trace of knowledge in it after death (Bṛ. 2, 4, 12). What this means is that the object of sight, etc. is the individual soul endowed with cognitions and not the highest Ātman. And further at the end of the dialogue, Yājñavalkya refers to the individual soul again, when he raises the question as to how one should 'know the knower'; for the knowing involves the cognitional aspect of the individual soul alone. As to how one may know everything else by knowing the individual soul, the pūrvapakṣin says that this is not to be taken in a literal sense, but must be understood as meaning that the world of objects is to be known through its relation to the soul.

To this we reply. If we look to the mutual connection of the passages in the dialogue, we shall find that the object of sight etc. is the highest Ātman. We must remember that it is only after Maitreyī was found to be thoroughly dissatisfied with riches which she thought was unable to carry her to immortality, that her husband Yājñavalkya imparted her the knowledge of the Ātman (Bṛ. 2, 4, 2 and 3). And as Śruti and Smṛti tell us, immortality cannot be attained without the knowledge of the Ātman. Nor can everything else be known without such knowledge ; for the Ātman is the highest cause of all. Therefore the view of the pūrvapakṣin, that it is not a literal truth that everything else becomes known when the Ātman is known, is not adequate. On the contrary, it is to point out that it is a literal truth, and that therefore it is inadequate to hold that the objects of the world are different from the Ātman, that we are told in the subsequent passage, that those who erroneously think that the castes of Brahmins etc. and the objects of the world are different from the Ātman are abandoned by them all. This means what is immediately stated further in the passage, viz. that all these things in the world are non-distinct from the Ātman (2, 4, 6). Just as the different sounds of the musical instruments can be said to be included in the prominent sound of the drum, even so, all these things are the Ātman. To say that 'Ṛgveda is the breath of this great Being' (2, 4, 10) is only to point out that the Ātman is the cause of names, forms and actions. It is this Ātman again which is further declared as the support or the destination of the whole world including the objects, the senses and the mind, and is characterized as neither having inside nor outside, and as one, full, homogeneous mass of intuitive knowledge. From all this it is clear that the object of sight etc. is the highest Ātman alone.

As for the argument of the pūrvapakṣin that the introductory part of the dialogue contains a reference to the individual soul, let us examine it in the next three Sūtras.

प्रतिज्ञासिद्धेर्लिंगमाश्मरथ्यः । २०

[Pratijñā—statement; siddheḥ—of proof; lingaṁ—mark; Āśmarathyaḥ.]

ĀŚMARATHYA THINKS (THAT THE REFERENCE TO THE INDIVIDUAL SOUL AS THE OBJECT TO BE SEEN ETC.) INDICATES THE PROOF OF THE STATEMENT. 20

If the individual soul having cognitions were to be different from the highest Ātman, then the knowledge of the latter will not involve the knowledge of the former as also of the other things in the world; nor will the other statement, 'all this is the Ātman,' will be fulfilled. It is therefore to secure the fulfilment of this statement as well as of the knowledge of all other things by the knowledge of the Ātman, that Āśmarathya thinks that the individual soul mentioned in the beginning is intended to imply its non-difference from the highest Ātman.

उत्क्रमिष्यत एवंभावादित्यौडुलोमिः । २१

[Utkramiṣyataḥ—of one who rises up; evaṁ—so; bhāvāt—because of being; iti—thus; Auḍulomiḥ]

AUḌULOMI (THINKS THAT THE FACT THAT THE INDIVIDUAL SOUL IS NON-DIFFERENT FROM THE HIGHEST ĀTMAN IS REFERRED TO IN THE BEGINNING OF THE SECTION) BECAUSE THE SOUL WILL BE SUCH WHEN IT DEPARTS (FROM THE BODY). 21

In view of the Upaniṣadic statement that 'The serene Being appears in its own form, as it departs from the body and meets the resplendent light' (Chā. 8, 12, 3), as also the statement that 'Like rivers running into the sea,' the wise man loses his name and form and becomes united with the highest Person' (Mu. 3, 2, 8), Auḍulomi thinks, that the reference to the individual soul as non-different from the highest Ātman, in the beginning of the Maitreyī-brāhmaṇa is appropriate. The individual soul is contaminated by the upādhis of body, senses mind etc. ; but when it becomes pure by means of knowledge, devotion etc., it leaves behind all the adjuncts of body and other things and is united with the highest Ātman. It is in view of this future condition which is acquired by the individual soul, that it is described in the beginning as non-different from the highest Ātman, in spite of the fact that the soul is described as if possessing name and form, only to make it comparable with the river which loses its name and form when it runs into the sea.

अवस्थितेरिति काशकृत्स्नः । २२

[*Avasthiteḥ*—*because of existence*; *iti*—*thus*; *Kāśakṛtsnaḥ.*]

KĀŚAKṚTSNA (THINKS THAT THE REFERENCE TO THE INDIVIDUAL SOUL AS NON-DIFFERENT FROM THE HIGHEST ĀTMAN IS ADMISSIBLE) BECAUSE (IT IS THE HIGHEST ĀTMAN WHICH) EXISTS IN THE CONDITION (OF THE INDIVIDUAL SOUL). 22

In view of the Brāhmaṇa-text that 'The divinity of the Ātman wished to manifest the names and forms by entering into the created elements under the form of the individual soul' (Chā. 6, 3, 2), and in view of the mantras, such as, 'The omniscient Ātman, having created the names and forms of things after first entering into them as the individual soul, calls them by these names' (Tai. 3, 12, 7), Kāśakṛtsna thinks that the individual soul is nothing else but the highest Ātman. The soul is neither a modification of the Ātman, nor a created thing like the five elements. The names and forms do not in reality belong to the soul, but are imposed upon it on account of the upādhis of avidyā. Āśmarathya, too, it may be said, believes in the non-difference of the individual soul from the highest Ātman; but he believes so for the sake of believing in something else, viz. the possibility of the knowledge of all things consequent on the knowledge of the Ātman, and the unity of the Ātman in spite of apparent diversity. Besides, his belief in the non-difference is not absolute but relative ; for, he does believe to some extent at least in the relation of cause and effect between the highest Ātman and the individual soul, and not in their identity. Auḍulomi goes a step further and admits that the soul and the Ātman are different in the condition of ignorance, though they become identical when knowledge arises. Kāśakṛtsna alone puts forth the correct view of Śruti viz. 'Thou art that'; and it is on this view alone that immortality can be said to follow from the realization of the Ātman. For if the soul were a modification of the Ātman, it will simply be lost by being merged in its cause, and there would be left no soul to experience the immortal life. Similarly, if immortality is to be construed as the vanishing of the names and forms, they ought to have truly belonged to the individual soul ; but it is seen that they disappear with the body, the senses etc., meaning thereby, that they are falsely attached to the soul. Nay, the very creation of the souls from the highest Ātman, as if they are sparks emanating from the fire, has no basis in reality but refers to the work of the upādhis of avidyā.

As for the refutation of the second point of the pūrvapaṣkin, viz., the great Being which emerges in the form of the individual soul from the elements, and which, in the form of the soul itself, is therefore declared in the middle of the Maitreyī-Brāhmaṇa, as the object to be seen, etc., the three Sūtras will again give three different answers thus. According to Āśmarathya, the emergence of the highest Ātman in the form of the soul is an indication of the proof of the statements that all the things of the world arise and dissolve in the Ātman, and so are known through the knowledge of the Ātman, and that they are non-different from the Ātman, as their cause. To Auḍulomi, it is the future possible condition of the soul which is responsible for its being described as non-different from the Ātman. The soul becomes purified by means of knowledge, devotion, etc. and becomes one with Ātman, at the time of its departure from the body. It is with reference to this future, non-different condition of the soul that it is conceived that the Ātman emerges as the soul. Kāśakṛtnsa, on the other hand, thinks that the soul is described as non-different from the Ātman, because it is verily the Ātman itself who lives in the form of the soul.

One may say however, that the soul is described as vanishing after the elements and as being destitude of all knowledge after death. How, then, it may be asked, can the soul be said to be non-different from the Ātman? But the reply is that it is the destruction of the specific cognitions of the soul, and not of the soul or the Ātman. This reply comes from Yājñavalkya himself when he finds that his wife was similarly bewildered at the extinction of knowledge and the consequent destruction of the soul after its departure from the body. 'The eternal, steadfast, ever-conscious Ātman is imperishable; what was conjoined by avidyā is merely disjoined by vidyā. It is simply the dissociation of the individual soul from the mātrās, i.e., the elements and the sense-organs' (Bṛ. 2, 4, 13).

The third point of the pūrvapakṣin should also be refuted only by what Kāśakṛtsna says. The argument of the pūrvapakṣin was that the word 'knower' in, 'how should one know the knower?' in the concluding portion of the dialogue, implies a subject as the knower as distinct from the object known, and therefore the action of knowing etc. must be ascribed to the individual soul. But as the Bṛhadāraṇyakopaniṣad says, 'One can see the other, so long as there is duality'; there will exist till then the various specific cognitions of the individual soul. But when, on account of vidyā, 'all this becomes the Ātman, then who should see whom?' (2, 4, 14). Except the fact that the word 'knower' is used to mean the great Being or the Ātman or the Self-consciousness itself, there remains in this non-dualistic condition, no specific cognition, nor the empirical distinction of the subject and object, nor again the difference of the individual soul from the highest Ātman.

This view of the Vedānta is fully supported by Śruti and Smṛti. 'Being only was in the beginning; one without a second' (Chā. 6, 2, 1); 'The Ātman alone is all this' (Chā. 7, 25, 2); 'Brahman alone is all this' (Mu. 2, 2, 11); 'There is no other seer but he' (Bṛ 3, 7, 23; 3, 8, 11). Smṛti too says: 'Know me to be the knower in all bodies' (B. G. 13, 27). There are other Śruti passages which support the above view by denying all difference: 'He who considers himself and Ātman as different is like a beast who does not know anything' (Bṛ. 1, 4, 10); 'He who sees mere multiplicity moves from death to death' (Bṛ. 4, 4, 19). The same conclusion is again strengthened by denying every kind of action or modification on the part of the Ātman. 'This great unborn Ātman is without old age and death; he is the fearless immortal Brahman' (Bṛ. 4, 4, 24). Besides, there will be no certain knowledge, release or satisfaction of desires, as are vouchsafed for those who have 'fixed themselves in the knowledge of the Ātman' (Mu. 3, 2, 6). 'What infatuation, or what sorrow will there be for him who sees the unity of the Ātman in all?' (Īs. 7). The Bhagavadgītā too mentions similar characteristics of one who is fixed in the higher knowledge of the Brahman (2, 54-69).

If, therefore, right knowledge, according to us, is the absolute identity of the individual soul and the highest Ātman, there would be no sense in admitting the plurality of souls, or difference, except in name, between the soul and the Ātman. That is why the cave in which the real, infinite, omniscient Brahman is said to reside (Tai. 2, 1), does not refer to any other cave except the heart of the soul. Neither can it be said that something other than the Brahman resides in the cave; for we are further told that the 'creator himself entered into the things after creating them' (Tai. 2, 6). Those therefore who insist on making a difference between the soul and the Brahman not only go against right knowledge, but also make the final beatitude impossible. Release to them is the fruit of actions. Naturally release to them is temporary; or, if assumed to be eternal, they will contradict their previous position viz. that it is the fruit of action.

७ प्रकृत्याधिकरणम् । (२३-२७)

प्रकृतिश्च प्रतिज्ञादृष्टान्तानुपरोधात् २३

[*Prakṛtiḥ*—*material cause*; *ca*—*and*; *pratijñā*—*statement*; *dṛṣṭānta*—*example*; *anuparodhāt*—*not being contradictory.*]

(BRAHMAN IS) THE MATERIAL CAUSE ALSO; FOR (TO HOLD THIS VIEW ALONE) DOES NOT CONTRADICT THE STATEMENT AND EXAMPLE OF IT. 23

We have already said that an inquiry about the nature of Brahman is essential, because it leads to mokṣa, just as an inquiry about religious duty is essential because it leads to prosperity. We have also characterised the Brahman as that from which the world has come, and in which it rests and is absorbed. But a question may arise as to whether the Brahman is the efficient cause of the world like a potter of the vessels of clay, or the material cause like the clay itself.

The pūrvapakṣin holds that Brahman is the efficient cause only. For just as a potter, who is merely an efficient cause of the vessels, reflects before producing the vessels, Brahman too is regarded as having first 'reflected before creating prāṇa' (Pra. 6, 3 ; 4). Or, like kings of different places, Brahman too can be considered as the Lord of this world and so possessing only efficient power. Besides, this world, which is the effect of the creator's activity, is non-intelligent, impure and consists of parts ; therefore, its cause too must be of the same nature. But as we learn from Śruti, Brahman is 'without parts, inactive, faultless and taintless' (Śve. 6, 19). Brahman therefore is not the material cause of the world. So, the only alternative that remains is to say, in the first place, that something different from Brahman, viz. the pradhāna of the Sāṁkhyas is the material cause of the world; and that secondly, Brahman is the efficient cause only.

As against this, we say in reply that Brahman is not merely the efficient but the material cause also; for it is only then that there will be no contradiction with what is given as illustration. When Āruṇi asks his son, Śvetaketu, if he had inquired from his preceptor as to 'what it was, which when known, one hears that which was not previously heard, and perceives and knows that which was not previously perceived or known' (Chā. 6 1, 3), he gives us the knowledge of the truth, that to know the Ātman is to know everything else. And this is possible only in the case of the material cause; for the effect is not different from its material cause. But we cannot say the same thing with reference to the efficient cause; for we find that the palace is different from the carpenter who constructed it. The illustrative examples too have a reference to the material cause alone. 'It is by one clod of clay that all that is made of clay is known; for whatever the modifications or the effects are, they are only names and have their origin in speech' (Chā. 6, 1, 4); or again, all that is made of gold or iron is known by one lump of gold or iron. Just as 'the plants grow in their cause, viz. the earth,' so there is the Ātman as the cause of all (Mu. 1, 1, 3 and 7); or just as 'when the drum is seized the sound is seized,' even so, 'everything else is known when the Ātman is known' (Bṛ. 4, 5, 6 and 8). All these and similar examples prove that Brahman is the material cause of the world. The ablative case also in 'That from which (yataḥ) these beings are born' indicates the material cause of the beings (Tai. 3, 1).

That, besides being the material cause, Brahman is also the efficient cause of the world, can be inferred from the fact that there is no other agent or operative cause responsible for guiding the creation, just as over and above clay or gold as the material cause, there are the potters and goldsmiths as efficient causes responsible for turning the clay or gold into vessels or ornaments. Śruti also says that prior to creation Brahman was one, without a second. On the other hand, if there were some additional guiding principle distinct from the material cause, both the statement and the illustrative examples would be false, inasmuch as, the knowledge of everything else would not follow from the knowledge of one thing. So in the absence of any other operative or material cause, Brahman alone is both the efficient and the material cause of the world.

Other reasons which support this view are :

अभिध्योपदेशाच्च । २४

[*Abhidhyā—volition; upadeśāt—because of statement.*]

AND BECAUSE OF THE STATEMENT REGARDING VOLITION (ON THE PART OF THE ĀTMAN). 24

The freedom to desire to 'become many etc.' shows that the Atman is the efficient cause. And since the growth and the manifold nature of the world spring forth from the Ātman, it is also the material cause (Tai. 2, 6, 1; Chā. 6, 2, 3).

साक्षाच्चोभयाम्नायात् । २५

[*Sakṣāt—directly; ca—and; ubhaya—both; āmnāyāt—as stated by Śruti.*]

AND BECAUSE (BRAHMAN) IS DIRECTLY MENTIONED BY ŚRUTI, (AS THE MATERIAL CAUSE OF) BOTH (THE ORIGIN AND DISSOLUTION OF THE WORLD). 25

It is said that that from which something comes into being and in which it is reabsorbed, is the material cause of that thing. The earth is considered as the material cause of rice and barley for the same reason. Even so, the Ākāśa, which means the Brahman, is said to give rise to and absorb all these beings in it (Chā. 1, 9, 1); and therefore the Ākāśa or the Brahman alone is the material cause of the world. Besides, it must be remembered that the effects can never be absorbed by anything else but their material cause.

आत्मकृतेः परिणामात् । २६

[*Ātmakṛteḥ—on account of action concerning itself; pariṇamāt—due to transformation.*]

(BRAHMAN IS THE MATERIAL CAUSE) ON ACCOUNT OF ACTION REFERRING TO ITSELF; (THIS IS POSSIBLE) ON ACCOUNT OF TRANSFORMATION. 26

'The Ātman transformed itself into its own self' (Tai. 2, 7), and thus being itself the agent, became its own effect. No doubt the Ātman was full and perfect before its activity, but just as the clay is changed into effects, even so, the Ātman has simply got itself modified into the things of the world. The word 'itself' excludes the possibility of any other cause.

The word 'pariṇāmāt' may be taken to constitute a separate Sūtra by itself,—and then it means that Brahman became 'sat,' and 'tyat', i.e. the visible beings of earth, water and light, and the invisible beings of wind and ākāśa, or the defined and the undefined beings. In short, it is the Brahman alone which has become all this world of effects.

योनिश्च हि गीयते । २७

[*Yoniḥ—origin; ca—and; hi—because; gīyate—is sung.*]

AND BECAUSE (BRAHMAN) IS MENTIONED AS THE SOURCE (YONI) ALSO. 27

We are told that 'The wise regard the Brahman as the source of all beings, and as the maker and the lord of all' (Mu. 1, 1, 6 ; 3, 1, 3) ; and we know from usage that the word 'source' means the material cause. The earth, for instance, is said to be the source of plants and herbs. No doubt, in some passages, the word 'yoni' means a place ; for instance, Indra is told that a yoni was made for him to sit upon (Ṛg. 1, 104, 1). But in the same passage quoted above, the word 'yoni' means the material cause; for in the example given a little further (Mu. 1, 1, 7), the spider is said to be the cause of the threads which he sends forth and draws in.

It is not, however, true that whatever is observed in everyday experience must hold true in Vedānta also. So the argument that Brahman must, like the potter, be the efficient cause only, because its activity is preceded by reflection, is not adequate. The evidence of Śruti and not of inference is the final word regarding the nature of Brahman.

८ सर्वव्याख्यानाधिकरणम् । (२८)

एतेन सर्वे व्याख्याता व्याख्याताः । २८

[*Etena—by this ; sarve—all ; vyākhyātāḥ—are refuted.*]

HEREBY ALL (THE NON-VEDĀNTIC DOCTRINES) ARE REFUTED. 28

We had several occasions to refute the Sāṁkhya doctrine of pradhāna and we gave special attention to it because the less intelligent people are likely to be attracted by it. The doctrine comes close to the Vedānta doctrine on account of certain views, like non-difference of cause and effect, being common ; it is accepted by authorities like Deval and others ; and the Vedānta-passages too contain something which may mislead some people. There are other non-Vedāntic doctrines such as, atomism and others. But the adherents of these are virtually vanquished by the vanquishing of the greatest of the antagonists, viz. the Sāṁkhya. These doctrines too are not founded on Śruti and are contradicted by Vedānta-passages. The repetition of the phrase 'are refuted' indicates the end of the first adhyāya.

ADHYĀYA SECOND

PĀDA FIRST

In the first adhyāya known as 'Samanvaya', it was shown that the omniscient Lord of all is not only the efficient but also the material cause of the universe, just as gold and clay are the material causes of the vessels made out of them. Like a magician of his world of magic, He was shown to be the controller of the universe, and like the earth which takes back within it the bodies of all the living creatures, He was shown to be the absorber of it in himself. It was further established that He alone is the Ātman of us all. This is indeed the samanvaya, the cumulative effect of all the Śruti-passages. Besides, opinions like 'pradhāna is the cause of the universe,' were shown to lack the authority of Śruti. Now, in this second adhyāya, known as 'Avirodha', will first be discounted, in the first pāda, the apparent contradictions of the conclusions of the first adhyāya with what is stated in certain Smṛtis; secondly, it will be shown, in the second pāda, that opinions regarding pradhāna and others are based on false reasoning; and thirdly, it will be shown, in the third and the fourth pādas, that the Śruti-passages do not at all contradict when they deal with the cosmology, the individual soul and the organs of sense.

१ स्मृत्याधिकरणम् । (१-२)

स्मृत्यनवकाशदोषप्रसंग इति चेन्नान्यस्मृत्यनवकाशदोषप्रसंगात् ।१

[Smṛti; an—not; avakāśa—room; doṣa—defect; prasaṅgaḥ —occasion; iti—that; cet—if; na—not; anya—other; Smṛti-anavakāśadoṣaprasaṅgāt—there being occasion for other defects.]

IF IT BE SAID THAT (THE VEDĀNTA DOCTRINE WILL BE) DEFECTIVE ON ACCOUNT OF THERE BEING NO ROOM FOR CERTAIN SMṚTIS, (WE REPLY), NOT SO; BECAUSE (EVEN OTHERWISE) THERE WILL BE THE DEFECT OF THERE BEING NO ROOM FOR CERTAIN OTHER SMṚTIS. 1

The pūrvapakṣin says : If the omniscient Brahman is accepted as the cause of the universe, then Kapila's Sāṁkhya Smṛti as also the Smṛtis of Āsuri and Pancaśikha which are written after its model and which propound that the cause of the universe is the non-intelligent, independent pradhāna, will be useless. These Smṛtis are not composed like the Manu Smṛti in order to make us aware of our various duties and rules in life, regarding the thread-ceremony, study, marriage, the keeping of sacrificial fire, the four-fold [1] end of human life and the different castes and stages of life. They are composeed with the deliberate intention of imparting the knowledge of liberation; and so, if as the Vedāntin would show that they contain no reference to Brahman, they would all have to be admitted as useless. But if, as we hold, they serve the purpose of liberation, the Śruti passages must be so interpreted as will not contradict their philosophical import.

The Vedāntin may contend that an objection of this sort is out of place when it has been already proved by reference to the word "seeing", (Adhyāya 1, Pāda 1, Sūtra 5) that Śruti is emphatic on the point that the omniscient Brahman alone is the cause of the universe. But we submit that some extraordinary persons may interpret the Śruti by the mere aid of their intellect; the ordinary persons however have to fall back upon Smṛtis and puraṇas for a proper interpretation of it. They do so because they have a great regard for the sages like Kapila for their intuitive, unhindered knowledge. Kapila, for instance, is considered even by the author of the

[1] The four ends of human life are dharma, artha, kāma and mokṣa.

Śvetāśvatara Upaniṣad (5, 2) as the first among the created beings and as one who was seen and instructed by God. Therefore it is that we say that the Vedānta-passages must be interpreted in accordance with the teachings of Smṛtis.

To this we reply. This is not correct. For if certain Smṛtis become useless, if Brahman is the cause of the universe, certain other very important Smṛtis would be useless if pradhāna is accepted as the cause of the universe. The Śāntiparva of the Māhābhārata (334,29) tells us that the avyakta or pradhāna which consists of three qualities comes into being and is absorbed in that nirguṇa Puruṣa who alone is the Ātman and the knower of all that is created. In the Bhagavadgītā again, we are told that the Lord Śrī Kṛṣṇa is the cause of the origin and the dissolution of the whole world. Similarly, in many other Smṛtis it has been maintained that God is both the efficient and the material cause of the universe.

As to the question, which of the conflicting Smṛtis should be accepted and which rejected, Jaimini tells us in the Mīmāṁsā Sūtras (1, 3, 3) that we should reject that Smṛti which is in conflict with Śruti; and if there is no conflict, because there is no Śruti with which it should be in conflict, we should suppose that there must have been a corresponding prior Śruti as once lending its authority and support to the Smṛti in question, though unfortunately that Śruti is lost to us. Kapila-Smṛti however not only has not got a corresponding Śruti prior to it but also goes against the existing Śrutis, and so deserves to be rejected. Kapila's own intuitive experience cannot be said to be the authority for his Smṛti; for it is to be remembered that this intuitive experience of the suprasensuous reality is itself the result of religious practices based on the Śruti injunctions. So we can never dispense with the authority of the Śruti.

Again, the word 'Kapila'[1] occuring in the Śvetāśvatara Upaniṣad need not necessarily mean the author of Kapila-Smṛti. It may mean another person known as Kapila or Vāsudeva by name, who, as the story goes in the Mahābhārata, burnt the sons of Sagara. So, when, on the one hand, the reference to Kapila, as the author of the dualistic Sāṁkhya philosophy is doubtful, Manu on the other hand, is mentioned with honour by the Taittirīya Sāṁhitā (2, 2, 10,2) as one whose words are as beneficial as medicine. And Manu himself appears to have cesured the opinion of Kapila while he is eulogizing the person who has realized the Ātman in all things (Manu Smṛ. 12, 91). The Mahābhārata too (1, 2, 360, 1-3 and 361, 4-5) goes against the Sāṁkhya-yoga doctrine of the plurality of souls, and holds that the one highest Ātman alone is the internal self of all beings, and that it is he who is all-heads, all-arms, all-feet, all-eyes, and who moves through all beings and goes wherever he likes. The Īśāvāsyopaniṣad also (7) declares the unity of the universal Self, realizing which there will be neither sorrow nor infatuation. These and similar passages go to prove that the doctrine of Kapila is faulty in every way. It contradicts the Veda and contradicts the Manu Smṛti which follows the Veda, by assuming not only the hypothesis of independent pradhāna but also that of the plurality of selves.

As to the validity of The Śruti it is as direct and independent as that of the Sun due to whose light we get the knowledge of form and colour. The validity of human statements, Smṛtis and purāṇas, on the other hand, is dependent on the validity of the Śruti. The authors of Smṛtis were endowed with sound memory. They wrote from what they learnt and remembered from Śruti. So, the objection that certain Smṛtis which

---

1 Besides, the important point to be noted in the Śvetāśvatara Upaniṣad is not the incidental reference to the imparting of knowledge by God to the sage Kapila, but the mystical fact of the "seeing of God." In view of the recommendation of this mystical knowledge, the word 'Kapila' means nothing but the Hiraṇyagrabha, the tawny-coloured being.

contradict the doctrine of the Vedas (viz. that Brahman is the cause of the universe) would be useless, is no real objection at all.

इतरेषां चानुपलब्धेः । २

[*Itareṣām̐-of others ; ca ; anupalabdheḥ-not being found.*]

AND ON ACCOUNT OF ABSENCE OF OTHERS (I. E. OF THE OTHER EFFECTS OF PRADHĀNA). 2

Another reason for believing that the objection is futile is given in the second Sūtra. A Smṛti is believed if it tells about the five elements and the organs of sense for we have an experience of these in our daily life, and we find them mentioned in the Veda. The Kapila Smṛti, on the other hand, is not believable because the principles such as, mahat and ahaṁkāra to which it refers as the products of pradhāna, are unknown to the Veda and to experience. They are as impossible as the objects of the sixth sense, which if assumed to exist, contradict both experience and the Veda.

If the purvapakṣin points out that in the Kāṭhaka Upaniṣad there is a reference (1, 3, 11) to the technical Sāṁkhya terms, mahat and avyakta, we reply that we have already shown in our discussion of Sūtra 1, 4, 1, that the words 'mahat,' and 'avyakta' denote the intellect of the Hiraṇyagarbha, and the body respectively, and not the Great one and pradhāna of the Sāṁkhya philosophy. So if the Kapila Smṛti is not to be trusted in its treatment of the effects (e.g. mahat and ahaṁkāra), it follows that it cannot be trusted in its treatment of the cause also (viz. the pradhāna).

योगप्रत्युक्त्यधिकरणम् । (३)

एतेन योगः प्रत्युक्तः । ३

[*Etena—by this ; yogaḥ ; pratyuktaḥ—is refuted.*]

THEREBY IS REFUTED THE YOGA-PHILOSOPHY (SMṚTI) ALSO. 3

Like the Sāṁkhya, the yoga-philosophy also maintains that pradhāna is the independent cause of the universe and 'that the great principle' etc. are its effects. This is, as we have already seen, contrary to both experience and the Vedas and therefore stands refuted by our arguments in Adhikaraṇa 1. Where then, it may be asked, is the necessity of pointing this out explicitly in this Sūtra?

The reply is that we are able to remove thereby an additional doubt that may arise, viz. whether we should accept or not the doctrine of the yoga-system, which it has in common with the Sāṁkhya, that pradhāna is the cause of the universe. The yoga-Smṛti and its teaching of the eight-fold discipline are not only not contrary to the Vedas, but are also considered as pointing out the way of realizing the Real. The Bṛhadāraṇyaka (2, 4, 5) recommends that the Ātman is to be heard, thought and meditated upon. The Śvetāśvatara (2, 8), speaks of the erect posture of the body with the head, the neck and the chest in a straight line. Kaṭhopaniṣad (2, 6, 11, 18) refers to yoga as the unswerving one-pointedness of the senses. The position of yoga, and that of Sāṁkhya-have been strengthened by Śvetāśvataropaniṣad (6,13) when it says that it is the knowledge of God as the cause of the universe, which can be had by the study of Sāṁkhya-yoga, and which makes a man free from all bondage. In view of this, one is likely to conclude that because there is partial agreement between yoga and the Veda, the whole of the yoga may be relied upon just as the Smṛti known as aṣṭakā, is relied upon.[1] But as the same Upaniṣad

[1] Aṣṭakā is the name of a ceremony which is recommended to be performed on the day of death anniversary. Corresponding to this Smṛti there is no existing Śruti. And yet the Mīmāṁsakas accept it because it does not offend the teaching of any of the existing Śrutis.

says (Śve. 3, 8), it is impossible to get at the highest bliss by the mere knowledge of the Sāṁkhya philosophy or by the mere yogic practices, without at the same time being helped by the Śruti. 'The way to go beyond death is to know the Ātman; there is no other way.' In this passage, there is the definite mention of the unity of the Ātman, a fact which is denied by the Sāṁkhya-yoga. Therefore it is that the Sūtra refers to the efutation of the Yoga philosophy too, so far as its teachings are contrary to those of Śruti.

In short, if the Sāṁkhya-yoga philosophies tell us something which is also found in Śruti, we do admit their authority ; but if they go against it, we reject them. The Sāṁkhya description of the Puruṣa as pure and free from qualities is acceptable to us, because the Bṛhadāraṇyaka also mentions the Puruṣa as 'unattached' to anything (4, 3, 16). In its prescription of rules for sanyāsin and in commending the path of renunciation, the yoga too has followed the Śruti, according to which it is possible for a man who has worn discoloured dress, is shaven, and is without any possession to attain liberation. (Jābāla, 4).

All that we have said above is also applicable to other Smṛtis which have a claim to truth. It may be that they are useful to us in the discovery of truth, but the knowledge of that truth, we assert, can only be had from the Vedāntic passages, such as, 'No one who does not know the Veda knows the highest Self' (Tai. Brā. 3, 1,2, 9, 7), 'I ask about that Puruṣa who is described in the Upaniṣads' (Bṛ. 3, 9, 26).

३ विलक्षणत्वाधिकरणम् । (४-११)

न विलक्षणत्वादस्य तथात्वं च शब्दात् । ४

[*Na—not ; vilakṣaṇatvāt—being different in nature; asya—of this; tathātvam—its being like that; ca—and; śabdāt—from Śruti.*]

(BRAHMAN) CANNOT (BE THE CAUSE OF THE WORLD); BECAUSE (THE WORLD) DIFFERS IN NATURE (FROM THE BRAHMAN); AND THAT IT IS SO (IS KNOWN) FROM ŚRUTI. 4

After having refuted the objections based on Smṛti, let us now refute those based on reasoning.

The pūrvapakṣin holds that over and above the authority of Śruti, reasoning also is possible as a means of knowledge in the case of Brahman ; for it is already a fact that exists and is not to come into existence as a result of some religious duties, in which case we may depend entirely on Śruti alone. The conflict between several Śruti-passages ought to be resolved by making them all consistent with a particular passage; and this is possible if we resort to means of knowledge other than Śruti, such as reasoning. Besides, reasoning appears to come very near to experience because it enables us to know an unseen object on the strength of its having some similarly with a seen object ; Śruti, on the other hand, appears to be removed from experience, because it conveys its meaning by reference to tradition only. Reasoning, then, is applicable to Brahman, because the knowledge of Brahman is said to culminate in an actual experience which dispels all ignorance and causes release. It does not simply end in a general knowledge about an unseen result, like that of a religious practice, and is therefore not based on the knowledge of Śruti only. The Bṛhadāraṇyaka recommends reasoning in addition to hearing in the passage (2, 4, 5) " The Ātman is to be heard, to be thought etc." Hence the objection to the theory that Brahman is the cause of the universe is set forth as based on reasoning, in the following manner.

Brahman cannot be the cause of the universe ; for whereas Brahman is conscious and pure, the universe lacks consciousness and is impure. Cause and effect cannot be different in nature. Golden ornaments are the effects of gold and not of earth; and earthen pots are the effects of earth and not of gold. The universe is impure, because it consists of pleasure, pain and infatuation, and as such is the cause of joy, sorrow and gloom. Besides it consists of different grades of abodes such as heaven, hell, mortal world etc. It lacks consciousness also; for like the physical body and the senses, it is useful as an instrument for the conscious soul. Had the universe been equally conscious, it would not have been of any use to the other, just as one lamp cannot be of any use to another lamp. Even in the case of a servant and a master, where both are alike on account of their being human beings, it is the non-intelligent part of the servant, viz. his body, senses etc. which are of any use to the master. The consciousness of one person by itself cannot be of any service or disservice to the consciousness of another person. The conscious principle is incapable of growth or decay, of service or disservice, and is therefore devoid of any activity. Hence it follows that what is non-intelligent can be useful as an instrument to the intelligent being. Neither is there any evidence of common experience to show that things like wood or clod of earth are of the nature of consciousness. The world therefore being heterogeneous in nature, cannot have Brahman as its material cause.

A Vedāntin may bring an objection to this. Accepting what the Śruti tells viz. that the material cause of the world is intelligence, he may infer that the world too is intelligent in nature like its cause. The apparent absence of intelligence in the world may be said to be due to a sort of modification in the intelligence itself, as may occur during the conditions of sleep and swoon. Things like wood and clod of earth may not exhibit intelligence, even though there is as much intelligence in them as in the individual souls. It is on account of this modification of intelligence that the souls appear to be endowed with intelligence but devoid of form and qualities, and the things of the world appear as endowed with form and qualities but devoid of intelligence. So, it is not necessary that the things of the world must be absolutely non-intelligent in order that they should be useful to the souls as instruments of action, or as servants to their masters. Just as cooked rice, flesh and soup are usefully combined, even so the two apparently distinct but really homogeneous parts, viz: the things of the world including the body and the senses, and the souls may have between them the relation of the subordinate to the superior.

Such a reasoning may do away with the distinction to a certain extent between the intelligent Brahman and the non-intelligent world; but it will not, says the pūrvapakṣin do away with the distinction between the purity of the one and the impurity of the other. Nay, it will not, as a matter of fact, explain away even the first kind of distinction. For, as stated in the Sūtra, 'Śruti itself tells us that the world is such', that is, different from Brahman. For example, in the Taittirīyopaniṣad (2, 6), the Brahman is spoken of as manifesting itself in two forms, the intelligent and the non-intelligent. This may, no doubt, be objected by a Vedāntin. He may quote the Śruti and try to prove intelligence on the part of bodily organs and the elements which are generally considered as non-intelligent. For example, the passages: 'The earth spoke', 'the waters spoke' (Śat. Brā. 6, 1, 3 2; 4), 'Fire thought', 'Waters thought', (Chā. 6, 2, 3, 4) 'The prāṇas quarrelled and went to Brahman to decide who of them was the best' (Bṛ. 6, 1, 7), 'Do thou, oh speech, sing for us' (Br. 1, 3, 2). All these speak directly about the intelligence of the elements and the organs, and not about the manifestation or otherwise of intelligence.

To this the pūrvapakṣin replies in the following Sūtra.

अभिमानिव्यपदेशस्तु विशेषानुगतिभ्याम् । ५

[*Abhimāni—vyapadeśaḥ—reference to presiding deities; tu— but; viśeṣa—anugatibhyāṁ—because of distinctive nature and relatedness.*]

THE REFERENCE HOWEVER IS TO THE PRESIDING (DEITIES OF THE ELEMENTS ETC.) BECAUSE OF THE DISTINCTIVE NATURE AND RELATEDNESS. 5

The intelligence implied in the activities of speaking, discussing etc. refers however not to the physical elements and the sense-organs but to the deities which govern them. For, as was pointed out already, there is the clear distinction between souls and the elements etc. in point of intelligence itself, which is present in the one and absent in the other. Besides, the Kaushītaki Upaniṣad expressly uses the word 'deities' to denote the intelligent governing souls and not the material elements or organs. 'After disputing as to who among them was the best, all the deities recognized prāṇa as the most prominent of them all' (Kau. 2, 14). And we learn from mantra, arthavāda, itihāsa and purāṇas that these governing deities are intimately connected with the elements and the organs. The passage, for example, 'Agni became speech and entered into the mouth' (Ait. Ār. 2, 4, 2, 4), shows that a particular organ is favoured by a particular deity. In another passage we read how, after being advised by Prajāpati, the sense-organs left the body one after another, and yet the activity of the body continued because prāṇas had not left the body; but how when the prāṇas left the body, it ceased to be active even though the sense-organs continued to stay in it. (Chā. 5, 1, 7). This shows by the method of agreement and difference not only the superiority of prāṇas over the indriyas but also the relation of the governing deities with the sense-organs. This is confirmed in another passage which refers to the offerings made to prāṇa by the organs of speech and others (Br. 6, 1, 13). Similarly, the 'seeing' done by the fire (Chā. 6, 2, 3.-4) indicates that it is an act done by the highest governing deity, viz. the Brahman, with reference to its effects, the world. In short, the world being different in nature, the Brahman cannot be its material cause.

To this objection of the pūrvapakṣa the reply comes in the next Sūtra.

दृश्यतेतु । ६

[[*Dṛśyate–is seen*; *tu–but*]].

BUT (THE EFFECT) IS SEEN (TO BE DIFFERENT IN NATURE FROM THE CAUSE). 6

That the world cannot proceed from the Brahman because the two are different in nature, cannot be accepted as a universal rule. For it is a common experience that non-intelligent hair and nails proceed from intelligent beings like men, and that scorpions and other animals come into being out of cowdung. Even granting that the hair and the nails come out of the bodies and not out of the souls themselves, and that it is the bodies of scorpions and not their souls which come out of the cow-dung, the difference in nature still remains between the cause and the effect, inasmuch as it is the non-intelligent body which is the abode of the intelligent soul, though neither the cow-dung nor the hair and nails are the abodes of it. Besides, it is due to the presence of the soul that the body is seen to undergo a vast change in colour, form etc. before it manifests as the hair and nails, or the cow-dung changes into the body of the scorpion. Further, there would be no distinction of cause and effect, if there were complete identity of nature between the two. If a partial identity is allowed, as for example, the identity of the element of earth in the body of the scorpion and the cow-dung, then a similar identity in nature can be established between the world and the Brahman, *viz.* that of the fact of existence itself.

But what after all does the opponent mean by the difference in nature between the world and the Brahman? Does he mean that there is no characteristic of Brahman which reappears in the world or does he mean that some characteristics are present in the one but absent in the other, or that the two are different only in the point of intelligence? To accept the first alternative is to negate the very existence of causal relation; for unless there is some difference between two things they will not be causally connected. The second alternative cannot be proved in the presence of an actual fact, *viz.* the reappearance of the quality of existence from the Brahman into the world. The third is incapable of proof because no instance which will be admitted by the Vedāntin can be shown to illustrate the absence of intelligence so that that particular thing may not be produced from Brahman. For the Vedāntin does hold that everything that exists whether intelligent or not is the effect of Brahman as its material cause. Besides, the view of the opponent is against the teaching of Śruti according to which, as we have already seen, Brahman is both the efficient and the material cause of the world.

As for the contention that, unlike religious duty, Brahman being an existing fact, there should be available other means of proof besides the Śruti, we reply that it is merely a wishful thinking. For Brahman being devoid of form and other sensible qualities cannot be the object of perception. Nor can it be the object of inference or comparison, because there is no perceivable sign or similarity in it. Brahman also, like religious duty, is to be known solely through the vedic teachings. This is what the Lord of Death tells Naciketas; 'This knowledge of the Ātman cannot be achieved by argument; it is achieved only after another person speaks about it' (Ka. 1, 2, 9). Or, as the Ṛgveda puts it, 'who indeed can know it or say whence this world comes ?' (10, 130, 6). It is clear from these two mantras that the cause of the world remains incomprehensible even to gods who have acquired great power and knowledge. Smṛti too says the same thing. 'One should not employ reasoning with reference to things which go beyond cognition', 'He is said to be unmanifest, unknowable and unchangeable'. Not all the gods and ṛṣis have known my origin' (B. G. 2, 25, 10, 2).

As for the opponent's view that thinking also is explicitly mentioned in Śruti after śravaṇa or hearing as useful for attaining the knowledge of the Ātman (Bṛ. 2, 4, 5), we say that it is not the mere dry, independent reasoning which we can introduce under some guise. On the contrary, it is such reasoning which comes after the hearing of Śruti and is therefore favourable to its teaching that is recommended in the above passage. It is reasoning which is subservient to anubhava or spiritual experience. We can see this illustrated in the following manner: (1) Since the states of dream and wakeful life are exclusive of each other, the Ātman is not connected with either of them; (2) Inasmuch as during deep sleep the jīva becomes one with the Ātman after leaving the consciousness of the world, the jīva is in reality the Ātman itself; (3) The world has come out of Brahman; and because the effect is not different from the cause, the world cannot be different from the Brahman. All these reasonings are useful to know the import of the Śruti, *viz.* the Ātman or the Brahman is one, without a second and that it transcends the phenomenal world and the three states of dream, sleep and wakefulness. Futility of mere independent reasoning, on the other hand, will be also shown further in Sūtra 11 of this Pāda.

Now, if an opponent were to believe in an intelligent cause of the world and thereby infer that the world too is intelligent, then it would be possible for him to interpret the Śruti passage (Tai. 2, 6) 'The Brahman itself became divided into two portions, intelligent and non-intelligent', as meaning the manifestation and the non-manifestation of intelligence in the two portions. But the Sāṁkhyas who believe that the non-intelligent pradhāna is the cause, will not be able to make any sense of the Śruti passage, because it mentions that the ultimate cause of all remains steadfast as the Ātman of all.

So, the charge against us that we believe that the intelligent Brahman assumes the form of what is different from it, *viz.* the non-intelligent world, can be equally laid at the door of the Sāṃkhyas who believe that the non-intelligent pradhāna assumes the form of what is different from it, *viz.* the intelligent souls. But, as seen above, and in conformity with Śruti, the cause of the world can be said to be an intelligent one, in spite of its being different from its effect.

असदिति चेन्न प्रतिषेधमात्रत्वात् । ७

⟦*Asat—non-existent; iti cet—if said; na—not; pratiṣedha—negation; mātratvāt—because it is merely so*⟧.

IF (THE EFFECT BE SAID TO BE) NON-EXISTENT (BEFORE ITS ORIGINATION, WE SAY THAT) IT IS NOT SO; FOR IT IS A MERE NEGATION (WITHOUT ANYTHING WHICH IS TO BE NEGATED). 7

The pūrvapakṣin may say that to suppose that Brahman which is intelligent, pure and without qualities is the cause of a world which is non-intelligent, impure and full of qualities, is to suppose, against the satkārya theory of the Vedāntin, that the effect did not exist.

We reply that the objection is baseless. It is a mere negation without any object to be negatived; *i. e.*, when the effect does not exist prior to its origination in its own form, there is nothing which can be negatived. For prior to its coming into being, the effect does exist in the form of its cause, and so cannot be negatived at all. And even after its coming into being the effect has no separate, independent existence of its own except being in the form of the cause. In other words, at any moment in the past or in the present, the effect by itself is a non-entity without the cause. Hence, to say that the effect was non-existent in the form in which it appears (prior to it so appearing), is meaningless. On the other hand, the effect being always an existential fact, so far as it is looked upon as the one or the other form of the cause, it will never be negatived. Hence, the world which is full of qualities, neither existed before nor exists now without its being a form of cause. It is therefore, in truth, that we hold that the intelligent Brahman alone is the cause of the world. Or else 'Whoever will think this all to be separate from the Ātman will be forsaken by all' (Bṛ. 2, 4, 6) !

We shall deal with this topic in details while dealing with the non-difference of the effect from the cause in Sūtra 14.

अपीतौ तद्वत्प्रसंगादसमंजसम् । ८

[*Āpītau–in dissolution; tadvat–of the same nature; prasangāt–because of an occasion; asamanjasaṁ–inadequate.*]

(THE VEDĀNTA-VIEW) IS INADEQUATE, BECAUSE AT THE TIME OF DISSOLUTION, (BRAHMAN WILL BE) OF THE SAME NATURE (AS THAT OF THE WORLD). 8

The pūrvapakṣin says that, in the first place, it is inadequate to hold the Vedānta-view that the cause of the world is the omniscient Brahman, because at the time of the dissolution when the effect becomes one with the cause, Brahman will be polluted by the impurity, grossness, non-intelligence and limitation of the world. How can we call such a defective Brahman as omniscient ? Secondly, if all the distinctions are wiped out, and there remains one Brahman at the time of dissolution, there is left no special cause due to which again a new world with its distinctions of souls and objects should arise. Thirdly, when the souls become merged in the Brahman, their actions and the fruits thereof also become merged and so cease to be active. If, in spite of this, we believe that souls are born again, we may as well believe that the liberated souls too are born again. And finally, if, in order to get away from these defects in his theory, the Vedāntin would say that the world remains separate from

Brahman even during its dissolution, then he contradicts his own view *viz.*, the effect is non-different from the cause. Besides, there would be no dissolution worth the name.

To this we get the reply in the next Sūtra.

न तु दृष्टान्तभावात् । ९

[*Na-not: tu-but; dṛṣṭānta-instances; bhāvāt-being available*].

BUT NOT SO; FOR INSTANCES ARE AVAILABLE (TO SHOW THAT THE CAUSE IS NOT AFFECTED BY THE NATURE OF THE EFFECT) 9

The Vedānta-view is not inadequate; for, just as pots of clay or ornaments of gold do not impart their qualities of size, and shape to the clay or gold in which they are absorbed, or just as the fourfold beings which come into being from the earth do not impart their qualities to the earth when they are finally absorbed in it, even so, in dissolution the world will not affect the Brahman in any way. The pūrvapakṣin, on the other hand, will not be able to advance any instance in favour of his statement. As a matter of fact, if we speak of dissolution, we cannot speak of the effect retaining its own qualities apart from the cause. How the effect is non-different from the cause, (though not *vice versa*) is a point which shall be made clear while dealing with Sūtra II, 1, 14.

The objection of the pūrvapakṣin that the cause may be polluted by the effect need not have been restricted to the period of dissolution only. It could have been extended to the period of the subsistence of the world also; because our doctrine of the identity of cause and effect holds good at all times, as is clear from the Śruti passages : 'All this is what this Ātman is; (Bṛ. 2, 4, 6)

'The Ātman alone is this all' (Chā. 7, 25, 2); 'The immortal Brahman alone is all this that is before us' (Mu. 2, 2, 11); 'Verily all this is Brahman' (Chā. 3, 14, 1). And the refutation too of the objection is the same on both the occasions. The effect and the qualities are mere false appearances due to avidyā, and so do not affect the cause in any way, either during dissolution or subsistence of the world in Brahman. Just as a magician is himself never affected by the illusion he creates for others, even so the highest Ātman is not affected by the illusions of this worldly existence. Or, just as a person does not become affected by the illusions of his dream, because they do not continue to exist either in his dreamless sleep or wakeful life, even so, the one Ātman who is the eternal witness of the three states of the world, is not affected by any one of them, because each is exclusive of the other two. That he appears to be connected with the three conditions of the world is as illusory as the appearance of a snake on a rope. This traditional truth of the Vedānta has been expressed by some well-known teachers thus : 'The moment the individual soul is aroused from the beginningless slumber of Māyā, that very moment he realizes the non-dual condition which is beyond birth, dream and sleep' (Gauda. Kā. 1, 16).

As for the second objection, we offer the explanation that just as in the case of a man who goes into deep sleep or yogic samādhi there remains no consciousness of any worldly distinctions, and yet he becomes conscious of them all the moment he comes out of sleep or samādhi, even so there may arise a new creation and all the distinctions thereof, although they seem to disappear in Brahman during the dissolution of the world. Ignorance persists both in sleep and in dissolution; and so arise the false distinctions of the phenomenal world even after dissolution. It is due to ignorance that 'in spite of their being merged in the one Reality, the creatures do not realize that they are so merged, and are therefore born again as lion, wolf, etc.' (Chā. 6, 9, 2-3). This removes the further doubt regarding the rebirth of the liberated souls. They are not born again, because their false knowledge is wiped out by the knowledge of the Real. And finally the suggestion, that the Vedāntin may hold the view, that the world remains distinct from Brahman even in dissolution, is to be simply rejected because the Vedāntin will never accept the dualistic position implied by the suggestion. Hence the Upaniṣadic doctrine is free from every objection.

स्वपक्षदोषाच्च । १०

[*Sva*—*one's own* ; *pakṣa*—*side* ; *doṣāt*—*due to defect* ; *ca*—*and.*]

And because the objections (brought against the Vedānta-view) apply also to the (Sāṁkhya) view. 10

Besides the objections are as much against the Vedānta as against the Sāṁkhya doctrine. For even supposing pradhāna to be the cause, we do find that the world which possesses form, sound, etc. is altogether different in nature from pradhāna which does not possess form and other qualities. This means that the objection that the effect was non-existent before its origination, is common to both the Sāṁkhya and Vedānta schools, both of which are Satkāryavādins. Secondly, inasmuch as the Sāṁkhya too believes that in dissolution the effect becomes one with the cause, he shall have also to accept that the cause becomes polluted by the qualities of the effect. And thirdly, the specific reasons which are responsible for the joys and sorrows of different persons being all destroyed in dissolution, there remains no reason why a new creation should arise; or if there can be a creation without any cause, there can as well be the rebirth of those who have achieved their release. And in order to avoid these objections, if it be said that some distinctions remain unabsorbed even in dissolution, then, we say that it is these very distinctions which must not have been the effects of pradhāna; for otherwise they would have been non-distinct from pradhāna.

The objections being common cannot be brought against the Vedānta view alone. And yet we have answered them and shown that they are not real objections at all.

तर्काप्रतिष्ठानादप्यन्यथानुमेयमिति चेदेवमप्यविमोक्षप्रसंगः । ११

[*Tarka*-reasoning; *apratiṣṭhānāt*—being unsound; *api*—even; *anyathā*—in another way; *anumeyaṁ*—be inferred; *iti cet*—if so; *evaṁ*; *api*; *avimokṣa*—absence of release; *prasaṅgaḥ*—occasion.]

NOTWITHSTANDING THE UNSOUND NATURE OF (SOME ONE) REASONING, IF IT BE SAID THAT ONE MAY INFER IN SOME OTHER WAY, THEN THERE WILL BE ALSO NO POSSIBILITY OF MOKṢA. 11

There being no hindrance to human imagination mere reasoning cannot be depended upon in matters which must be understood in the light of Śruti statements alone. The thoughts of some clever men are pointed out as fallacious by some other clever persons; while the thoughts of these latter too are turned down by some others cleverer still. Even men of eminence and philosophical importance, such as Kapila and Kaṇāda, are seen to contradict one another.

It may be contended that not all reasoning is unsound; for even this contention must be proved by reasoning alone. And unless we admit the soundness of some kind of reasoning, our whole practical life will be of no value. Men seek pleasure and avoid pain on the supposition that nature is uniform in the past, the present and the future. Even in the Vedic sphere, whenever there arises a conflict among different interpretations of

Śruti-passages, it is reasoning alone which ends the conflict by refuting the unreal and by fixing the correct meanings of words and sentences. Manu asks us 'to know well three things, *viz.* perception, inference and śāstra, and to apply such reasoning as cannot be contradicted by Veda', in order that we should know what Dharma is (Manu Smṛ. 12, 105-106). In a way, the fallacy is a point of attraction in reasoning. For we require reasoning both for detecting and avoiding fallacies. It does not follow that because the argument of the pūrvapakṣa is fallacious, therefore the argument of the siddhāntin is also fallacious, just as a man does not become stupid because his forefathers were so.

To this we reply. Reasoning may appear to hold good in certain cases; but with regard to the unfathomable nature of Reality upon the knowledge of which depends the final release of man, there will be no use of reason unless it is backed up by Śruti. For, as already noticed, Brahman is neither the object of perception nor of inference; it has neither form nor sound to be seen or heard, nor any sign on account of which it is to be inferred.

Besides, all those who believe in the doctrine of mokṣa say that it is the result of the right kind of knowledge which has a constant and uniform nature. It is knowledge about which there will be no different opinions; a knowledge like that of fire *viz.* 'that it is hot.' A mere inference may take different forms, and so may leave us in doubt as to the exact nature of object. It need not be universal and constant like the perception of heat in fire. The Sāṁkhya who puts his faith in reasoning is not accepted by all as the best among logicians, so that we can trust in what he tells, irrespective of space and time. The Vedic knowledge, on the other hand, being self-evident and eternally the same is incapable of being challenged by any logician. Mokṣa therefore is impossible to be attained by any other means except through the right kind of knowledge given to us by the Upaniṣads.

We have thus proved by means of Śruti and by reasoning which is faithful to Śruti that the intelligent Brahman is both the efficient and the material cause of the universe.

४ शिष्टापरिग्रहाधिकरणम्। (१२)

एतेन शिष्टापरिग्रहा अपि व्याख्याताः। १२

[*Etena—by this; siṣṭha—authority; aparigraāḥ—things not accepted by; api—even; vyākhyātāḥ—are refuted.*]

This refutes other (theories) too which have not been accepted by competent authorities. 12

So far we have refuted the objections against the Vedānta doctrine, as also refuted the Sāṁkhya theory that pradhāna is the cause of the world. We refuted the latter because, in the first place, it comes very close to Vedānta in the account it gives of certain of its beliefs, such as the satkāryavāda, the identity of cause and effect, and the independent existence of the Ātman; secondly, because it has used in its support some powerful arguments; and thirdly, because some competent authorities who follow the Vedas, like Devala for example, are amongst its adherents. But when other half-witted persons, such as the atomists or the naturalists, also raise their heads and bring forth their arguments, the Sūtrakāra suggests that he has virtually vanquished them all, inasmuch as he has already vanquished the most powerful of the opponents.

५ भोक्त्रापत्त्यधिकरणम्। (१३)

भोक्त्रापत्तेरविभागश्चेत्स्याल्लोकवत्। १३

[*Bhoktṛ—enjoyer; āpatteḥ—being reduced to plight; avibhāgaḥ—no distinction; cet—if; syāt—may be; lokavat—like ordinary experience.*]

IF IT BE SAID THAT (ON THE VEDĀNTIC VIEW) THERE WILL BE NO DISTINCTION BETWEEN (THE INDIVIDUAL SOULS AND THEIR OBJECTS OF EXPERIENCE) ON ACCOUNT OF THE ENJOYERS (i. e. THE SOULS) BEING REDUCED TO THE CONDITION (OF THE OBJECTS AND VICE VERSA, WE SAY THAT THE DISTINCTION) MAY CONTINUE TO REMAIN AS IS SEEN IN ORDINARY EXPERIENCE. 13

There comes another objection from the side of reason alone against the view that Brahman is the cause of the world. It is true, says the pūrvapakṣin, that Śruti is authoritative in its own sphere; but where the meaning of a Śruti-passage is to be ascertained, and where, according to the available other means of knowledge, the meaning appears to be different, we have to construe the passage as not having the primary meaning but only the secondary. For example, when it is said that the 'sacrificial post is the sun', we have to understand that the post is like the sun and not the sun itself, because it is contrary to actual perception. It is in this way that mantra and arthavāda are to be explained. Reasoning too is not authoritative except in its own sphere. For example, it is not competent to say what is dharma and what is adharma. Suggesting, therefore, that reasoning and Śruti have got equal claims to discuss the nature of Brahmavidyā, the pūrvapakṣin tells us that if there is a conflict between Śruti and reasoning or between Śruti and some other means of knowledge, it is not proper that Śruti should refute what has been established by reason or other means; otherwise it may lead to some absurd conclusion. The pūrvapakṣin illustrates what he means. The distinction between the intelligent, embodied souls and the objects of experience is so obvious and persisting from the viewpoint of ordinary experience, that any attempt to remove it will be objected to. But this exactly is being done on the theory that the world is non-different from Brahman. Even the distinction between the subject and the object, between Devadatta and the cooked rice he eats would be removed, because both Devadatta and the cooked rice are identical with Brahman. The view that Brahman is the cause would make the subjects and objects pass into each other.

To this we reply that the distinctions may remain from the phenomenal point of view even though we accept Brahman as the cause of the world. Modifications of the sea, such as waves, foam and bubbles are not different from the water and yet they do not pass over into each other ; they are all related to each other, inasmuch as all of them are in essence water only, and yet they are distinct from each other. Even so the subjects and the objects may remain distinct without passing into one another, and yet be non-different from Brahman. No doubt, the souls cannot be said to be the effects of Brahman in the sense in which the modifications of water are ; for as Śruti tells us, Brahman it is 'which enters into them after having created them' (Tai 2, 6). Just as the one ākāśa appears to be many on account of jars and other limiting adjuncts, even so the effects i.e. the subjects and the objects appear to be many and distinct although they are in essence nothing but Brahman.

६ आरंभणाधिकरणम् । (१४-२०)

तदनन्यत्वमारंभणशब्दादिभ्यः । १४

[*Tad—that; ananyatvaṁ—non-difference; ārambhaṇa—beginning; śabdādibhyaḥ—from words and others.*]

WORDS LIKE 'ĀRAMBHA' AND OTHERS (PROVE) THE IDENTITY BETWEEN THEM (VIZ. THE CAUSE AND THE EFFECT). 14

The distinction we allowed to exist in the previous Sūtra between the subjects and the objects, from the view-point of ordinary experience, does not however exist as a matter of fact. For both the subjects and the objects along with ākāśa and other things are included in the world which is non-distinct from its cause, namely, the Brahman. The effect cannot exist, in other words, apart from and in the absence of the cause. In the Chāndogyopaniṣad we are told that all the modifications of clay, such as jars and dishes, are in reality nothing but clay, and are real only when looked at from the view-point of clay. But so far as they appear to exist as different individual things apart from clay, they are names only as 'originating from speech,' and as such are unreal. It is therefore said that to know one clod of clay is to know all its modifications; for there is nothing else but clay (6, 1, 4). Similarly, apart from Brahman existing in it as its cause, the world cannot have its independent existence. Other Śruti-passages where the word 'āraṁbha' is not used, tell us about the unity of the Ātman. The effects of fire, water and earth do not exist apart from them; naturally, these elements too represented by the colours red, white and black, in their turn 'do not exist apart from Brahman which is their cause' (Chā. 6, 4, 1). 'All this is the Ātman, the Real ; thou art that '; 'the Ātman is all this ' (Chā. 6, 8, 7; 7, 25, 2). 'All this is the Ātman', 'There is no diversity in it' (Bṛ. 2, 4, 6 ; 4, 4, 25); 'Brahman alone is all this ' (Mu. 2, 2, 11). In no other way, then, except believing in the theory that the things of this world have no existence apart from Brahman, can we prove our thesis that to know one thing is to know everything else. So just as the several portions of ākāśa, limited as they are by jars and other things, are not different from one universal ākāśa, or just as the appearance and disappearance of water in a mirage[1] are not different from the salty expanse of a desert, even so, the innumerable things of the world, including the experiencing subjects and their objects, have no independent existence apart from Brahman at any time.

Objection 1. It may be said that just as a tree, though one, presents the aspect of many branches, or the

[1] The illustration of ākāśa shows the identity of jīva and Brahman; that of mirage shows that Saṁsāra is mere appearance hiding the Brahman.

one sea of many waves, or one clay of many jars, even so, the Brahman may present both the aspects of unity and multiplicity. Its unity will be useful from the view-point of achieving mokṣa, and its multiplicity viz. its various activities and powers will be useful to explain the activities of human life as recommended by the Vedic Karma-kāṇḍa.

We reply that the theory that Brahman may be both one and many is not tenable. For the proposition 'clay alone is real', asserts not only the reality of the cause viz. the clay, but also the unreality of things other than clay. All other things have their 'origin' in speech, are mere names, and so are unreal. And again, the passage, 'That is the Ātman; that is the Reality; thou art that, oh Śvetaketu', tells us that the highest cause or the Brahman is the only Reality and that the individual soul is nothing else but Brahman. Especially, the sentence 'Thou art that,' shows that the identity between jīva and Brahman is a fact which is already existing and not one which is to become on account of some efforts on the part of jīva. Hence it is that this Vedānta doctrine will do away with the idea of the independent existence of the jīva, just as the recognition of the rope will remove the illusion of the snake on it. And then, along with the idea of the independent existence of the jīva, also goes away, *ipso facto*, the independent existence of the entire phenomenal world and its dealings and efforts which, according to our opponent, constitute the aspect of manifoldness of Brahman. 'When in the case of some one all this becomes one with the Ātman, who should see whom, and by what means?' (Bṛ. 2, 4, 11). This is a fact which is eternally true and it does not point to any particular state. Śruti tells us that the unity of the Brahman is the reality, and that the manifoldness of it is unreal. It warns us further by telling us that while a truth-speaking man is released, a liar is punished. If now the unity and plurality be both real, how can Śruti call that man who is engrossed with the manifold dealing of this world, as a liar? Nay it declares that 'one who sees that there is diversity moves from death to death' (Bṛ. 4, 4, 19). Again, if unity and multiplicity are both true, there will neither be bondage as the result of multiplicity, nor release as the result of the removal of multiplicity by the knowledge of the unity of Brahman.

Objections 2-5. (2) If unity alone is real and multiplicity unreal, preception and other means of knowledge will be null and void, because there will be no objects with which they will be connected. (3) The entire Karmakāṇḍa too will be impossible, because what it enjoins and prohibits is related with the plural aspect of things. (4) Even mokṣa is, in a way, dependent on the recognition of more than one thing, viz. the teacher, the disciple, etc. (5) And therefore, finally, if mokṣa too becomes impossible in the absence of the aspect of manifoldness, what guarantee is there for the trustworthiness of the science of mokṣa so far as its teaching of the unity of the Ātman is concerned?

We reply that our position is in no way disturbed by the objections. For so long as the real knowledge of the identity of the jīva and the Brahman has not dawned, it is inevitable that the course of the world should go on undisturbed both with reference to mundane and extra-mundane or Vedic activities. A man who dreams never doubts, so long as the dream lasts, that his experience of the various perceptions is false. Similarly, it is under the influence of avidyā that a man forgets that he is Brahman in reality, that Brahman alone is all this ; and so he identifies himself with everything he calls as belonging to him. It is natural therefore that he should never think of this world of distinctions and effects, and of the means and obj cts of ordinary knowledge as unreal.

Objection 6. If Brahman alone is real, how can the Vedānta-passages, which are then presumably false, lead one to the knowledge of the identity of the jīva and Brahman ? No one dies on account of being bitten by the illusory snake which appears on a rope; nor is anybody seen using the water in a mirage for the purpose of drinking or bathing.

We reply that the objection is futile. For we do see that death occurs sometimes as a consequence of the mere suspicion that a venomous snake has bitten. And the snake-bite and drinking of water in a dream, from the view-point of the dreamer himself, are real so long as the dream lasts. Nay, even after the dream is over, and the events of the dream are contradicted by the waking life and seen to be false, the knowledge about them as events in the dream persists in the waking life also without being contradicted. This continuity of consciousness or knowledge shows not only the emergence[1] of truth from falsehood but also the futility of the view of the Laukāyatikas that the Ātman is nothing but the body; for on that theory, the disappearance of the subtle body in the dream would mean the disappearance of the knowledge of the dream. Events in the dream, though unreal, are sometimes, we are told, indications of actual future events in life. The sight of a woman in a dream is a sign of prosperity for one who undertakes to perform a sacrifice to fulfil some desire (Chā. 5, 2, 8). Similarly, the sight of a black man with black teeth indicates death (Ait. Āra, 3, 2, 4, 7). That dreams are further causally connected with happy or unhappy consequences is shown by some experts by means of positive and negative instances. The written representation of an alphabet, though conventional and unreal, is able to make us pronounce the eternal sound of that alphabet.

This Upaniṣadic statement of the unity of the Ātman is moreover the crown of all other arguments ; for there is left nothing else with reference to which we may raise questions in order to get ourselves satisfied. The statement 'one should perform a sacrifice' makes us desirous

[1] Emergence, on the Vedānta view, means the manifestation of what already exists, and not the coming into existence of new knowledge.

to know the purpose as to why or how it should be performed; but the statements 'thou art that', 'I am the Brahman', leave us in no doubt regarding the unity of the Ātman; for there is nothing else which remains to be known over and above this unity. Nor can it be said that no one can have such a knowledge; for Śvetaketu, for example, did possess it and did realize what his father had told him (Chā. 6, 7, 6), viz. that Brahman is Ānanda. Even the way to the realization of this knowledge is mentioned; for instance, the hearing and the reading of the Vedas. It is not useless, for it removes all avidyā. Nor is it of an illusory nature, for there is nothing else which can sublate it. No doubt, so long as there is no awakening of it, there will continue to exist the ordinary consciousness which will recognize all the distinctions of the world. But the moment there arises the knowledge of the unity of the Ātman, all the distinctions of the Vedic or the ordinary life vanish, and there remains no room for the supposed aspect of multiplicity in the Brahman.

Objection 7. It appears from the illustration of clay cited by Śruti that, like clay, Brahman too is capable of being modified into other things.

Not so, we reply. Brahman is not capable of modifications, for it has been declared to be 'the great unborn Ātman which is without decay or death, is fearless and immortal', and is described only in negative terms 'as not big, not small etc.' (Bṛ. 4, 4, 25; 3, 9, 26; 3, 8, 8). Passages like this deny activity and change on the part of Brahman. Capacity to become modified and changelessness being contradictory in nature cannot belong to Brahman at the same time; nor can they be conceived to belong to it in succession,—changelessness, for instance, during the time of absorption, and modality during subsistence of the world. For changelessness alone being true, all modality is appearance on the Brahman. Besides, in the Vedic passages, which deal with the nature of Brahman as changeless and as devoid of attributes and distinctions, it is clearly stated that the vision of it as the universal Ātman leads to mokṣa. Janaka, for example, is stated 'to have attained the condition of fearlessness' in the same passage in which the Ātman is first described in negative terms (Bṛ. 4, 2, 4). No such result nor any other is mentioned to have followed from the knowledge that Brahman is modified in the form of this world. This means that the latter kind of knowledge must be supposed to be only subservient to the former; for we have the Mīmāṁsā rule that a thing or act which has no result of its own but is mentioned in connection with something else which has its own specific result, must be supposed as subservient to the other. Still, if some one were to say that the knowledge that Brahman is capable of being modified may result in a corresponding modification of the individual soul, because the soul is said to become that which it worships or believes, we say that it will be a very poor substitute for the mokṣa which can be had from the knowledge that Brahman is changeless and without qualities.[1]

Objection 8. The doctrine of the changeless Brahman allows no room for the distinction of a God who rules, and the world and the souls as ruled by Him. How then can it be maintained that God is the cause of the world?

We reply that there is no contradiction between the original assertion we made while discussing the Sūtra 'janmādyasya yataḥ' (Brah. Sū. 1, 1, 4) and the present assertion of the Śruti-passages regarding the unity of the Brahman. We do maintain even now the original statement we made in connection with the Śruti-passage, 'From that Ātman alone has sprung the ākāśa' (Tai. 2, 1), that the creation, subsistence and absorption of the world is due not to pradhāna but to the omniscient and omnipotent Lord who is at the same time eternally pure,

1 To know that clay is modified into vessels is only useful to know that clay alone is the reality; even so, the knowledge that Brahman as capable of producing the world is only useful to know that the changeless and qualitiless Brahman alone is real.

intelligent and free. And we have now said nothing to contradict this, even though we hold the doctrine of the unity of the changeless Brahman.

To explain the same. The infinite names and forms are born of avidyā and are no doubt the root-cause of the phenomenal world; but they cannot be said to be of the nature of God, for while God is intelligent, they are non-intelligent. Nor can they be said to be different from him; for if they are supposed to exist apart from him, they will lose their non-intelligent nature. They are therefore said to be indescribable ; or as Śruti and Smṛti would call them, they are the māyā, the śakti or the prakṛti of the omniscient God. And yet God is different from them as is clear from the passages : 'Ākāśa (Brahman) indeed is the revealer of name and form ; that is Brahman in which these are contained ' (Chā. 8, 14, 1); ' Let me produce name and form ' (Chā. 6, 3, 2); ' The wise Ātman produced the forms and after giving them names, is calling them by these names' (Tai. Ār. 3, 12, 7); 'He who turns one seed into many' (Śve. 6, 12). Just as ākāśa, which is independent and different from jars, appears to be limited on account of them, even so, God who is independent and different from names and forms only appears to be dependent on them for the purpose of ruling over them. And just as the portions of ākāśa, notwithstanding their being one with the universal ākāśa, are limited by the walls of the jars, even so, the individual souls, though one with the Ātman, appear different on account of the bodies or the names and forms of avidyā. Naturally, God too appears in relation to them in the phenomenal world as a ruler, and as being omniscient and omnipotent. Otherwise, from the view-point of one who is liberated from upādhis by means of knowledge, the Ātman will never be conceived as presenting the distinction of the ruler and the ruled, or appear as omniscient, omnipotent, etc. 'Where one sees, hears or understands nothing else, that is the infinite' (Chā. 7, 24, 1) ; ' When the Ātman only has become all this, what else should one see, and by what means?' (Bṛ. 2, 4,14). As is clear from these passages, the entire phenomenal world does not exist for him who has realized the Ātman. The Bhagavadgītā too tells us that in reality there is no such relation of the ruler and the ruled. 'God is not the author of the actions or the fruits thereof, nor does he receive anybody's sins or merits. People are deluded because their knowledge is enveloped by ignorance' (B. G. 5, 14-15). The practical point of view, on the other hand, admits the distinctions of the phenomenal world. God is spoken of as 'the king and the protector of all things; the support and the bridge of the worlds, so that they may not be confounded' (Bṛ. 4, 4, 2). 'He resides in the hearts of all beings, and by his power turns them all, as if they are mounted on a machine' (B. G. 18, 61). It is from the viewpoint of the highest reality, then, that the Sūtrakāra too has established the identity of cause and effect. What was asserted by him in the previous Sūtras, viz Brahman is the ocean, and the world is the waves, was with reference to the phenomenal world; and this was allowed to be considered as real from the practical point of view. The pariṇāmavāda is accepted by the Sūtrakāra (Brah. Sū.1, 4, 46; 2, 1, 24), so far as it is subservient for the purpose of devotion to saguṇa Brahman. For it is only then that the world becomes real and God is considered as omniscient, omnipotent and omnipresent.

भावे चोपलब्धेः । १५

[[*Bhāve—when it exists; ca—and; upalabdheḥ—because it is found.*]]

AND BECAUSE (THE EFFECT) IS FOUND ONLY WHEN (THE CAUSE) EXISTS. 15

It is possible for a jar to exist only when the clay exists and not otherwise; similarly a piece of cloth can exist only when the threads exist and not otherwise. The effect, in other words, is non-different from the material cause. The presence or absence of a thing, on the other hand, which has no causal connection with another, is not at all dependent on the presence or absence of that other thing. The presence of a horse is equally possible whether the bull is present or not. The potter is the efficient cause of the jar, but the jar can exist in the absence of the potter. The effect can never, however, be independent and different from its material cause.

It may be said that fire and smoke continue to be two different things, though smoke is seen only when the fire exists. But this is wrong; for smoke may be observed in a jar in which it is collected even though fire is extinguished. The argument is not improved even if it be said that a particular kind of smoke which, for example, is seen springing forth from an object does not exist unless fire exists. For what is required in establishing identity is not only the presence of the cause, but also the presence of the consciousness of the cause along with the presence of the consciousness of the effect. The jar inevitably makes us aware of its material cause, the clay ; smoke, on the other hand, does not make us conscious of fire.

Or the Sūtra may be taken to read as भावाच्च उपलब्धेः। (Bhāvāt ca upalabdheḥ), and then it means that the non-difference of effect from cause is not only to be believed as true because Śruti says so, but also because it is a fact of perception. What we call cloth is nothing but threads which we perceive crossing each other breadth-wise and length-wise. The threads again are nothing but collections of finer threads which we can perceive; and the fine threads again, in their turn, are made up of still finer threads, and so on. It is these perceived facts which enable us further to infer that the smallest parts of things are ultimately nothing but the three elements of fire, water, and earth, represented by the three colours of red, white and black (Chā. 6, 4). These three colours further are nothing but their cause, the wind: the wind is nothing but ākāśa; and finally the ākāśa is nothing but the highest cause *viz.* the one, non-dual Brahman. Therefore Brahman alone and not pradhāna or any other thing is the object of all the means of proof.

सत्त्वाच्चावरस्य । १६

[*Sattvāt—owing to existence; ca-and; avarasya-of what is afterwards.*]

AND BECAUSE THE (EFFECT) WHICH COMES INTO BEING AFTERWARDS (IS SAID TO) EXIST (IN THE FORM OF CAUSE BEFORE). 16

The effect, the present world referred to in the Śruti passages, 'All this was existing before' (Chā. 6, 2, 1,), 'In the beginning, this was verily the one Ātman only' (Ait. Ār. 2, 4, 1, 1), is stated to have existed before its appearance in the form of its cause, the Ātman only. In other words, Śruti tells us that the effect is non-different from its cause. Reasoning also favours this conclusion. How can one thing emerge from another unless it is present in that other in some form? Can oil be produced by crushing the sand? If the world did not exist in the Ātman prior to its beginning, it would never have existed in the form in which it is. Besides, just as the Brahman remains the same in all times, even so, the world which was one with Brahman before, will also continue to be one with it after its emergence from the Brahman. What exists now as before is the only one Reality *viz.* the Brahman; the world,[1] in other words, is non-different from its cause, the Brahman.

असद्व्यपदेशान्नेति चेन्न धर्मान्तरेण वाक्यशेषात् । १७

[*Asat—non-existence; vyapadeśāt—being mentioned; na—not; iti cet—if so; na; dharmāntareṇa—due to another quality; vakyaśeṣāt-on account of complementary sentence.*]

[1] The world is unreal if only it is thought of as existing independently of Brahman.

If it be said that (the effect does) not (exist prior to its being produced) on account of its being mentioned as non-existent, (we reply) that it is not so; for with reference to what follows (the mention of non-existence is to be interpreted as only meaning) another quality. 17

When the Chāndogyopaniṣad speaks of 'non-existence alone in the beginning' (3, 19, 1), it does not mean absolute non-existence of the effect, but means the non-existence of only names and forms which evolve later on in course of time. For that which was first referred to as non-existent, was afterwards referred to as existent. A thing which is absolutely non-existent can never become an existent; nor can it assume any form. But a thing which is non-existent on account of the unevolved condition of name and form, can exist later on, on account of the evolution of some name and form. When the effect therefore is said to be non-existent, it only means that the name and form of the effect was non-existent during the time when the effect was existing in the form of cause. Besides, the words 'this' and 'was' clearly point out that predication made in the Śruti passage is not with reference to absolute non-existence, but with reference to the world of names and forms.

Similarly, the being which is spoken of as 'non-existent' in the Taittiriyopaniṣad (2, 7, 1) does not mean absolute non-existence; for it is further said about that non-existent being that it got itself manifested into the world. This means that there was something, *viz.* the Brahman, before the world of names and forms came into existence. In short, if by the word 'sat' we mean the world of names and forms, by the word 'asat' we do not mean the non-existence of it, but the existence of it without the names and forms.

युक्तेः शब्दान्तराच्च । १८

[*Yukteḥ—from reasoning; sabdāntarāt—from another Śruti passage; ca—and*].

FROM REASONING AND FROM OTHER ŚRUTI PASSAGE. 18.

That the effect exists before its production and that it is not different from the cause can be ascertained from reasoning as well as from Śruti. To proceed to reasoning first.

Our ordinary experience tells us that milk, clay and gold are taken by people in order to produce out of them curds, jars and ornaments, respectively. No one who wants curds will expect to have it out of clay, nor will any one expect to have jars out of milk. This means that the effect exists in the cause prior to its production. For had the effect been really non-existent before its production, there is no reason why curds be produced out of milk alone or jars out of clay. Besides, all the effects being equally non-existent, anything might come out of anything else.

In order to explain the origin of effects, an asatkāryavādin may say that there exists in each cause a special power to produce a special effect; *e.g.*, milk has the specific capacity to produce curds; clay has got the specific capacity to produce jars. But this is to abandon the asatkāryavāda and to assume something prior to the effect which forthwith becomes the effect. If, on the other hand, the specific power also is conceived as non-existent before its appearance, or as different from both the cause and the effect, then as said above, anything may come out of anything else. In other words, just as there is no reason why a jar only may be produced out of clay, even so, there would be no reason why it should be produced on account of the specific power. if the latter is either non-existent before its appearance or is different from both cause and effect, *viz.* the clay and the jar. So, once again, we are led to believe that the effect is nothing but the cause, even though we introduce a third something *viz.* the causal power between the two. No one, as a matter of fact, is ever conscious of the cause and effect or of substance and qualities etc. in the manner in which one is conscious of two distinct and separate things like a horse and a buffalo.

It may be said that the cause and the effect or the substance and the qualities etc. do not appear different because they are held together by the connection known as samavāya, and not because they are identical with each other. But the so-called samavāya must itself either be connected with the terms between which it exists or be independent of them entirely. In the first case, to explain the one connection of samavāya we have to postulate a second connection; and in order to explain the second connection we have to postulate a third, and so on *ad infinitum.* In the second case, the cause and the effect or the substance and the qualities will fall apart from each other, and appear as totally disconnected. To avoid this, if it be said that samavāya can act alone without being further connected, then saṁyoga too being a connection between two things may not likewise require the further support of samavāya, as the Nyāya-Vaiśeṣikas hold. As a matter of fact, the notion of the relation of samavāya is useless because experience tells us that substance and qualities, cause and effect etc. are identical in essence.

Again, if the relation between the cause and effect is considered as that which exists between the parts and the whole, and the two are said to be held up together by samavāya, we may very well raise the question regarding the manner in which this takes place. If the whole resides in all the parts simultaneously, then the whole may not be perceptible at all; for instance, the other side of a jar will not be in contact with the eye at all. If, on the other hand, the whole is said to reside in some portions or the parts successively, then no doubt the knowledge of the whole is inferrable from the perception of a part; for instance, the knowledge of a part of a sword held in hand makes us aware of the whole of it, even though we have no visual or tactual knowledge of it, on account of the sword being hidden in the sheath. Yet the hidden parts of the sword which come in contact with the inside parts of the sheath are admittedly different from those of the sheath. This means that we introduce a new series of parts between the original parts and the whole, or between the cause and the effect. To pervade the second series of parts, the whole will again have to be conceived as consisting of a third series of parts of its own, and so on *ad infinitum.* In short, the effect will be further and further removed from the cause.

The effect as a whole cannot be said to reside in each one of the parts, simultaneously; for otherwise it will be more than one whole. Devadatta cannot reside in Srughna and Pāṭaliputra at the same time; that is possible only when there are two men, Devadatta and Yajñadatta. Nor can the whole reside in each one of the parts simultaneously, in the manner in which the one sāmānya or jāti of cow is said to reside in each of the cows at the same time. For just as every cow manifests the sāmānya, every part of the cause might manifest the whole of the effect. But this is not invariably experienced. Besides if the whole were to reside fully in each part, one may as well have the milk of cow from her horns.

Morever, if the effect be non-existent before its origination, there would be no action of origination itself because origination implies a reference to the particular effect and to the substratum in which it takes place. Walking is understood as an action with reference to the man who walks. The origination of a jar implies that the jar alone is being produced out of clay; it does not imply that the efficient cause like potter is being originated. For it is there already as a fact. So unless the existence of the jar is assumed before it is produced, in the form of its cause, *viz.*, the clay, the very sentence 'the jar is originated' will have absolutely no meaning. To say, in reply, that origination instead of being an action in some substratum is simply the fact of the effect's being connected with existence, is to speak what is impossible. For, as experience tells us, there can be some connection between two existing things, and not between two things which do not exist at all, nor between two things one of which exists and the other does not. How can a jar which has not come into existence be connected, in a moment prior to its existence, with clay which already exists? Moreover, existing things alone, such as fields and houses, can be spoken of as having certain limitations. But how can absolute non-existence or that which is absolutely featureless be spoken of as 'being prior to' origination? To say that the son of a barren woman was the king before the coronation of Pūrvavarman, has no meaning. For the son of a barren woman is not only non-existent, but is an unreality; and therefore no temporal limitation can be set to him. Even so, at no time, will the absolute non-existence of the effect, e. g. a jar, be a reality, though there may be the efforts of the potter.

If the non-existent can never become existent, then the asatkāryavādin may say that there would be no purpose for the operative causes like potter and others which bring the effect into existence. If the effect exists in the cause and is non-different from it, where is the need of the potter to bring out a jar into existence, just as there is no need of him to bring into existence the clay which already exists without any reference to him? But what happens as a matter of fact is that people do strive to bring about the effects, and so it is that one must assume the non-existence of the effect prior to its origination.

We reply that the purpose of the operative agents is simply to arrange the cause in the form of the effect. No doubt, the form of the effect too is present in the cause;

for we have already said that there cannot be any effect without a cause. The form too is not altogether new; and so a mere change in form does not transform one thing into an altogether different thing. Devadatta may bring his arms and legs close to his body, or may stretch them out, and yet he is recognized as the same man. Similarly, people may be seen in changing moods and conditions, and yet they are always recognized as the same, whether as, father, mother, or brother. It may be said that they are recognized as the same persons because their different conditions are not separated by death; the jar on the other hand is said to be different because the clay is as good as being destroyed. But we reply that this is not correct. Milk continues to exist under a different form, when we say that it has become curd. And even where this continued existence of the cause is not perceivable, for instance, when the seed is not seen to exist in the tree, we have to direct our att ntion to the earlier stages of the tree, such as the sprouts, and find that they are nothing but the later stages of the seed. Because we choose to call arbitrarily the appearance and the disappearance of the sprouts as birth and death of the seed respectively, it does not follow that the seed really dies and the sprouts come into existence as something altogether new. What takes place, as a matter of fact, is that it is the seed which becomes visible in the form of sprout, with the accumulation of particles of matter; and it is the seed again which becomes invisible and not non-existent, when the sprouts or the particles of matter change into something else. If, in spite of this, we believe that the non-existent becomes existent, and the existent becomes non-existent, we may as well believe that the unborn child in the womb of the mother and the same child in the cradle after it is born are altogether two different children or that the same person is different altogether in his childhood, youth and oldage. Hereby we have incidentally refuted the Bauddha doctrine of momentary existence; for we have proved the eternal, continued existence of cause.

That the operative agents have no purpose to serve is a charge which can be laid at the door of the asatkārya-vādin himself. For non-existence cannot be the object of any activity. It cannot be modified in any way by activity, just as the sky is not modified in any way by weapons. Nor can the cause *e. g.*, the clay, which is said to be samavāyī and existent, be the object of the activity of the operative agents; for if the effect, which was non-existent, is to arise from a cause which is different in nature, then anything may arise from anything else. And if to avoid these unpleasant conclusions, the asatkārya-vadin would say that the effect is nothing but a specific power of the cause, then he would thereby only accept the position of the satkāryavādin. The conclusion we reach, therefore, is that causes like milk and clay become known as effects when they assume the form of curds and jars, and that it is impossible to establish even after hundreds of years that the effect is different from the cause. This leads us to the further conclusion that Brahman is the ultimate cause of all, and that it is Brahman alone which appears like an actor in this or that form of effect and so becomes the explanation of the whole of the phenomenal world.

We have proved so far by means of reasoning that the effect exists prior to its origination and that it is non-different from the cause. A passage from the Chāndogyopaniṣad, unlike the passage referred to in the preceding Sūtra, refers directly to the 'existence of the Being which alone was in the beginning, without a second' (6, 2, 1). Then a subsidiary reference is made to the opinion of others who call the Being as non-existent, but it is immediately pointed out that the existent cannot come out of the non-existent, and that therefore 'all this was existent alone in the beginning'. But the word 'this' which indicates the world refers by way of identity to the word 'existent' which means the Being or the cause of the world. In other words, this passage also shows that the effect exists prior to its origination in the form of cause and is identical with it, and proves thereby the earlier assertion made in the same Upaniṣad (6, 1, 3) that the Brahman or the cause being known, everything else becomes known. On the asatkāryavāda theory, on the other hand, the cause may be known, but the effect being different will remain unknown.

पटवच्च । १९

[*Paṭavat—like a piece of cloth; ca—and.*]

AND JUST AS A PIECE OF CLOTH (IS NOT DIFFERENT FROM THREADS). 19

Just as a rolled piece of cloth is not different from what it becomes when it is spread out, similarly the effect is not different from the cause. The only difference between the two conditions is that what is not manifest in the cause becomes manifest in the effect. The length and breadth of the rolled piece of cloth which were not manifest, become manifest only after it is spread out. Similarly, the piece of cloth which is not manifest in the threads becomes manifest on account of the operative agents such as the shuttle, the loom and the weaver.

यथा च प्राणादि । २०

[*Yathā—just as; ca—and; prāṇādi—breath and others.*]

AND JUST AS THE PRĀṆAS (FUNCTION DIFFERENTLY IN DIFFERENT CONDITIONS). 20

The different prāṇas such as prāṇa, apāna vyāna etc. are not really different from their causal condition *viz.* the wind; yet, so long as they are contained within their cause, their only function is to keep the body alive. But when they manifest as separate from one another, they not only keep the body alive. but also cause the limbs to move. This means that movement which was not manifest in the cause becomes so in the effect. The whole world then being an effect of the Brahman is not different from it; and so Brahman being known, everything else becomes known (Chā. 6, 1, 3).

७ इतरव्यपदेशाधिकरणम् । (२१ २१)

इतरव्यपदेशाद्धिताकरणादिदोषप्रसक्तिः । २१

[*Itara*–*the other; vyapadeśāt*–*being mentioned; hita (benefit)*–*akaraṇādi (things like not-doing)*–*dośa (defect)*–*prasaktiḥ (would follow).*]

THE OTHER (i. e. THE INDIVIDUAL SOUL) BEING MENTIONED (AS NON-DIFFERENT FROM THE BRAHMAN), THE DEFECTS (OF THE FORMER), AS, FOR INSTANCE, OF NOT DOING WHAT IS BENEFICIAL WOULD BELONG TO (BRAHMAN). 21

Whether 'the other' means the individual soul according to the passage 'That thou art, oh Śvetaketu,' (Chā. 6, 8, 7) or the Brahman according to the passage, 'having entered into the products, such as, earth, water and light, in the form of jīva, it thought of conceiving names and forms' (Chā. 6, 3, 2), what Śruti wants to convey is that the individual soul and the Brahman are identical. It follows from this identity therefore that the power of creation belongs to the individual soul also. But instead of producing things which might be beneficial, how is it that the individual soul has produced a network of suffering, *viz.*, birth, death, oldage and disease? No free person would like to build a prison as his house. How would that pure Ātman look upon the physical impure body as part of itself? Would it not free itself of the evil consequences of its actions and enjoy only the rewards? The individual soul would have remembered itself as the author of creation, and therefore withdrawn into itself the entire magical illusion of creation. But the pity is that the individual soul cannot withdraw his own body even. All this therefore goes against the view that the world has been created by an intelligent cause.

अधिकं तु भेदनिर्देशात् । २२

[*Adhikaṁ–what is more; tu–but; bheda–difference; nirdeśāt–being pointed out.*]

BUT (BRAHMAN) IS DIFFERENT (FROM THE INDIVIDUAL SOUL), FOR THE DIFFERENCE IS POINTED OUT (BY ŚRUTI. AND SO THE DEFECTS DO NOT BELONG TO BRAHMAN). 22

But as against the view of the pūrvapakṣin, the creator of the world as we consider him is not the jīva but the Brahman which is declared by Śruti as different from the jīva, and as being omniscient, omnipotent, eternal, pure, intelligent and free. From the view-point of such Brahman, there is nothing beneficial to be done or harmful to be avoided. There is nothing which it cannot know or do; creation or destruction it can do with great ease. The individual soul, on the other hand, being different in nature, the various defects mentioned by the pūrvapakṣin belong to it. That jīva and Brahman are different is evident from various Sruti passages, such as, 'The Ātman indeed is to be seen, heard, thought of and meditated upon' (Bṛ. 2, 4, 5); 'He should be the object of the desire to know, and of careful seeking' (Chā, 8, 7, 1); 'Then, during sleep, the jīva becomes one with the Brahman' (Chā. 6, 8, 1); 'The embodied soul becomes lodged in the prājña Ātman' (Bṛ. 4, 3, 35). In all these and similar other passages, actions such as seeking, seeing, and meditating on the part of the jīvātman point to him as the subject and the Paramātman as the object.

It may be pointed out that non-difference also of the jīva and Brahman is stated by Śruti in the passage 'That thou art'; and so difference and non-difference being contradictory, they cannot both be true. But, we say in reply that they can co-exist in spite of the apparent contradiction. Just as the false limited ākāśa in the jar can co-exist with its contradictory *viz.* the one unlimited ākāśa, even so as explained already more than once, the limiting adjuncts of the self such as body, manas and senses, which arise out of the names and forms of avidyā, are felt to be real. But they are seen to be mere illusions, the moment the consciousness of the non-difference of the jīva and Brahman arises in us. Then there comes an end to all the practical distinctions of wrong knowledge, and with them vanish also the saṁsāric condition of the soul and the notion of creation on the part of Brahman. Where is the room, then, for the defect of not doing what is beneficial? And where is the room for the creation of the world at all? But so long as the illusion lasts, there is room for the wrong notions such as the self is hurt, or the soul dies. So long too Brahman is different from the jīva, and becomes the object of inquiry and search. So long, too, the jīva is only a creature and not the creator. The defects therefore do not belong to the Brahman

अश्मादिवच्च तदनुपपत्तिः । २३

[*Aśmā-ādi-vat-like stone and others; ca—and; tad-that: anupapattiḥ--cannot be had.*]

(THE CREATION) BEING (WONDERFUL AND DIFFERENT) LIKE STONES AND OTHERS, THESE (DEFECTS) CANNOT BE CONCEIVED. 23

Just as stones present a great variety among them, some of them being more or less valuable like diamonds, lapis lazuli, and 'sūryakānta', and some so ordinary and valueless as can be thrown at dogs and crows; or just as the same piece of ground yields different trees like sandal and cucumber, which have different leaves, flowers, fruits, fragrance and juice; or just as the same food assumes the form of blood, hair etc; even so, within the same Brahman there may seem to arise the distinctions of various effects, such as the jīva and the Īśvara. Brahman however is not at all affected by the defects of the jīva and the world; for as Śruti declares all these distinctions have their origin in speech only, and are like the phantoms of a dreaming person.

८ उपसंहारदर्शनाधिकरणम् । (२४-२५)

उपसंहारदर्शनान्नेति चेन्न क्षीरवद्धि । २४

[*Upasaṁhāra—collection; darśanāt–being observed; na–not; iti cet—if it is said; na; kṣīravat—like milk; hi—for.*]

IF IT BE SAID THAT (BRAHMAN) IS NOT (THE CAUSE) BECAUSE IT IS (ELSEWHERE) OBSERVED THAT (INSTRUMENTS) ARE BEING COLLECTED (FOR PRODUCTION OF SOMETHING), (WE SAY) NO; FOR LIKE MILK, (BRAHMAN MAY ACT ALONE). 24

Potters and weavers are seen to collect the material and the means such as clay, wheels, thread and shuttle before they produce the jars and cloth. But Brahman, on the other hand, though intelligent like a potter, cannot be thought of as first providing itself with material and instruments, because it is conceived to be without a second. Brahman, therefore, it may be said, cannot be the cause of the world.

To this we reply. Brahman can be conceived to be the cause in much the same way as milk or water can be said to be of curds or ice. It may appear that milk must be heated first before it is turned into curds. But had there been no original capacity in milk whereby it changes into curds, no amount of heat will be able to do so. Otherwise one could have turned ākāśa or wind into curds by heating it. What heat does is only to hasten the process of turning milk into curds. Brahman, on the other hand, does not even require this much help of extraneous circumstances to transform itself into manifold effects. For as Śruti says, ' Nothing remains to be done by him, for He is already perfect; nor does He require any instrument, for there can be none else who is equal unto him, much less superior to him. Various and supreme are His powers; knowledge and strength are natural with him' (Śve. 6, 8).

देवादिवदपि लोके। २५

[*Deva-ādt-vat—like gods and others; api—also; loke—in Sāstra, etc.*]

AND LIKE GODS AND OTHER BEINGS AS MENTIONED IN SĀSTRAS, (BRAHMAN) TOO (MAY BE ABLE TO PRODUCE). 25

The opponent may admit that non-intelligent things like milk may change of themselves without any extraneous help into curds and other things; but he may point out that Brahman being intelligent like potter cannot be conceived to create without other external means. We reply that just as gods and sages are reported to have the ability to produce palaces and chariots by the power of their mere will; or just as the spider creates the web of the threads he emits out of his body; or just as the female crane conceives without the contact of the male; or just as, without being transplanted, the lotus travels from one pond to another, even so, Brahman may create the world without any extraneous means.

Our opponent may find flaw in our reply and say, that the material causes of the things produced in all the above instances are not the intelligent souls but the non-intelligent bodies. The palaces and chariots are due to the bodies of gods etc; the web of the spider due to its hardened saliva, the conception of the female crane as due to the hearing of the sound of thunder, and the wandering of the lotus from pond to pond is like the climbing up of the creeper on a tree. To this we reply that Brahman is intelligent like potters and gods, but unlike them is not dependent on any extraneous means for the act of creation. Brahman is unconditionally free to create.

९ कृत्स्नप्रसक्त्यधिकरणम्। (२६-२९)

कृत्स्नप्रसक्तिर्निरवयत्वशब्दकोपो वा। २६

[*Kṛtsna (entire)-prasaktiḥ (will result); niravayatva—without parts; śabda (Śruti)-kopaḥ (violation), vā—or.*]

THERE WILL RESULT EITHER (THE CHANGE) OF THE ENTIRE (BRAHMAN) OR THE VIOLATION OF THE ŚRUTI WHICH TELLS THAT (BRAHMAN) IS WITHOUT PARTS. 26

To emphasize Vivarta as against Pariṇamā, the Sūtrakāra raises another objection. Quoting Śruti the objector says that there are no distinctions in Brahman. 'It is partless, actionless, tranquil, faultless and taintless' (Śve. 6, 19); 'That heavenly Puruṣa is without body, is both inside or outside, and is unborn' (Mu. 2, 1, 2); 'This great being is endless, unlimited, and consists of knowledge alone'; 'He is to be described in negative terms only, as neither big nor small' (Bṛ. 2, 4, 12; 3, 9, 26; 3, 8, 8). As Brahman is partless, it cannot be said that it undergoes a change in one part alone; therefore it may be pointed out that the entire Brahman undergoes the change. But this would mean that Brahman as the cause of all will cease to exist; and then there would be no meaning in the exhortation that one should 'see' the Brahman. There would also be no meaning in the exhortation, if by seeing the Brahman we are to understand seeing the world or the transformed Brahman; for the world is seen even without anybody's telling. If the world alone exists, then what does Śruti mean by saying that Brahman is unborn? If to escape the faults due to transformation of the entire Brahman, the Vedāntin would accept that Brahman consists of parts, he would contradict all the Śruti passages which deny parts to Brahman. Besides, that which consists of parts is of a perishable nature The Vedānta doctrine therefore appears to be wholly untenable.

श्रुतेस्तु शब्दमूलत्वात् । २७

[*Śruteḥ*–of Śruti; *tu*–but; *Śabdamūlattvāt*–because Śruti is the ground.]

BUT (IT IS NOT SO), ON ACCOUNT OF ŚRUTI (BEING AVAILABLE AND) BEING THE GROUND (OF BELIEF IN BRAHMAN). 27

We discard the objection. In the first place, the entire Brahman cannot undergo transformation For Brahman is not only spoken of by Śruti as the source of the world, but as existing apart from the world. *E.* g.: 'the Divine Being thought of entering into the other three divinities by its own self and manifest their names and forms' (Chā, 6,3,2); 'Such is the greatness of Gāyatri; greater than it is the Puruṣa; for one foot of him is all these bhūtas, while his three other feet are in the immortal heaven' (Chā. 3; 12, 6). Again, had the whole of the Brahman been transformed, there would have been no meaning in its being described as 'residing in the heart' and the jīva being described as 'being one with it during sleep' (Chā. 6, 8, 1). Besides, if Brahman were completely transformed, it would have been visible, just as the world is; but that it is not the object of perception proves that it exists in an unmodified form.

Secondly, we do not see any contradiction between the partless nature of Brahman and its not undergoing transformation as a whole, though both these facts are declared by Śruti, and though Śruti is the only infallible source which will make us know the nature of Brahman. For even when the ordinary things such as gems and herbs produce different and opposite effects on different occasions and in different places and times, and thereby baffle the intellect of man if it is not properly instructed, how much more difficult it must be to fathom the powers of Brahman by mere intellect? Reasoning cannot be applied to what is unthinkable; we must resort to Śruti alone to know the supra-sensuous.

The opponent may then wish the Śruti itself to remove the contradiction. The contradiction, he may point out. is not of the nature of two alternatives suggested in Karma-Kāṇḍa so that the adoption of one of them would remove the contradiction altogether. For instāce, to accept or not the 'Ṣodaśin-cup at the atirātra is left to the option of the man; and so there is no contradiction between the two Vedic injunctions. But there is real contradiction between the partless nature of Brahman and its being transformed in the form of this world. Brahman is either partless or is transformed partially; if it is partless then it must get itself wholly transformed or not at all; and if it is only partially transformed, then it consists of parts. The contradictory statements are not like alternative actions which may be dependent on the choice of man, but relate to the nature of an already accomplished fact, *viz.* the Brahman, and therefore present a real difficulty.

But this is no real difficulty, we say in reply. A man of defective vision may see more than one moon; but there is only one moon. Similarly, though, in reality, Brahman ever remains the same, without any change, it is still the ground of the multiplicity of name and form of the phenomenal world. These distinctions of names and forms are the effects of avidyā, and originate from speech alone. They are so illusory that they appear now as manifest, and now as unmanifest; now as different from Brahman and now as non-different from it; and yet they cannot change the nature of Brahman as being without parts. Even the Śruti-passages which refer to the transformation of Brahman have the only aim of directing us beyond the fact of creation or transformation to the knowledge of Brahman as being the Ātman of all; for it is only this knowledge which will carry us beyond the saṁsāra. The knowledge of the mere transformation by itself, on the other hand, will lead us nowhere. It is this interest in the Ātman rather than in any particular effect of creation or transformation which is obviously seen in such a passage of the Śruti : 'He is not this, He is not that, etc.' The negative description is useful to draw our attention from the phenomenal world, and fix it on the Brahman, which when known will make us fearless like Janaka (Bṛ. 4, 2, 4).

आत्मनि चैवं विचित्राश्च हि । २८

[*Ātmani—in one's self*; *ca—and*; *evaṁ—thus*; *vicitrāḥ—wonderful*; *ca*; *hi—even.*]

AND EVEN WITHIN THE SELF WONDERFUL (CREATION) LIKE THIS (IS MENTIONED). 28

We learn from Śruti that 'There are no chariots, horses and roads' during the state of dream, but that the dreamer creates them (Bṛ. 4, 3, 10). Gods and magicians too create elephants etc. without losing their own unity of being. Even so, there may exist a manifold creation in Brahman, without affecting its real nature and unity.

स्वपक्षदोषाच्च । २९

[*Sva-own*; *-pakṣa-side*; *doṣāt-due to defects*; *ca—and.*]

AND BECAUSE (THE SAME) OBJECTIONS CAN BE RAISED AGAINST (THE OPPONENTS') OWN VIEW. 29

The pradhāna of the Sāṁkhyas, too, it may be said, must either change into the world wholly or partially; and then there remains either no pradhāna at all, or the view that it is partless must be given up. If, to avoid this difficulty, it be said that the three guṇas themselves are the three parts of pradhāna, we say in reply that in no way it saves the position. For, in the first place as the Sāṁkhyas believe, the creation is the combination of all the three guṇas; and so it cannot be said that some one or two of them evolve, and the remaining do not. Secondly, none of the three guṇas is considered by the Sāṁkhyas as consisting of parts, so that we may say that some of the parts evolve and some do not. Thirdly, pradhāna will not be eternal, if it consists of parts. And finally to say that pradhāna may be considered as consisting of various powers is only to say what the Vedāntin believes and not anything special.

The same is the case with the atomists. On the one hand, if two partless atoms combine, they can do so only by entering into each other and by occupying the same space, *i. e.* together they would form one atom again. If, on the other hand, the atom be conceived as coming in contact with another in some of its parts, the atomists shall have to give up their own view that the atom is partless.

The objections, therefore, which the Vedāntin has already refuted, cannot be laid against him alone.

१० सर्वोपेताधिकरणम् । (३०-३१)

सर्वोपेता च तद्दर्शनात् । ३०

[*Sarva—all ; upetā—endowed with ; ca—and ; taddarśanāt—for Śruti tells so.*]

AND (BRAHMAN) IS ENDOWED WITH ALL (POWERS); FOR (ŚRUTI) TELLS US SO. 30

The following Śruti-passages describe Him as endowed with all powers. 'He is the doer of all and desires all, he is all fragrance and all tastes, he envelopes this all, he is without organs of sense or action, and he is fearless' (Chā. 3, 14, 4); 'Whatever he wishes and desires is always true' (Chā. 8, 7, 1); 'He is omniscient' (Mu. 1, 1, 9); 'It is by the command of the imperishable Being that the sun and the moon are held up' (Bṛ. 3, 8, 9).

विकरणत्वान्नेति चेत्तदुक्तम् । ३१

[*Vikaraṇatvāt—on account of absence of organs ; na—not; iti cet—if it be said; tad—then; uktaṁ—has been said.*]

IF IT BE SAID (THAT BRAHMAN CANNOT BE THE CAUSE) ON ACCOUNT OF THE ABSENCE OF ORGANS, (WE REPLY THAT) THIS HAS BEEN (ALREADY) EXPLAINED. 31

How can Brahman, it may be asked, be endowed with all power, if it is described only in negative terms? And granting that it possesses such powers, how can it produce the world, because it is 'without eyes, ears, speech or mind' (Bṛ. 3, 8, 9)?

We have already considered this objection while discussing Adhyāya I Pā. 2, Sū. 18-20, and Adhyā. II Pā. 1, Sū. 4. The capacity of one being may not be the same as that of another. Brahman cannot be fathomed by mere reasoning; we must know it by means of Śruti alone. Besides we have already seen that in spite of its being without qualities, Brahman can be conceived as being endowed with powers so long as it is wrongly believed that Brahman is connected with the various distinctions of names and forms of avidyā. Śruti says in support of this: 'He holds the things, even though he has no hands, runs without feet, sees without eyes, and hears without ears' (Śve. 3, 19).

११ प्रयोजनत्वाधिकरणम् । (३२–३३)

न प्रयोजनत्वात् । ३२

[*Na—not; prayojanatvāt—there being the motive.*]

(CREATION IS) NOT (POSSIBLE FOR BRAHMAN) BECAUSE THERE MUST BE MOTIVE (FOR THE ACTIVITY OF INTELLIGENT BEINGS). 32

The objector may again point out that no intelligent and thoughtful person begins even an unimportant work without some selfish motive; much less will it be in such a very important work as creating the universe with all the varied contents in it. Śruti tells us that 'everything becomes dear to us for the sake of the self' (Bṛ. 2, 4, 5). If therefore we attribute some selfish motive to the intelligent highest Ātman for his act of creation, we shall be doing violence to his self content nature; if, on the other hand, we say that there is no such motive, there will be no activity at all, except the activity of a mad man, which of course can never belong to the Ātman on account of his admitted omniscience. Hence, it follows that creation cannot proceed from the intelligent Ātman.

लोकवत् लीलाकैवल्यम् । ३३

[*Lokavat*–*as in experience; līlā*–*sport; kaivalyaṁ*–*mere.*]

(THE CREATIVE ACTIVITY OF BRAHMAN) HOWEVER IS MERE SPORT, AS WE FIND IN (OUR) LIFE. 33

Just as kings are sporting for no special reason, or just as the breathing goes on naturally (even during sleep), even so, God's activity in creation is a natural sport with him and so cannot be shown to be due to any other motive, even if we resort to Śruti or reasoning. Nor can we assign any special reason for this peculiar nature or svabhāva of God. It is possible that one may find some motive, however trifling or unconscious, even in the sport of kings or in breathing; but there may not be any motive for the activity of God. For the Śruti says that he has no desire which is unfulfilled. And yet, we cannot compare his activity to that of a senseless man; for the Śruti says that he is both omniscient and creator. The following points must not therefore be forgotten in this connection:–(1) That creation is not real from the point of view of the highest Reality; (2) That it is only an appearance, and so consists of the names and forms of avidyā; and (3) that the only purpose, which the Śruti-passages dealing with creation serve, is to show that Brahman alone is the soul of all the created things.

१२ वैषम्यनैर्घृण्याधिकरणम् । (३४–३६)

वैषम्यनैर्घृण्ये न सापेक्षत्वात्तथाहि दर्शयाति । ३४

[*Vaiṣamya*–*nairghṛnye—inequality and cruelty; na*–*not; sāpekṣatvāt—being dependent; tathā—same; hi—also; darśayati—Śruti says.*]

Inequality and cruelty cannot (be attributed to God); for (his activity) is dependent (on merit and demerit); besides (Śruti) tells the same. 34

Just as a pole is shaken in order to see if it is firmly fixed or not, even so, an objection is again raised to make the Vedānta theory unshakeable. It is pointed out that because God has made the deities extremely happy, animals extremely unhappy, and men partly happy and unhappy it appears that he too like ordinary persons possesses passion and malice; but this is contrary to the goodness which is ascribed to him by Śruti and Smṛti. He may be considered as being very cruel because he causes pain and the ultimate destruction of all creatures. Brahman therefore need not be considered as the cause of the world.

The blame could have been ascribed to him, we say in reply, had God created the inequality without any reference to anything outside him. But being dependent on the unequal merits and demerits of the creatures, he is free from it. God is like rain, the uniform cause of production. The difference lies in the various seeds of rice barley etc. and not in the rain. Similarly, the various beings have differences among them on account of differences in their merits and demerits, and not on account of inequality on the part of God. Śruti tells us that 'whomsoever he wishes to take up from this world, God makes him do good deeds and whomsoever he wishes to take down makes him do bad deeds' (Kau. 3, 8). But once again, it is not the unequal wishes of God, but the unequal previous deeds of merit and demerit and the desires of beings that make them good or bad (Bṛ. 3, 2, 13). Smṛti too informs us that the punishment or the grace, coming from God, depends on the quality of the deeds of men, and not on God; for he 'treats men in the way in which they show their attitude' towards him (B. G. 4, 11).

न कर्माविभागादिति चेन्नानादित्वात् । ३५

[*Na—not; karma;–avibhāgāt–owing to absence of duality; iti cet–if it be said; na; anāditvāt–being without beginning.*]

IF IT BE SAID THAT THERE WAS NO KARMA (BEFORE THE FIRST CREATION) ON ACCOUNT OF THE ABSENCE OF DUALITY, (WE SAY THAT) IT IS NOT SO; FOR (SAṀSĀRA IS) WITHOUT BEGINNING. 35

If, prior to creation, there was only 'One being, without a second', then it may be pointed out that there was no merit too on account of which the creation might be unequal. And to say that God is guided by the merits of the actions is to argue in a circle; *viz.* action is dependent on body and other conditions, and that the body and other conditions are dependent on action. Indeed, God can be said to depend on the merits, once the distinctions are granted to be there; but the first creation, at least, must be perfectly uniform, because there was no action or merit prior to it.

But the objection is not valid; because the world has no beginning. The seed and sprout appear to be dependent on each other; yet there is no logical flaw because both of them have no beginning. Similarly merits and inequality may continue to operate upon each other because both are without any beginning.

उपपद्यते चाप्युपलभ्यते च । ३६

[*Upapadyate—is ascertained*; *ca—and*; *upalabhyate—is found*; *ca*; .]

(THAT SAṀSĀRA IS WITHOUT BEGINNING) IS ASCERTAINED (BY REASON) AND IS FOUND (IN ŚRUTI). 36

For if there be a beginning to samsāra, there is no reason why it may begin to exist at a particular moment and no reason why the souls once released may not be born again. And there being again no reason for the inequality of pleasure and pain, rewards and punishments may come without merit or demerit of previous actions. That God is not the cause of this inequality we have already seen. Avidyā also cannot by itself be the cause ; for it remains the same in all the conditions of life, such as sleep, swoon etc. But the cause of inequality may be avidyā, provided it comes in contact with the merits or demerits of actions which the people are urged to do owing to anger, hatred and desires. Moreover to assume that the cause of inequality is the body, is to fall into a circular reasoning : for there will be no physical body without action, and no action without physical body. But if we believe the saṁsāra to be without any beginning, like the seed and the sprout, the causal connection between actions and the inequality appears reasonable.

Śruti and Smṛti also favour the view that the world is without a beginning. The very word 'jīva' used for the Ātman in the passage, 'Let me enter with this jīva etc.' (Chā. 6, 3, 2), shows that it has been used to denote the function of sustaining the prāṇas in the body of an individual being. It is clear therefore that the prāṇas and along with them the bodies of the creatures ever existed without a beginning, if at all the use of the word 'jīva' is to be justified. The word is not used in order to indicate a future relation with the prāṇas ; for the future is only a possibility, while the past is already a fact. Similarly, the mantra, 'As the creator thought of the former creation, he created the sun and the moon etc.' (Ṛg. 10, 190, 3) ; and the passage, 'Neither the support and form (viz the Brahman), nor the beginning nor the end of this is known' (B. G. 15, 3), show us that the saṁsāra is without a beginning.

१३ सर्वधर्मोपपत्त्यधिकरणम् । (३७)

सर्वधर्मोपपत्तेश्च । ३७

[*Sarva—all; dharma—qualities; upapatteḥ—being available; ca.*]

AND BECAUSE ALL THE QUALITIES ARE AVAILABLE (BRAHMAN IS THE CAUSE OF THE WORLD). 37

So far, the Sūtrakāra has removed all the objections, such as the difference in the nature of the world and the Brahman, and has proved that Brahman alone is the efficient and the material cause of the world. That this cause is at once, omniscient and omnipotent, and the ground of Māyā, is sufficient to show that no further doubt be entertained regarding the Upaniṣadic foundations of the Vedānta doctrine.

He will now proceed to the Second Pāda where the main concern will be to refute the opinions held by other teachers.

———

ADHYĀYA SECOND

PĀDA SECOND

१ रचनानुपपत्त्यधिकरणम् । (१-१०)

रचनानुपपत्तेश्च नानुमानम् । १

[*Racanā-an-upapatteḥ—owing to impossibility of design ; na—not ; anumānaṁ—inference.*]

AND BECAUSE THE ORDERLY ARRANGEMENT (OF THE WORLD) IS NOT POSSIBLE, THE INFERENCE (OF THE SĀṀKHYAS THAT PRADHĀNA IS THE CAUSE) CANNOT BE (MAINTAINED). 1

The purpose of the Vedānta system is to expound the meaning of the Upaniṣadic passages, and not to support or refute by means of logic any particular view. And yet, it is the duty of every student of the Vedānta to refute the Sāṁkhya and other systems of thought, because they are merely obstacles to right knowledge. Therefore it is that a new pāda is begun, after having, so far, established our own position, which affords the means of mokṣa to those who desire it. One may counsel us to remain satisfied with our own position and not to incite hate and anger by refuting other views. But the refutation too has a purpose of its own. It is to prevent the ordinary people of no great intellect from putting their faith in systems which are intrinsically worthless. The Sāṁkhya system, for instance, is very likely to mislead the ignorant people into believing that it contains right knowledge, because it appears weighty on account of subtle reasoning used by competent authorities. No doubt, we have already refuted the Sāṁkhya and some others on different occasions (while dealing with, 1, 1, 5 and 1, 4, 28). But this was done only to show that the interpretations which they put on the Vedānta-passages, which they too advanced for establishing their position, were all fallacious. The refutation which we are now going to do will exclusively deal with the reasonings which they have adopted, and not with the Śruti-passages which they have taken for support.

To begin with the arguments of the Sāṁkhyas. Just as vessels made of clay have clay alone as their cause even so, the external or the internal world of effects, whether house, body, or mind, endowed as it is with the characteristic marks of pleasure, pain and infatuation must be supposed to have arisen from a cause which must also possess these three characteristics. It is these three qualities which together go to form the cause known as the three-fold pradhāna. Like clay, it is non-intelligent ; but it evolves spontaneously into various modifications, for the sake of fulfilling the purposes of the soul, viz. the enjoyment of worldly pleasures and mokṣa. That pradhāna is the cause can also be inferred on account of other reasons,[1] such as the characteristic that things have measurement or dimensions.

---

[1] The Sāṁkhya Kārikā (15) mentions five such reasons:

भेदानां परिमाणात्समन्वयाच्छक्तितः प्रवृत्तेश्च ।
कारणकार्यविभागादविभागाद्वैश्वरूप्यस्य ॥

(1) The discrete and finite things in the world are the effects of eonjunctions of the several parts of these things. A piece of cloth is the effect of conjunction of several threads. There can be no room for conjunction in the homogeneous one Brahman. Pradhāna, on the other hand, consists of three guṇas and so affords room for their conjunction. The finite things of the world therefore have the threefold unevolved pradhāna as their cause. (2) Pradhāna is the common origin of all; for just as clay is found in all the vessels produced out of it, pradhāna is involved in all its products. (3) The activity of movement or action is seen only in things which are non-intelligent; for instance, a chariot moves on account of presence in it of wood and iron, which are non-intelligent things, God can not be the cause, because he is intelligent; therefore the non-intelligent pradhāna must be the source of all activity. (4) Cause and effect are of the same nature, clay is as non-intelligent as its effects, viz. the vessels. Therefore the ultimate cause of the world must be as non-intelligent as the world itself. It is, pradhāna and not God. (5) The absorption of the effect too is possible in a cause of similar nature. Vessels of clay can only be absorbed in clay. The non-intelligent world therefore requires for its absorption a non-intelligent cause viz. the pradhāna.

To this we reply. It is nowhere observed in the world that a non-intelligent thing like a stone produces of its own accord anything which may be of use, unless it is guided by some intelligent being. Palaces and pleasure-grounds are prepared by intelligent workmen, and do not come into being of their own accord. How then can this wonderful world which consists of the five elements, and of the internal things such as mind, intellect etc., and which baffles the imagination of even the most talented architects on account of the various species of beings and the arrangement of their organs, and the appropriate fruits for them contained in it, be created by a non-intelligent principle? Vessels of particular form and size are produced out of clay, only if a potter is there; even so, the pradhāna must be assumed to evolve only under the guidance of an intelligent being. For the production of a jar, it is not simply the material cause, viz. the clay that is responsible; the efficient cause too, viz. the potter is equally required. Even so the original cause of the world need not be taken to be simply the non-intelligent mixture of pleasure, pain and infatuation; it is rather the efficient cause of an intelligent being. To say so is not to offend any canon of reasoning.[1] On the contrary, we are in agreement with the teaching of Śruti which tells us that there is an intelligent cause of the world.

The word 'and' in the Sūtra is intended to state additional reasons for not believing in pradhāna as the cause. In the first place, the external and the internal objects of the world cannot be said to be of the nature of pleasure, pain and infatuation, because the latter are mental states while the former are the causes of these. Sound, for instance, as a sense-object is one and the same.

---

1 Just as we go beyond the presence of smoke in a mountain to the presence of fire in it, on account of similar observation in a kitchen, even so, we may go to an efficient intelligent cause of the world viz. the Brahman beyond the so-called material cause of it viz. the pradhāna, on account of similar going beyond to an intelligent potter, over and above the accepted material cause of a jar, viz the clay.

It is neither pleasant nor painful in itself; yet it affects one person as pleasant, another as painful, and a third as neither pleasant nor painful, on account of the mental condition of the persons. In other words, it only means that objects such as sound. are only the occasions of rousing the feelings on account of the desires and mental disposition of men. The objects themselves do not consist[1] of pleasure, pain and infatuation, which correspond to the three guṇas of the pradhāna. Secondly, if the Sāṁkhyas can argue from the partial observation that some distinct and limited things like roots, sprouts etc. are the result of conjunction of several things, to a generalization that all the objects of the world are the effects of conjunction of several things, we too can say against them that the three constituent qualities of the pradhāna, viz. the sattva-rajas and tamas, also arise on account of previous conjunction of several things; for they too are distinct and separate, and therefore limit one another.[2] Thirdly, as already pointed out, not all the effects are due to a non-intelligent prior condition ; they are also due to an intelligent principle beyond it.

प्रवृत्तेश्च । २

[*Pravṛtteḥ—because of tendency to activity; ca— and.*]

AND BECAUSE THE TENDENCY TOWARDS ACTIVITY (BEING IMPOSSIBLE, PRADHĀNA IS NOT THE CAUSE). 2

---

1 If things were to consist of pleasure, pain and infatuation, sandal-paste which is cool in summer would be so in winter too: and thistles which are eaten by camels, would have been eaten by men also with pleasure.— Bhāmati.

2 Limitation may arise in three ways, due to dimensions, duration and inherent nature. The spatial limitation has in reality no meaning with reference to ākāśa which is one: the temporal too does not exist. for in the scheme of the twentyfive principles of the Sāṁkhyas there is no place for time· the three guṇas. on the other hand, may be conceived as each having a separate inherent nature of its own: but then the Sāṁkhyas consider these as infinite and eternal aspects of pradhāna.

Let us leave aside the consideration of the orderly arrangement of the world. Even the original disturbance of the three guṇas from their equipoised condition during the dissolution of the world, and the consequent subordination of two of them to the third one, so necessary for the production of the things of the world as classified into sāttvika, rājasa and tāmasa, cannot be attributed to the non-intelligent, independent pradhāna. We never see the clay changing itself into pots without the help of a potter, nor a chariot moving itself without a horse. So we say that unless there is an ultimate intelligent principle, pradhāna can never be the cause of the world.

No doubt, it is true that the intelligent principle also is not actually seen to be active; but it is a matter of common observation that the non-intelligent chariot is seen to be moving only when it is joined with an intelligent being, such as a horse. And yet it may be said by the Sāṁkhyas that we see the activity in the non-intelligent chariot as certainly as we see the chariot itself, and that, on the other hand, we neither see the intelligent principle nor the activity located in that principle. At best, according to them, only the existence of the intelligent principle, and not its activity, is inferred on account of the actions which take place in a living body, which is dissimilar in nature to inanimate things like chariots. And so far as the existence of the intelligence also is concerned, it is found only when there exists a body; but when there exists no physical body, no intelligence too is found. In other words, as the Lokāyatikas consider, intelligence is a mere attribute of the body. Activity therefore belongs only to what is non-intelligent.

To this we reply. We do not mean to deny activity to non-intelligent things where it is observed. Let it belong to them. What we want to assert is that it is due to an intelligent principle. For just as the capacity to burn and shine which exists in wood, and which is not manifested in mere fire as such, requires for its manifestation the conjunction of wood with fire, even so, the activity of any non-intelligent thing is seen only when the intelligent principle is present and not otherwise. That is why, as the Lokāyitikas also admit, it is present in a living body and not in a corpse; present in a chariot drawn by a horse, and not in a mere chariot. Intelligence therefore possesses the power to move, without any contradiction.

It may still be said that because the Ātman is, according to the Vedāntins, pure consciousness and nothing else, it must itself be incapable of activity and incapable of making others active. But the objection does not stand. For a thing may be devoid of motion and yet capable of moving other things. A magnet may not move itself, but moves a piece of iron; colours and other objects of sense do not move themselves, but make the eyes and other senses active. So, the omnipresent, omnipotent, omniscient God too, being the Ātman of all, can move the universe, himself remaining unmoved. It is no objection to suggest that there being only one Brahman and nothing else, there can be no motion at all. For we have repeatedly said that inasmuch as the entire world consisting of names and forms has been the work of Māyā or avidyā, God too is imagined to be connected with it as the substratum on which the illusion exists. Thus there is room for activity if the ultimate cause of all is taken to be the all-knowing Brahman; but not when it is taken to be the non-intelligent pradhāna.

पयोम्बुवच्चेत्तत्रापि । ३

[*Payaḥ—milk, aṁbu—water; vat—like; cet—if; tatra—then; api—even.*

If it be said that (pradhāna may be active) like water and milk, (we reply that) then, too, (the activity is due to intelligence). 3

Citing further instances of the non-intelligent milk and water which flow themselves naturally for the nourishment of the calf and for the benefit of mankind, the Sāṁkhya may wish to prove that the pradhāna also, in like manner, transforms itself into the world so that men should achieve the highest end of life.

The argument however is not adequate ; for both the parties now agree in saying that activity is not observed in merely non-intelligent things such as chariots. The activity of the non-intelligent milk and water like that of the non-intelligent chariot, must be said to be equally guided by intelligence, and therefore cannot be cited as affording a new argument. Besides, it is the loving wish of the intelligent cow for the calf, and the sucking of milk by the intelligent calf, which make possible the flow of the milk. The flowing of water too is dependent on the low level of the ground. Besides, in a general way, it is dependent on the intelligent principle viz. the Brahman which is present everywhere. Śruti also supports what we say : 'He dwells and rules the water from within' (Bṛ. 3, 7, 4) ; 'By the command of the Akṣara some rivers flow to the east' (Bṛ. 3, 8, 9).

The present Sūtra may be shown to contradict Sūtra 24 of adhyāya second, pāda first. For there, the natural change of milk into curds without any extraneous cause was used by us as an illustration to show that God can create the universe out of himself without the help of any other instrument ; while here we say that all activity is guided by intelligence. But there is no contradiction between the practical way of explaining things, as we did on the former occasion, and the logical way of explaining them, as in the present Sūtra. For even the natural way of the changing of milk into curds requires the guidance of God.

व्यतिरेकानवस्थितेश्चानपेक्षत्वात् । ४

[*Vyatireka-anavasthiteḥ— there being nothing beyond; ca; anapekṣatvāt— there being no purpose.*]

(AND BECAUSE THERE IS NOTHING BEYOND (PRADHĀNA AS THE CAUSE OF ACTIVITY, THE PRADHĀNA) CANNOT HAVE ANY PURPOSE (TO BE ACTIVE OR INACTIVE). 4

According to the view of the Sāṁkhyas, pradhāna means the equipoised condition of the three guṇas. And there being no other principle beyond pradhāna, there is nothing which could make it active or inactive. For puruṣa, in their view, is indifferent and so cannot be said either to cause action or the cessation of action. Pradhāna thus being utterly independent, it is impossible to know why it should sometimes transform itself into mahat and other things, and why at other times it should not.[1] God, on the other hand, can be active or not as he pleases, because he is omniscient and omnipotent and can make use of his māyā, whenever he wants.

अन्यत्राभावाच्च न तृणादिवत् । ५

[*Anyatra-elsewhere; abhāvāt-because of absence, ca, na; tṛṇa-ādi-vat-like grass and other things*]

NOR (DOES PRADHĀNA MODIFY ITSELF) LIKE GRASS ETC. (WHICH CHANGE INTO MILK); FOR (EXCEPT IN THE FEMALE ANIMAL, *e. g* A COW THE CHANGE OF GRASS INTO MILK) DOES NOT EXIST ELSEWHERE. 5

The Sāṁkhya may again argue that just as grass, herbs and water get themselves naturally transformed into milk, even so the pradhāna may transform itself into mahat

1 If the activity is uncontrolled, there is no knowing when it may continue to exist, and when it may stop. Supposing the activity to create is once starting it may continue to be without any end or dissolution of the world. Or supposing the world is at an end, there may not be any beginning of it.

and other things. For had there been any other cause responsible for transforming grass into milk, men could have employed it to produce as much milk as they liked. But as this is not done, the process must be considered as natural; and so one may expect the same in the case of pradhāna.

We do not admit this ; because we know that some other cause is responsible for changing grass into milk, It is only that grass, which is eaten by a cow, that changes into milk, and not that which is not eaten, nor that which is eaten by an ox. Besides, an event need not be said to be natural, simply because man cannot accomplish it. For things not brought about by men, are brought about by divine activity. And we do find that men too feed the cows with plenty of grass etc. if they want plenty of milk. Hence it is not correct to say that pradhāna modifies itself spontaneously like grass and other things.

अभ्युपगमेऽप्यर्थाभावात् । ६

[*Abhyupagame–admitting; api–even; artha–abhāvāt—there being no purpose.*]

EVEN ADMITTING (THE SPONTANEOUS ACTIVITY OF PRADHĀNA, THERE REMAINS THE DEFECT OF) THERE BEING NO PURPOSE (FOR SUCH ACTIVITY). 6

Now, if by saying that pradhāna is spontaneously active, it is meant that it is not in need of any other principle beyond it, it must also mean that it acts independently of any purpose. But to say so is to go against the very tenet of the Sāṁkhya view that the pradhāna becomes active for fulfilling the purposes of man. If, on the other hand, the Sāṁkhya says that the spontaneous activity of pradhāna is necessarily purposive, though not dependent on some other principle, we must search what that purpose is. If, in the first place, that purpose is to provide with appropriate pleasures and pains to the Puruṣa, we have to suppose, what is impossible on the Sāṁkhya hypothesis, that the Puruṣa who is eternally unchanging undergoes corresponding modifications of increase or decrease in his nature [1]. Besides, there would be no release, because experience of pleasure and pain has been now accepted as the only motive for the activity of pradhāna. If, in the second place, the purpose is to achieve the liberation of the puruṣa, it is merely to conceive the superfluous that is, something which has already been realized; for the puruṣa was in the condition of liberation even before the activity of pradhāna. Besides, if the motive is not to provide with the pleasures and pains of life, there would be no empirical experience of worldly life, such as sounds, colours etc. If, again, in the third place the purposes be conceived as both mundane pleasures and pains, and liberation, we shall find that in reality neither is possible. Liberation is not possible[2] because the objects produced by pradhāna are infinite and so there would be no occasion at all for final release. Satisfaction of the desire to fulfil the human ends cannot, as a matter of fact, be attributed to pradhāna, because it is not intelligent; nor can any desire be attributed to the puruṣa because he is said to be pure and partless.[3]

If, to avoid all these difficulties, the pradhāna is said to be active on account of its inherent power to produce, and on account of the inherent power of the puruṣa to 'look on' at things produced, we observe that there will be endless existence of this saṃsāra on account of the

---

1Even a phenomenal change cannot be ascribed to the puruṣa, inasmuch as the conception of adhyāsa or superimposition of one thing on another, as in the Vedānta, is foreign to the theory of the Sāṁkhyas.—Ratnaprabhā.

2As said above, liberation is already an accomplished fact; it does not require the activity of pradhāna for its coming into being.

3Desire is a kind of dirt of the mind, which is otherwise pure and is endowed with the capacity to know the distinction between, good and bad. right and wrong etc. Desire obstructs this capacity just as dust on a mirror obstructs its capacity to reflect things.

imperishable nature of these two powers. In other words, once again, there will be no liberation at all. Hence it is incorrect to say that pradhāna becomes active for the sake of fulfilling the purposes of the puruṣa.

पुरुषाश्मवदिति चेत्तथापि । ७

[*Puruṣa; aśmavat–like magnet ; iti ; cet ; tatha-api—even then.*]

IF IT IS SAID THAT (PURUṢA MOVES THE PRADHĀNA, AS A (LAME) MAN (MAY LEAD A BLIND MAN) OR AS THE MAGNET (MAY ATTRACT THE IRON), EVEN THEN (THE DIFFICULTY REMAINS). 7

If the puruṣa is said to move the pradhana, then, in the first place, the Sāṁkhya has to abandon his own position, *viz.*, that the pradhāna is active on its own account, and that the puruṣa possesses no moving power. How indeed should the indifferent, inactive puruṣa move the pradhāna ? A lame man, no doubt, may lead a blind man by mounting on his back; but he leads him by means of words etc. How can the puruṣa who is devoid of action and qualities be expected to move the pradhāna ? Similarly, the magnet comes near the iron and then attracts it. But the puruṣa and the pradhāna are permanently near each other; and so there would be perpetual activity and no final release. Besides, the magnet is required to be made clean before it can be expected to attract iron. The puruṣa, on the other hand, is already pure. Hence the illustrations are inadequate. So, between the non-intelligent pradhāna and indifferent puruṣa, there being no third principle, there can be no connection at all between the two. Besides, as proved in the preceding Sūtra, there can be no purpose of the activity of pradhāna, even though it is now assumed that that activity is caused by puruṣa. The highest Ātman, on the Vedāntic doctrine, is only indifferent so far as its own nature is concerned. Still it is considered as active in its relation to māyā;

and that is why there is no inconsistency[1] to say that the Ātman is both active and inactive.

अंगित्वानुपपत्तेश्च । ८

[*Angitva-relation of principal (and subordinate); anupapatteḥ-being impossible, ca-and.*]

AND BECAUSE (THE THREE GUṆAS) ARE NOT RELATED AS PRINCIPAL (AND SUBORDINATE, PRADHĀNA CANNOT BE ACTIVE). 8

Pradhāna means the equipoised, eternal condition of the three co-ordinate, independent guṇas of sattva rajas and tamas. So, the moment any one of them becomes superior to others, the very characteristic nature of the guṇas and therefore of the pradhāna itself will be lost.[2] And as there exists no external principle to disturb the guṇas, the evolution of the universe will not be possible.

अन्यथानुमितौ च ज्ञशक्तिवियोगात् । ९

[*Anyathā-in another way; anumitau-if inferred; ca; jñaśakti-intelligence; viyogāt-being devoid of.*]

AND THOUGH ANOTHER INFERENCE BE MADE (THE DEFECTS REMAIN) BECAUSE (PRADHĀNA) IS DEVOID OF INTELLIGENCE. 9

The Sāṁkhya may say that as he has no proof to hold that qualities are unchangeable and without relation,

---

1 The Sāṁkhya view is contradictory, because the puruṣa is conceived to be both inactive and the mover of pradhāna. The Vedānta view, on the other hand, has no such contradiction, because there is the conception of adhyāsa (superimposition) arising out of ignorance or Māyā. The Ātman appears to be the creator of the world and the subject of empirical experience, on account of ignorance. But from the point of view of one who has real knowledge, there being no plurality, the Ātman is neither the creator nor the subject of empirical experience.

2 Pradhāna will therefore neither be considered as Kūṭasthanitya (eternal by itself) nor pariṇāminitya (eternal as a process).

he may infer from the nature of the effects that the qualities have got, in spite of their equipoise, the capacity to change and produce the effects. Even then, we reply that the argument will contain the defect we have already pointed out, *viz*., that there will be no orderly arrangement of the world, if the pradhāna is non-intelligent. And if, to avoid this difficulty, the Sāṁkhya would say that pradhāna too is intelligent, then he will not differ from us at all. For what we call Brahman, he will call pradhāna. And there will be only one intelligent principle which will also be the material cause of this multiform universe. Granting further that the guṇas are capable of undergoing inequality in spite of their equipoise, they will never be unequal in the absence of an adequate cause. So there may not be any evolution of the world at all. Or if the guṇas somehow happen to be unequal without any cause, they will always remain so, and there will be perpetual sāṁsara and no release.

विप्रतिषेधाच्चासमंजसम् । १०

[*Vipratiṣedhāt–owing to contradictions ; ca–and ; asamañjasaṁ–not satisfactory.*]

BESIDES, (THE SĀṀKHYA DOCTRINE) IS UNSATISFACTORY ON ACCOUNT OF ITS CONTRADICTIONS. 10

The Sāṁkhya doctrine, moreover, contains many contradictions. Sometimes, they say that there are seven senses, sometimes eleven.[1] In some places, they tell us that the five subtle elements (tanmātras) evolve from the great principle (mahat), while in other places, they are said to evolve from the consciousness of the ego (ahaṁkāra). Sometimes, they speak of one internal organ *viz*., the intellect (antaḥkaraṇa), sometimes of three *viz*. mind, intellect and egoism. Besides, it is well known that

1 Five senses of action, five of knowledge, and mind; or five senses of action mind, and the sense of touch which functions for the five senses of knowledge.

their doctrine contradicts the Śruti teaching that God is the cause of the world.

At this, the Sāṁkhya too, brings a counter attack. The Vedānta doctrine also, says he, cannot be accepted, because even the practical distinction which the whole world is making between a person who suffers and his suffering is not possible on the Brahmanic theory. The sufferer and the suffering will be considered as the attributes of Brahman itself, and therefore the teaching of the Śruti that knowledge should be attained for the purpose of putting an end to all suffering, loses its significance. A little consideration however will show that these are different though connected. Just as the flame though distinct cannot exist apart from its light and heat, or just as, even in the illustration used by the Vedāntin,[1] the sea-water, can never be conceived to be permanently different from the waves and foam, which are sometimes manifest and sometimes not, even so the Ātman must be thought of as essentially connected with its attributes of jīva and saṁsāra, or which is the same thing, as the sufferer and the suffering. In other words, if the Ātman is essentially and permanently bound up with the sufferer and the suffering, though not the same as the latter, there will be no release at all.

That the sufferer and the suffering are two different things from the practical point of view can be seen in another way also. An object of desire is different from the person who desires it; otherwise there will be on desire at all. A flame *e. g.*, does not desire to have light, for it possesses it already. Nor can it be said that the object of desire desires itself; for this is nowhere seen. The relation implied in desire, cannot be established with reference to one thing or person only; it requires two terms to relate, *viz.*, the object of desire and the person

---

[1]The Vedāntin shows that the Ātman may remain the same even though the attributes pass away.

desiring it. The same holds good if instead of desire there is aversion. Now there being a far greater number of objects of aversion or dislike than that of like. both of them are generally known as the objects that cause suffering to man.[1] To return to the point, if both the sufferer and the suffering go to form one self, there would be no release. But if they are two, then there is the possibility of release, inasmuch as the cause of bondage, *viz.*, wrong knowledge may be removed.

We reply that all this reasoning is pointless. For Brahman being the only reality, there can neither be the sufferer and the suffering as two distinct things, nor any relation between them. Fire can neither burn nor illumine itself, even though it may be said that it possesses the attributes of heat and light, and grows in volume etc. No doubt from the practical point of view, it may be said that the Sun is the cause of suffering, while the living body which is scorched by the heat is the sufferer. Yet we cannot admit the argument of the Sāṁkhya that the suffering or pain may in reality belong to the intelligent being alone, and not to the non-intelligent body, on the ground, as he says, that if it were to belong to the latter, it would, as the Cārvākas hold, cease with the cessation of the body, and that there would therefore be no need to search for the means of liberation of the soul. For, apart from the fact that nobody can ever imagine a disembodied being becoming the object of suffering, the Sāṁkhya too, on his own theory, cannot admit the soul or puruṣa who is essentially pure to be affected by pain, either directly by itself or indirectly through the connection of the body. Nor, again, can the connection of pain and puruṣa be established through the connection of puruṣa and sattvaguṇa, and through the affection of

[1] Things which are liked and are dear to man are in the first place few in number. Secondly these are hard to be acquired. Further they cause great anxiety while protecting them, and if lost cause great sorrow. Besides, it is not always that they are loved and liked Sandal is good in summer, but not in winter.—Marathi Trans. by Abhyankar Śāstri Vol II. Page 628.

sattva by rajas. For there can be no connection between the non-intelligent guṇas and the intelligent and partless puruṣa. And finally if the puruṣa be supposed to suffer as it were, simply because he is said to be reflected in the sattva, we have no objection to his being so imagined to suffer, as it were. But to suppose that an amphisbena is like a serpent is not to make it poisonous, nor is it to make a serpent non-poisonous by supposing it to be like an amphisbena. Thus, on the theory of the Sāṁkhyas, too, the relation between the sufferer and the suffering is not real; or which is the same thing as the Vedāntin says, it is the effect of avidyā. The fact of suffering and the distinction between the sufferer and the suffering are in other words, inexplicable and unreal.

The Sāṁkhya may again take a new line of thought and argue that the puruṣa is capable of suffering on account of the non-discrimination of the fact that he is different from pradhāna, and that therefore there will be release for him as soon as there will be the separation from him of the cause of non-discrimination, *viz.* the tamoguṇa. But this is to make the release all the more impossible. For, as the Sāṁkhya believes, the tamoguna, which is the root cause of non-discrimination and non-release, is as eternal as sattva; and as the conquest or defeat of one guṇa by the other is neither fixed nor everlasting, the tamas may at any time again overpower the sattva, and thus clouding the intellect of man may again bind him.[1]

To the Vedāntin, on the other hand, mokṣa, or final release is an undoubted fact. For the Ātman alone being the one existing entity, and the so-called plurality having its origin in speech, as the Chāndogyopaniṣad says there cannot be any such distinction or relation as exists

---

1 The Saṁkhya argues that the intellect or the sattvaguṇa becomes clouded by the non-discrimination of tamas, and so the puruṣa experiences the suffering enhanced by rajas. The puruṣa becomes overpowered, in other words, by the qualities of pradhana. When, however, the non-discrimination comes to an end by the dominance of sattva over tamas, there arises the release.

between subject and object or between sufferer and suffering in spite of the cognition of these in practical life.

२ महद्दीर्घाधिकरणम् । (११)

To refute now the atomic theory of the Vaiśeṣikas who argue as follows: White threads produce a white piece of cloth, and not of any other colour. From this we can infer that qualities which are found in the cause reappear in the effect. So, if we assume the intelligent Brahman as the cause of the world, we should expect the same quality of intelligence in the world also. But, as this is not, we conclude that Brahman is not the cause of the world.

It is this reasoning which the Sūtrakāra shows to be fallacious, by taking his stand on the theory of the Vaiśeṣikas themselves.

महद्दीर्घवद्वा ह्रस्वपरिमण्डलाभ्याम् । ११

[*Mahat-dīrgha-vat—as having dimensions known as 'mahat' and dīrgha; vā—or; ṛhsva-parimandalābyāṁ—from what is minute and spherical.*]

AND, JUST AS (DYADS AND TRIADS POSSESSING DIMENSIONS OF) 'MAHAT' AND 'DIRGHA' (ARISE FROM ATOMS POSSESSING) MINUTENESS AND SPHERICITY, (EVEN SO, THE WORLD MAY ARISE OUT OF BRAHMAN). 11

The theory of the Vaiśeṣikas is as follows:-'The atoms are spherical; though specific atoms have got specific[1] qualities. During the time of dissolution, they do not produce anything; but at the time of a new creation, they come together on account of the force of the unseen

1 Earth atoms have got, for instance, the four qualities of colour, taste smell and touch; water atoms have three except smell; fire atoms have two viz. colour and touch; while air atoms have only one quality viz. touch.

merits and demerits of the actions of the souls, and being combined with the will of God, produce the entire world of effects. Along with this production, the qualities of the causes are reproduced in the effects. Thus when two atoms produce a dyad, the white colour of the atoms is produced in the dyad, but not the original sphericity or 'pārimāṇḍalya' of the atom. For the dyad is said to assume the new dimensions of 'aṇutva' (smallness) and 'rhasvatva' (shortness). When two (four) dyads, in their turn, combine to produce a tetrad, it is the whiteness of the cause which is found to be repeated in the effect, but not the dimensions; for the tetrad assumes the new dimensions of 'mahatva' (largeness) and 'dirghatva' (length). Similar is the case when many simple atoms, or many dyads, or an atom and a dyad combine to produce new effects.

So, if at every stage, while passing from atom to dyad, or from dyad to triad and tetrad, dissimilar qualities are produced on the Vaiśeṣika theory, we have to say that on the Vedānta theory also, there may arise the non-intelligent world from the intelligent Brahman.

At this, the Vaiśeṣika may say that the products like dyads, triads etc. being endowed with qualities opposed in nature to those of the causes, it is not possible for the latter to overcome the former and reappear in their place. But non-intelligence is not a quality opposed in nature to intelligence; it is merely the negation or absence of intelligence, and so there is nothing to prevent the Brahman from reproducing its quality of intelligence in the world.

But the argument is not correct. For, in the first place, the intelligence of the Brahman is not produced in the world, just as sphericity of the atoms is not produced in their effects. It cannot be said, in the second place, that the old qualities cannot be repeated because the effect is being endowed with new qualities. For, as the Vaiśeṣikas hold, substances are, in the first instant, devoid of qualities, but become endowed with them only in the second instant; and so, it is possible that the old qualities can reproduce themselves in the effects during the period in which the latter are without any qualities. Nor can it be said, in the third place, that the old qualities like sphericity etc. are incapable of reproducing themselves inasmuch as it is these which create new and dissimilar qualities in new effects. As Kaṇāda says, the new qualities such as 'mahatva' (largeness), and 'dīrghatva' (length) arise out of plurality or largeness contained in the cause; aṇutva (smallness) and rhasvatva (shortness), on the other hand, arise when there is neither plurality nor largeness in the cause. In other words, as Kaṇāda himself tells, these new qualities do not come out of the original qualities of sphericity etc. (Vai. Sū. 7, 1, 9 and 10 and 17). Nor finally can it be said that the plurality of the constituent members of a cause or the duality of them being contiguous[1] with the effects produces the 'mahatva' or 'aṇutva' in them, though it is not so with sphericity etc. because these qualities of the cause instead of being contiguous with the effects, are, on the contrary, remote from them. As a matter of fact, all the qualities of the cause must reside in it in exactly the same manner, that is, either on all or on some of the parts of the cause, and are therefore equally contiguous or not with the effect. The reason then why sphericity etc. are not seen reproduced in the effects is not that they are not contiguous,

---

1 When two atoms combine to make a dyad, the number 'two' is said to be contiguous with the dyad, while the 'pārimāṇḍalya' or the sphericity of the atoms is not said to be so contiguous with the dyad. And further, just as the dyad is dependent for its existence on two atoms taken together, and not on each of the two atoms taken separately, so also the number 'two' exists on the two atoms taken together and not on each of them taken separately. The 'sphericity' of the atom, however, exists on each atom separately, and not on two or more atoms taken together. Therefore it is that sphericity is said to be away or not contiguous with the dyad. Similarly, the 'mahat' (largeness) of triad, is simultaneously present on the plural number of the dyads—out of which the triad arises—and so is contiguous with the triad. The 'aṇutva' of the dyad, on the other hand, resides on only one dyad and not on several dyads taken together, and so is not contiguous with the triad. Ve. Sū; Marathi Trans. Abhyankar Śastri Vol. II Page. 639.

but that they have this natural mode of behaving. Why then can we not say with reference to the intelligence of the Brahman that it has the natural way of not being reproduced in the world ?

Besides, we do find that from the quality known as conjunction, (saṁyoga) of the threads, there results the substance viz. a piece of cloth ; and so the statement that the cause and effect are similar in nature is not true. If the Vaiśeṣika would object to comparing a quality with substance and thereby prevent us from saying that the Brahman, as substance, can produce a dissimilar effect, we reply that we are only interested in pointing out that the effect is dissimilar from the cause. Besides, there is no rule that while adducing examples one must choose the example of a quality, when the quality is under discussion or choose that of a substance when the substance is under discussion. Kaṇāda himself cites the example of a quality when substance is under discussion, as in Sūtra, 4, 2,2, 'Inasmuch as the conjunction of things perceivable and things imperceivable, is itself imperceivable, the body is not composed of the five elements.' The meaning of the Sūtra is that just as the quality of conjunction which is said to be inherent in the perceptible earth and the imperceptible ākāśa, is itself imperceptible, even so, if the physical body were to reside or inhere in its constituent five elements some of which (viz. the earth, water and fire) are perceptible, and some (viz. air and ākāśa) are not, it too would have been imperceptible. But the body is perceived, and hence it is not composed of the five elements. It is thus that Kaṇāda himself has given the lead in comparing the quality of conjunction with the substance, viz. the body. Besides in Sūtra 6 of Pāda 1 of Adhyāya 2, we have shown that the effect may be different from the cause. And though this is a repetition and we could have avoided it, (as we once did avoid a repetition while dealing with II, 1, 3 and 12) what we wished to do here is to refute the Vaiśeṣikas on their own ground.

३ परमाणुवादनिराकरणाधिकरणम् । (१२-१७)

उभयथापि न कर्मातस्तदभावः । १२

[*Ubhayathāpi—both ways; na; karma—activity; ataḥ—hence; tat-abhāvaḥ—absence of that.*]

No activity (is possible) notwithstanding both ways; hence the absence of that (viz. the creation of the world). 12

Now begins the refutation of the atomic theory which can be stated thus. A piece of cloth is connected with the threads which are contained in it by the relation known as 'samavāya'; and the several threads are brought together by 'saṁyoga'. In general, we may say that the parts inherent in any whole are brought together by conjunction; and that all things which consist of parts such as mountains and seas, or the four elements of earth, water, fire and air come out of the different combinations of four kinds of atoms. It is these things which can be considered as wholes of parts and which can ultimately be said to be produced out of atoms and disintegrated back into the atoms, at the time of the dissolution of the universe. But the atom being the limit of divisibility cannot be dissolved or destroyed. At the time ofcreation therefore the atoms of air first come together on account of the motion caused in them by the unseen merits and demerits of the souls, and thus it is that dyads, triads etc. of the element of air are produced only to give rise to the air itself. Similar is the production of the other three elements of fire, water and earth in succession, and of the physical body and the senses. This is how the whole universe has come out of atoms. As for the qualities of the successive products, they are, as already seen, like those of the earlier causes. The quality of whiteness for instance of a piece of cloth is the same as that of the threads. Such, in brief, is the view of Kaṇāda and his followers.

To this we reply. In the first place, it must be admitted that the conjunction which takes place between the several separate atoms at the time of creation is duc to some action, like the one required in bringing about the conjunction of threads into a piece of cloth. The action, in its turn, implies some effort on the part of the soul, or some impact of one thing against another, like the impact, for instance, of wind with the tree, or of the hand with the thing which is moved by it. The effort of the soul is possible only when the mind is joined with the soul, and the impact only after the creation of the products like wind etc. But neither is possible during the condition of dissolution, because there is neither the physical body, nor any evolved product or thing except in its atomic condition. Therefore the causes which are only possible to exist after the creation of the world cannot be thought of as existing before it and producing the initial action necessary for the conjunction of the atoms. Creation therefore out of the atoms is inexplicable.

If, in the second place, it is said that it is the principle of 'unseen' accumulation of merits and demerits that causes the original motion of the atoms, we reply that this is not possible at all, whether the principle resides in the soul or in the atoms. For it is a non-intelligent principle; and as already shown in our examination of the Śaṁkhya view, a non-intelligent thing cannot of itself be the cause of any action. Nor can we suppose that the principle is guided by the soul, because the soul too is not intelligent on the Vaiśeṣika view. Even if the 'unseen' principle is said to reside in the soul there will be no connection between the principle and the atom ; and if the scul is said to be connected with the atoms and so indirectly, if the unseen principle in the soul is said to be connected with them, there will be perpetual activity and perpetual creation [1] and therefore no dissolution at all. Hence.

1 This will occur especially when the Iśvara, who is according to the Vaiseṣika, eternal and self-conscious, is supposed to be the cause of the action in the atoms, on account of the guidance of the unseen principle in the individual soul.

in the absence of any definite cause of action, there will be no activity in the atoms. Hence, further, there will be no conjunction of different atoms and no formation of dyads, triads etc. In other words, there will be no creation at all.

Supposing the atoms combine, do they interpenetrate each other or are joined only partially? In the former case, there would be no increase in volume or size; and in the latter, the atoms shall have to be conceived as consisting of parts.[1] And even if they are imagined to be made up of parts, due to their position and direction in space, their conjunction will be an unreal thing of imagination, and so will not be useful as an efficient cause in producing dyads, triads, etc. And finally, as seen above, just as creation of things becomes impossible on account of any visible cause of motion and the consequent conjunction of the atoms, even so, the dissolution of the world will be impossible in the absence of any visible cause for the separation of the atoms. Nor can the situation be saved by resorting to the unseen principle as the cause of dissolution; for it may explain the occurrence of pleasures and pains in this world, but not the state of complete dissolution in which there is neither pleasure nor pain. In short, in the absence of any cause, seen or unseen, for the motion and conjunction of the atoms there will be neither creation nor dissolution possible on the Vaiśeṣika theory. It must therefore be rejected.

समवायाभ्युपगमाच्च साम्यादनवस्थितेः । १३

[*Samavāya; abhyupagamāt—being admitted; ca; sāmyāt—owing to resemblance; anavasthiteḥ—on account of regress ad infinitum.*]

AND BECAUSE THE INCLUSION OF SAMAVĀYA WHICH RESEMBLES (THE DYAD IN ITS RELATION TO THE ATOMS) LEADS TO REGRESS AD INFINITUM (THERE WILL BE NEITHER CREATION NOR DISSOLUTION). 13

---

1 Consequently, on the former view, there will be no production of any distinct effect; the latter is simply a contradiction of the Vaiseṣika hypothesis. —Ratnaprabhā.

The relation of samavāya (inherence) too in the doctrine of the Vaiśeṣika will not be sufficient to explain the creation and the dissolution of the world. For just as a dyad which resides or inheres in two atoms is absolutely different from them, even so the relation of inherence or samavāya which is equally different from the two atoms must reside in them on account of a second relation of samavāya. But this second relation will similarly require a third, and so on *ad infinitum*. It may be said that samavāya is never seen as an unconnected relation or as depending on some other connection, so that it may ultimately lead to the regress. On the contrary, it may be shown to be eternally present in the things which are seen here and before us.[1] But in that case, saṁyoga (conjunction) also, we reply, can be said to be eternally connected with things which are joined together, and need not therefore depend on a further connection viz. samavāya, as the Vaiśeṣika supposes. Like saṁyoga, samavāya is a distinct relation, and so ought to depend on some other relation. Nor can it be said that saṁyoga is dependent on another relation because saṁyoga is the name of a quality, while samavāya is self-sufficient because it is not a quality. But this is no proof. For categories other than the category of quality, such as 'karma' and 'sāmānya' are in need of the relation of samavāya. The one thing which is common to both saṁyoga and samavāya, and on account of which saṁyoga is dependent on another relation, is the fact that both of them are absolutely different from the terms they relate; and so, samavāya too is dependent on a second samavāya. Now, as seen above, this involves the regress and makes the last term of the series inexplicable inasmuch as there is no relation beyond it with which it must be connected to have its own being possible. But being connected with this inexplicable last relation of samavāya all the earlier relations of samavāya also are as good as naught. So ultimately, in the absence of samavāya there will be no

---

1 E.g. a piece of cloth on threads; qualities and actions in a substance; or existence in substance, quality and action etc.

production of a dyad out of any two atoms. There ill therefore be no creation on the atomic theory.

नित्यमेव च भावात् । १४

[*Nityaṁ—permanent; eva—only; ca—and; bhāvāt—because of existence*].

AND BECAUSE OF EXISTENCE (OF THE NATURAL ACTIVITY OR NON-ACTIVITY OF ATOMS) THERE WILL BE THE CONTINUATION OF IT. 14

Now the Vaiśeṣika may resort to four possibilities. Either the atoms are naturally endowed with activity, or with non-activity, or with both or with neither. If the first, there will be perpetual creation and no dissolution; if the second, there will be perpetual dissolution, and no creation: the third is a statement of contradiction; and if the fourth, the activity or otherwise of the atoms must be due to some other cause. Now if this cause be the 'unseen' accumulation of merits and demerits, the very proximity of it with the atoms will cause permanent activity; otherwise there will be inactivity again.

रूपादिमत्त्वाच्च विपर्ययो दर्शनात् । १५

[*Rūpādi-matvāt—on account of possessing colour and others; viparyayāḥ—opposite; darśanāt—because it is observed*]

AND OPPOSITE CONCLUSION (WILL FOLLOW) IF ATOMS ARE ENDOWED WITH COLOUR ETC., AS IS OBSERVED (IN DAILY EXPERIENCE), 15

Our ordinary experience tells us that things possessing colour and other qualities are more transitory and gross than their causes. A piece of white cloth is bigger and more easily perishable than the filaments. Therefore the atoms of the Vaiśeṣikas too, if admitted as having colour, taste, smell and touch, must be due to some other cause, and must be gross and transitory in comparison with that cause.

And if atoms have a cause, then Kaṇāda's definition of a permanent thing as 'That which has existence but no cause', (Vai. Sū. 4, 1, 1) cannot be made applicable to atoms. The second reason also which Kaṇāda gives for the permanency of the atoms, viz. that if they too, as causes, are not permanent then there would be no meaning in making a specific reference to the impermanence of the effects (4, 1, 4), is not at all adequate. No doubt the prefix 'im' (a) can never be applied to the word 'permanent' (nitya) and the word 'impermanent' can mean anything unless there is something which is permanent. But this is no reason to suppose that the atoms alone are permanent, for as we, the Vedāntins, hold the Brahman is the permanent cause. Besides, the mere use of a word need not be taken as a sufficient ground for the existence of a thing implied by that word; on the contrary, the thing which is the content or meaning of the word must be first established as existing by other means of knowledge. And if 'ignorance' of cause, that is the 'non-perception of the cause of atoms which exist themselves and which produce perceptible effects by their being combined,' is given as the third reason (4, 15) for believing that the atoms are permanent, we may say that this is too wide. For thereby we may believe that like atoms the dyads also are permanent, because they exist and produce perceptible effects like jars and cloth, and are themselves produced by atoms which are non-perceived. If to avoid this difficulty, the Vaiśeṣika would say that he means by 'ignorance' or 'non-perception' of cause only the non-existence of a material substance responsible for the production of the effects, and that thereby he would prevent the dyads from being considered as permanent on account of atoms being there as the material substance out of which the dyads have come into being, then this is nothing but a repetition of the earlier Sūtra (4, 1, 1) which speaks of the absence of cause as the ground of permanence of the atoms. In other words, the Sūtra, 4, 15, is superfluous.

The 'avidyā' or non-perception in the Sūtra, 4, 1, 5, may again be interpreted by the Vaiśeṣika in a new way. According to him a thing can be destroyed either by the destruction of its cause or by the disintegration of it. The atoms having no further cause cannot be destroyed in either of these two ways. And there is no third reason of destruction known to exist. So it is this absence of any additional reason of destruction that is meant by the word 'avidya,' And because there is no such reason, the atoms are said by him to be permanent.

This reasoning of the Vaiśeṣika may be said to be correct provided the thing that comes into being is the result of combination of several substances. In that case alone, that particular thing will be said to perish, if the several substances become separate from each other or are themselves destroyed. In either case, in other words, as the Vaiśeṣika holds, there will be the end of that particular thing on account of the end of the conjunction[1] of the several substances. But as the Vedāntins view it, destruction of the effect is possible only by a modification in its condition, just as the solidity of ghee is destroyed by its being transformed into the liquid condition. Similarly, atoms may not be destroyed or disintegrated but may be transformed into a prior non-atomic condition, which is the condition of the being of Brahman.

उभयथा च दोषात् । १६

[*Ubhayathā–both ways ; ca–and; doṣāt–due to defect*].

1 Conjunction is the asamavāyi cause on the Vaiśeṣika theory. Along with its own being it brings into existence new things; and so along with its destruction or disintegration of the several constituent causes, the thing also is destroyed. This may be true so far as Arambha-vāda is concerned. But on the Vivarta-vāda of the Vedāntin, destruction may take place due to modification of qualities or states. The Vedāntin does not hold that a jar is a new thing; it is, on

AND AS THERE ARISES THE DEFECT BOTH WAYS. 16

The four elements of earth, water, fire and air are seen to possess in decreasing number from four to one, the qualities of smell, taste, colour and touch, and are therefore endowed with increasing fineness[1] Water is subtler than earth because it does not contain smell; fire is subtler still because it lacks both smell and taste ; and air is the subtlest of all because it lacks all the qualities except touch. Now if the specific atoms also are likewise supposed to possess qualities in decreasing number, the atoms which have the largest number of qualities will, necessarily, in view of the principle just observed, be larger in volume and grosser in quality than those which have a small number of qualities. But, in that case, they will cease to be called atoms. And if, on the other hand, in order to maintain the equality of all kinds of atoms we suppose that they have each only one specific quality, the effect too will have only one quality. Fire will be devoid of touch, water of colour and touch, and earth of touch, colour and taste. Or again, to maintain the equality, we suppose that each kind of atom is endowed with four qualities, then contrary to actual experience, we shall have to believe that water has smell, or that fire has smell and taste,or that air has smell, taste and colour. Hence we conclude that the atomic theory is not acceptable.

अपरिग्रहाच्चात्यन्तमनपेक्षा । १७

[*Aparigrahāt—because not accepted; ca—and; atyantaṁ—completely; anapekṣā—disregard*].

AND AS IT IS NOT ACCEPTED (BY ANY COMPETENT PERSON) IT IS TO BE COMPLETELY DISREGARDED. 17

---

the other hand, non-distinct from the earth; and so the destruction of the jar means the destruction of a particular condition of the earth. It indicates only an avasthā-nāśa and not svarūpa-nāśa.

[1] Water enters through smallest pores where sand will never enter. A ray of light travels through water without disturbing the particles of water. Air moves through sunshine without disturbing the rays of the sun, and without casting any shadow of its own. Therefore air is the finest element of all.

The Sāṁkhya theory of pradhāna is at least acceptable to a certain extent to some of the Vedāntins like Manu, because both the Sāṁkhya and the Vedānta accept the satkāryavāda theory of causation and the nature of the self or puruṣa as being essentially transcendent, pure and conscious. But the atomic theory has not been accepted by any competent authority, and therefore deserves to be completely disregarded.

Besides, the Vaiśeṣika contradicts himself when he maintains that the six categories of substance, quality, activity, generality, particularity and inherence are absolutely as separate [1] from each other, as a man is from a horse, or a hare from grass, and at the same time holds, the view that it is on the first category of substance that all the remaining five are dependent. [2] Or if the dependence of qualities and other categories is to mean their presence or absence subsequent to the presence or absence of the substance, then like the Sāṁkhyas (and the Vedāntins) the Vaiśeṣika too may be supposed to believe that the qualities etc. are nothing but the different forms and conditions of one and the same substance, just as Devadatta is the same person in spite of changes in conditions. But this is to abandon the Vaiśeṣika view-point.

Upon this the Vaiśeṣika may point out that mere dependence of one thing upon another is not sufficient to show that both are one and the same thing. Smoke is dependent on fire and yet is distinct and separate from it. But we reply that smoke is believed to be separate because it is actually seen to be so. This is not however the case with substance and quality. A blanket which is white,

---

Bra-Sū. Marathi Trans. Abhyankar Sāśtri. Page 661, Footnote.

1 Substance is that in which the qualities reside. Quality is that which has neither activity nor quality, but in which the universal or jāti resides; e.g. redness in red. Activity is that which occasions conjunction and disjunction. Universal or sāmānya or jāti is that which is one and eternal and which resides or inheres in many things. Particularity or Viśeṣatva is the distinguishing mark of one substance as separate from others; e. g. touch is the exclusive sign of air-atom. Inherence is an everlasting relation; e. g. the relation of colour with a jar.

2 Saṁyoga and samavāya though depending on guṇas and Karma are ultimately dependent on dravya or substance.

or a cow which is red, or a lotus which is blue, is not at all seen separately without at the same time being white red, or blue. In other words, the adjective, white, red or blue can have its being only in some substance. Similarly, action, generality, particularity and inherence belong to and are found in substance or dravya alone.

Now what appears to the Vedāntin as an instance of non-difference or identity may appear to the Vaiśeṣika as an instance of mutual dependence or ayutasiddhatva. But what after all does the Vaiśeṣika mean by it? If he means thereby the existence of two things in one and the same place, he will contradict the authority of Kaṇāda, according to whom 'a substance begets a substance, and a quality begets a quality' (Vai. Sū. 1, 1, 10): the threads produce a piece of cloth ; and the colour of the threads produces the colour of the cloth. But this means that the piece of cloth occupies the space covered by the threads, while the colour of the cloth occupies the space covered by the cloth and not that covered by the threads; whereas by the hypothesis of ayutasiddha, the colour of the cloth and the cloth itself ought to have occupied one and the same space covered by the threads. If he were to mean by ayutasiddha, the existence of two things in one and the same moment of time, even the two horns of a cow would be an illustration of it. And finally, if he means by it identity in character, there would be no difference between substance and quality.

Equally fallacious is the view of the Vaiśeṣika regarding the relations of conjunction and inherence between things which are separate and between things which are mutually dependent respectively. For the cause (e.g. a piece of cloth) which exists one moment at least prior to its effect (viz. a quality) cannot be said to be inseparable from it. The Vaiśeṣika may say that it is the effect which is inherent in the cause; the quality, for instance, cannot exist independently and apart from a piece of cloth. But how can the quality which has not come into existence (and which, as the effect of cloth, comes into existence at least one moment afterwards) be related to the cause at all? Nor can it be said that the effect comes into existence first and is then related with the cause. For this is to admit that the effect exists prior to its coming into existence, and therefore to admit that the effect is not incapable of separate existence. This necessitates in spite of his belief the further admission that the connection between the two independent, separate terms of cause and effect is conjunction and not inherence. And if the ākāśa can be said to be related to all other things by means of saṁyoga and not samavāya, even if there is no activity on the part of the things to be so related, it will also, contrary to his belief, be readily accepted that there would likewise be the connection of saṁyoga and not samavāya between the cause and the effect also.

Besides, there exists no sound proof to show that saṁyoga and samavāya are themselves some actual entities beyond the things in which they exist as relations. That they have names of their own and produce peculiar cognitions in us, just as pots and other things are named and produce cognitions peculiar to them, is no sufficient reason to believe that they are actual things. For things in this world have first got an original nature of their own, before they acquire a name and a new nature on account of their being related with other things. Devadatta, for instance has always got one and the same original meaning, viz. that he is a man, though he may acquire new names and meanings on account of his social relations. He becomes known as a learned Brahmin, as a young or old man, or as father, son, brother etc. A numeral remains the same, though it may have different meanings when it occupies different positions such as the tenth or the hundredeth place. Saṁyoga and samavāya, on the other hand, do not indicate anything by which we can discern their own nature, apart the nature from which they accrue from the relatedness of the things. Devadatta is discerned and known distinctly as a 'man' even apart from his social relations or context. The names and meanings of saṁyoga and samavāya arise only out of the relatedness of things; apart from this relatedness or apart from the things related, they have no permanent meanings of their own, which might continue even in the absence of things so related.

An additional reason why the saṁyoga cannot exist between the atoms and the soul, or between the soul and the mind is that these are, as the Vaiśeṣika holds, without any parts.[1] And if, for the purpose of the theory, the existence of the parts is to be assumed, then anything can be assumed to exist. One may even assume that a hundred or a thousand things exist instead of merely six categories. Moved by compassion, a man may assume that this miserable worldly life may come to an end; a wicked person, on the other hand, may assume that even the liberated souls come back to saṁsāra.

And just as there cannot be any intimate connection or saṁavāya between a diad and the partless ākāśa, as is conceivable between wood and varnish even so there can be no such connection between a partite diad and impartite atoms. If in spite of this, the relation of samavāya is presumed to account for the dependence of effect on cause, there will creep in the defect of mutual dependence. For it is only when the difference between cause and effect is ascertained that there occurs the dependence of one on the other, and it is only when the dependence of effect on cause is ascertained that it indicates that there is difference between the two. Thus will arise the defect of mutual dependence or what is known as 'explanation in a circle.'[2] The Vedāntin, on the other hand, is free

1 The impossibility of saṁyoga between partless atoms, on the one hand, and the soul and the mind, on the other, excludes the possibility of knowledge as also the production of diads and other things.

2 This is known as Kuṇḍa-badara-nyāya, Where is the Kuṇḍa or the vessel? It is near the Badara-tree. And where is the Badara-tree? It is near the Kuṇḍa. This leads to no conclusion regarding the place of either of them.

from this defect because he neither believes in any difference between cause and effect nor in the dependence of one on the other. To him, the effect is nothing but a state of the cause.

Besides the atoms being limited they must have as many limbs as there are directions, six, eight or ten[1]; and if they have limbs or parts, they are perishable, in spite of the Vaiśeṣika claim that they are eternal and partless. To say that these parts themselves are the atoms does not improve the argument. For the atoms too being of the nature of the four elements must ultimately perish, just as the gross elements and the diads etc. perish. Now this destruction of the atoms, as we have already pointed out, need not take place by the disjunction of the parts. It may take place by mere transformation into the undifferentiated condition of the highest cause, *viz.* the Brahman, in the way in which the solid nature of ghee or gold is destroyed by mere change into liquid form. Similarly, things may come into being not by conjunction of parts, but in the manner in which curds and ice come into being out of the original condition of milk and water.

The atomic theory, in short, is based on weak arguments, is against the teaching of the Śruti that God is the highest cause, and is not accepted by competent authorities like Manu and others. Hence those who are intent on having their spiritual good should disregard it completely.

४ समुदायासिद्ध्यधिकरणम् । (१८-२७)

समुदाय उभयहेतुकेऽपि तदप्राप्तिः । १८

[*Samudāyaḥ—collection; ubhayahetuke—due to both the reasons; api—even, tad-aprāptiḥ—they cannot be had.*]

1 They are six viz. East, West, South and North, and upwards and downwards; eight, viz. the four main directions and the four corner directions; and ten, viz. these eight directions and the two directions of upwards and downwards.

NOTWITHSTANDING THE ASSUMPTION OF COLLECTIONS DUE TO BOTH THE REASONS, THEY ARE NOT PROVED. 18

Having shown the inadequacy of the semi-nihilistic[1] doctrine of the Vaiśeṣikas, we now proceed to show that the thoroughly nihilistic doctrine of the Buddhists is all the more unworthy of being taken into consideration. The doctrine assumes three main forms, either because Buddha himself held different opinions on different occasions, or because it was taught to three types of disciples who differed in their intellectual capacity.[2] The Realists (Sautrāntikas, and Vaibhāṣikas) are those who believe in the reality of everything; the Idealists or the Vijñānavādins are those who hold that thought alone is real; and the Nihilists or Śūnyavādins are those to whom everything is void or unreal.

To refute the realists first. According to them both the external world of elements, sense organs and qualities and the internal mental world are real. The external world arises out of four kinds of atoms, which are either hard, fluid, hot or mobile, according as they are of earth, water, fire and air, respectively. The internal world which constitutes the experience of man consists of the five groups (skandha) of sensations, knowledge, feelings, names and impressions (*i. e.* the skandhas of rūpa, vijñāna, vedanā, saṁjñā and saṁskāra).

As against this we observe that neither the atoms nor the skandhas are able to achieve the two-fold groupings as assumed by these realists. For the atoms as well as the skandhas are non-intelligent; and if at all they are assumed to be active of their own accord they will never

---

1 Everything except atoms, ākāśá, time, space, soul, mind, sāmānya, viśeṣa, samavāya and a few qualities, is perishable according to the Vaiśesikas. This is semi-nihilism. But the momentary character of all things is the common view of all the schools in Buddhism; and it is this which ultimately leads to perfect nihilism.

2 E. g. The Mādhyamikas are said to be of mediocre intelligence,

cease to be so, and hence there will be no nirvāṇa. Even the activity of the mind, which might be supposed to be the cause of the groupings, will not be possible on the Buddhist view, without the accomplishment of the groupings, that is, without the presence of the body. Nor does the theory allow the existence of any other permanent and intelligent being such as the soul which enjoys, or the Lord who governs. Nor again can a chain of cognitions of one's own self as 'I am' be the cause. For if the chain is different in character from the several momentary cognitions of which it is made, it is to admit the permanent Ātman of the Vedāntin. But if the chain too is momentary, there is left no scope for it to be active and to bring into being the external and the internal worlds.

इतरेतरप्रत्ययत्वादिति चेन्नोत्पत्तिमात्रनिमित्तत्वात् । १९

[*Itaretara—successive; pratyayatvāt—because of causal links; iti cet—if it be said; na; utpatti-origin; mātra—only; nimittatvāt—being the cause.*]

If it be said that (groupings of atoms and skandhas are formed) on account of successive causal links (of avidyā, saṁskāras etc., we say) it is not so; for they only explain the origin (of new successive links, and not the formation of the groupings). 19

It may be said that even in the absence of a permanent ruling principle, the saṁsāra is made possible, on account of the causal force of a series[1] which begins with avidyā and ends with death and return to life. These links in the chain follow upon each other as surely as water-pots on a wheel and explain the saṁsāra.

---

[1] The series consists of such members as : avidyā, saṁskāra, vijñāna, nāmarūpa, ṣadāyatana, sparṣa, vedanā, tṛṣṇā, upādāna, bhava, jāti, and oldage, death etc.

But the argument cannot be accepted, because it merely accounts for the origination of the several members in the series by reference to the preceding members in the same. It does not explain how the external and the internal groupings are formed. If, as we have already pointed out, it cannot be proved even on the Vaiśeṣika theory how the atoms are combined, in spite of the fact that the theory admits the existence of permanent atoms and of souls in which the unseen fruits of actions reside, how much more improbable it must be for the Buddhists to explain the combinations, when the atoms are said to be momentary, and are devoid of any connection with the souls and with the unseen fruit? The series of avidyā and other things, being itself dependent on the assemblage of atoms and skandhas, cannot be the cause of the latter. Avoiding these difficulties, if it be said that the series of avidyā and others as well as that of atoms and skandhas on which it depends are simultaneously responsible for the continued existence of saṁsāra, we have to ask a further question, whether the successive groupings of atoms and skandhas are like unto each other or unlike. In the first case, in spite of his good or bad actions, man will never be able to obtain the bodies of birds and animals or of angels and gods; in the second case, man may change, at any time, even while living, into an elephant or a god. Besides, if even the souls have got a momentary existence, it is inconceivable how they can wait till the objects of enjoyment are formed for their sake or till the time of final release Release or enjoyment too serves no purpose.

उत्तरोत्पादे च पूर्वनिरोधात् । २०

[*Uttar—subsequent ; utpāde—as it arises ; ca—and ; pūrva—preceding ; nirodhāt—on the destruction.*]

AS EVERY NEW (MOMENTARY THING) ARISES ON THE DESTRUCTION OF THE PRECEDING, (THERE CANNOT BE ANY CAUSATION TOO AMONG THE MEMBERS OF THE SERIES OF AVIDYĀ ETC.). 20

There cannot exist any causal relation between any two momentary things because it is only after the first has ceased to be that the second comes into existence. Howsoever the antecedent may become developed and possess power, it cannot produce the consequent unless contrary to the theory of universal momentariness, it is assumed that the antecedent lives for the second moment and actually exerts influence in order to be connected with the second thing. The existence of the antecedent by itself is not again sufficient to produce the consequent; for there can be no consequent worth the name which has not in it the essence of the antecedent. But to admit this is to give up the view of momentariness and to say that the essence of the antecedent continues to remain the same till the moment of the production of the consequent.

Besides what does the Buddhist mean by origin and destruction of things? If thereby we understand the nature of a thing, then whether the thing is destroyed or not, it is as good as saying that the thing is maintaining its own nature, in spite of the view of momentariness. If origin and destruction are the earlier and later stages of one and the same intermediate thing, even then it is as good as admitting that the thing lives at least during three moments of time. And finally, if they are absolutely distinct and separate from the thing just as a horse is different from a buffalo, even then we reach the same conclusion. The thing is eternal because it is not affected either by origin or destruction. And further, if origin and destruction were merely to imply the perception and the non-perception of a thing, they would then refer to a percipient being and not to the thing at all. Hence it is that the Bauddha view is untenable.

असति प्रतिज्ञोपरोधो यौगपद्यमन्यथा । २१

[*Asati—when absent; pratijñā—statement; uparodhaḥ—the contradiction; yaugapadyaṁ—simultaneity; anyathā—otherwise.*]

(IF THE EFFECT IS PRESENT, EVEN) WHEN (THE CAUSE IS) ABSENT, THERE WILL RESULT THE CONTRADICTION OF THE ADMITTED PRINCIPLE, OR ELSE SIMULTANEITY (OF CAUSE AND EFFECT). 21

If it be said that there may be an effect even if there is no cause, the original principle of the school that the mind and its states arise on account of four different causes[1] will have to be given up. Besides anything may come into being at any time, if no cause is required. If, on the other hand, it is said that the antecedent may continue to exist till the consequent is produced, it will simply mean the giving up of the theory of universal momentariness and the acceptance of the simultaneous existence of cause and effect.

प्रतिसंख्याऽप्रतिसंख्यानिरोधाप्राप्तिरविच्छेदात् । २२

[*Pratisaṁkhyā—voluntary* ; *apratisaṁkhyā—involuntary nirodha—destruction* ; *aprāpti—not to have* ; *avichedāt —being not discontinuous.*]

AS THERE IS NO DISCONTINUITY (IN THE SERIES), THERE CAN BE NEITHER VOLUNTARY NOR INVOLUNTARY DESTRUCTION. 22

The nihilists further maintain that all the objects of knowledge except ākāśa and the voluntary and the involuntary types of destruction, are produced and are momentary in character. The three excepted things are not only non-substantial but are also negative in character. Ākāśa, which will be considered in Sūtra 24, indicates the absence of anything which will occupy space. Destruction, whether voluntary as in the case of a jar which is intentionally broken by means of a stick, or natural, which takes place on account of continual decay of things,

1 The four causes are: Material (ālambana), Impressional (samanantara), sensory (adhipati), and auxiliary (sahakāri): e. g. the jar, prior impressions of it,

must refer either to the stream of things as a whole or to the things themselves. But the stream or the series of things and events cannot be destroyed, because the members in the series are connected together as cause and effect in an unbroken manner. Nor are the things themselves capable of being destroyed. For in the various conditions or states of a thing there remains something[1] by which that thing itself is recognized, either actually or by inference. Hence, there is no kind of destruction possible, as is upheld by the nihilists.

उभयथा च दोषात् । २३

[*Ubhayathā—both ways; ca—and; doṣāt—due to defect.*]

AND BEING DEFECTIVE BOTH WAYS. 23

Besides, if the destruction of avidyā and other things, as involved in the two kinds of destruction, were to result on account of perfect knowledge and other ethical means, the Bauddha teaching that destruction takes place without any cause will have to be given up. And if avidyā etc. are destroyed of their own accord, what then is the use of the path to salvation which consists in knowing, that everything is momentary, painful, and void?

आकाशे चाविशेषात् । २४

[*Ākāśe—in the case of ākāśa; ca; aviśeṣāt—there being no difference.*]

AND ON ACCOUNT OF ITS BEING NOT DISSIMILAR (WITH THE TWO KINDS OF DESTRUCTION) ĀKĀŚA (TOO CANNOT BE SAID TO BE A NON-ENTITY). 24

the eye, and the light, are the four causes in the case of the perception of a jar.

1 Clay is recognized as the indestructive common element of the different states of a jar, such as the pieces or the powder of it. Where it is not so seen, it is inferred to be so; e. g. in the case of the different states of the seed, such as the sprout, the plant, the flower etc.

Ākāśa too cannot be said to be devoid of positive characteristics, and therefore a non-entity. That it is a real thing can, first of all, be seen from the Śruti passage, 'From Ātman came forth the ākāśa '(Tai. 2, 1). Secondly, it can be inferred from the specific quality of sound, just as earth and other elements are considered to be real on account of smell and other qualities. Besides, if ākāśa means simply un-covered space, the existence of any flying bird in the sky would render the space covered, and so may prevent any other bird from flying in the sky. If, in reply to this, it be said that another bird may fly in another portion of the sky, then this is nothing but to admit, with reference to that second portion of the sky, that there is first a portion of the sky or ākāśa which exists independently of its being covered or not by the body of the flying bird, and that it is not simply the uncovered space. And if ākāśa is to be defined only negatively, it will contradict Buddha's own reply, in another place, that ākāśa is the support of wind. If, according to him, a positive entity like wind is the support of the earth, how is it possible that the wind should have its support in a non-entity like ākāśa? Besides, there is a further contradiction involved in saying that ākāśa, like the two kinds of destruction, is a non-entity and is at the same time eternal. How can that which is unreal be either eternal or non-eternal? For the attributes can be predicated or not of real things only.

अनुस्मृतेश्च । २५

[*Anusmṛteḥ—On account of recollection; ca—and.*]

AND BECAUSE THERE IS RECOLLECTION, (THE EXPERIENCING SUBJECT CAN NOT BE A MOMENTARY THING). 25

The nihilist who believes in the universal momentariness of things shall have consistently to believe in the momentary existence of the experiencing subject. But the fact of recollecting makes this impossible. For recollection or recognition of a thing belongs to the same person who has first cognized that thing. We never observe that one man cognizes things and another recognizes them. Even the distinction between a thing seen today and a thing seen yesterday cannot be noticed, unless both the things are seen by one and the same person. Even the nihilist cannot possibly deny that the perceptions which he now remembers belonged to himself in the past; he is as certain of this as of the fact that fire is hot and gives light. If then the nihilist must connect in himself the two moments of perception and rememberance, and must think that from his cradle to the grave all his perceptions and the subsequent recollection of them must belong to himself as one and the same person, will he not be ashamed of having held the view that everything is momentary in character?

Should he argue that the belief in one and the same experiencing subject arises from similarity of two or more cognitions of the self, we reply that even for the cognition of similarity there is required a person who will be permanent enough to discern the similarity of two successive things. But from the point of view of the nihilist, there being only momentary things, to say that recognition is based on similarity is to utter sheer nonsense. Should he again argue that the knowledge of similarity is altogether a new cognition, and is therefore neither based on the prior cognitions of two things occupying two different moments of time, nor on the existence of a permanent experiencing subject, we reply that the expression 'this is similar to that' not only points to the 'this' and the 'that' as two distinct things but also to the common third thing of the similarity between them expressed in one single act of judgment. If similarity were to be altogether a distinct object of knowledge and unconnected with things which are similar, then the expression 'this is similar to that' would serve no purpose; we should be able in that case to speak of 'similarity' only without any reference to the 'this' or the 'that'. To refuse to admit a well-known fact, whether for the purpose of establishing one's own position or for the purpose of refuting the position of others, is not only not to carry conviction to oneself or others, but also to expose oneself to the charge of being vainly talkative. It is therefore not proper to say, if we attach any value to our everyday life and thought, that what we apprehend is due to similarity only; for in recognition, what we are aware of is the sameness of the thing apprehended before and not of similarity of one thing with another. No doubt, it is likely that with reference to external things, a doubt may sometimes arise whether a thing is the same as seen before or as simply similar. But there cannot arise any such doubt with reference to the conscious subject; for everyone is distinctly and clearly aware that he is the same subject who remembers today what he has apprehended yesterday.

नासतोऽदृष्टत्वात् । २६

(Na–not ; asataḥ–from non-existence ; a-dṛṣṭatvat–since it is not observed.)

SINCE IT IS NOT OBSERVED, (AN EXISTING THING) DOES NOT ARISE FROM NON-EXISTENCE. 26

The nihilists must further believe that existence arises from non-existence, because they propound the view that the effect does not arise without the destruction of the cause. There comes forth the sprout after the seed is destroyed; curds is formed only when milk ceases to be milk, and the clay ceases to be a mere lump of clay, before we see a jar out of it. If changeless causes were to produce effects, then we may, says the Buddhist, as well expect all the effects at once and without any delay.

To this we reply. If non-existence were to produce existence, then there would be no meaning in assigning special causes for special effects, such as seed for sprouts, clay for jars or milk for curds. For there will be no difference between non-existence as indicated by the expression 'The horn of a hare' and the non-existence indicated by the destruction of clay or seed. We need not even posit so much that there is first the non-existence of seed and then the existence of sprout; for a sprout may come out of the non-existence indicated by 'The horn of a hare.' If, on the other hand, we assume that different kinds of non-existence have different characteristics of their own, then like several things with their peculiar properties, non-existence too will lose its character of being a nonentity. It will be an entity with a quality of its own, just as a lotus has the quality of being blue. Besides, will not the effects of non-existence participate in the nature of their cause and become non-existent? But we do not find this in our experience. On the contrary, we find every effect wearing a peculiar aspect of existence. The jars of clay are like clay and not like threads of cotton, indicating thereby that the jars participate in their appropriate existing cause viz. the clay and not in their non-existent cause viz., .the threads of cotton. So the Baudha view that nothing which does not change can become a cause, is false. Gold does not change, though it is made into ornaments. Even in the case of seeds, where there is apparent change, the seed is not destroyed; the small particles of the seed are not destroyed and it is these which are the real cause of the sprout. In short, because we see that nothing originates from non-existence which is like the idea of the horn of a hare, and that, on the contrary, every entity originates from some other entity which has an enduring nature like gold or clay we conclude that the Baudha doctrine is fit to be rejected. It is to be rejected for the additional reason that the Baudhas contradict themselves by saying first that the mind and its modifications arise from four skandhas, and the material things from atoms, and by saying again that existence is due to non-existence. Their doctrine is nothing but bewilderment to others.

उदासीनानामपि चैवं सिद्धिः । २७

[*Udāsīnānāṁ-of idle persons; api-even; ca-and; evaṁ-thus; siddhiḥ-success.*]

AND IDLE PERSONS ALSO WILL THUS ACHIEVE (THEIR ENDS). 27

If the doctrine 'entity arises from non-entity' were admitted, lazy persons also would achieve their ends; for non-existence can be had without any effort. Corn would grow even if the farmer did not till the land; vessels would come into being without the moulding of clay by the potter; and cloth will be available even if the weaver was lazy and did not weave. No body will be required to put in any efforts for the attainment of the heaven or of release. All this is absurd and unacceptable. Therefore the doctrine referred to is false.

५ अभावाधिकरणम् । (२८-३२)

नाभाव उपलब्धेः । २८

[*Na—not; abhāvaḥ—non—existence; upalabdheḥ—being available.*]

NON-EXISTENCE (OF EXTERNAL THINGS) CANNOT (BE MAINTAINED), ON ACCOUNT OF (THEIR) BEING PERCEIVED. 28

Now that the Baudha view that the external world is real though momentary is refuted on the ground that it is impossible to account for the groupings of atoms and skandhas, there comes forward for consideration another view known as the Subjective idealism of the Vijñānavādins. The reality of the external world is believed to have been adopted by Buddha, in order to make it suitable to some of his disciples who were, according to him, too much attached to the things of the external world. His real view however was different. It was to maintain the reality of cognitions or ideas and nothing else.

According to this doctrine known as Vijñānavāda, all experience, whether in the form of cognition, or in the form of the subject, the object and the means of cognitions is mental in character. Supposing that things exist in the outside world, we can have no experience of them unless they assume the form as determined by intellect. And if the external things are to be admitted, they must either be of the nature of atoms or of their groupings. Obviously, things like pillars cannot be apprehended as atoms, because the latter are imperceptible. Nor can they be apprehended as aggregates of atoms ; for if these aggregates are different from atoms, they can be no longer considered as made up of atoms ; and if they are non-different, they will be as imperceptible as the atoms, and hence there will be no cognition of pillars as pillars, or of any other gross objects. In the same way, one can show that the external objects have neither universality [1] nor any other category.

Now the various differences we feel in our general, uniform awareness or experience, on account of the various references to objects of knowledge such as, a pillar, a wall or a pot, are, as a matter of fact, mental in character. They are differences in our ideas or cognitions, and are found to conform to things. This is to admit, in other words, that the forms of objects of our knowledge are determined by our ideas, [2] and not given by the reality of the external world. Besides, our knowledge of objects in the form of ideas and of the objects themselves being always simultaneously presented, they must in reality be one and the same. [3] For had they been different, we

---

1 If the universality or jāti viz the pillarness is different from pillar, then they are two separate things: and if it is non-different, then just as the pillar will be either atomic and imperceptible or mental, the universality will also be either imperceptible or mental in character,

2 Instead of believing in the various forms of objects, and corresponding to them in similar various forms of our ideas of objects, the subjective idealist wants us to believe in our own ideas only as the source of our belief in the external world.

3 Though the idea and the thing are one and the same thing, the subjective dealist, it must be noted, says that the idea alone is real,

might have been conscious of one and not of another ; but this is never the case. Hence, too, we may say that the world of external things is not real.

One more reason for not believing in the external world is the similarity of the perceptions of our waking life to our experience in dreams and illusions. If our experience of the latter type appears to us as twofold, that as, as made up of subject and object, inspite of the fact that there is no external world in dreams and illusions, our experience of the waking life also may be independent of the external world. Our perceptions of objects are nothing but simple ideas. As for the reason of the variety of ideas, it need not be sought in the existence of the external world, but in the saṁskāras or the impressions of past ideas. The ideas and the impressions succeed[1] each other as necessarily as the seed and the sprout succeed and cause this endless Sāṁsāra. That the ideas or cognitions are caused not by external objects but by impressions can be proved by reference to positive and negative assertions we can make regarding the relation between them. The Vedāntins too admit with us that in dreams, when there are no external objects, knowledge or ideas arise on account of prior mental impressions. But in the absence of impressions, there cannot be as we hold, any knowledge or ideas. We therefore conlude that there is no external world of things.

To this we, the Vedāntins, make the following reply. It is wrong to hold that the external world does not exist ; for we are aware that corresponding to our ideas our perceptions point out to us external things like pillars and walls. Nobody will listen to a man who, while he is enjoying his dinner, says that he is neither eating anything nor having any satisfaction out of it. Let the Baudha

---

1 That this succession of ideas and impressions is not an example of mutual dependentance upon each other, is admitted even by the Vedāntin. Mutual dependence (anyonyāsraya) is a defect; as it determines nothing. But when the succession denotes a causal and endless succession it is no defect.

arbitrarily explain that what he means by saying that there is no object is that there is no consciousness of object apart from the act of consciousness. But the truth is that consciousness itself points out to us that what we are aware of in perception, for instance, is not the perception itself, but the objects of perception. The Baudhas themselves tacitly acknowledge this fact when they say that the internal object of cognition appears 'like something external.' How can there be something 'like external' if there is really nothing external? Is it possible that Viṣnumitra should ever appear like the son of a barren mother? Besides, whether objects of perception are possible to be external or not is to be judged by reference to the means of knowledge; the means of knowledge are never said to exist or not to exist by reference to our preconceived[1] notions about things. That is possible which is capable of being apprehended by perception or other means of knowledge; that is impossible which is not so capable. So when, as a matter of fact, the external things are apprehended by means of knowledge, to say that they are only mental on the ground that they are neither different nor non-different from atoms, is to indulge in idle talk.

Again, if there are no external objects how can the ideas have the form of objects? And, if the ideas have the forms of the objects, does it mean that forthwith the objects whose forms the ideas have, are all reduced to these forms only? The truth is that objects are apprehended as external and distinct from ideas; and therefore the invariable concomitance of the idea and the object should be construed as the expression of the causal connection between them and not as that of identity. That the idea and the object are distinct from each other can moreover be shown by reference to the difference between a substantive and the attributes or aspects which belong to it. The perception

1 The vijñānavādins first take it for granted that external things do not exist, and then run to the conclusion that not only these objects are mental in character, but that even the means of knowledge are also mental.

of a white ox differs from the perception of a black ox, though the knowledge of an ox in general is the same. The two kinds of knowledge as specified by the differing attributes 'white' and 'black' are also further different from the generic knowledge of an ox as such. Similar is the distinction between the perceptions of a jar and a pot, or between the perception and rememberance of a jar, or between the smell and taste of milk, even though the generic knowledge in each case may be simply some indefinite thing, or simply a jar of milk. Neither the attributes nor the substantive be said to be non-distinct and non-separate from each other. And if the ideas occupy different moments of time, and vanish immediately after they have been felt in consciousness, it will not be said about any one of them that it is either the knower or known. If the idea does not last even for two consecutive moments, then there ought not to be any talk about the ideas being different from each other, about everything being momentary and void, about the distinction between individuals and classes, or between existence and non-existence due to avidyā, and about bondage and release. [1]

The vijnānavādin may further argue that while an idea illumines by itself as a lamp, the external objects do not, and hence we become conscious of the idea and not of the external world. But it looks strange that he should readily believe in something absurd enough like 'fire burns itself,' and not believe in the altogether common and rational view that the ideas make us aware of the external things. He may object to this by saying that this involves the *regress ad infinitum*; for if the idea is to depend for its apprehension on something else, that something also has to be dependent for its

---

1 All this is possible on the supposition that there exists a knower who can compare one idea with another, and that ideas last at least for two moments to allow such comparasion. But the Buddhist has no such belief.

apprehension on something else and so on. But so far as the knowledge of ideas, is concerned he may tell us, that just as a lamp does not require another lamp to illumine it, even so one cognition may not require another cognition to cognize it. But we reply that both the arguments are wrong. The regress need not arise ; for, there is no other cogniser of the self[1] who cognizes the ideas ; and the self and the cognitions are of different nature. They are related to each other as the knower and the known, or as the subject and object. As for the witnessing self, he exists by himself and cannot be doubted.

The lamplike, self-illuminating idea of the vijñānavādin appears therefore neither in need of any means of proof nor of any other being beyond it. But this is like believing that a thousand lamps are burning in the interior of an impenetrable rock. To say that the self-conscious nature resembles the view of the Vedāntin is not correct; for just as the light of a lamp is dependent for its being known on the eye of an intelligent being, even so the idea manifests itselt through some intelligent principle beyond it. Besides, whereas the witnessing self of the Vedāntin is one, permanent and self-illuminating, the ideas of the Vijñāvavādin are transitory and many, and therefore require for their manifestation an intelligent principle beyond them.

वैधर्म्याच्च न स्वप्नादिवत् । २९

[*Vaidharmyāt–on account of difference in nature; ca–and; na–not; svapna-ādi-vat—like dream and others.*]

AND ON ACCOUNT OF DIFFERENCE IN NATURE (IDEAS OF THE WAKING LIFE) CANNOT BE LIKE THOSE IN A DREAM ETC. 29

1 According to the Vedāntin, the Ātman alone is the only self-illuminating cognizer of all ideas or knowledge.

We now refute the Buddhist view that the ideas of the waking life may arise, in the absence of the external objects, in the same manner in which the ideas in a dream arise. The two kinds of ideas, we contend, are different in nature. The ideas in a dream arise falsely because the mind is infatuated by sleep. That is why the experience of having met a great person in a dream is cancelled in the waking life. Similar is the case with illusory experience. But the things of which we become conscious in the waking life continue to exist without being negated. Besides, what we experience in dreams is due to memory, while what we experience in the waking life is immediate apprehension. The difference between the two states is the difference marked by the presence or absence of objects. Notwithstanding this obvious, self-evident truth regarding the difference between the two states, if the Baudha proceeds to infer that the knowledge of the waking life is like that of the dreaming state, simply on the ground that there is a kind of knowledge in both the states, he will thereby show that he has neither logic nor wisdom. What is contrary to experience, viz. the knowledge of the external world without the existence of the external world, he hopes to demonstrate by reference to a partial resemblance of consciousness between the wakeful and dreaming states. But how can an attribute which does not naturally belong to a thing, be ascribed to it, simply because that thing has a partial similarity with some other thing? Can fire be cold, because like water, fire is one of the five elements? Therefore it is that we say that the waking life is different from a dream.

न भावोऽनुपलब्धेः । ३०

[*Na*—not; *bhāvaḥ*— existence; *an*—*upalabdheḥ*—being not available.]

IN THE ABSENCE OF EXISTENCE (OF EXTERNAL THINGS, THE MENTAL IMPRESSIONS) DO NOT EXIST. 30

To refute now the possibility of knowledge due to impressions, even if there is no external world. We may ask, in the first place, as to how the impressions may arise at all if there are no external objects as their causes. To say that they are due to prior cognitions in addition to the belief that cognitions are due to prior impressions, and to say that this has been going on without any beginning, is to rest satisfied with a fruitless regress ad infinitum.[1] Like one blind man leading another, it will only cut the entire practical life. It will not also help the Buddhist to uphold his position, viz. that cognitions are due to impressions and not to external objects. The anvaya and vyatireka, that is the positive and the negative method of argument which he uses[2] is really in our favour. For cognitions arise if there exist the external objects; and they do not arise if there are no such objects. As opposed to this, people believe in the existence of the external world even in the absence of the impressions.[3] Moreover the impressions do require a substratum[4] in which they reside, though such a substratum from the view-point of the Buddhist cannot be cognized by any means of knowledge.

क्षणिकत्वाच्च । ३१

[*Kṣaṇikatvāt—on account of being momentary; ca—and.*]

AND ON ACCOUNT OF (THE ĀLAYAVIJNĀNA) BEING MOMENTARY, (IT CANNOT BE THE SUBSTRATUM OF MENTAL IMPRESSIONS). 31

1 The Buddhist is not prepared to call the regress as fruitless, because he imagines that it is beginningless and inevitable like the causal chain of seed and sprout. But this is not correct. For it is simply taken for granted without regard to the external objects that there exists a causal connection between cognitions and impressions.

2 If there are impressions there arise cognitions, and if there is no impression there does not arise any cognition,

3 The external world being the cause of the impressions can exist without the effects.

4 That this substratum cannot be the 'Ālayavijñāna' will be shown in the next Sūtra,

If the pravṛttivijñāna or the cognitions having the form of external things cannot be the substratum of impressions, the ālayavijñāna [1] also, that is, the cognitions which have the form of 'I am', cannot be the substratum because it is also momentary in character. Unless there be something which continues to exist and is therefore connected with the past, the present and the future, or unless there is the absolutely permanent on-looker of all things, there will be no proper explanation of the whole of the practical life which consists of memory, recognition and the various impressions. The ālayavijñāna being as momentary in character as any other thing in the Buddhist scheme, the objections we raised against the realists in Sūtra 20 (adhyāya 2, pāda 2) can also be raised against it.

As for the refutation of the Śūnyavāda, which goes against all means of knowledge, no regard may be shown. For a complete denial of everything is not possible except on the recognition of some truth which cannot be denied.

सर्वथाऽनुपपत्तेश्च । ३२

[*Sarvathā–in all ways; anupapatteḥ–on account of being defective; ca–and*]

AND ON ACCOUNT OF BEING DEFECTIVE IN ALL WAYS. 32

To say in short, the more we search to find out some good point in the Buddhist system, the more it gives way on all hands, as the sandy walls of a well fall when we begin to dig it deep. By propounding the different views of realism, idealism and nihilism, Buddha has merely exposed himself as a man given to teach contradictory things. Or thereby he has shown his hatred

1 Even if the cognitions are considered as stream or series, they do not form an enduring substratum,

to all people, so that they may be bewildered and lost. Therefore what the Sūtra indicates is that the Baudha doctrine should be completely discarded by those who wish to achieve their spiritual good.

६ एकस्मिन्नसंभवाधिकरणम् । (३३–३६)

नैकस्मिन्नसंभवात् । ३३

[*Na*–*not*; *ekasmin*–*in one*; *asaṁbhavāt*–*on account of not being possible.*]

ON ACCOUNT OF THE IMPOSSIBILITY OF (CONTRADICTORY ATTRIBUTES) IN ONE THING, (THE JAINA VIEW) CANNOT (BE ACCEPTED). 33

Having refuted the Buddhists, we now turn to the Jainas. According to them there are seven[1] entities, viz. jīva, ajīva, āsrava, saṁvara, nirjara, bandha and mokṣa. Or subsuming[2] the last five under the first two, they may be said to believe only in two entities, viz. the soul and the objects (jīva and ajīva). Or they may be said to believe in five entities which they consider as varieties of these two, and which they call as 'astikāyas', with reference to jīva, pudgala,[3] dharma, adharma and ākāśa. All these varieties, they again subdivide in various imaginary ways.[4] And to all these things

1 These seven entities are: the soul, the objects of experience, the movement of the senses towards the objects, the restraint of this activity, the work itself constituting the bondage, and the release which means either the attainment of the condition of Iśvara who is eternally released, or ascending the highest heaven.

2 Mokṣa however may come under both the categories. If it means to become Isvara, it belongs to jiva, but if it means the ascending to heaven, it belongs to ajīva.

3 'Pud'–joining, and 'gal'–fall away. Pudgala means therefore the atom; for it is the atoms which join together and fall away.

4 Jīvāstikāya is divided into those that are bound, those that are released, and those that are released without being previously bound; pudgalāstikāya into earth, water, fire, wind, moveable and immoveable things; ākāsāstikāya into lokākāśa and alokākāśa; bandha into eight varieties due to karma.

they apply the reasoning known as 'saptabhangīnaya'[1] which is:-somehow it is; somehow it is not; somehow is is and is not; somehow it is indescribable; somehow it is and yet is indescribable; somehow it is not and yet is indescribable; somehow it is and is not, and yet is indescribable. They apply this reasoning even to such conceptions as unity and eternity.

Against this doctrine we say the following. The reasoning itself is faulty; for it is impossible that contradictory attributes, like hot and cold, may belong to the same thing at one and the same time. To apply the saptabhangīnaya to the seven entities is to have confused an indefinite knowledge about them; for they may either have a particular nature or not have it. In other words, all assertions about them will end in doubt and not in any definite knowledge. To say that the cognition of a thing can assume more than one nature and is a definite piece of knowledge, is itself unture; for applying the same reasoning this so-called definite knowledge may or may not be definite. If, in short, this indefiniteness belongs to all things without exception, that is, if it belongs to knowledge and the means of knowledge, as also to the knowing subject and the objects of knowledge, how indeed can it be said that the Jain Tīrthakara teaches anything which is undoubtable or definite? Or how indeed can his followers be said to accept his words. which being thoroughly indefinite, appear to be uttered by a madman or a drunken person?

If we extend the application of the same reasoning to the five astikāyas, they may be seen to be more or less

1 The first bhanga is the reply to the Sāṁkhya realist. Because the potter works, the jar cannot be said to have its existence necessarily. The second is the reply to the Śunyavādi nihilist. Why should the potter work at all? The third is the reply to the Vaisesika, according to whom a thing was non-existent first, but existent afterwards, which as the Jains think, is inexplicable. The fourth is the reply to the Vedāntin who says that things are real and unreal or anirvacanīya. The fifth, sixth and the seventh modes of reasoning arise out of the combinations of the first and the fourth, the second and the fifth, and the third and the fourth respectively.

than five. To call them indescribable and yet to describe them is to contradict oneself. And to go on saying that they can be known or not known, that their knowledge is perfect or imperfect, inspite of its being imperfect or not, is certainly to talk like a drunken or a mad person. Nobody will ever act to achieve his release or to ascend the heaven, if these things mean nothing definite, so far as their existence or duration are concerned. As a matter of fact, being excludes non-being, and non-being excludes being; but if nothing definite can be said regarding soul or unity, whether it is one or many, permanent or non-permanent, separate or non-separate, we must reject the doctrine of the Arhat. As for the Jain doctrine of the atoms or pudgalas, we need not refute it again, as we have already refuted the atomic doctrine of the Vaiśeṣikas.

एवं चात्माऽकार्त्स्न्यम् । ३४

[*Evam—thus* ; *ca—and* ; *ātmā—the soul* ; *akārtsnyaṁ—nonpervasiveness.*]

AND LIKEWISE (THERE OCCURS) THE NON-PERVASIVENESS OF THE SOUL. 34

The Jains believe that the soul has the same size as that of the body. But this means that being limited in extension, the soul is as non-eternal as jars and other things. Besides, if the soul of man were to enter into the body of an elephant as a consequence of its previous deeds, it will not occupy the whole of it; nor will it find sufficient space for it in the body of an ant. Similar will be the difficulty if we take into consideration the bodies of one and the same person, in his childhood, youth and oldage. The Jain may explain away the difficulty by saying that the soul consists of infinite number of parts, which are capable of being compressed in a small body, and of being expanded to fill the space in a large body. But if the infinite particles occupy different places, they cannot be contained in a small body; and if they occupy the same place, that is the place occupied by one particle only, the size of the soul will always, in all cases, be very minute. Besides, there will be no reason why he should believe in the particles being infinite in number, when the soul has a limited extent of the body.

The Jain may say in reply that the particles join or fall away as the occasion for the soul is to enter into a large or a small body. To this the reply is given in the next Sūtra.

न च पर्यायादप्यविरोधो विकारादिभ्यः । ३५

[*Na–not; ca–and; paryāyāt–by turns; api–also; avirodhaḥ–non-contradiction; vikārādibhyaḥ–because of change etc.*]

NOR IS THERE NON-CONTRADICTION (IF PARTICLES JOIN AND FALL AWAY FROM THE SOUL) BY TURNS; BECAUSE OF (DEFECTS LIKE) CHANGE ETC 35

The Jain theory that the soul has the size of the body cannot be shown to be free from contradiction, even if it is supported by another theory, viz. according as the size of the body is large or small, the soul gains new particles or loses some of those which are already there. For this new theory implies that the soul is capable of undergoing change, and is therefore non-permanent like the skin of body. But this goes against the Jain doctrine of the soul's release which is likened to the coming up to the surface of water of a gourd (freed from dirt) which was previously immersed in saṁsāra on account of the eightfold bonds of karma. Besides, like the body which comes into being and is destroyed, these particles too have got origin and destruction, and therefore cannot be said to be of the nature of the self. If some one permanent part is to be said as the self, we do not know which one is meant. Nor do we know whence the particles come when they join the soul, and whither they go when they fall away. The soul being immaterial, they cannot be said to have sprung from the material elements so that they may return back into them. Nor do we know any storehouse of these particles. Besides, on the Jain view, the soul and the particles of it will both be indefinite in character. For all these reasons, the theory that the particles join and fall away from the soul cannot be accepted.

The Sūtra may be interpreted differently. To the objection that the soul will not be permanent if it is to be considered as having the size of the body, the Jain may be supposed to reply that the soul may be considered to be permanent in spite of its changes; just as a stream of water is said to be permanent in spite of the changing water, or just as, in the opinion of the Raktāmbaras, a stream of ideas is permanent, though individual ideas pass away. To this the present Sūtra contains the reply: if the stream is not real, there will be the theory of the void; and if the stream is real, the defects such as the changing nature of the soul, etc. will follow. The Jain view, in short, will be inadequate.

अंत्यावस्थितेश्चोभयनित्यत्वादविशेषः । ३६

[*Antya-avasthiteḥ-on account of permanency of the final ; ca-and; ubhaya-nityatvāt-due to permanence of both; aviśeṣaḥ-without difference.*]

AND BECAUSE THE FINAL (SIZE OF THE SOUL) IS CONSIDERED PERMANENT AND BECAUSE OF THE PERMANENCY OF THE TWO (EARLIER SIZES), THERE IS NO DIFFERENCE (OF SIZE). 36

Moreover, because the Jains believe that the final size of the soul is permanent during its condition of release, it follows that the initial and the intervening sizes also must be permanent; otherwise there will be three different conditions of one and the same soul. But this means that the different bodies of the soul will have one and the same size, and that the soul will not be required to enter into bigger and smaller bodies.

Or the Sūtra may be explained in a different way. The dimensions of the soul being the same in its three conditions, as noted above, the soul must be either small or large, and must not vary according to the size of the body. Hence the doctrine of the Arhat, like that of the Buddhist, is inadequate and therefore deserves to be rejected.

७ पत्यधिकरणम् । (३७–४१)

पत्युरसामंजस्यात् । ३७

[*Patyuḥ*—*of the Lord*; *asāmanjasyāt*—*because inadequate.*]

(IT IS IMPOSSIBLE TO THINK) OF THE LORD (AS ONLY THE EFFICIENT CAUSE OF THE WORLD), BECAUSE THIS IS INADEQUATE. 37

In the Sūtras 23 and 24 of the fourth pāda of the first adhyāya, it was shown that God is both the material and the efficient cause of the world. And if the Sūtrakāra is not inconsistent, the present Sūtra cannot be meant to show that God is neither the efficient nor the material cause. It should therefore be understood that the Sūtra intends to attack what is contrary to the unity of Brahman, viz. the view that God is merely the efficient and not the material cause of the world.

There are many who are opposed to the Vedānta view regarding the nature of God. Some rely on the Sāṁkhya and the yoga systems and say that God is only the efficient cause, and that he is therefore different from both pradhāna and puruṣa. The Māheśvaras hold that Paśupati (Śiva) is the efficient cause, and say that there are four other things as taught by Paśupati himself, viz. the effect, the yoga, the ritual and the end of pain[1]. In a like manner, the Naiyāyikas, the Vaiśeṣikas and others have told us that God is only the efficient cause of the world.

All these opinions are however inadequate. For in supposing that the Lord is the cause of the differences in the various beings, such as low, intermediate and the best, we shall merely ascribe to him human motives of hatred and passion. Then he will be no real God, but like one of us. If, in order to get over this difficulty, it is said that God's choice is determined by the merits and demerits of the beings themselves, then it is to fall in another difficulty, viz. that God's choice and the works of beings will be mutually dependent on each other. To suggest that this mutual dependence is without any beginning is no solution of the difficulty; for this mutual dependence was as much a fault[2] in the past as it is the present time. Like one blind man leading other blind men, it will lead us nowhere. Moreover, the Naiyāyika canon that 'it is some kind of imperfection that leads to action' (Nyā. Sū. 1, 1, 18), and our experience that all persons, whether egoistic or altruistic, become active because they are imperfect, lead us to believe in a God who in spite of his benevolence and the consequent activity is imperfect still. The inadequacy of such a view becomes all the more apparent when the Pātañjala-yoga tells us that God is a peculiar indifferent type of puruṣa.

---

1 The effect means the world: yoga is the meditation on God; ritual consists in taking three baths in a day; and the end of pain is the mokṣa.

2 This mutual dependence or anyonyāsraya is no fault only when the two things are causally connected; e. g. the seed and the sprout, though mutually dependent on each other ever since the beginning of time, are causally connected and are therefore allowed by logicians as not involving the regress. In the case of God's choice and the karma, however there is mere endless sequence and not causal connection For the initial choice of God if considered as the first cause will be arbitrary; and the works being non-intelligent in nature cannot move the God to make his choice.

संबंधानुपपत्तेश्च । ३८

[*Sam̐bandha*-*connection* ; *anupapatteḥ*-*being impossible*; *ca*-*and*.]

AND THE CONNECTION BEING IMPOSSIBLE. 38

Moreover the doctrine we are considering is not satisfactory for some additional reasons. The God, the pradhāna and the soul being all infinite and without parts, no one can be related with the other two by the connection known as sam̐yoga; for sam̐yoga can take place only betweeṇ objects which consist of parts. It cannot be samyāya also; for we do not know which of them is the substratum. Nor can we establish any special kind of relation between God and the world. For this would have been possible, if the world were admitted to be the product of pradhāna; but as yet this has not been proved.

It may be suggested that the Vedāntin also is sailing in the same boat; because according to him Māyā which is the cause of this world is in no way connected with the Brahman. But this is wrong; because the relation between the Māyā and the Brahman, according to him, is that of identity. He comes to know that Brahman is the cause of the world, because he relies upon Śruti, and does not think it necessary that what he believes must always conform to what he observes. His opponents, on the other hand, rely upon only what is observed and upon inference which is conformable to it. Besides, there is a fundamental difference between what the Vedāntin thinks about the nature of Śruti and what the opponents think. According to the former, the authority of Śruti or 'Āgama' is valid by itself; while according to the latter, it is due to some omniscient being[1]. This

[1] The Sām̐khyas believe that sages like Kapila are omniscient. Naturally, whatever they have written, e. g. the Sām̐khya-Sūtras, have got all the force of Āgama. The Vedāntin, on the other hand, believes that the Ājama is valid by itself, and is not the work of any human agency.

however creates a logical difficulty for the opponent, viz. the authority of the āgama is to be referred to an omniscient being, and the omniscience is to be inferred by reference to āgama. For all these reasons, the Sāṁkhya-yoga view about the nature of God[1], as also other theories which make no reference to the Vedas, are to be rejected.

अधिष्ठानानुपपत्तेश्च । ३९

[*Adhiṣṭhāna—support; anupapatteḥ-being impossible; ca- and*]

SUPERVISION BEING IMPOSSIBLE (THE LORD CANNOT BE THE MAKER). 39

People who resort to inference only may put forth the argument that just as the potter deals with clay while producing the jars, even so the Lord may be doing with reference to pradhāna. But this is not possible; because pradhāna being devoid of colour and other qualities is not capable of being preceived just as clay is, and will therefore not be a fit object to be dealt with and shaped into the world by the Lord.

करणवच्चेन्न भोगादिभ्यः । ४०

[*Karaṇavat—like the senses ; cet—if ; na—not; bhogādibhyaḥ—because of enjoyment of fruits etc.*]

IF IT BE SAID (THAT PRADHĀNA IS GUIDED BY THE LORD) JUST AS THE SENSES (ARE BY THE SOUL), IT IS NOT SO; FOR (THE LORD WILL BE SUBJECT) TO ENJOYMENTS ETC. 40

It may be supposed that the Lord guides the pradhāna in the same way in which the soul guides the organs of sight etc., even though the organs lack colour

[1] The Sāṁkhya system referred to here is one which affords a place for God.

and other qualities and are not objects of perception. The supposition however proves nothing. For whereas the soul is pleased or displeased on account of the activity of the senses, and affords us reason to infer that it must be guiding the senses, we do not get any such evidence for believing that the Lord derives pleasure or pain by the activity of the pradhāna to enable us to infer that he rules over it.

Or this and the preceding Sūtra may be explained in a different way. Sūtra 39: If kings can rule over a country only if they are endowed with a body, and not otherwise, even so the Lord of all must have got some kind of body to which his senses must belong, and on account of which he should be able to rule. But bodies can exist only subsequent to creation and not prior to it. So a body can never be said to belong to the Lord, and therefore it can never be said that he is able to act and rule. Sutra 40 : And if we assume that the Lord possesses a body which he can create for himself even before creation, and which he can utilize for guiding his own senses as well as the pradhāna, he remains no longer the Lord, but becomes like one of us subject to pleasure and pain.

अंतवत्त्वमसर्वज्ञता वा । ४१

[*Antavattvaṁ*—*liable to perish*; *asarvajñatā*—*non-omniscience*; *vā*—*or*.]

(THE LORD WILL THEN BE) EITHER PERISHABLE IN NATURE OR NON-OMNISCIENT. 41

For an additional reason too, the theory of those who rely on mere inference becomes invalid. They teach that God is eternal and omniscient, and that pradhāna and the souls also live for infinite duration. Now let us suppose, in the first place, that the omniscient God must have measured the duration, the extent and the number of himself, of pradhāna and of the souls. But as experience tells us all measured things, like jars and the like, are of finite duration only. No doubt the number of souls is too great; still it is limited from the view-point of the omniscient Lord. That is why, gradually and one after another, the souls get the release from saṁsāra. But when all of them get released, the saṁsāra itself comes to an end. In other words, it is nothing but the end of pradhāna itself; for it is the pradhāna which, under the guidance of the Lord, had modified and manifested itself as the saṁsāra, for the good of the souls. And when the pradhāna thus comes to an end, what remains there for the Lord to supervise or to rule? It is as good as saying that he too comes to an end;— and then, we are landed in a general void. If to avoid these unpleasant conclusions, we suppose, in the second place, that God did not or could not measure himself or the pradhāna or the souls, we shall deprive him of his omniscience. Thus the, doctrine that God is only the efficient cause of the world, is untenable.

८ उत्पत्त्यसंभवाधिकरणम् । (४२--४५)

उत्पत्त्यसंभवात् । ४२

[*Utpatti—origination ; asaṁbhavāt—on account of impossibility.*]

THE ORIGINATION (OF THE INDIVIDUAL SOUL) BEING IMPOSSIBLE, (THE BHĀGAVATA DOCTRINE CANNOT BE ACCEPTED.)

Having refuted the Śaiva doctrine that God is only the efficient and not the material cause of the world, we shall now refute the doctrine of the Bhāgavatas or the Vaiṣṇavas. Their smṛti is no doubt faithful to Śruti in believing that God is both the efficient and the material cause of the world, but differs from it in certain respects; and it is in these respects that we have to examine the doctrine.

Their theory can be stated thus : Vāsudeva is the highest reality; he alone exists and is pure knowledge. Dividing himself in four forms this Vāsudeva or Nārāyaṇa appears as Vāsudeva, Sañkarṣaṇa, Pradyumna and Aniruddha, or appears, in other words, as the highest Ātman, the individual soul the mind and ahaṁkāra, respectively. Vāsudeva represents the primal cause, and the three others are the effects. If a man goes to the temple and worships this Vāsudeva for hundred years by means of offerings, prayers and meditation, he will thereby be able to overcome affliction and reach the Vāsudeva himself.

Now we have no desire to dispute over the doctrine that Nārāyaṇa who transcends the avyakta, and who is the highest and the internal Ātman of all divides himself and manifests in various forms. For Śruti also tells us that the highest Ātman appears in many forms, that 'he is one, he becomes three' (Chā. 7, 26, 2). Nor do we wish to contend against the devotional approach and the unceasing one-pointed meditation on God; for this has been recommended both by Śruti and Smṛti.[1] But we do take objection to the origination of the individual soul (Sañkarṣaṇa) from the highest Ātman (Vāsudeva), as also to the origination of mind and ahaṁkāra from the soul and the mind respectively. For in that case, like all other things which are originated, the soul also will be perishable in nature. Besides there will be no mokṣa for the soul, because it will be simply destroyed and will not therefore reach the highest Being. That the soul does not originate will be shown later on in II, 3, 17. Hence it is that the doctrine of the Bhāgavatas is untenable.

न च कर्तुः करणम् । ४३

[*Na—not; ca—and; kartuḥ—of the doer; karaṇam—instrument.*]

1 Vide Bṛ. 4, 4, 23, and B. G. 11,55.

NOR IS THE MEANS (OF DOING SEEN TO BE PRODUCED) FROM THE DOER. 43

We never observe that an instrument of doing some work, springs forth by itself from the doer[1] of that work. Devadatta may use an axe, but the axe does not come out of Devadatta. The Bhāgavatas teach us however that the mind (Pradyumna) arises out of the individual soul (Saṅkarṣaṇa), and that ahamkāra (Aniruddha) arises out of the mind. But as said above, experience goes against their teaching. Nor have they any support from Śruti.

विज्ञानादि भावे वा तदप्रतिषेधः । ४४

[*Vijñāna-adi-bhāve—when knowledge and other things exist; vā—or; tat-a-pratiṣedhaḥ—non-exclusion of that.*]

AND THERE WILL BE NO EXCLUSION OF THAT (DEFECT OF NON-ORIGINATION,) EVEN IF (ALL OF THEM ARE SUPPOSED AS) POSSESSING KNOWLEDGE AND OTHER (QUALITIES.) 44

The Bhāgavatas may now take a different line of thought and say that Saṅkarṣaṇa etc. are not the soul, the mind or the ahaṁkāra, but are, all of them, gods endowed with the divine qualities of knowledge, glory, might, power, valour and lustre. They are, in other words, prototypes of Vāsudeva, all of them being without any defects, self-supporting and permanent. Therefore the Bhāgavatas may think that the defect regarding origination (referred to, in Sūtra 42) does not at all apply to these divinities.

To this we reply that objection does remain in spite of this argument. Does the Bhāgavata mean, in the first place, that the four divinities have the same attributes, but are different in form? If so, it is a useless addition of multiple forms when the act of

1 As if the doer is the material cause, and not simply the efficient cause.

governance can be performed by one only. Besides, it is only to relinquish his own hypothesis, viz, that Vāsudeva alone is the one real Being. Or if, in the second place, the Bhāgavata means that the divinities, though possessing the same attributes, have sprung in succession from one highest Being, then, as shown already while discussing Sūtra 42, the objection does remain valid. Besides, we learn from experience that there must be some kind of difference[1] between the cause and the effect; or to put it negatively, wherever such difference does not exist, there exists no causal relation. Accordingly we should expect some kind of difference between one divinity and another, because one springs forth from another. But the Pañcarātrikas[2] acknowledge no such difference; They say, on the contrary, that all the divinities are forms of Vāsudeva.

Further, there is no reason why the forms of Vāsudeva be limited only to four in number. As a matter of fact, the whole world, from Brahmadeva down to a blade of grass, is the manifestation of God.

विप्रतिषेधाच्च । ४५

[*Vipratiṣedhāt—on account of contradictions; ca—and.*]

AND ON ACCOUNT OF CONTRADICTIONS. 45

The qualities mentioned above as belonging to the divinities are also mentioned, by way of contradiction, elsewhere as different selves or forms of Vāsudeva.[3] Besides the statement that Śāṇdilya acquired this knowledge of the Pañcarātra school, when he became despaired of winning the highest bliss by the study of the four Vedas, is certainly an obloquy of the Vedas. Hence too the doctrine of the Bhāgavatas cannot be accepted.

---

1 The jar is different from clay in its form and function.

2 The Bhāgavatas are known as Pañcarātrikas because they accept the philosophy contained in the treatise known as Pañcarātra.

3 Even the divinities which are once mentioned as separate, i. e. as soul mind and ahaṁkāra, are again mentioned as non-distinct from each other.

SUMMARY

ADHYĀYA FIRST

Pāda First

The nature of Adhyāsa: Extreme opposition of the asmad and yuṣmad, the subject and the object in experience. Yet the mutual superimposition, i.e., the apprehension of something in something else, does take place on account of avidyā. Adhyāsa is the root cause of all evil; knowledge of the unity of the Ātman will remove this evil.

Sūtra.

1 The word 'now' indicates succession and not a mere auspicious beginning. This antecedent condition is neither the study of the Vedas, nor the knowledge of dharma. For Brahma-jñāna may be had without that of dharma. The real antecedents are the discrimination between the real and the unreal, non-attachment, possession of tranquility and desire to have liberation. Brahma-jñāna is the Summum Bonum of life. Different opinions about the nature of self.

2 Origin, subsistence and dissolution of the world are due to Brahman. Difference between Dharma-jijñāsā and Brahma-jijñāsā.

3 Śruti is the means of knowing that Brahman is the cause.

4 If as Jaimini holds no Vedic passage has any meaning unless it is subservient to action, there is no direct reference to Brahman as an accomplished fact.

But the Sūtrakāra holds that the direct cumulative and harmonious result of all the Vedānta passages is that Brahman is the cause of the world. Brahman is not an object of perception or other means of knowledge, nor of meditation. Difference between Karma-vidyā and Brahma-vidyā. Mokṣa is Kūṭastha-nitya, and is the same as Brahma-jñāna. The knowledge of the identity of jīva and Brahman is neither a make-believe, nor due to superimposition; neither the result of acts of purification nor the indication of any functional resemblance. The Ātman is not amenable to change. To deny it is to posit it. It is the in-dwelling witness of all. The connection of a thing with action does not change that thing into action. Function of a negative proposition is to indicate the neutral condition of indifference to actions. Propositions like, 'This is a rope, not a snake', are useful in removing fear. Disembodied condition is possible on this side of death; description of this condition. Had Brahman been subservient to action, Jaimini would have incorporated it in Pūrva-Mīmāṁsā.

5 Non-intelligent pradhāna cannot possess 'seeing', i.e. intelligence, knowledge etc. Nor it is omniscient, because sattva is equipoised by rajas and tamas. A yogin is omniscient, because he is a conscious subject, and not due to excess of sattva. By deriving causal activity from Brahman, pradhāna cannot be said to be the cause. Omniscience and freedom of Brahman are not incompatible. Contradictory predicates reconciled in God. Difference of soul from God, due to ignorance. Cannot pradhāna be said to be the cause in a secondary or figurative sense?

6 Not figurative also; for the word 'jīvātman' which means intelligent ruler cannot refer to pradhāna, but to Brahman. Cannot pradhāna be the cause if it helps the soul in having bhoga or mokṣa? Cannot the word Ātman refer to both intelligent and non-intelligent beings?

7 Mokṣa is possible on account of devotion to Ātman as recommended by spiritual teacher, and not due to pradhāna. The word Ātman refers to Śvetaketu and to 'sat' according to context, and so cannot be transferred to pradhāna.

8 The word 'sat' is not used to denote pradhāna even as a preliminary step, so that this may be discarded afterwards, and 'sat' used to denote Brahman. Besides, knowledge of pradhāna as the cause would mean knowledge of souls as effects; but this is impossible because pradhāna is non-intelligent, and the soul is intelligent.

9 The conscious soul will find no rest in the unconscious pradhāna during sleep, but will find it in the conscious Ātman.

10 The consensus of opinions as contained in the Vedānta-passages is that Brahman is the cause.

11 Is Brahman the object of knowledge or devotion?

12 Ānandamaya, according to pūrpapakṣa, is the jīvātman, because it is the last of the series and has joy as its head. The Vedāntin holds that it is Brahman, because it is of the nature of flavour which if once tasted, makes one fearless. The mention of the various false ātmans is simply an aid to understand the real ānandamaya Ātman. To conceive the Ātman as having limbs is only an imagination.

13 Ānandamaya means 'abounding in bliss', and not 'made up of bliss'. Various blisses upto that of Brahman measured in ascending degrees.

14 Knowledge of Ātman results in bliss because the Ātman is full of bliss.

15 The mantra, the Brāhmaṇa and the Bhārgavi Vāruṇī vidyā, are all consistent is saying that Brahman is the innermost Ātman and is blissful.

16 Creation of the world on the pattern of his thought and non-different from himself is possible for the highest Ātman only.

17 The ānandmaya Ātman is to be searched and attained. The individual soul though illusory is non-distinct from God; but God being the ground of avidyā and souls is different from either.

18 Neither the desire to create and become many, nor the 'ānanda' belongs to pradhāna.

19 Ānandamaya is not jīva, because salvation occurs when the jīva is joined with the ānandamaya. Ānandamaya is one of the five sheaths: the tail or support of ānandamaya is the Brahman. Ānandamaya is Saguṇa Brahman, which no doubt must be first attained, in order to reach the Nirguṇa Brahman.

20 The person on the sun and in the eye is Saguṇa Brahman.

21 Even the sun does not know who dwells in him and controls him.

22 Ākāśa means Brahman; for the latter is the cause of all the elements including that of ākāśa. Words 'only' and 'all' would be useless, if ākāśa would mean the element. Infinity, exculsive mark of Brahmaṇ. The Udgītha or Om owes its eternity or greatness to Ākāśa or Brahman. Synonyms for ākāśa are used for Brahman.

23 Does prāna mean the breath in which organs of sense and action merge during sleep? As the beings themselves who have the senses merge, prāna

means Brahman. Mere contiguity of words viz the prāṇa, the sun and the food is no key to interpret the meaning. Grammatical position and context will be useful.

24 Can jyoti mean the physical light? 'Heaven' in the Gāyatrī passage and in this jyoti passage is the same. Brahman is the topic of the earlier Gāyatrī and the latter Śāndilya passages. Brahman is the meaning of the word jyoti. Brahman spoken of as jyoti for purpose of meditation.

25 Gāyatrī means the Brahman and not the metre. The four feet of Gāyatrī are those of Brahman.

26 The passage following that of Gāyatrī mentions the door-keepers of the heart in which Brahman with four feet resides.

27 The words 'divi' and 'divaḥ' make no difference so far as the nature of Brahman is concerned.

28 Prāṇa means Brahman. It cannot be the breath; for the highest Good of man cannot be of the changing nature. Bliss and immortality are the marks of Brahman and not of air. Prāṇa is Brahman because it is unaffected by good and bad actions.

29 Can prāṇa mean Indra, because he is the resident of heaven and so has ānanda, and because he is the object of devotion and unaffected by oldage, death and action? It is Brahman, because it has the power of bestowing and taking away life; it is described as the nave with the spokes of senses etc. fixed in it.

30 Indra's reference to himself is the awareness of intuitive knowledge of Brahman. Reference to killing the son of Tvaṣṭā glorifies the redeeming nature of Self-realization.

31 Brahman is the topic of knowledge and devotion; it is neither the prāṇa nor the jīva.

ADHYĀYA FIRST

Pāda Second

Sūtra

1-8 The resplendent Ātman described as manomaya, with prāṇa as its body; and as the object of meditation it is Brahman and not the individual soul

9-10 Brahman alone is the consumer of the whole movable and immovable world.

11 The two beings in the cave of the heart are the jīva and Brahman; for both are intelligent as indicated by 'Ṛtapāna'.

12 One eats the sweet fruit, and the other looks on. Or, the two birds may be considered as buddhi and the released soul.

13-17 The person in the eye is the stainless highest Ātman, and is recommended as the object of meditation. He is not the perishable reflection of some person in the eyes of another; for he is said to be immortal and fearless. The person is one's own eye is capable of being seen by meditation.

18 The internal ruler must be the Ātman.

19-20 It cannot be pradhāna, because though the Ātman is itself unseen like pradhāna, it sees the entire world. Neither ean it be the individual jīva whose existence is due to avidyā.

21 Bhūtayoni means the highest God; for omniscience cannot belong to pradhāna or to the individual soul.

22 The Upaniṣadic person who is the same as bhūtayoni is described, unlike jīva and pradhāna, as effulgent, bodiless, unproduced, without mind or prāṇa and pure.

23 That bhūtayoni has got a form in spite of being invisible shows that it is the Ātman of all.

24-25 In view of its description as 'lustrous heaven' and of the result of meditation on it, viz the eating of all the food, Vaiśvānara means the Ātman and not the abdominal fire or the jīva.

26-27 Vaiśvānara is said to be the Puruṣa and at the same time inside the body of man; so it is neither the deity nor the element of fire.

28-32 Jaimini and Āśmarathya think him to be the object of meditation and as measured from chin to forehead.

ADHYĀYA FIRST

Pāda Third

Sūtra

1. The word 'setu' (bridge) with reference to Brahman does not indicate that there is another bank which is to be reached. It indicates the idea of holding together or lending support or of attaining immortality.

2 The wise man fixes his mind on the Ātman; for to talk much is weariness.

3-7 In Ātman alone, the heaven, the earth and the sky are woven.

8 Bhūman means Brahman and not prāṇa. The quality of being an ativādin refers to Brahman, and not to prāṇa on account of the series of 'truth' and other things. Prāṇa is not the last word of Sanat-kumāra's teaching.

9 The bliss of deep sleep does not refer to prāṇa. Similarly, qualities such as immortality, truth, omnipresence etc. belong to Brahman or Bhūman.

10-12 Akṣara being imperishable and all-pervading means Brahman. Qualities of ākṣara such as 'unseen', 'unheard' etc. may be common with pradhāna, but the other qualities of 'seeing', 'hearing' etc. do not belong to pradhāna but to Brahman.

13 Nirguṇa Brahman alone is the object of meditation on Om and of sight; it transcends the transcendent jīva-ghana.

14-17 Daharākāśa, though located in the heart, is as large as the elemental ākāśa; and yet it is not the elemental ākāśa because qualities belonging to the Ātman are ascribed to it.

18-21 Dahara also does not mean the individual soul; for the qualities like freedom from sin belong to the Ātman. It refers to the real nature of the jīva which is gradually being shown to be identical with Brahman, and which is therefore described as rising beyond the body and as appearing in its own form. The bearing of this on Karma-Kāṇḍa.

22-23 The Prājña-ātman is the cause of the light of the sun, the moon etc.

24-25 The Ātman is said to be of the size of the thumb, only with the view to show the identity of jīva and Brahman.

26-27 Gods too have got the capacity to have the knowledge of Brahman.

28. Words like 'vasu', 'āditya' are connected with the eternal species and not with transitory objects. The words connote some permanent meanings. According to grammarians, the words perish, and it is the 'sphota' which manifests the meaning of words and which alone is real. As opposed to this, Upavarṣa holds that it is not necessary to imagine the existence of sphota to explain the manifestation of meaning from the letters of the word.

29 The Veda (or the word) is the source of the universe.

30 The Veda is as eternal as Saṁsāra, and it was available to Hiraṇyagarbha by the grace of the highest God.

31-32 Jaimini's opinion regarding incapacity of gods.

33 The Upaniṣadic testimony regarding the hankering of gods after knowledge of the Ātman; Indra and Virocana as instances. The arthavāda is as complete a unity as vidhi-vākya, but has got the additional function of praising some thing or person. It is from these that we know that gods have bodily forms and that they desire to have the knowledge of Brahman.

34 The word Śūdra may mean the grief and not the caste.

35 Jānaśruti may be a Kṣatriya.

36-38 A Śūdra is unfit, because he is not a twice-born. Yet they may learn through itihāsa and purāṇas.

39 Prāṇa is Brahman; for to make the whole world tremble through fear is possible for the latter; and again, mokṣa is due to knowledge of Brahman.

40 Similarly, light means Brahman; for release and disembodied condition can belong to Brahman and not to the sun and other luminous bodies,

41 Ākāśa means Brahman, because ultimately it is the cause of names and forms.

42-43 The conditions of sleep and of departure of the soul show it to be different from the Brahman or Ātman who is really the Lord.

ADHYĀYA FIRST

Pāda Fourth

Sūtra

1 Avyakta does not mean the pradhāna; it means the body mentioned in the metaphor of the chariot, which aims at showing us the final destiny of the soul, viz. the abode of Viṣṇu.

2 Avyakta means the subtle, causal body; it is the non-manifest condition of the world.

3 It is premordial power of God known as avidyā, māyā, ākāśa, akṣara etc.

4 Not being mentioned as subject of knowledge or meditation, it serves no human purpose.

5 The object of perception referred to in the same Upaniṣad (Katha, 2,3,15) is the intelligent, highest Ātman.

6 The dialogue between Naciketas and Death refers to three things alone, viz. the fire, the individual soul and the highest Ātman, and does in no way mention the pradhāna.

7 The Vedic meaning of 'mahat' as opposed to that of the Sāṁkhyas is Puruṣa or the Ātman.

8-9 Just as 'camasa' or the cup may mean the 'head' even so, 'ajā' may not mean pradhāna, but may mean that the three elements with their three colours have come out of the highest God.

10 Prakṛti being composed of three elements is poetically known as a she-goat.

11-13 'Pañcapañca janaḥ' does not mean the categories of the Sāṁkhyas, but particular types of beings. Various reasons for holding this view.

14 There may be contradictions regarding the accounts of creation; but inasmuch as the welfare of man does not depend on this, all the Vedānta-passages are directed in the search of Brahman alone.

15 If the word 'sat' indicates the world or the Brahman with names and forms, the word 'asat' indicates the same Brahman, without any names and forms. Brahman is both the efficient and the material cause of the world.

16-18 The work of creation refers to God as the creator.

19-22 The object of sight is the Ātman alone. While Āśmarathya believes in relative non-difference of the jīva and the Brahman, while Audulomi thinks they are identical in the condition of knowledge, Kārśakritsnya voices forth the correct view embodied in 'Thou art that.' The Ātman, as the object of sight, is not some future condition of the soul. On the contrary, the soul is a form of the Ātman.

23–28 Brahman is also the material cause of the universe.

ADHYĀYA SECOND

Pāda First

Sūtra

1 To accept pradhāna as the cause is to make Smṛtis like the Bhagavadgītā as useless; for nirguṇa Brahman is considered by them as the efficient and material cause. A Smṛti which goes against Śruti is to be rejected. Reference to Kapila is ambiguious and incidental; the main fact is the 'seeing of God'.

2 Kapila Smṛti cannot be trusted in its reference to mahat, avyakta etc. because these are unknown to the Veda and to experience.

3 Because yoga Smṛti is useful and partially true, it cannot be accepted as wholly true, especially in its reference to pradhāna as the independent cause.

4 Believing that reasoning comes very near to experience, the pūrvapakṣa contends that Brahman which is pure and conscious cannot be the cause of the universe which is impure and unconscious. Absence of intelligence in the things of the world cannot simply be said to be apparent.

5 Though the elements are represented as thinking, 'seeing' etc. the pūrvapakṣin points out that the reference is to the presiding deities and not to the non-intelligent elements.

6 To the Vedāntin, whatever exists, whether intelligent or not, is the effect of Brahman. Experience

corroborates this. As for the knowledge of Brahman, argument cannot achieve it; it is achieved only when another person speaks about it. Reasoning which is favourable to Śruti is welcome; illustrations of this. Disparity of nature is no reason why Brahman should not be the cause, especially when pradhāna can be said to be the cause of intelligent souls.

7 To say that the effect was non-existent (in the form in which it appears) is meaningless. For it is a negation of nothing. The effect always exists in some form of the cause.

8-9 Size and shape of a jar can never be found in clay; the world therefore will never make the Brahman impure. The effect and its qualities are due to avidyā. The Ātman is the eternal spectator of the three states, and so is not affected by avidyā. New creation is due to the persistence of avidyā even in dissolution; in the case of the liberated souls, false knowledge is completely wiped out.

10 Objections against the Vedānta can be equally levelled against the Sāṁkhya, if pradhāna is without form and qualities.

11-12 One may say that reasoning is faulty is itself proved by reason, and that fallacy is a point of attraction which leads to more reason. But reasoning may not lead to right knowledge, and so may not lead one to mokṣa.

13 From the practical point of view, there remains the distinction between subjects and objects, though they are, in reality, non-different from the Brahman, just as waves, foam etc. are distinct from each other, though they are, in essence, nothing but water.

14 Nothing exists apart from Brahman; names and forms have their origin in speech only, To know

the Brahman is to know all. Multiplicity is unreal, yet it is believed as true so long as the knowledge of the identity of jīva and Brahman does not arise. Notwithstanding the fact that nothing is real except Brahman, the Vedic knowledge is useful to point out what is real. Though the dream is unreal, the knowledge that there was a dream continues to be real in the waking life. We need not be sceptic about having such knowledge; for Śvetaketu did possess it and realized that Brahman is ānanda. The motive in having the knowledge of Brahman as the cause of the world is not to know that it is modifiable, but to know that it alone is the reality. In order to negate this modal character, Brahman is described negatively knowing which, Janaka is said to have achieved mokṣa. In no way the unity of Brahman contradicts its being the cause of the origin, subsistence and dissolution, or its being the ruler and protecter. The pariṇāmavāda too is accepted by the Sūtrakāra so far as it is subservient to the purpose of devotion to Saguṇa Brahman.

15 The perception of the jar makes us inevitably aware of the clay. Besides it will not exist apart from clay.

16 Either before or after its coming into being, the world is one with its cause viz. the Brahman.

17 The so-called non-existence of the effect before its origination means only a relative and not absolute non-existence; it means that during the period when the effect was in the form of the cause, it had not got its present names and forms.

18 Had the effect been really non-existent before its origination, there is no reason why curds should be produced out of milk alone; as a matter of fact, anything may come out of anything else. To say that curds has a specific power is to abandon asatkāryavāda and to

admit the immediate prior condition of effect. Difficulties of samavāya and saṁyoga; the cateogory of whole and parts. Absolute non-existence, such as the existence of the son of a barren woman, can never become a reality in spite of the efforts of potters etc. The operative agents arrange the cause in the form of effect. Devadatta is the same person, whether with limbs stretched out or drawn in.

19–20 What is not manifest in the cause becomes manifest in the effect.

21-23 Jīva and Brahman are different and non-different from each other.

24-25 Brahman is self-sufficient to produce the world.

26-29 Not pariṇāma but vivarta is the correct view. Besides Brahman is both immanent and transcendent; it is the ground of names and forms which are both different and non-different from it. The negative description leads us from phenomena to God.

30-31 Contradictions reconciled in Brahman.

32-33 Rational activity may be motivated by the desire to sport merely. Creation is not real from the view-point of the highest reality.

34-36 God is neither cruel nor unjust. Law of Karma is alone responsible.

ADHYĀYA SECOND

Pāda Second

Sūtra

1 A potter is necessary to produce a jar; mere clay is not sufficient. Even so, the pradhāna will require an intelligent principle for its guidance.

2 Intelligence possesses the power to move a non-intelligent thing like a chariot, though itself it may remain unmoved.

3 The love of the cow for the calf and the sucking of the milk are responsible for the flow of milk. God is the ultimate intelligent principle.

4 If there is no intelligent principle beyond pradhāna, neither activity nor cessation of activity will be explained.

5 Neither is there the spontaneous transformation of pradhāna into the world, like grass into milk. For that grass alone which is eaten by a cow changes into milk.

6 Either there is no purpose for the activity of pradhāna which is against the Sāṁkhya hypothesis, or there is some purpose, in which case the Puruṣa shall have to undergo change. Thus, there will be no liberation.

7 If the Puruṣa is inactive, it cannot move the pradhāna; the inadequacy of the illustration of the lame and the blind.

8-9 The moment the equipoised condition of the three guṇas in disturbed, pradhāna itself is in danger of being lost. Either there will be perpetual Saṁsāra or no evolution at all.

10 Besides, the Sāṁkhya doctrine is full of contradictions. On the Vedāntic view, the distinction between sufferer and suffering is due to avidyā; but when the Sāṁkhya makes tamoguṇa the cause of non-discrimination, release is impossible; for the tamoguṇa is as eternal as the sattva and may overtake a man at any time.

11 Atomism explained and criticized. Intelligence of Brahman is not produced in the world, just as sphericity of the atoms is not produced in their effects.

12 The original motion of the atoms is neither explained by some impact which can take place after creation, nor by the principle of 'unseen accumulation of merits' which is non-intelligent.

13 The relation of samavāya like saṁyoga must depend on another samavāya and so on *ad infinitum*.

14 If atoms possess qualities like colour and sound, they must be gross and transitory. Besides, they may not be destroyed or disintegrated, but be transformed into a prior non-atomic condtiion.

16 Atoms will not be atoms if they increase in volume and possess many qualities. And to maintain uniformity, if the four kinds of atoms have only one or four qualities, we shall have to say something against experience.

17 The Vaiśeṣika contradicts himself when he says that the six categories are independent, and that

five of them are dependent on one of them, viz. the substance. His view of ayutasiddhatva either in space, time or character, is equally faulty; for he will thereby go aainst the authority of Kaṇāda, or say that there is no difference between substance and quality. His view about saṁyoga and samavāya is riddled with contradictions, and involves mutual dependence.

18 The two-fold world of the Buddhist realists cannot be explained by reference to the non-intelligent atoms and skandhas. And if there is no mind, there is no chain of mental cognitions; nor a lord who will govern. Nirvāṇa is impossible.

19 The series of avidyā, saṁskāras etc., being dependent on atoms and skandhas, cannot be the cause of the latter.

20 If everything is momentary, there will be no causal connection at all; and words like origin, destruction will have no meaning.

21 If the effect were to exist without cause, anything may come into existence; and if it has a cause, the view that everything is momentary shall have to be given up.

22 The voluntary and the involuntary types of destruction as well as ākāśa are non-substantial and negative in character.

23 Ākāśa cannot be a non-entity; its existence is inferrable from the quality of sound. Buddha himself accepts it as the support of wind. Besides a non-entity cannot be eternal.

24 Recollection and recognition of things as same will be impossible, if the experiencing subjects are momentary in character. The belief in the experiencing subjects as the same cannot be the result of

similarity of cognitions; for cognition of similarity itself is due to a permanent subject.

26-27 Nothing originates from non existence; or else, the lazy persons would get what they want.

28 The external world is not mental in character; for our ideas point to perceptions and the perceptions point to external things. No one will be satisfied by a mental dinner. If ideas are only momentary in character, all practical life will be robbed of its meaning. It will be more reasonable for the Vijñānavādins to believe in the commonsense external world than in the self-luminous ideas. Besides, as against the Vedānta view, such ideas are transitory and many.

29 Waking life is real and is to be distinguished from the dream, because it consists of immediate experience and is not due to memory, and because it consists of objects and is not capable of being negated by any other state.

30 Cognitions are not, unlike the Buddhist opinion, due to impressions, but are due to external objects; for in the absence of objects cognitions do not arise.

31 Like the pravṛttivijñāna, the ālayavijñāna also cannot be the substratum because it is momentary.

32 Buddhism is not only contradictory but leads to no spiritual good.

33 To apply the saptabhagīnaya to the seven entities is to have indefinite and confused knowledge.

34 To consider that the soul has got the size of the body is to make it limited and perishable. Difficulties of considering it as having parts.

35-36 The particles too like the body have got origin and decay and so are not of the nature of self; or, the soul may have different bodies of the same dimensions.

37 The God of the Naiyāyikas and the Māheśvaras is only imperfect like us, howsoever benevolent he may be. God is not merely the efficient cause.

38 God, souls and pradhāna being, all of them, infinite and partless, neither saṁyoga nor samavāya will establish any relation amongst them.

39 Pradhāna is not to God as clay is to the potter.

40 Nor is there any evidence to show that the Lord guides the pradhāna and is therefore pleased or displeased.

41 With the release of all souls there will be no purpose left either for pradhāna or for the Lord.

42 Notwithstanding the manifestation of the Ātman in several forms and the devotional approach to it, the soul, on the Bhāgavata view, will be perishable in nature.

43 Experience does not bear testimony to the production of ahaṁkāra out of the mind and of the mind out the soul.

44 To suppose that the soul, the mind and ahaṁkāra are, all of them, divinities like the highest Ātman, is to rest satisfied with an arbitrary multiplication of unity.

45 To say that Śāndilya got knowledge from the Pañcarātra school is only to cast doubt on the Vedic lore.

Extracts from Upanishads and other sources as found in Śaṁkarā's commentary

Aitareya Āraṇyaka

2, 1, 2, 6 — अहमुक्थमस्मीति विद्यात्।

2, 4, 1, 1–2 (cf. Ar. Up. 1, 1) — आत्मा वा इदमेक एवाग्र आसीत्। नान्यत्किंचन मिषत्। स ईक्षत लोकान्नु सृजा इति। स इमांल्लोकानसृजत।

2, 4, 2, 4 — अग्निर्वाग्भूत्वा मुखं प्राविशत्।

3, 2, 4, 7 — अथ यः स्वप्ने पुरुषं कृष्णं कृष्णदन्तं पश्यति स एनं हन्ति।

Ait. Brāhmaṇa, 3, 8, 1 — यस्मै देवतायै हविर्गृहीतं स्यात्तां मनसा ध्यायद्वषट्करिष्यन्। संध्यां मनसा ध्यायेत्।

Bhagavadgītā

2, 24–25 — अच्छेद्योऽयमदाह्योऽयमक्लेद्योऽशोष्य एव च। नित्यः सर्वगतः स्थाणुरचलोऽयं सनातनः॥ अव्यक्तोऽयमचिन्त्योऽयमविकार्योऽयमुच्यते। तस्मादेवं विदित्वैनं नानुशोचितुमर्हसि॥

2, 55 — प्रजहाति यदा कामान्सर्वान्पार्थ मनोगतान्। आत्मन्येवात्मना तुष्टः स्थितप्रज्ञस्तदोच्यते॥

4, 11 — ये यथा मां प्रपद्यन्ते तांस्तथैव भजाम्यहम्। मम वर्त्मानुवर्तन्ते मनुष्याः पार्थ सर्वशः॥

4, 37 — ज्ञानाग्निः सर्वकर्माणि भस्मसात्कुरुते॥

5, 14–15 — न कर्तृत्वं न कर्माणि लोकस्य सृजति प्रभुः। न कर्मफलसंयोगं स्वभावस्तु प्रवर्तते॥ नादत्ते कस्यचित्पापं न चैव सुकृतं विभुः। अज्ञानेनावृतं ज्ञानं तेन मुह्यन्ति जन्तवः॥

7, 6 — अहं कृत्स्नस्य जगतः प्रभवः प्रलयस्तथा॥

7, 19 — वासुदेवः सर्वमिति स महात्मा सुदुर्लभः॥

8, 6 — यं यं वापि स्मरन्भावं त्यजत्यन्ते कलेवरम्। तं तमेवैति कौन्तेय सदा तद्भावभावितः॥

8, 24 — अग्निर्ज्योतिरहः शुक्लः षण्मासा उत्तरायणम्। तत्र प्रयाता गच्छन्ति ब्रह्म ब्रह्मविदो जनाः॥

10, 2—न मे विदुः सुरगणाः प्रभवं न महर्षयः। अहमादिर्हि देवानां महर्षीणां च सर्वशः॥

10, 41-42—यद्यद्विभूतिमत्सत्त्वं श्रीमदूर्जितमेव वा। तत्तदेवावगच्छ त्वं मम तेजोंऽशसंभवम्॥ विष्टभ्याहमिदं कृत्स्नमेकांशेन स्थितो जगत्॥

13, 2— क्षेत्रज्ञं चापि मां विद्धि सर्वक्षेत्रेषु भारत॥

13, 13—सर्वतःपाणिपादं तत्सर्वतोऽक्षिशिरोमुखम्। सर्वतः श्रुतिमल्लोके सर्वमावृत्य तिष्ठति॥

13, 27—समं सर्वेषु भूतेषु तिष्ठन्तं परमेश्वरम्। विनश्यत्स्वविनश्यन्तं यः पश्यति स पश्यति॥

13, 31—अनादित्वान्निर्गुणत्वात्परमात्मायमव्ययः। शरीरस्थोऽपि कौन्तेय न करोति न लिप्यते॥

14, 17—सत्त्वात्संजायते ज्ञानम्॥

15, 3—न रूपमस्येह तथोपलभ्यते। नान्तो न चादिर्न च संप्रतिष्ठा॥

15, 6—न तद्भासयते सूर्यो न शशांको न पावकः। यद्गत्वा न निवर्तन्ते तद्धाम परमं मम॥

15, 12—यदादित्यगतं तेजो जगद्भासयतेऽखिलम्। यच्चन्द्रमसि यच्चाग्नौ तत्तेजो विद्धि मामकम्॥

15, 20—एतद् बुद्ध्वा बुद्धिमान् स्यात्कृतकृत्यश्च भारत।

18, 61—ईश्वरः सर्वभूतानां हृद्देशेऽर्जुन तिष्ठति। भ्रामयन्सर्वभूतानि यन्त्रारूढानि मायया॥

Bṛhadāraṇyakopaniṣad

1, 3, 2—ते ह वाचमूचुस्त्वं न उद्गायेति तथेति तेभ्यो वागुदगायत्।

1, 4, 6-8—इदं सर्वमन्नं चैवमन्नादश्च सोम एवान्नमग्निरन्नादः। तद्धेदं तर्ह्यव्याकृतमासीत्तन्नामरूपाभ्यामेव व्याक्रियतासौ नामायमिदंरूप इति तदिदमप्येतर्हि नामरूपाभ्यामेव व्याक्रियतेऽयमिदंरूप इति। स एष इह प्रविष्टः। आनखाग्रेभ्यः। यथा क्षुरः क्षुरधानेऽवहितः स्याद्विश्वंभरो वा विश्वंभरकुलाये तं न पश्यन्ति। आत्मानमेव प्रिय उपासीत।

1, 4, 10—ब्रह्म वा इदमग्र आसीत्तदात्मानमेवावेत्। अहं ब्रह्मास्मीति तस्मात्तत्सर्वमभवत् ।

1, 4, 15—यदिह वा अप्यनेवंविन्महत्पुण्यं कर्म करोति तद्धास्यान्ततः क्षीयत एवात्मानमेव लोकमुपासीत स य आत्मानमेव लोकमुपास्ते न हास्य कर्म क्षीयते।

2, 2, 3—अर्वाग्बिलचमस ऊर्ध्वबुध्न इतीदं तच्छिर एष ह्यर्वाग्बिलचमस ऊर्ध्वबुध्नस्तस्मिन्यशो निहितं विश्वरूपमिति प्राणा वै यशो विश्वरूपम्।

2, 4, 5-6—न वा अरे पत्युः कामाय पतिः प्रियो भवत्यात्मनस्तु कामाय पतिः प्रियो भवति । जायायै० पुत्राणा०, वित्तस्य०, ब्रह्मण०, क्षत्रस्य०, लोकानां०, देवानां०, भूतानां० सर्वस्य, । आत्मा वा अरे द्रष्टव्यः श्रोतव्यो मन्तव्यो निदिध्यासितव्यः। आत्मनो वा अरे दर्शनेन श्रवणेन मत्या विज्ञानेनेदं सर्वं विदितम्। ब्रह्म तं परादाद्योऽन्यत्रात्मनो ब्रह्म वेद, क्षत्रं तं०, लोकास्तं०, देवाः०, भूतानि०, सर्वं०। इदं ब्रह्मेदं क्षत्रमिमे लोका इमे देवा इमानि भूतानीदं सर्वं यदयमात्मा।

2, 4, 10—अरेऽस्य महतो भूतस्य निःश्वसितमेतद्यदृग्वेदो यजुर्वेदः सामवेदोऽथर्वाङ्गिरस इतिहासः पुराणं विद्या उपनिषदः श्लोकाः सूत्राण्यनुव्याख्यानान्यस्यैवैतानि निःश्वसितानि ।

2, 4, 12—इदं महद्भूतमनन्तपारं विज्ञानघन एव।

2, 4, 14—यत्र हि द्वैतमिव भवति तदितर इतरं जिघ्रति, पश्यति, शृणोति, अभिवदति, मनुते, विजानाति। यत्र वा अस्य सर्वमात्मैवाभूत्तत्केन कं जिघ्रेत्तत्केन कं पश्येत्तत्केन कं शृणुयात्तत्केन कमभिवदेत्तत्केन कं मन्वीत तत्केन कं विजानीयात्। येनेदं सर्वं विजानाति तं विज्ञातारमरे केन विजानीयादिति ।

2, 5, 18—स वा अयं पुरुषः सर्वासु पूर्षु पुरिशयो नैनेन किंचनानावृतं नैनेन किंचनासंवृतम्

2, 5, 19—तदेतद्ब्रह्मापूवमनपरमनन्तरमबाह्यमयमात्मा ब्रह्म सर्वानुभूरित्यनुशासनम्।

3, 1, 9—अनन्तं वै मनोऽनन्ता विश्वेदेवा अनन्तमेव स तेन लोकं जयति।

3, 3, 2—वायुरेव व्यष्टिर्वायुः समष्टिरप पुनर्मृत्युं जयति य एवं वेद।

3, 4, 2 — न दृष्टेर्द्रष्टारं पश्येर्न श्रुतेः श्रोतारँ शृणुया न मतेर्मन्तारं मन्वीथा न विज्ञातेर्विज्ञातारं विजानीयाः। एष त आत्मा सर्वान्तरोऽतोऽन्यदार्तम्।

3, 7, 1—-—य इमं च लोकं परं च लोकं सर्वाणि च भूतानि योऽन्तरो यमयति। वायुर्वै तत्सूत्रं वायुना वै सूत्रेणायं च लोकः परश्च लोकः सर्वाणि च भूतानि।—यः पृथिव्यां तिष्ठन्पृथिव्या अन्तरो यं पृथिवी न वेद यस्य पृथिवी शरीरं यः पृथिवीमन्तरो यमयत्येष त आत्मान्तर्याम्यमृतः। योऽप्सु तिष्ठन्नद्भ्योऽन्तरो यमापो न विदुर्यस्यापः शरीरं योऽपोऽन्तरो यमयत्येष त आत्माऽन्तर्याम्यमृतः।

3, 7, 9 — य आदित्ये तिष्ठन्नादित्यादन्तरो यमादित्यो न वद यस्यादित्यः शरीरं य आदित्यमन्तरो यमयत्येष त आत्माऽन्तर्याम्यमृतः।

3, 7, 23 — अदृष्टो द्रष्टाऽश्रुतः श्रोताऽमतो मन्ताऽविज्ञातो विज्ञाता नान्योऽतोस्ति द्रष्टा, श्रोता, मन्ता विज्ञातैष त आत्मान्तर्याम्यमृतोऽतोऽन्यदार्तम्।

3, 8, 7-11 — कस्मिन्नु खल्वाकाश ओतश्च प्रोतश्चेति। स होवाचैतद्वै तदक्षरं गार्गि ब्राह्मणा अभिवदन्ति अस्थूलं, अनणु, अह्रस्वं, अदीर्घं, अलोहितं, अच्छायं, अतमः, असंगं, अरसं, अगंधं, अचक्षुष्कं, अश्रोत्रं, अवाक्, अमनः, अप्राणं, अमुखं, अनंतरं, अबाह्यं, न तदश्नाति किंचन। एतस्य वा अक्षरस्य प्रशासने गार्गि सूर्याचंद्रमसौ विधृतौ तिष्ठतः, द्यावापृथिव्यौ विधृते तिष्ठतः, प्राच्योऽन्या नद्यः स्यन्दंते श्वेतेभ्यः पर्वतेभ्यः प्रतीच्योऽन्या यां यां दिशमनु। तद्वा एतदक्षरमदृष्टं द्रष्ट्रश्रुतं श्रोतमतं मंत्रविज्ञातं विज्ञातृ। नान्यदतोऽस्ति दृष्टृ, श्रोतृ, मन्तृ, विज्ञातृ।

3, 9, 10 — पृथिव्येव यस्यायतनमग्निर्लोको मनो ज्योतिर्यो वै तं विद्यात्सर्वस्यात्मनः परायणम्।

3, 9, 26 — स एष नेतिनेत्यात्माऽगृह्यो न हि गृह्यतेऽशीर्यो न हि शीर्यतेऽसितो न हि सज्यतेऽसितो न व्यथते न रिष्यति।

3, 9, 28 — विज्ञानमानंदं ब्रह्म रातिर्दातुः परायणं तिष्ठमानस्य तद्विद इति।

4, 2, 4 — अभयं वै जनक प्राप्तोसि।

4, 3, 5-7 — वागेवास्य ज्योतिर्भवति वाचैवायं ज्योतिषास्ते पल्ययते कर्म कुरुते विपल्येति यत्र स्वः पाणिर्न विनिर्ज्ञायतेऽथ यत्र वागुच्चरत्युपैव तत्र न्येति। अस्तमित आदित्ये याज्ञवल्क्य चंद्रमस्यस्तमिते शान्तेऽग्नौ शांतायां वाचि किंज्योतिरेवायं पुरुष इत्यात्मैवास्य ज्योतिर्भवती-

स्यात्मनैवायं ज्योतिषास्ते पल्ययते कर्म कुरुते विपल्यतीति। कतम आत्मेति सोऽयं विज्ञानमयः प्राणेषु हृद्यन्तर्ज्योतिः पुरुषः।

4, 3, 10—न तत्र रथा न रथयोगा न पन्थानो भवन्त्यथ रथारथयोगान्पथः सृजते स हि कर्ता।

4, 3, 15-16—स वा एष एतस्मिन्संप्रसादे रत्वा चरित्वा दृष्ट्वैव पुण्यं च पापं च पुनः प्रतिन्यायं प्रतियोन्याद्रवति स्वप्नायैव, बुद्धान्तायैव स यत्तत्र पश्यत्यन्वागतस्तेन भवत्यसंगो ह्ययं पुरुषः।

4, 3, 21—अयं पुरुषः प्राज्ञेनात्मना संपरिष्वक्तो न बाह्यं किंचन वेद नान्तरं तद्वा अस्यैतदाप्तकाममात्मकाममकामं रूपं शोकान्तरम्।

4, 3, 30—न हि विज्ञातुर्विज्ञातेर्विपरिलोपो विद्यतेऽविनाशित्वान्न तु तद्द्वितीयमस्ति ततोऽन्यद्विभक्तं यद्विजानीयात्।

4, 3, 32—एतस्यैवानन्दस्यान्यानि भूतानि मात्रामुपजीवन्ति।

4, 3, 35—तद्यथाऽनः सुसमाहितमुत्सर्जध्यायादेवमेवायं शारीर आत्मा प्राज्ञेनात्मनाऽन्वारूढ उत्सर्जन्याति यत्रैतदूर्ध्वोच्छ्वासी भवति।

4, 4, 7—यदा सर्वे प्रमुच्यन्ते कामा यस्य हृदि श्रिताः। अथ मर्त्योऽमृतो भवत्यत्र ब्रह्म समश्नुत इति। तद्यथाऽहिनिर्ल्वयनी वल्मीके मृता प्रत्यस्ता शयीतैवमेवेदं शरीरं शेतेऽथायमशरीरोऽमृतः प्राणो ब्रह्मैव तेज एव।

4, 4, 12—आत्मानं चेद्विजानीयादयमस्मीति पूरुषः। किमिच्छन्कस्य कामाय शरीरमनुसंज्वरेत्।

4, 4, 16-18—यस्मादर्वाक्संवत्सरोऽहोभिः परिवर्तते। तद्देवा ज्योतिषां ज्योतिरायुर्होपासतेऽमृतम्॥ यस्मिन्पंच पंचजना आकाशश्च प्रतिष्ठितः। तमेव मन्य आत्मानं विद्वान्ब्रह्मामृतोऽमृतम्॥ प्राणस्य प्राणमुत चक्षुषश्चक्षुरुत श्रोत्रस्य श्रोत्रं मनसो ये मनो विदुः। निश्चिक्युर्ब्रह्म पुराणमग्र्यम्॥

4,4, 21-25—तमेव धीरो विज्ञाय प्रज्ञां कुर्वीत ब्राह्मणः। नानुध्यायाद्बहूञ्छब्दान्वाचो विग्लापनं हि तत्। एष भूताधिपतिरेष भूतपाल एष सेतुर्विधरण एषां लोकानामसंभेदाय॥ एष नित्यो महिमा ब्राह्मणस्य न वर्धते कर्मणा नो कनीयान्॥ स वा एष महानज आत्माऽजरोऽमृतोऽभयो ब्रह्माभयं वै ब्रह्म भवति य एवं वेद॥

4, 5, 13—स यथा सैंधवघनोऽनन्तरोऽबाह्यः कृत्स्नो रसघन एवैवं वा अरेऽयमात्माऽनन्तरोऽबाह्यः कृत्स्नः प्रज्ञानघन एव।

Bṛ. 4, 5, 15—Refer Bṛ. 2, 4, 14.

5, 8-9—वाचं धेनुमुपासीत ॥ अयमग्निर्वैश्वानरो योऽयमन्तःपुरुषे येनेदमन्नं पच्यते यदिदमद्यते तस्यैव घोषो भवति ॥

6, 1, 7—ते हेमे प्राणा अहंश्रेयसे विवदमाना ब्रह्म जग्मुस्तद्धोचुः को नो वसिष्ठ इति तद्धोवाच यस्मिन्वः उत्क्रान्त इदं शरीरं पापीयो मन्यते स वो वसिष्ठ इति।

6, 2, 9—असौ वै लोकोऽग्निर्गौतम तस्यादित्य एव समिद्रश्मयो धूमोऽहरर्चिर्दिशोऽङ्गारा अवान्तरदिशो विस्फुलिङ्गास्तस्मिन्नेतस्मिन्नग्नौ देवाः श्रद्धां जुह्वति।

Chāndogyopaniṣad

1, 6, 6, and 7—य एषोंतरादित्ये हिरण्मयः पुरुषो दृश्यते हिरण्यश्मश्रुर्हिरण्यकेश आप्रणखात् सर्व एव सुवर्णः ॥ तस्य यथा कप्यासं पुण्डरीकमेवमक्षिणी तस्योदिति नाम स एष सर्वेभ्यः पाप्मभ्य उदित उदेति ह वै सर्वेभ्यः पाप्मभ्यो य एवं वेद ॥

1, 7, 5—अथ य एषोऽन्तरक्षिणि पुरुषो दृश्यते सैवर्क्तत्साम तदुक्थं तद्यजुस्तद्ब्रह्म तस्यैतस्य तदेव रूपं यदमुष्य रूपं यावमुष्य गेष्णौ तौ गेष्णौ यन्नाम तन्नाम।

1, 7, 6—तद्य इमे वीणायां गायन्त्येतं ते गायन्ति तस्मात्ते धनसनयः।

1, 9, 1—अस्य लोकस्य का गतिरित्याकाश इति होवाच सर्वाणि ह वा इमानि भूतान्याकाशादेव समुत्पद्यन्त आकाशं प्रत्यस्तं यन्त्याकाशो ह्येवैभ्यो ज्यायानाकाशः परायणम्।

1, 9, 2—स एष परोवरीयानुद्गीथः स एषोऽनन्तः परोवरीयो हास्य भवति परोवरीयसो ह लोकाञ्जयति य एतदेवं विद्वान्परोवरीयांस-मुद्गीथमुपास्ते।

1, 11, 4-5—कतमा सा देवतेति प्राण इति होवाच सर्वाणि ह वा इमानि भूतानि प्राणमेवाभिसंविशन्ति प्राणमभ्युज्जिहते सैषा देवता प्रस्तावमन्वायत्ता।

3, 1—असौ वा आदित्यो देवमधु तस्य द्यौरेव तिरश्चीनवंशो-न्तरिक्षमपूपो मरिचयः पुत्राः।

3, 11, 3—न ह वा अस्मा उदेति न निम्लोचति सकृद्दिवा। हैवास्मै भवति य एतामेवं ब्रह्मोपनिषदं वेद ॥

3, 12, 1 — गायत्री वा इदं सर्वं भूतं यदिदं किंच वाग्वै गायत्री, गायति च त्रायते च ।

3, 12, 5, 9 — सैषा चतुष्पदा षड्विधा गायत्री तदेतदृचाऽभ्यनूक्तम् ॥ तावानस्य महिमा ततो ज्यायांश्च पूरुषः पादोऽस्य सर्वा भूतानि त्रिपादस्यामृतं दिवि ॥ यद्वै तद्ब्रह्मेतीदं वाव वहिर्धा पुरुषादाकाशः, स योऽयमन्तःपुरुष आकाशः स योऽन्तर्हृदय आकाशस्तदेतत्पूर्णमप्रवर्ति पूर्णामप्रवर्तिनीं श्रियं लभते य एवं वेद ॥

3, 13, 6 — ते वा एते पंच ब्रह्मपुरुषाः स्वर्गस्य लोकस्य द्वारपाः ।

3, 13, 7 — अथ यदतः परो दिवो ज्योतिर्दीप्यते विश्वतः पृष्ठेषु सर्वतः पृष्ठेष्वनुत्तमेषु लोकेष्विदं वाव तद्यदिदमस्मिन्नन्तःपुरुषे ज्योतिस्तस्यैषा दृष्टिर्यत्रैतदस्मिञ्छरीरे संस्पर्शेनोष्णिमानं विजानाति तस्यैषा श्रुतिर्यत्रैतत्कर्णावपिगृह्य निनदमिव नदथुरिवाग्नेरिव ज्वलत उपशृणोति तदेतद्दृष्टं च श्रुतं चेत्युपासीत चक्षुष्यः श्रुतो भवति य एवं वेद ।

3, 14, 1 — सर्वं खल्विदं ब्रह्म तज्जलानिति शान्त उपासीत । अथ खलु क्रतुमयः पुरुषो यथाक्रतुरस्मिंल्लोके पुरुषो भवति तथेतः प्रेत्य भवति स क्रतुं कुर्वीत ।

3, 14, 2 — (Cf. 3, 14, 4) मनोमयः प्राणशरीरो भारूपः सत्यसंकल्प आकाशात्मा सर्वकर्मा । सर्वकामः सर्वगन्धः सर्वरसः सर्वमिदमभ्यात्तोऽवाक्यनादरः ॥

3, 14, 3 — एष म आत्माऽन्तर्हृदयेऽणीयान्व्रीहेर्वा यवाद्वा सर्षपाद्वा श्यामाकाद्वा श्यामाकतण्डुलाद्वैष म आत्माऽन्तर्हृदये ज्यायान्पृथिव्या ज्यायानन्तरिक्षाज्ज्यायान्दिवो ज्यायानेभ्यो लोकेभ्यः ।

3, 18, 1 — मनो ब्रह्मेत्युपासीत ।

3, 19, 1 — आदित्यो ब्रह्मेत्यादेशः ।

4, 2, 3 — अह हारेत्वा शूद्र तवैव सह गोभिरस्तु ।

4, 4, 5 — नैतदब्राह्मणो विवक्तुमर्हति समिधं सोम्याहरोप त्वा नेष्ये न सत्यादगाः ।

4,10,5 — स होवाच विजानाम्यहं यत्प्राणो ब्रह्म कं च तु खं च न विजानामीति ते होचुर्यद्वाव कं तदेव खं यदेव खं तदेव कमिति प्राणं च हास्मै तदाकाशं चोचुः ।

4 15, 1–2 — य एषोऽक्षिणि पुरुषो दृश्यत एष आत्मेतिहो वाचैतदमृतमभयमेतद्ब्रह्मेति तद्यद्यप्यस्मिन्सर्पिर्वोदकं वा सिंचति वर्त्मनी एव गच्छति । एतंसंयद्वाम इत्याचक्षत एतं हि सर्वाणि वामान्यभिसंयन्ति ।

4, 15, 5 — अथ यदु चैवास्मिञ्छव्यं कुर्वन्ति यदि च नार्चिषमेवाभिसंभवन्त्यर्चिषोऽहरह्न आपूर्यमाणपक्षमापूर्यमाणपक्षाद्यान्षडुदङ्ङेति मासास्तान्मासेभ्यः संवत्सरं संवत्सरादादित्यमादित्याच्चन्द्रमसं चन्द्रमसो विद्युतं तत्पुरुषोऽमानवः स एनान्ब्रह्म गमयत्येष देवपथो ब्रह्मपथ एतेन प्रतिपद्यमाना इमं मानवमावर्तं नावर्तन्ते नावर्तन्ते ।

5, 2, 8 — यदा कर्मसु काम्येषु स्त्रियं स्वप्नेषु पश्यति । समृद्धिं तत्र जानीयात्तस्मिन्स्वप्ननिदर्शने ॥

5, 18, 1-2 — तान्होवाचैते वै खलु यूयं पृथगिवेममात्मानं वैश्वानरं विद्वांसोऽन्नमत्थ यस्त्वेतमेव प्रादेशमात्रमभिविमानमात्मानं वैश्वानरमुपास्ते स सर्वेषु लोकेषु सर्वेषु भूतेषु सर्वेष्वात्मस्वन्नमत्ति । तस्य ह वा एतस्यात्मनो वैश्वानरस्य मूर्धैव सुतेजाः ।

6, 1, 2-6 — तं पितोवाच श्वेतकेतो यन्नु सोम्येदं महामना अनूचानमानी स्तब्धोऽस्युत तमादेशमप्राक्ष्यः । येनाश्रुतं श्रुतं भवत्यमतं मतमविज्ञातं विज्ञातमिति । कथं नु भगवः स आदेशो भवतीति ॥ यथा सोम्यैकेन मृत्पिण्डेन सर्वं मृण्मयं विज्ञातं स्याद्वाचारंभणं विकारो नामधेयं मृत्तिकेत्येव सत्यम् ॥ यथा सोम्यैकेन लोहमयं विज्ञातं स्याद्वाचारंभणं विकारो नामधेयं लोहमित्येव सत्यम् ॥ यथा सोम्यैकेन नखनिकृन्तनेन सर्वं कार्ष्णायसं विज्ञातं स्याद्वाचारंभणं विकारो नामधेयं कृष्णायसमित्येव सत्यमेव सोम्य स आदेशो भवतीति ॥

6, 2, 1-4 — सदेव सोम्येदमग्र आसीदेकमेवाद्वितीयम् ॥ कुतस्तु खलु सोम्यैवं स्यादिति होवाच कथमसतः सज्जायतेति । सत्त्वेव सोम्येदमग्र आसीत् ॥ तदैक्षत बहु स्यां प्रजायेयेति तदपोऽसृजत । ता आप ऐक्षन्त बह्व्यः स्याम प्रजायेमहीति ता अन्नमसृजन्त ।

6, 3, 2-3 — सेयं देवतैक्षत हन्ताहमिमास्तिस्रो देवता अनेन जीवेनात्मनानुप्रविश्य नामरूपे व्याकरवाणीति । तासां त्रिवृतं त्रिवृतमेकैकां करवाणीति । सेयं देवतेमास्तिस्रो देवता अनेनैव जीवेनात्मनानुप्रविश्य नामरूपे व्याकरोत् ।

6, 4, 1 — यदग्ने रोहितं रूपं तेजसस्तद्रूपं यच्छुक्लं तदपां यत्कृष्णं तदन्नस्य ।

6, 8, 1-2 — यत्रैतत्पुरुषः स्वपिति नाम सता सोम्य तदा संपन्नो भवति स्वमपीतो भवति तस्मादेनं स्वपितीत्याचक्षते । स यथा शकुनिः सूत्रेण प्रबद्धो दिशं दिशं पतित्वान्यत्रायतनमलब्ध्वा बन्धनमेवोपा श्रयत

एवमेव खलु सोम्य तन्मनो दिशं दिशं पतित्वान्यत्रायतनमलब्ध्वा प्राणमेवोपाश्रयते प्राणबंधनमेव सोम्य मन इति ।

6, 8, 4 — सोम्य अन्नेन शुंगेनापो मूलमन्विच्छाद्भिः सोम्य शुंगेन तेजो मूलमन्विच्छ तेजसा सोम्य शुंगेन सन्मूलमन्विच्छ सन्मूलाः सोम्येमाः सर्वाः प्रजाः सदायतनाः सत्प्रतिष्ठाः ।

6, 8, 7 — स य एषोऽणिमैतदात्म्यमिदं सर्वं तत्सत्यं स आत्मा तत्त्वमसि श्वेतकेतो इति ।

6, 9, 2–3 — इमाः सर्वाः प्रजाः सति संपद्य न विदुः सति संपद्यामह इति । त इह व्याघ्रो वा सिंहो वा वृको वा वराहो वा कीटो वा पतंगो वा दंशो वा मशको वा यद्यद्भवन्ति तदाभवन्ति ।

6, 14, 1–2 — यथा सोम्य पुरुषं गंधारेभ्योऽभिनद्धाक्षमानीय तं ततोऽतिजने विसृजेत्स यथा तत्र प्राङ्वोदङ्वाऽधराङ्वा प्रत्यङ्वा प्रध्मायीताभिनद्धाक्ष आनीतोऽभिनद्धाक्षो विसृष्टः । तस्य यथाभिनहनं प्रमुच्य प्रब्रूयादेतां दिशं गन्धारा एतां दिशं व्रजेति स ग्रामाद्ग्रामं पृच्छन्पण्डितो मेधावी गन्धारानेवोपसंपद्येतैवमेवेहाचार्यवान्पुरुषो वेद तस्य तावदेव चिरं यावन्न विमोक्ष्येऽथ संपत्स्य इति ।

6, 16, 2–3 — अथ यदि तस्याकर्ता भवति तत एव सत्यमात्मानं कुरुते स सत्याभिसंधः सत्येनात्मानमन्तर्धाय परशुं तप्तं प्रतिगृह्णाति स न दह्यतेऽथ मुच्यते । एतदात्म्यमिदं सर्वं तत्सत्यं स आत्मा तत्त्वमसि श्वेतकेतो ।

7, 1, 1 — अधीहि भगव इति होपससाद सनत्कुमारं नारदः ।

7, 1, 3 — सोऽहं भगवो मंत्रविदेवास्मि नात्मविच्छ्रुतं ह्येव मे भगवद्दृशेभ्यस्तरति शोकमात्मविदिति सोऽहं भगवः शोचामि तं मा भगवाञ्छोकस्य पारं तारयत्विति ।

7, 15, 1 — यथा वा अरा नाभौ समर्पिता एवमस्मिन्प्राणे सर्वं समर्पितं प्राणः प्राणेन याति प्राणः प्राणं ददाति प्राणाय ददाति प्राणो ह पिता प्राणो माता प्राणो भ्राता प्राणः स्वसा प्राण आचार्यः प्राणो ब्राह्मणः ।

7, 15, 4 — प्राणो ह्येवैतानि सर्वाणि भवति स वा एष एवं पश्यन्नेवं मन्वान एवं विजानन्नतिवादी भवति तं चेद्ब्रूयुरतिवाद्यसीत्यतिवाद्यस्मीति ब्रूयान्नापह्नुवीत ।

7, 16, 1 — एष तु वा अतिवदति यः सत्येनातिवदति ।

7, 23—यो वै भूमा तत्सुखं नाल्पेसुखमस्ति भूमा त्वेव विजिज्ञासितव्यः।

7, 24, 1—यत्र नान्यत्पश्यति नान्यच्छृणोति नान्यद्विजानाति स भूमाथ यत्रान्यत्पश्यत्यन्यच्छृणोत्यन्यद्विजानाति तदल्पं यो वै भूमा तदमृतमथ यदल्पं तन्मर्त्यं स भगवः कस्मिन्प्रतिष्ठित इति स्वे महिम्नि यदि वा न महिम्नीति।

7, 26, 2—स एकधा भवति त्रिधा भवति पंचधा सप्तधा नवधा चैव पुनश्चैकादशः स्मृतः शतं च दश चैकश्च सहस्राणि च विंशतिः। आहारशुद्धौ सत्वशुद्धिः सत्वशुद्धौ ध्रुवा स्मृतिः स्मृतिलम्भे सर्वग्रन्थीनां विप्रमोक्षस्तस्मै मृदितकषायाय तमसस्पारं दर्शयति भगवान्सनत्कुमारः।

8, 1, 1-6—अथ यदिदमस्मिन्ब्रह्मपुरे दहरं पुण्डरीकं वेश्म दहरोऽस्मिन्नन्तराकाशस्तस्मिन्यदन्तस्तदन्वेष्टव्यं तद्वाव विजिज्ञासितव्यम्। तं चेद्ब्रूयुः किं तदत्र विद्यते यदन्वेष्टव्यं। स ब्रूयात् यावान्वा अयमाकाशस्तावानेषोऽन्तर्हृदय आकाश उभे अस्मिन्द्यावापृथिवी अन्तरेव समाहिते उभावग्निश्च वायुश्च सूर्याचन्द्रमसावुभौ विद्युन्नक्षत्राणि यच्चास्येहास्ति यच्च नास्ति सर्वं तदस्मिन्समाहितमस्ति। तं चेद्ब्रूयुर्यदैतज्जरा वाप्नोति प्रध्वंसते वा किं ततोऽतिशिष्यत इति इति। स ब्रूयान्नास्य जरयैतज्जीर्यति न वधेनास्य हन्यत एतत्सत्यं ब्रह्मपुरमस्मिन्कामाः समाहिता एष आत्माऽपहतपाप्मा विजरो विमृत्युर्विशोको विजिघत्सोऽपिपासः सत्यकामः सत्यसंकल्पो यथा ह्येवेह प्रजा अन्वाविशन्ति यथानुशासनं यं यमन्तमभिकामा भवन्ति यं जनपदं यं क्षेत्रभागं तं तमेवोपजीवन्ति। तद्यथेह कर्मजितो लोकः क्षीयत एवामेवामुत्र पुण्यजितो लोकः क्षीयते तद्य इहात्मानमननुविद्य व्रजन्त्येतांश्च सत्यान्कामांस्तेषां सर्वेषु लोकेष्वकामचारो भवत्यथ य इहात्मानमनुविद्य व्रजन्त्येतांश्च सत्यान्कामांस्तेषां सर्वेषु लोकेषु कामचारो भवति।

8, 3, 2—अथ ये चास्येह जीवा ये च प्रेता यच्चान्यदिच्छन्न लभते सर्वं तदत्र गत्वा विन्दतेऽत्र ह्यस्यैते सत्याः कामा अनृतापिधानास्तद्यथाऽपि हिरण्यनिधिं निहितमक्षेत्रज्ञा उपर्युपरि संचरन्तो न विन्देयुरेवमेवेमाः सर्वाः प्रजा अहरहर्गच्छन्त्य एतं ब्रह्मलोकं न विन्दन्त्यनृतेन प्रत्यूढाः।

8, 3, 4—अथ य एष संप्रसादोऽस्माच्छरीरात्समुत्थाय परं ज्योतिरुपसंपद्य स्वेन रूपेणाभिनिष्पद्यत एष आत्मेति होवाचैतदमृतमभयमेतद्ब्रह्मेति तस्य ह वा एतस्य ब्रह्मणो नाम सत्यमिति।

8, 4, 1—(Cf Br. 4, 4, 22)–अथ य आत्मा स सेतुर्विधृतिरेषां लोकानामसंभेदाय नैतं सेतुमहोरात्रे तरतो न जरा न मृत्युर्न शोको न सुकृतं न दुष्कृतं सर्वे पाप्मानोऽतो निवर्तन्तेऽपहतपाप्मा ह्येष ब्रह्मलोकः।

8, 7, 1—य आत्माऽपहतपाप्मा विजरो विमृत्युर्विशोको विजिघत्सोऽपिपासः सत्यकामः सत्यसंकल्पः सोऽन्वेष्टव्यः स विजिज्ञासितव्यः।

8, 12, 1—मघवन्मर्त्यं वा इदं शरीरमात्तं मृत्युना तदस्यामृतस्याशरीरस्यात्मनोऽधिष्ठानमात्तो वै सशरीरः प्रियाप्रियाभ्यां न ह वै सशरीरस्य सतः प्रियाप्रिययोरपहतिरस्त्यशरीरं वाव सन्तं न प्रियाप्रिये स्पृशतः।

8, 12, 3—एष संप्रसादोऽस्माच्छरीरात्समुत्थाय परं ज्योतिरुपसंपद्य स्वेन रूपेणाभिनिष्पद्यते स उत्तमः पुरुष स तत्र पर्येति जक्षत्क्रीडन्रममाणः स्त्रीभिर्वा यानैर्वा ज्ञातिभिर्वा नोपजनं स्मरन्निदं शरीरं सः।

8, 14, 1—आकाशो वै नाम नामरूपयोर्निर्वहिता ते यदन्तरा तद्ब्रह्म तदमृतं स आत्मा।

Gauḍapādakārikā

1, 16—अनादिमायया सुप्तो यदा जीवः प्रबुध्यते। अजमनिद्रमस्वप्नमद्वैतं बुध्यते तदा॥

3, 15—मृल्लोहविस्फुलिंगाद्यैः सृष्टिर्या चोदिताऽन्यथा। उपायः सोऽवितारा़य नास्ति भेदः कथंचन॥

Iśāvāsyopaniṣad

7–8—यस्मिन्सर्वाणि भूतान्यात्मैवाभूद्विजानतः। तत्र को मोहः कः शोक एकत्वमनुपश्यतः॥ स पर्यगाच्छुक्रमकायमव्रणमस्नाविरँ शुद्धमपापविद्धम्। कविर्मनीषी परिभूः स्वयम्भूर्याथातथ्यतोऽर्थान्व्यदधाच्छाश्वतीभ्यः समाभ्यः।

Jābālopaniṣad

1—अथ हैनमत्रिः पप्रच्छ याज्ञवल्क्यं य एषोऽनन्तोऽव्यक्त आत्मा तं कथमहं विजानीयामिति। स होवाच याज्ञवल्क्यः सोऽविमुक्त उपास्यो य एषोऽनन्तोऽव्यक्त आत्मा सोऽविमुक्ते प्रतिष्ठित इति। सोऽविमुक्तः कस्मिन्प्रतिष्ठित इति। वरणायां नास्यां च मध्ये प्रतिष्ठित इति। सर्वानिन्द्रियकृतान्दोषान्वारयतीति तेन वरणा भवति। सर्वानिन्द्रियकृतान्पापान्नाशयतीति तेन नासी भवति। कतमं चास्य स्थानं भवतीति। भ्रुवोर्घ्राणस्य च यः संधिः स एष द्यौर्लोकस्य परस्य च संधिर्भवतीति। एतद्वै संधिं संध्यां ब्रह्मविद उपासत इति॥

4—अथ परिव्राड्विवर्णवासा मुण्डोऽपरिग्रहः शुचिरद्रोही भैक्षणो ब्रह्मभूयाय भवति।

Jaimini Sūtra (Pūrva-Mīmāmsā).

1, 1, 1-2 (Śābara-bhāṣya) दृष्टो हि तस्यार्थः कर्मावबोधनम्। चोदनेति क्रियायाः प्रवर्तकं वचनम्।

1, 2, 1—आम्नायस्य क्रियार्थत्वादानर्थक्यमतदर्थानाम्।

1, 2, 7—विधिना त्वेकवाक्यत्वात्स्तुत्यर्थेन विधीनां स्युः।

1, 3, 3—विरोधे त्वनपेक्षं स्यादसति ह्यनुमानम्।

6, 1—वसन्ते ब्राह्मणोऽग्नीनादधीत ग्रीष्मे राजन्यः शरदि वैश्यः।

Kaṭhopaniṣad:

1, 1, 13—स त्वमग्निं स्वर्ग्यमध्येषि मृत्यो प्रब्रूहि त्वं श्रद्दधानाय मह्यम्। एतद्द्वितीयेन वृणे वरेण।

1, 1, 20—येयं प्रेते विचिकित्सा मनुष्येऽस्तीत्येके नायमस्तीति चैके। एतद्विद्यामनुशिष्टस्त्वयाहं वराणामेष वरस्तृतीयः॥

1, 2, 4—दूरमेते विपरीते विषूची अविद्या या च विद्येति ज्ञाता। विद्याभीप्सिनं नचिकेतसं मन्ये न त्वा कामा बहवोऽलोलुपन्त।

1, 2, 9—नैषा तर्केण मतिरापनेया प्रोक्ताऽन्येनैव सुज्ञानाय प्रेष्ठ।

1, 2, 12—तं दुर्दर्शं गूढमनुप्रविष्टं गुहाहितं गह्वरेष्ठं पुराणम्। अध्यात्मयोगाधिगमेन देवं मत्वा धीरो हर्षशोकौ जहाति॥

1, 2, 14—अन्यत्र धर्मादन्यत्राधर्मादन्यत्रास्मात्कृताकृतात्। अन्यत्र भूताच्च भव्याच्च यत्तत्पश्यसि तद्वद॥

1, 2, 18—न जायते म्रियते वा विपश्चिन्नायं कुतश्चिन्न बभूव कश्चित्। अजो नित्यः शाश्वतोऽयं पुराणो न हन्यते हन्यमाने शरीरे॥

1, 2, 22—अशरीरं शरीरेष्वनवस्थेष्ववस्थितम्।

1, 2, 25—यस्य ब्रह्म च क्षत्रं च उभे भवत ओदनः। मृत्युर्यस्योपसेचनं क इत्था वेद यत्र सः॥

1, 3, 1—ऋतं पिबन्तौ सुकृतस्य लोके गुहां प्रविष्टौ परमे परार्ध्ये। छायातपौ ब्रह्मविदो वदन्ति पंचाग्नयो ये च त्रिणाचिकेताः॥

1, 3, 3-4—आत्मानं रथिनं विद्धि शरीरं रथमेव तु। बुद्धिं तु सारथिं विद्धि मनः प्रग्रहमेव च॥ इंद्रियाणि हयानाहुर्विषयांस्तेषु गोचरान्। आत्मेन्द्रियमनोयुक्तं भोक्तेत्याहुर्मनीषिणः॥

1, 3, 9-12—विज्ञानसारथिर्यस्तु मनःप्रग्रहवान्नरः। सोऽध्वनः पारमाप्नोति तद्विष्णोः परमं पदम्॥

इंद्रियेभ्यः परा ह्यर्था अर्थेभ्यश्च परं मनः। मनसस्तु परा बुद्धिर्बुद्धेरात्म महान्परः॥

महतः परमव्यक्तमव्यक्तात्पुरुषः परः। पुरुषान्न परं किंचित्सा काष्ठा सा परा गतिः॥

एष सर्वेषु भूतेषु गूढोऽऽत्मा न प्रकाशते। दृश्यते त्वग्र्यया बुद्ध्या सूक्ष्मया सूक्ष्मदर्शिभिः॥

1,3,15—अशब्दमस्पर्शमरूपमव्ययं तथाऽरसं नित्यमगन्धवच्च यत्। अनाद्यनन्तं महतः परं ध्रुवं विचाय्य तन्मृत्युमुखात्प्रमुच्यते॥

(Ncte. The Vallis of chapter second of the Kaṭha are sometimes counted as 1, 2, 3 etc. or as 4, 5, 6 etc. beca´use they are subsequent to three vallis of the first chapter. So, 2, 1, 10 =2, 4, 10).

2, 4, 4—स्वप्नान्तं जागरितान्तं चोभौ येनानुपश्यति। महान्तं विभुमात्मानं मत्वा धीरो न शोचति॥

2, 4, 10—यदेवेह तदमुत्र यदमुत्र तदन्विह। मृत्योः स मृत्युमाप्नोति य इह नानेव पश्यति॥

2, 4, 12-13—अङ्गुष्ठमात्रः पुरुषो मध्य आत्मनि तिष्ठति। ईशानो भूतभव्यस्य न ततो विजुगुप्सते॥ अङ्गुष्ठमात्रः पुरुषो ज्योतिरिवाधूमकः।

2, 5, 5—न प्राणेन नापानेन मर्त्यो जीवति कश्चन। इतरेण तु जीवन्ति यस्मिन्नेतावुपाश्रितौ॥

2, 5, 15—न तत्र सूर्यो भाति न चंद्रतारकं नेमा विद्युतो भान्ति कुतोऽयमग्निः। तमेव भान्तनुभाति सर्वमिदं विभाति॥

2, 6, 2—यदिदं किंच जगत्सर्वं प्राण एजति निःसृतम्। महद्भयं वज्रमुद्यतं य एतद्विदुरमृतास्ते भवन्ति॥

2, 6, 3 (Cf. Tai. 2, 8, 1)—भयादस्याग्निस्तपति भयात्तपति सूर्यः। भयादिन्द्रश्च वायुश्च मृत्युर्धावति पंचमः॥

2, 6, 11—तां योगमिति मन्यन्ते स्थिरामिन्द्रियधारणाम्।

2, 6, 17—अंगुष्ठमात्रः पुरुषोऽन्तरात्मा सदा जनानां हृदये संनिविष्टः। तं स्वाच्छरीरात्प्रवृहेन्मुंजादिवेषिकां धैर्येण। तं विद्याच्छुक्रममृतम्॥

2, 6, 18 — मृत्युप्रोक्तां नाचिकेतोऽथ लब्ध्वा विद्यामेतां योगविधिं च कृत्स्नम् । ब्रह्मप्राप्तो विरजोऽभूद्विमृत्युरन्योऽप्येवं यो विद्ध्यात्ममेव ॥

Kauṣītak – Brāhmana – Upaniṣad:

2, 14 — ता वा एताः सर्वाः देवताः प्राणे निश्रेयसं विदित्वा प्राणमेव प्राज्ञात्मानमभिसंभूयास्माच्छरीरादुच्चक्रमुः ।

3, 1–3 — सत्यं हीन्द्रः होवाच यो मां विजानीयान्नास्य केन च कर्मणा लोको मीयते न मातृवधेन न पितृवधेन न स्तेयेन न भ्रूणहत्यया नास्य पापंचन चक्रुषः मुखान्नीलं वेति ॥ स होवाच प्राणोस्मि प्रज्ञात्मा तं मामायुरमृतमित्युपास्वायुः प्राणः प्राणो वा आयुः प्राण एवामृतम् । यत्रैतत्पुरुषः सुप्तः स्वप्नं न कंचन पश्यत्यथास्मिन्प्राण एवैकधा भवति तदैनं वाक्सर्वैर्नामभिः सहाप्येति चक्षुः सर्वैं रूपैः सहाप्येति श्रोत्रं सर्वैः शब्दैः सहाप्येति मनः सर्वैः ध्यानैः सहाप्येति स यदा प्रतिबुध्यते यथाग्नेर्ज्वलतः सर्वा दिशो विस्फुलिङ्गा विप्रतिष्ठेरन्नेवमेवैतस्मादात्मनः प्राणाः यथायतनं विप्रतिष्ठन्ते प्राणेभ्यो देवा देवेभ्यो लोकाः ॥

3, 8 — यथा रथस्यारेषु नेमिरर्पिता नाभावरा अर्पिता एवमेवैता भूतमात्राः प्रज्ञामात्रास्वर्पिताः प्रज्ञामात्राः प्राणेऽर्पिताः ॥ स एष प्राण एव प्रज्ञात्मानन्दोऽजरोऽमृतो न साधुना कर्मणा भूयान्नो एवासाधुना कर्मणा कनीयानेष ह्येवैनं साधु कर्म कारयति तं यमेभ्यो लोकेभ्य उन्निनीषत एष उ एवैनमसाधु कर्म कारयति तं यमधो निनीषते एष लोकपाल एष लोकाधिपतिरेष सर्वेशः स म आत्मेति विद्यात् ॥

4, 19–20 — यो वै बालाक एतेषां पुरुषाणां कर्ता यस्य वैतत्कर्म स वै वेदितव्यः ॥ तद्यथा श्रेष्ठी स्वैर्भुंक्ते यथा वा स्वाः श्रेष्ठिनं भुंजन्त्येवमेवैष प्रज्ञात्मैरात्मभिर्भुंक्ते एवमेवैत आत्मानः एतमात्मानं भुंजन्ति ॥

Kenopaniṣad:

1, 3–5 — अन्यदेव तद्विदितादथो अविदितादधि ॥ यद्वाचानभ्युदितं येन वागभ्युद्यते । यन्मनसा न मनुते येनाहुर्मनो मतम् । तदेव ब्रह्म त्वं विद्धि नेदं यदिदमुपासते ॥

2, 3 — यस्यामतं तस्य मतं मतं यस्य न वेद सः । अविज्ञातं विजानतां विज्ञातमविजानताम् ॥

Mahābhārata (Śāntiparva)

47, 68 — यस्याग्निरास्यं द्यौर्मूर्धा खं नाभि चरणौ क्षितिः । सूर्यश्चक्षुर्दिशः श्रोत्रं तस्मै लोकात्मने नमः ॥

233, 24–25 — अनादिनिधना नित्या वागुत्सृष्टा स्वयंभुवा। आदौ वेदमयी दिव्या यतः सर्वाः प्रवृत्तयः॥ नाम रूपं च भूतानां कर्मणां च प्रवर्तनम्। वेदशब्देभ्य एवादौ निर्ममे स महेश्वरः॥

303, 115 — अतश्च संक्षेपमिमं शृणुध्वं नारायणः सर्वमिदं पुराणः। स सर्गकाले च करोति सर्वं संहारकाले च तदत्ति भूयः॥

336, 28–30 — यत्तत्सूक्ष्ममविज्ञेयम्॥ स ह्यंतरात्मा भूतानां क्षेत्रज्ञश्चेति कथ्यते॥ तस्मादव्यक्तमुत्पन्नं त्रिगुणं द्विजसत्तम॥

बहवः पुरुषा राजन्सांख्ययोगविचारिणाम्॥ बहूनां पुरुषाणां हि यथैका योनिरुच्यते। तथा तं पुरुषं विश्वमाख्यास्यामि गुणाधिकं॥ ममान्तरात्मा तव च चान्ये देहसंस्थिताः। सर्वेषां साक्षीभूतोऽसौ न ग्राह्यः केनचित्क्वचित्॥ विश्वमूर्धा विश्वभुजो विश्वपादाक्षिनासिकः। एकश्चरति भूतेषु स्वैरचारी यथासुखम्॥

Vana parva, 3, 297, 17 — अथ सत्यवतः कायात्पाशबद्धं वशं गतं। अंगुष्ठमात्रं पुरुषं निश्चकर्ष यमो बलात्॥

Manu Smṛti :

1, 2—सर्वेषां तु नामानि कर्माणि च पृथक्पृथक्। वेदशब्देभ्यः एवादौ पृथक्संस्थाश्च निर्ममे॥

10, 4—शूद्रश्चतुर्थो वर्ण एकजातिः।

10, 126—न शूद्रे पातकं किंचिन्न च संस्कारमर्हति।

12, 91—सर्वभूतेषु चात्मानं सर्वभूतानि चात्मनि। संपश्यन्नात्मयाजी वै स्वाराज्यमधिगच्छति॥

12, 105–126—प्रत्यक्षमनुमानं च शास्त्रं च विविधागमं। त्रयं सुविदितं कार्यं धर्मशुद्धिमभीप्सता॥ आर्षं धर्मोपदेशं च वेदशास्त्राविरोधिना। यस्तर्केणानुसंधत्ते स धर्मं वेद नेतरः॥

Muṇḍakopaniṣad :

1, 1, 1—स ब्रह्मविद्यां सर्वविद्याप्रतिष्ठामथर्वाय ज्येष्ठपुत्राय प्राह।

1, 1, 3—कस्मिन्नु भगवो विज्ञाते सर्वमिदं विज्ञातं भवति।

1, 1, 5, 6—तत्रापरा ऋग्वेदो यजुर्वेदः सामवेदोऽथर्ववेदः शिक्षा कल्पो व्याकरणं निरुक्तं छन्दो ज्योतिषमिति। अथ परा यया तदक्षरमधिगम्यते॥ यत्तदद्रेश्यमग्राह्यमगोत्रमवर्णमचक्षुःश्रोत्रं तदपाणिपादम्। नित्यं विभुं सर्वगतं सुसूक्ष्मं तदव्ययं यद्भूतयोनिं परिपश्यन्ति धीराः॥

1, 1, 7—यथोर्णनाभिः सृजते गृह्णते च यथा पृथिव्यामोषधयः संभवन्ति। यथा सतः पुरुषात्केशलोमानि तथाऽक्षरात्संभवतीह विश्वम्॥

1, 1, 9—यः सर्वज्ञः सर्वविद्यस्य ज्ञानमयं तपः । तस्मादेतद्ब्रह्म नाम रूपमन्नं च जायते ॥

1, 2, 7—प्लवा ह्येते अदृढा यज्ञरूपा अष्टादशोक्तमवरं येषु कर्म। एतच्छ्रेयो येऽभिनन्दन्ति मूढा जरामृत्युं ते पुनरेवापि यन्ति ॥

1, 2, 12—परीक्ष्य लोकान्कर्मचितान्ब्राह्मणो निर्वेदमायान्नास्त्यकृतः कृतेन । तद्विज्ञानार्थं स गुरुमेवाभिगच्छेत्समित्पाणिः श्रोत्रियं ब्रह्मनिष्ठम् ॥

1, 2, 13—तस्मै स विद्वानुपसन्नाय सम्यक्प्रशान्तचित्ताय शमान्विताय । येनाक्षरं पुरुषं वेद सत्यं प्रोवाच तां तत्वतो ब्रह्मविद्याम् ॥

2, 1, 2-10—दिव्यो ह्यमूर्तः पुरुषः सबाह्याभ्यन्तरो ह्यजः। अप्राणो ह्यमनाः शुभ्रो ह्यक्षरात्परतः परः ॥ एतस्माज्जायते प्राणो मनः सर्वेन्द्रियाणि च। खं वायुर्ज्योतिरापः पृथिवी विश्वस्य धारिणी॥ अग्निर्मूर्धा चक्षुषी चन्द्रसूर्यौ दिशः श्रोत्रे वाग्विवृताश्च वेदाः। वायुः प्राणो हृदयं विश्वमस्य पद्भ्यां पृथिवी ह्येष सर्व भूतान्तरात्मा ॥ तस्मादग्निः समिधो.... तस्मादृचः साम यजूंषि दीक्षा यज्ञश्च सर्वे..देवा बहुधा..मनुष्याः पशवः.. सप्त प्राणाः..समुद्रा गिरयश्च..॥ पुरुष एवेदं विश्वं कर्म तपो ब्रह्म परामृतम्। एतद्यो वेद निहितं गुहायां सोऽविद्याग्रन्थिं विकिरतीह सोम्य ॥

2, 2, 5—यस्मिन्द्यौः पृथिवी चान्तरिक्षमोत मनः सह प्राणैश्च सर्वैः। तमेवैकं जानथ आत्मानमन्या वाचो विमुंचथामृतस्यैष सेतुः ॥

2, 2, 8—भिद्यते हृदयग्रन्थिश्छिद्यन्ते सर्वसंशयाः । क्षीयन्ते चास्य कर्माणि तस्मिन्दृष्टे परावरे ॥ Cf B. G. 4, 37—ज्ञानाग्निः सर्वकर्माणि भस्मसात्कुरुतेऽर्जुन।

2, 2, 9—हिरण्मये परे कोशे विरजं ब्रह्म निष्कलम् । तच्छुभ्रं ज्योतिषां ज्योतिस्तद्यदात्मविदो विदुः॥

2, 2, 10-11—(Cf. Ka. 2, 5, 15)—न तत्र सूर्यो भाति न चन्द्रतारकं नेमा विद्युतो भान्ति कुतोऽयमग्निः। तमेव भान्तमनुभाति सर्वं तस्य भासा सर्वमिदं विभाति ॥ ब्रह्मैवेदममृतं पुरस्ताद्ब्रह्म पश्चाद् ब्रह्म दक्षिणतश्चोत्तरेण । अधश्चोर्ध्वं च प्रसृतं ब्रह्मैवेदं विश्वमिदं वरिष्ठम् ॥

3, 1, 1-3—द्वा सुपर्णा सयुजा सखाया समानं वृक्षं परिषस्वजाते। तयोरन्यः पिप्पलं स्वाद्वत्त्यनश्नन्नन्यो अभिचाकशीति ॥

समाने वृक्षे पुरुषो निमग्नोऽनीशया शोचति मुह्यमानः। जुष्टं यदा पश्यत्यन्यमीशमस्य महिमानमिति वीतशोकः ॥

यदा पश्यः पश्यते रुक्मवर्णं कर्तारमीशं पुरुषं ब्रह्मयोनिम्। तदा विद्वान्पुण्यपापे विधूय निरंजनः परमं साम्यमुपैति ॥

3, 3, 6 — वेदान्तविज्ञानसुनिश्चितार्थाः संन्यासयोगाद्यतयः शुद्धसत्त्वाः। ते ब्रह्मलोकेषु परान्तकाले परामृताः परिमुच्यन्ति सर्वे ॥

3, 2, 8 — यथा नद्यः स्यन्दमानाः समुद्रेऽस्तं गच्छन्ति नामरूपे विहाय। तथा विद्वान्नामरूपाद्विमुक्तः परात्परं पुरुषमुपैति दिव्यम् ॥

3, 2, 9 — स यो ह वै तत्परमं ब्रह्म वेद ब्रह्मैव भवति नास्याब्रह्मवित्कुले भवति। तरति शोकं तरति पाप्मानं गुहाग्रन्थिभ्यो विमुक्तोऽमृतो भवति ॥

Nyāya-sūtra

1, 1, 2 — दुःखजन्मप्रवृत्तिदोषमिथ्याज्ञानानामुत्तरोत्तरापाये तदनंतरापायादपवर्गः।

1, 1, 18 — प्रवर्तनालक्षणा दोषाः।

Pras'nopanisad

1, 1 — ते हैते ब्रह्मपरा ब्रह्मनिष्ठाः परं ब्रह्मान्वेषमाणा एष ह वै तत्सर्वं वक्ष्यतीति ते ह समित्पाणयो भगवन्तं पिप्पलादमुपसन्नाः।

1, 10—अथोत्तरेण तपसा ब्रह्मचर्येण श्रद्धया विद्ययात्मानमन्विष्यादित्यमभिजयन्ते। एतद्वै प्राणानामायतनमेतदमृतमभयमेतत्परायणमेतस्मान्न पुनरावर्तन्ते।

2, 3—तान्वरिष्ठः प्राण उवाच। मा मोहमापद्यथाहमेवैतत्पंचधात्मानं प्रविभज्यैतद्बाणमवष्टभ्य विधारयामि।

3, 3—आत्मन एष प्राणो जायते।

4, 2, 3—यथा गार्ग्य मरीचयोऽर्कस्यास्तं गच्छतः सर्वा एतस्मिंस्तेजोमण्डल एकीभवन्ति। ताः पुनः पुनरुदयतः प्रचरन्त्येवं ह वै तत्सर्वं परे देवे मनस्येकीभवति। तेन तर्ह्येष पुरुषो न शृणोति न पश्यति न जिघ्रति न स्पृशते नाभिवदते नादत्ते नानन्दयते न विसृजते नेयायते स्वपितीत्याचक्षते। प्राणाग्नय एवैतस्मिन्पुरे जाग्रति ॥

4, 6—अत्रैष देवः स्वप्नान्न पश्यत्यथ तदैतस्मिञ्शरीर एतत्सुखं भवति।

5, 2—एतद्वै सत्यकाम परं चापरं च ब्रह्म यदोंकारः। तस्माद्विद्वानेतेनैवायतनेनैकतरमन्वेति ॥

5, 5—यः पुनरेतं त्रिमात्रेणोमित्येतेनैवाक्षरेण परं पुरुषमभिध्यायीत स तेजसि सूर्ये संपन्नः। यथा पादोदरस्त्वचा विनिर्मुच्यत एवं ह वै स पाप्मना

विनिर्मुक्तः स सामभिरुन्नीयते ब्रह्मलोकं स एतस्माज्जीवघनात्परात्परं पुरिशयं पुरुषमीक्षते ॥

5, 7—ऋग्भिरेतं यजुर्भिरन्तारिक्षं सामभिर्यत्क.वयो वेदयन्ते । तमोंकारेणैवायतनेनान्वेति विद्वान्यत्तच्छान्तमजरममृतमभयं परं चेति ॥

6, 2, 4—इहैवान्तःशरीरे सोम्य स पुरुषो यस्मिन्नेताः षोडश कलाः प्रभवन्ति । स ईक्षांचक्रे स प्राणमसृजत ॥

6 8—ते तमर्चयन्तस्त्वं हि नः पिता योऽस्माकमविद्यायाः परं पारं तारयसीति ।

Ṛgveda-Saṁhitā:

1, 98, 1—वैश्वानरस्य सुमतौ स्याम राजा हि कं भुवनानामभिश्रीः ।

1, 104, 1—योनिष्ट इन्द्र निषदे अकारि ।

1, 164, 39—ऋचो अक्षरे परमे व्योमन्यस्मिन्देवा अधि विश्वे निषेदुः ।

8, 53, 7—यत्पांचजन्यया विशा ।

9, 46, 4—गोभिः श्रीणीत मत्सरम् ।

10, 71, 3—यज्ञेन वाचः पदवीयमायन्तामन्वविंदन्नृषिषु प्रविष्टाम ।

10, 88, 3—यो भानुना पृथिवीं द्यामुतेमामाततान रोदसी अंतरिक्षम् ।

10, 88, 12—विश्वस्मा अग्निं भुवनाय देवा वैश्वानरं केतुमह्नामकृण्वन् ।

10, 90—पादोऽस्य सर्वा भूतानि त्रिपादस्यामृतं दिवि ।

10, 121, 1—हिरण्यगर्भः समवर्तताग्रे भूतस्य जातः पतिरेक आसीत् । स दाधार पृथिवीं द्यामुतेमां कस्मै देवाय हविषा विधेम ॥

10, 129, 6—कोऽद्धा वेद क इह प्रवोचत् । इयं विसृष्टिर्यत आबभूव ।

10, 190, 3—सूर्याचंद्रमसौ धाता यथापूर्वमकल्पयत् । दिवं च पृथिवीं चान्तरिक्षमथो स्वः ॥

Sāmkhya-Kārikā:

3—मूलप्रकृतिरविकृतिर्महदाद्याः प्रकृतिविकृतयः सप्त । षोडशकश्च विकारो न प्रकृतिर्न विकृतिः पुरुषः ॥

Śatapatha Brāhmana:

6, 1, 3, 2, 4—मृदब्रवीत् । आपोऽब्रुवन् ।

10, 3, 3, 6 — यदा वै पुरुषः स्वपिति प्राणं तर्हि वागप्येति प्राणं चक्षुः प्राणं श्रोत्रं प्राणं मनः। स यदा प्रबुध्यते प्राणादेवाधि पुनर्जायन्ते ॥

10, 6, 1, 11 — स एषोऽग्निर्वैश्वानरः।

10, 6, 3, 2 — यथा व्रीहिर्वा यवो वा श्यामाको वा श्यामाकतंडुलो वैवमयमंतरात्मन्पुरूषो हिरण्मयः।

Śvetāśvataropaniṣad:

1, 1 and 3 — ब्रह्मवादिनो वदन्ति। किं कारणं ब्रह्म कुतः स्म जाता जीवाम केन क्व च संप्रतिष्ठा ॥ ते ध्यानयोगानुगता अपश्यन्देवात्मशक्तिं स्वगुणैर्निगूढाम्। यः कारणानि निखिलानि तानि कालात्मयुक्तान्यधितिष्ठत्येकः ॥

2, 8 — त्रिरुन्नतं स्थाप्य समं शरीरं हृदीन्द्रियाणि मनसा संनिवेश्य। ब्रह्मोडुपेन प्रतरेत विद्वान्स्रोतांसि सर्वाणि भयावहानि ॥ Cf. B. G. 6–13.

2, 12 — पृथ्व्यप्तेजोऽनिलखे समुत्थिते पंचात्मके योगगुणे प्रवृत्ते। न तस्य रोगो न जरा न मृत्युः प्राप्तस्य योगाग्निमयं शरीरम् ॥

3, 8 — वेदाहमेतं पुरुषं महान्तमादित्यवर्णं तमसः परस्तात्। तमेव विदित्वातिमृत्युमेति नान्यः पन्था विद्यतेऽयनाय ॥

3, 19 — अपाणिपादो जवनो ग्रहीता पश्यत्यचक्षुः स शृणोत्यकर्णः। स वेत्ति वेद्यं न च तस्यास्ति वेत्ता तमाहुरग्र्यं पुरुषं महान्तम् ॥

4, 3 — त्वं स्त्री त्वं पुमानसि त्वं कुमार उत वा कुमारी। त्वं जीर्णो दण्डेन वंचसि त्वं जातो भवसि विश्वतोमुखः ॥

4, 5 — अजामेकां लोहितशुक्लकृष्णां बह्वीः प्रजां सृजमानां सरूपाः। अजो ह्येको जुषमाणोऽनुशेते जहात्येनां भुक्तभोगामजोन्यः ॥

4, 10–11 — मायां तु प्रकृतिं विद्यान्मायिनं तु महेश्वरम्। तस्यावयवभूतैस्तु व्याप्तं सर्वमिदं जगत् ॥ यो योनिं योनिमधितिष्ठत्येको यस्मिन्निदं सं च वि चैति सर्वम्। तमीशानं वरदं देवमीड्यं निचाय्येमां शांतिमत्यन्तमेति ॥

5, 2 — यो योनिं योनिमधितिष्ठत्येको विश्वाणि रूपाणि योनीश्च सर्वाः। ऋषिं प्रसूतं कपिलं यस्तमग्रे ज्ञानैर्बिभर्ति ज्यायमानं च पश्येत् ॥

5, 8 — अंगुष्ठमात्रो रवितुल्यरूपः संकल्पाहंकारसमन्वितो यः। बुद्धेर्गुणेनात्मगुणेन चैव आराग्रमात्रो ह्यपरोऽपि दृष्टः ॥

6, 8–9 — न तस्य कार्यं करणं च विद्यते न तत्समश्चाभ्यधिकश्च दृश्यते। परास्य शक्तिर्विविधैव श्रूयते स्वाभाविकी ज्ञानबलक्रिया च॥ स कारणं करणाधिपाधिपो न चास्य कश्चिज्जनिता न चाधिपः॥

6, 11–13 — एको देवः सर्वभूतेषु गूढः सर्वव्यापी सर्वभूतान्तरात्मा। कर्माध्यक्षः सर्वभूताधिवासः साक्षी चेताः केवलो निर्गुणश्च॥ प्रहिणोति तस्मै। तं ह देवमात्मबुद्धिप्रकाशं मुमुक्षुर्वै शरणमहं प्रपद्ये॥

6, 15 — Refer 6, 8.

6, 18 — यो ब्रह्माणं विदधाति पूर्वं यो वै वेदांश्च प्रहिणोति तस्मै।

— एको वशी निष्क्रियाणां बहूनामेकं बीजं बहुधा यः करोति। तमात्मस्थं येऽनुपश्यन्ति धीरास्तेषां सुखं शाश्वतं नेतरेषाम्॥ नित्यो नित्यानां चेतनश्चेतनानामेको बहूनां यो विदधाति कामान्। तत्कारणं सांख्ययोगाधिगम्यं ज्ञात्वा देवं मुच्यते सर्वपाशैः।

6, 19 — निष्कलं निष्क्रियं शान्तं निरवद्यं निरंजनम्। अमृतस्य परं सेतुं दग्धेन्धनमिवानलम्॥

Taittirīya Āraṇyaka:—

3, 12, 7 — सर्वाणि रूपाणि विचित्य धीरो नामानि कृत्वाऽभिवदन्यदास्ते।

Taittirīya Brāhmaṇa:—

2, 2, 4, 2 — स भूरिति व्याहरस्य भूमिमसृजत।

3, 1, 4, 1 — अग्निर्वा अकामयत अन्नादो देवानां स्यामिति। स एतमग्नये कृत्तिकाभ्यः पुरोडाशमष्टाकपालं निरवपत्॥

3, 12, 3, 7 — नावेदविन्मनुते तं बृहन्तं येन सूर्यस्तपति तेजासिद्धः।

Taittirīya Samhitā:—

2, 1 — वायव्य श्वेतमालभेत भूतिकामः। वायुर्वै क्षेपिष्ठा देवता वायुमेव स्वेन भागधेयेनोपधावति स एवैनं भूतिं गमयति।

2, 2, 10, 2 — यद्वै किं च मनुरवदत्तद्भेषजम्।

7, 1, 1, 6 — तस्माच्छूद्रो यज्ञेऽनवक्लृप्तः शूद्रो विद्यायामनवक्लृप्तः।

Taittirīyopaniṣad:—

2, 1–2—ब्रह्मविदाप्नोति परम् । तस्माद्वा एतस्मादात्मन आकाशः संभूतः । आकाशाद्वायुः । वायोरग्निः । अग्नेरापः । अद्भ्यः पृथिवी । पृथिव्या ओषधयः । ओषधीभ्योऽन्नम् । अन्नात्पुरुषः ।

2, 5, 9—तस्माद्वा एतस्माद्विज्ञानमयात् । अन्योऽन्तर आत्मानंदमयः । तस्य प्रियमेव शिरः । मोदो दक्षिणः पक्षः । प्रमोद उत्तरः पक्षः । आनन्द आत्मा । ब्रह्म पुच्छं प्रतिष्ठा ॥

असन्नेव स भवति । असद्ब्रह्मेति वेद चेत् । अस्ति ब्रह्मेति चेद्वेद । सन्तमेनं ततो विदुः ॥

सोऽकामयत बहु स्यां प्रजायेयेति । स तपोऽतप्यत । इदं सर्वमसृजत । तत्सृष्ट्वा तदेवानुप्राविशत् । तदनुप्रविश्य । सच्च त्यच्चाभवत् । निरुक्तं चानिरुक्तं च । निलयनं चानिलयनं च । विज्ञानं चाविज्ञानं च । सत्यं चानृतं च सत्यमभवत् । यदिदं किंच । तत्सत्यमित्याचक्षते ॥

असद्वा इदमग्र आसीत् । ततो वै सदजायत ॥ (Cf. Chā. 3, 19, 1) रसो वै सः । रसं ह्येवायं लब्ध्वानन्दी भवति । को ह्येवान्यात्कः प्राण्यात् । यदेष आकाश आनन्दो न स्यात् ।

यदा ह्येवैष एतस्मिन्नदृश्येऽनात्म्येऽनिरुक्तेऽनिलयनेऽभयं प्रतिष्ठां विन्दते । अथ सोऽभयं गतो भवति । यदा ह्येवैष एतस्मिन्नुदरमन्तरं कुरुते । अथ तस्य भयं भवति ॥

भीषाऽस्माद्वातः पवते । भीषादेति सूर्यः । भीषाऽस्मादग्निश्चेन्द्रश्च । मृत्युर्धावति पंचमः ॥

सैषानन्दस्य मीमांसा भवति । युवा स्यात्साधुयुवाऽध्यायकः । आशिष्ठो द्रढिष्ठो बलिष्ठः । तस्येयं पृथिवी सर्वा वित्तस्य पूर्णा स्यात् । स एको मानुष आनन्दः । ते ये शतं मानुषा आनंदाः । स एको मनुष्यगंधर्वाणामानंदः । श्रोत्रियस्य चाकामहतस्य । ते ये शतं०. स एको देवगंधर्वाणामानंदः । ते ये शतं० स एकः पितॄणां०; ते ये शतं० देवानां०; ते ये शतं० इन्द्रस्य०, बृहस्पतेः०, प्रजापतेः०; ते ये शतं० स एको ब्रह्मणः आनंदः ॥

स यश्चायं पुरुषे । यश्चासावादित्ये । स एकः ॥ यतो वाचो निवर्तन्ते । अप्राप्य मनसा सह । आनंदं ब्रह्मणो विद्वान् । न बिभेति कुतश्चनेति ॥

3, 1—यतो वा इमानि भूतानि जायन्ते । येन जातानि जीवन्ति । यत्प्रयन्त्यभिसंविशन्ति । तद्विजानस्व । तद्ब्रह्मेति ॥

3, 6 — आनंदो ब्रह्मेति व्यजानात्। आनंदाद्ध्येव खल्विमानि भूतानि जायन्ते। आनंदेन जातानि जीवन्ति। आनंदं प्रयन्त्यभिसंविशंति। सैषा भार्गवी वारुणी विद्या॥

3, 10, 5 - 6 — स य एवंवित्। अस्माल्लोकात्प्रेत्य। एतमन्नमयमात्मानमुपसंक्रम्य। एतं प्राणमयं०, मनोमयं०, विज्ञानमयं०, आनंदमयमात्मानमुपसंक्रम्य। इमाँल्लोकान्कामान्नी कामरूप्यनुसंचरन्। एतत्साम गायन्नास्ते। हा ३ वु हा ३ वु हा ३ वु। अहमन्नमहमन्नमहमन्नम्। अहमन्नादोऽ ३ हमन्नादोऽ ३ हमन्नादः। अहं श्लोककृदहं श्लोककृदहं श्लोककृत्। अहमस्मि प्रथमजा ऋता ३ स्य। पूर्वं देवेभ्योऽमृतस्य ना ३ भायि। यो मा ददाति स इदेव मा ३ ऽऽवाः। अहमन्नमहन्नमदन्तमद्मि। अहं विश्वं भुवनमभ्यभवा ३ म्। सुवर्न ज्योतीः॥

Vaiseiṣka – Sūtras

1, 1, 10 — द्रव्याणि द्रव्यान्तरमारभन्ते गुणाश्च गुणान्तरम्।

4, 1, 1 — सदकारणवन्नित्यम्।

4, 1, 4 — अनित्यमिति च विशेषतः प्रतिषेधाभावः।

4, 1, 5 — अविद्या च।

4, 2, 2 — प्रत्यक्षाप्रत्यक्षाणामप्रत्यक्षत्वात्संयोगस्य पंचात्मकं न विद्यते।

7, 1, 9 — कारणबहुत्वात्कारणमहत्त्वात्प्रचयविशेषाच्च महत्।

7, 1, 10 — तद्विपरीतमणु।

7, 1, 17 — एतेन दीर्घत्वह्रस्वत्वे व्याख्याते।

Yoga – Sūtras

2, 44 — स्वाध्यायादिष्टदेवतासंप्रयोगः।

Sūtra-wise Index of Upaniṣadic and other References.

ADHYĀYA FIRST

Pāda First

Sūtra.		
1	Chā.	8, 1, 6;
	Tai.	2, 1; 3, 1;
2	Tai.	3, 1; 3, 1, 6;
3	Bṛ.	2, 4, 10;
4	Ait. Ār.	2, 4, 1, 1;
	Ait. Brā.	3, 8, 1;
	Bṛ.	1, 4, 10; 1, 4, 15;
		1, 7, 8; 2, 4, 5;
		2, 4, 14; 2, 5, 19;
		3, 1, 9; 3, 4, 2;
		3, 9, 26; 3, 9, 28;
		4, 2, 4; 4, 3, 15;
		4, 4, 7; 4, 4, 12;
	Chā.	3, 18, 1; 3, 19, 1;
		4, 3, 3; 4, 3, 7;
		5, 7, 1; 5, 8, 1;
		5, 10, 5; 6, 2, 1;
		6, 8, 7; 7, 1, 3;
		7, 26, 2; 8, 7, 1;
		8, 12, 1;
	Iś.	7; 8
	Ka.	1, 2, 14; 1, 3, 11;
		2, 18; 2, 22;
		3, 1, 4;

Sūtra.		
	Ke.	1, 3; 1, 4 & 5; 2, 3;
	Mu.	1, 9; 2, 1, 2;
		2, 2, 8; 2, 2, 11;
		3, 1, 1; 3, 2, 9;
	Nyā. Sū.	1, 1, 2;
	Pr.	6, 8;
	Pū. Mīm.	1, 1, 5; 1, 1, 25;
	(Jai. Sū.)	1, 2, 1; 1, 2, 7;
		1, 2, 40; 4, 1, 1;
	Śat. Brā.	1, 1, 1 —2;
	Śve.	3, 11; 6, 11;
	Tai.	2, 9;
	Yaj. Saṁ.	1, 1, 1;
5	Ait.	1, 1, 1;
	B. G.	14, 17;
	Bṛ.	3, 7, 23;
	Chā.	4, 6, 2-3;
	Mu.	1, 1, 9;
	Pr.	6, 3;
	Śve.	3, 19; 6, 8;
6	Chā.	6, 2; 6, 8, 7;
7	Ait. Ār.	2, 1; 2, 6;
	Chā.	6, 8, 7; 6, 14, 2;
		6, 16, 3;

Sūtra.		
8	Chā.	6, 1, 2-6;
9	Bṛ.	6, 3, 21;
	Chā.	6, 8, 1; 6, 8, 3, 5; 8, 3, 3;
10	Chā.	7, 26, 1;
	Kau.	3, 3;
	Pra.	3, 3;
11	Śve.	6, 9;
12	Ait. Ār.	2, 3, 2;
	B. G.	8, 6; 10, 41;
	Bṛ.	2, 3, 6; 3, 8, 8; 3, 9, 28; 4, 5, 15;
	Chā.	3, 14, 1; 7, 24, 1;
	Tai. Ār.	3, 12, 7;
	Tai.	2, 5; 2, 6; 2, 7–9; 3, 6;
	Śve.	6, 19;
13	Tai.	2, 8;
	Pā. Sū.	5, 4, 21;
14	Tai.	7;
15	Tai.	2, 1 & 5;
16	Tai.	2, 6;
17	Bṛ.	3, 7, 23;
	Tai.	2, 7;
18	Tai.	2, 6;
19	Bṛ.	3, 9, 28; 4, 3, 32;
	Chā.	7, 24, 1;
	Śve.	6, 11;
	Tai.	2, 1; 2, 5-9; 3, 6;
	B. G.	10, 41;
20	Bṛ.	4, 4, 22;
	Chā.	1, 6, 6; 1, 6, 8; 1, 7, 5-6; 3, 14, 2; 7, 24, 2; 8, 7, 1; 10, 41;
	Kau.	1, 3, 15;
21	Bṛ.	3, 7, 9;

Sūtra.		
22	Bṛ.	3, 9, 28; 5, 1;
	Chā.	1, 8, 8; 1, 9, 1; 3, 14, 3; 4, 10, 5; 8, 14, 1;
	Ṛg. Saṁ	1, 164, 39;
	Tai.	2, 1; 2, 7; 3, 6;
23	Bṛ.	4, 4, 18;
	Chā.	1, 10, 9; 1, 11, 4-5; 6, 8, 2;
	Kau.	3, 3;
	Śat. Brā.	10, 3, 3, 6;
24	Bṛ.	4, 3, 5; 4, 4, 16;
	Chā.	1, 9, 4; 3, 12; 3, 12, 6; 3, 13, 7; 3, 13, 8; 6, 3, 3;
	Ka.	2, 5, 15;
	Tai. Brā.	3, 12, 9, 7;
	Tai. Saṁ.	1, 6, 3, 3;
25	Ait. Ār.	3, 2, 3, 12;
	Chā.	3, 11, 3; 3, 12, 6; 3, 14, 1; 4, 3, 8;
26	B. G.	10, 42;
	Chā.	3, 12, 7-8; 3, 13, 6-7;
	Ṛg. Saṁ.	10, 90;
28	Kau.	3, 1; 3, 1, 2, 3 & 8; 3, 8;
	Mu.	2, 2, 8;
	Śve.	3, 8;
29	Bṛ.	2, 5, 19; 3, 8, 8;
	Kau.	3, 2; 3, 8;
30	Bṛ.	1, 4, 10;
	Kau.	1, 3;
31	Chā.	3, 14, 2;
	Ka.	2, 5, 5;

Sūtra		
	Kau.	3, 3; 3, 4; 3, 4, 5; 3, 3;

Sūtra.		
	Ke.	1, 5;
	Pra.	2, 3;

ADHYĀYA FIRST

Pāda Second

Sūtra		
1	Chā.	3, 14; 3, 14, 3; 3, 14, 4;
	Mu.	2, 1, 2;
2	B. G.	13, 13;
	Chā.	3, 14, 2; 3, 14, 4; 8, 7, 1;
	Mu.	2, 1, 2;
	Śve.	4, 3;
3	Chā.	3, 14, 3;
4	Chā.	3, 14, 4;
5	Śat. Brā.	10, 6, 3, 2;
6	B. G.	13, 2; 18, 61;
	Bṛ.	3, 7, 23;
8	Bṛ.	3, 7, 23;
9	Bṛ.	1, 4, 6;
	Kaṭhavalli	1, 2, 25;
	Mu.	3, 1, 1;
10	Ka.	1, 2, 18;
11	Bṛ.	4, 4, 23;
	Ka.	1, 1, 20; 1, 2, 12; 1, 2, 14;
	Kaṭhavalli	1, 3, 1;
	Mu.	3, 1, 1;
	Tai.	2, 1;
12	B. G.	13, 2;
	Bṛ.	4, 5, 15;

Sūtra		
	Chā.	6, 8, 7;
	Ka.	1, 3, 3; 1, 3, 9;
	Mu.	3, 1, 1; 3, 1, 2;
13	Bṛ.	5, 5, 2;
	Chā.	4, 15, 1; 4, 15, 2; 6, 8, 7;
14	Chā.	1, 6, 7, 6;
15	Chā.	4, 10, 5; 4, 14, 1; 4, 15, 1-2;
16	B. G.	8, 24;
	Chā.	4, 15, 5;
	Pr.	1, 10;
17	Bṛ.	5, 5, 2;
	Chā.	8, 9, 1;
	Tai.	2, 8;
18	Bṛ.	3, 7, 1; 3, 9, 10;
19	Bṛ.	3, 4, 2; 3, 7, 23;
	Manu Smṛ.	1, 5;
20	Bṛ.	2, 4, 14; 3, 7, 22; 3, 7, 23; 4, 5, 15;
21	Mu.	1, 1, 1; 1, 1, 3; 1, 1, 5-7; 1, 1, 9; 1, 2, 7; 1, 2, 12, 13; 2, 1, 2;

Sūtra.		
22	Mu.	2, 1, 2;
23	Bṛ.	3, 9, 9;
	Mu.	2, 1, 3-4; 2, 1, 5-10;
	Ṛg.	10, 121,1;
	Tai.	3, 10, 6;
24	Bṛ.	5, 9;
	Chā.	5, 11, to 5,18: 5, 24, 3;

Sūtra.		
	Ṛg.	1, 98, 1, 10, 88, 12;
25	Ma. Bhā.	47, 68;
26	Chā.	3, 14, 2; 3, 18, 1; 5, 18, 2; 5, 19, 1;
	Ṛg. Sam.	10, 88, 3;
	Śat. Brā.	10, 6, 1, 11;
28	Śat. Brā.	10, 6, 1, 11;
31	Chā.	5, 11, to 5, 18;
	Śat. Brā.	10, 6, 1, 11;

ADHYĀYA FIRST

Pāda Third

Sūtra.		
1	Bṛ.	2, 4, 12; 3, 7, 2; 4, 5, 13;
	Chā.	6, 8, 4;
	Ka.	2, 1, 10;
	Mu.	2, 1, 10; 2, 2, 5; 2, 2, 11;
2	Bṛ.	4, 4, 7; 4, 4, 21;
	Mu.	2, 2, 8;
3	Mu.	1, 1, 9;
6	Mu.	1, 1, 3;
7	Mu.	1, 1, 5-6, 2, 2, 5; 3, 1, 1;
8	Bṛ.	4, 3, 15;
	Chā.	7, 1 to 15; 7, 1, 3; 7, 15, 1; 7, 15, 4; 7, 16, 1; 7, 23; 7, 24; 7, 24, 1; 7, 26, 1; 7, 26, 2;

Sūtra.		
	Kau.	3, 2;
	Pra.	4, 2-3; 4, 6;
	Śve.	6, 15;
	Tai.	2, 1;
9	Bṛ.	3, 4, 2; 4, 3, 32; 4, 5, 15;
	Chā.	7, 23, 1; 7, 24, 1;
10	Bṛ.	3, 8, 7-8;
	Chā.	2, 23, 4;
11	Bṛ.	3, 8, 9;
12	Bṛ.	3, 8, 8; 8, 3, 11,
13	Ka.	1, 3, 11;
	Pra.	5, 2; 5, 5;
14	Bṛ.	2, 5, 18;
	Chā.	8, 1, 8, 1, 3; 8, 1, 5; 8, 1, 6; 8, 2-3;
	Pra.	5, 5;
	Śat. Brā.	10, 6, 3 2;

Sūtra.		
	Śve.	5, 8;
15	Chā.	6, 8, 1; 8, 3, 2;
16	Bṛ	3, 8, 9; 4, 4, 22;
	Chā.	8, 4, 1;
17	Chā.	1, 9, 1; 8, 14;
18	Chā.	8, 3, 4;
19	B G.	13, 31;
	Br	3, 7, 23; 4, 3, 30;
	Chā.	8, 7, 1; 8, 7, 4;
		8, 10, 1; 8, 11, 1;
		8, 11, 3; 8, 12, 3;
	Ka.	1, 2, 22,
	Mu	3, 2, 9;
22	Bṛ.	4, 2, 4; 4, 3, 6;
		4, 4, 16;
	Chā.	3, 14, 2;
	Ka.	2, 5, 15;
	Mu.	2, 2, 5;
		2, 2, 9-10;
23	B. G.	15, 6 & 12;
24	Ka.	1, 2, 14;
		2, 4, 12, 13;
	Ma. Bhā.	3, 297, 17;
25	Ka.	2, 6, 17;
	Pū. Mīm. Sū.	6, 1;
26	Chā.	8, 11, 3;
	Pū. Mīm. Sū.	6, 1, 5,
	Tai.	3, 1;
27	Bṛ.	3, 9, 1, 2;
	Ma. Bhā.	12, 110, 62;
28	Bṛ.	1, 2, 4,
	Ma. Bhā. S. P	223, 24, 233, 25;
	Manu.	

Sūtra.		
	Smṛ.	1, 21;
	Pū. Mīm.	1, 1, 5;
	Ṛg.	9, 62;
	Tai. Brā	2, 2, 42.
29	Rg.	10, 71, 3;
30	Kau.	3, 3;
	Rg. Sam.	10, 190, 3;
	Śve.	6, 18;
	Tai.	3, 1, 4, 1;
31	Bṛ.	2, 4, 2;
	Chā.	3, 18, 2; 3, 19, 1;
		4, 3, 1;
32	Chā.	3, 6, 4;
33	Ait. Brā.	3, 8, 1;
	Bṛ.	1, 4, 10;
	Chā.	8, 7, 2;
	Ṣadviṁsa Brā.	1, 1;
	Tai.	2, 1;
	Yoga Sūtras	2, 12; 2, 44;
34	Chā.	4, 2, 3;
	Tai. Saṁ.	7, 1, 1, 6;
36	Chā.	5, 11, 7; 7, 1, 1;
	Manu. Sm.	10, 4; 10, 126;
	Pra.	1, 1;
	Śat. Brā.	11, 5, 3, 3;
37	Chā.	4, 4, 5;
38	Gau. dharmaśāstra	10, 1; 12, 4; 12, 5, 6;
	Manu.	4, 80;
39	Br	3, 3, 2; 4, 4, 18;
	Ka.	2, 5, 5; 2, 5, 8;
		2, 6, 6;
	Śve.	6, 15;
	Tai.	2, 8, 1;

Sūtra.		
40	Chā.	8, 6, 5; 8, 7, 1;
		8, 9, 3; 8, 12, 1;
		8, 12, 3;
41	Chā.	6, 3, 2; 8, 14, 1;

Sūtra.		
42	Bṛ.	4, 3, 7;
		4, 3, 14-16;
		4, 4, 22;
43	Bṛ.	4, 4, 22;

ADHYĀYA FIRST

Pāda Fourth

Sūtra.		
1	Bṛ.	3, 2;
	Ka.	1, 3, 3-4;
		1, 3, 10-11;
		1, 3, 12;
	Śve.	6, 18;
2	Bṛ.	1, 4, 7;
	Rg.	9, 46, 4;
3	Bṛ.	3, 8, 11;
	Mu.	2, 1, 2;
	Śve.	4, 10;
5	Ka.	2, 3, 15;
6	Kaṭhavalli	1, 1, 12-13;
		1, 1, 20; 1, 2, 4;
		1, 2, 14; 1, 2, 18;
		2, 5, 6-7;
7	Ka.	1, 2, 22;
	Śve.	3, 8;
8	Bṛ.	2, 2, 3;
9	Chā.	6, 4, 1;
	Śve.	1, 1; 4, 5;
		4, 10-11;
10	Bṛ.	5, 8; 6, 2, 9;
	Chā.	3, 1;
	Śve.	6, 11;
11	Bṛ.	4, 4, 17;
	Pāṇini	2, 1, 50;

Sūtra.		
	Tai. Saṁ.	1, 6, 2, 2;
12	Bṛ.	4, 4, 17; 4, 4, 18;
	Chā.	3, 13, 6; 7, 15, 1;
	Rg.	8, 53, 7;
14	Ait.	1, 1;
	Bṛ,	1, 4, 7;
	Chā.	3, 19, 1;
		6, 2, 1-3;
		6, 8, 4; 7, 1, 3;
	Mā, Gauda Kā:	3, 5;
	Pra:	6, 4;
	Śve.	3, 8;
	Tai.	2, 1; 2, 6; 2,7;
15	Bṛ.	1, 4, 7;
	Chā	3, 19, 1; 6, 2, 1;
		6, 3, 2;
	Tai.	2, 1; 2, 6, 1;
16	Bṛ.	3, 9, 9;
	Kau. Brā.	4, 1; 4, 18; 4, 20
17	Chā.	6, 8, 2,
	Kau.	4, 20;
18	Bṛ.	2, 1, 16-17;
		2, 1, 20;
	Chā.	8, 1, 1;
	Kau.	4, 19-20;

Sūtra.		
19	Bṛ.	2, 4, 2-3; 2, 4, 6;
		2, 4, 10; 2, 4, 12;
		3, 5, 6;
21	Chā.	8, 12, 3;
	Mu.	3, 2, 8;
22	B. G.	2, 54-69; 13, 27;
	Bṛ.	1, 4, 10;
		2, 4, 13-14;
		3, 7, 23;
		3, 8, 11; 4, 4, 19;
		4, 4, 24;
	Chā.	6, 2, 1; 6, 3, 2;
		7, 25, 2;
	Iś.	7;
	Mu.	2, 2, 11; 3, 2, 6;

Sūtra.		
	Tai.	2, 1; 2, 6;
		3, 12, 7;
23	Bṛ.	4, 5, 6 & 8;
	Chā.	6, 1, 3; 6, 1, 4;
	Mu.	1, 1, 3 & 7;
	Pra.	6, 3-4;
	Śve.	6, 19;
	Tai.	3, 1;
24	Chā.	6, 2, 3;
	Tai.	2, 6, 1;
25	Chā.	1, 9, 1;
26	Tai.	2, 7;
27	Mu.	1, 1, 6; 1, 1, 7;
		3, 1, 3;
	Rg.	1, 104,1;

ADHYĀYA SECOND

Pāda First

Sūtra.		
1	Iś.	7,
	Mahā-Bhā.	12, 334, 29;
		12, 360, 1-3
		& 361; 4-5;
	Manu-Smṛ.	12, 91;
	Mīm. Sū.	1, 3, 3;
	Śve.	5, 2;
	Tai. Sam.	2, 2, 10, 2;
2	Ka.	1, 3, 11;
3	Bṛ.	2, 4, 5; 3, 9, 26;
		4, 3, 16;
	Jābāla	4;
	Ka.	2, 6, 11-18;
	Śve.	2, 8; 3, 8; 6, 13;

Sūtras,		
	Tai. Brā.	3, 12, 9, 7;
4	Bṛ.	1, 3, 2; 2, 4, 5;
		6, 1, 7;
	Chā.	6, 2, 3 & 4;
	Śat. Brā.	6, 1, 3, 2 & 4;
	Tai. Brā.	3, 12, 9, 7;
	Tai.	2, 6;
5	Ait. Ār.	2, 4, 2, 4;
	Bṛ.	6, 1, 13;
	Chā.	5, 1, 7; 6, 2, 3-4;
	Kau.	2, 14;
6	B. G.	2, 25; 10, 2;
	Bṛ.	2, 4, 5;
	Ka.	1, 2, 9;
	Rg.	10, 130, 6;
	Tai.	2, 6;

Sūtra.				Sūtra.			
7	Bṛ.	2, 4, 6;		17	Chā.	3, 19, 1;	
9	Bṛ.	2, 4, 6;			Tai.	2, 7, 1;	
	Chā.	3, 14, 1;		18	Chā.	6, 1, 3;	6, 2, 1;
		6, 9, 2-3;		20	Chā.	6, 1, 3;	
		7, 25, 2;		21	Chā.	6, 3, 2;	6, 8, 7;
	Gaudakā.	1, 16;		22	Bṛ.	2, 4, 5;	4, 3, 35;
	Mu.	2, 2, 11;			Chā.	6, 8, 1;	8, 7, 1;
11	Manu Smṛ.	12, 105, 106;		24	Śve.	6, 8;	
13	Tai.	2, 6;		26	Bṛ.	2, 4, 12;	3, 8, 8;
14	Ait. Ār.	3, 2, 4, 7;				3, 9, 26;	
	B. G.	5, 14-15;	18, 61;		Mu.	2, 1, 2;	
	Bṛ.	2, 4, 6;	2, 4, 11;		Śve.	6, 19;	
		2, 4, 14;	2, 4, 19;	27	Bṛ.	4, 2, 4;	
		3, 8, 8;	3, 9, 26;		Chā.	3, 12, 6;	6, 3, 2;
		4, 2, 4;	4, 4, 2;			6, 8, 1;	
		4, 4, 19;	4, 4, 25;	28	Bṛ.	4, 3, 10;	
	Chā.	5, 2, 8;	6, 1, 4;	30	Bṛ.	3, 8, 9;	
		6, 3, 2;	6, 4, 1;		Chā.	3, 14, 4;	8, 7, 1;
		6, 7, 6;	6, 8, 7;		Mu.	1, 1, 9;	
		7, 24, 1;	7, 25, 2;	31	Bṛ.	3, 8, 9;	
		8, 14, 1;			Śve.	3, 19;	
	Mu.	2, 2, 11;		32	Bṛ.	2, 4, 5;	
	Śve.	6, 12;		34	B. G.	4, 11;	
	Tai. Ār.	3, 12, 7;			Bṛ.	3, 2, 13;	
	Tai.	2, 1;			Kau.	3, 8;	
15	Chā.	6, 4;		36	B. G.	15, 3;	
16	Ait. Ār.	2, 4, 1;			Chā.	6, 3, 2;	
	Chā.	6, 2, 1;			Ṛg.	10, 190, 3;	

ADHYĀYA SECOND

Pāda Second

Sūtras,				Sūtras,		
3	Bṛ.	3, 7, 9;	3, 8, 9;	17	Vai. Sū.	1, 1, 10;
15	Vai. Sū.	4, 1, 1;	4, 1, 4;			
		4, 15;				